Youth Court Guide

Youth Court Guide

Third Edition

Terry Moore BA LLM

Formerly Clerk to the Justices,
Avon & Somerset South Western Divisions

Tottel publishing

Tottel Publishing
Maxwelton House
41–43 Boltro Road
Haywards Heath
West Sussex
RH16 1BJ

British Library Cataloguing-in-Publication Data
A CIP Catalogue record for this book is available from the British Library.

ISBN 978 1 84766 141 8

Typeset by Etica Press Ltd, Malvern, Worcs (www.eticapress.com)
Printed in the UK by CPI William Clowes Beccles NR34 7TL

Preface

The *Youth Court Guide* has been in use now for 25 years since Tony Wilkinson and I wrote the first edition in 1984. Tony is no longer a co-author having moved his interests and his practice to other areas of the law and so I have taken on this edition as a solo project.

The objectives of the book remain the same, and that is to provide as comprehensive a guide as possible to all those using the Youth Court including legal advisers, defence lawyers, prosecutors, magistrates and youth offending teams. The text follows the typical progress of a case moving through from the police station procedures to appearance in court, bail, sentence and ancillary orders.

The last edition was published almost four years ago and since then case law alone has changed the way the Youth Court and those practising therein operate. Add to that a raft of different statutes affecting sentencing, bail, ancillary orders and mental health issues and the need for the guide appears to be a continuing one.

Case law was always going to be an important factor in how the Youth Court dealt with the dangerousness provisions and their interaction with grave crimes and that has proved to be so. As a result the chapter on the venue of proceedings has been substantially rewritten to take account of this.

The seemingly increasing number of young people appearing with mental health or associated problems has also been reflected in case law and a larger section dealing with these has been included, with the aim of assisting advocates and magistrates through this comparative minefield. In addition the chapter on mental health has been updated to reflect the changes in the the Mental Health Act 2007.

One of the frustrations of writing or editing a legal text used by practitioners is the habit of government to introduce legislation and then fail to bring it into force. In the last edition the community orders chapter had a whole section on new community orders that have never been brought into force. This time the government has brought in a youth rehabilitation order with many and extensive requirements. I am reliably informed that when this book comes into use in the spring of 2009 these orders will be introduced and so I have taken the decision to update the text as if the provisions in the Criminal Justice and Immigration Act 2008 were fully in force.

Amendments to the Bail Act and to referral orders and anti-social behaviour orders are also included in the text as if the Criminal Justice and Immigration Act 2008 is fully in force. Hopefully, if the Ministry of Justice keeps to its published timetable, that will be the case.

Numbers of important procedural changes are incorporated in the text including changes brought about by the Youth Court Constitution Rules 2007 and the Criminal Procedure (Amendment) Rules 2008.

Other than the Criminal Justice and Immigration Act 2008, as mentioned above, I have attempted to state the law as at 1 January 2009.

Terry Moore

North Somerset
January 2009

Acknowledgments

I have been extremely fortunate to have been assisted by a number of friends during the writing of this book and I would like to take this opportunity to thank them. Firstly, there is Tony Wilkinson, who although no longer a co-author, still found the time to read the text as it emerged and to make some very helpful comments.

Two regular and experienced practitioners in the Youth Court, Pakeeza Rahman and Fran Thornton, also offered to read the manuscript and both made invaluable comments and suggestions for improvements.

Lastly, but my no means least, is Fred Davies who spent most of his Christmas holiday proofreading and ensuring that the detail was correct.

It remains true of course that any defects the reader may find in the text are my responsibility alone.

I would also like to thank my wife Karen for her support and understanding during my many hours hunched in front of the computer and for her help in checking case references and statutory provisions.

Terry Moore

North Somerset
January 2009

Contents

Contents

Chapter 2

Prosecution and the constitution of the Court   27

Chapter 3

Attendance at Court   43

Chapter 4

The Youth Court and Human Rights Act   57

Chapter 5

Venue of proceedings   73

Chapter 8

Referral orders, deferment of sentence discharges, reparation orders, and financial orders   143

Chapter 9

Youth community rehabilitation orders and sentences   157

Chapter 10

Custodial orders   179

Chapter 11

Breach, revocation and amendment of youth rehabilitation orders and reparation orders 197

Chapter 12

Additional powers and ancillary orders in the Youth Court 209

Chapter 13

Common problems in the Youth Court 239

Chapter 14

Anti-social behaviour orders in the Youth Court   271

Chapter 15

The mentally ill juvenile   299

Chapter 16

Appeals   313

Appendix A

Magistrates' Courts (Children and Young Persons) Rules 1992 (1992 No 2071)   323

Appendix B

The Youth Courts (Constitution of Committees and Right to Preside) Rules 2007 (SI 2007 No 1611)   331

Appendix C

Criminal Procedure Rules 2005 (SI 2005 No 384)   337

Contents

Appendix D

Code for Crown Prosecutors   389

Appendix E

Final Warning Scheme
Guidance for the Police and Youth Offending Teams   403

Appendix F

Youth Court Asset Form

Appendix G

Maximum fines

Appendix H

Orders guide

Table of statutes

References at the right-hand side of the column are to paragraph numbers.

Table of cases

References at the right-hand side of the column are to paragraph numbers.

PARA

L

M

N

O

P

R

Chapter 1

Before charge

THE FRAMEWORK OF THE SYSTEM

1.01   The underlying philosophy of the legislation relating to persons under the age of 18 years who come before the courts is embodied in the Children and Young Persons Act 1933 (CYPA). Section 44 of this Act provides that every court in dealing with a child or young person who is brought before it, either as an offender or otherwise, shall have regard to his or her welfare. The 1933 Act has been amended frequently and may be overridden completely by the Crown Court imposing detention for life under s 226 of the Criminal Justice Act 2003. Section 37 of the Crime and Disorder Act 1998 (CDA) provides that the principal aim of the youth justice system shall be to prevent offending by children and young persons. This text is written as if the whole of the Criminal Justice and Immigration Act 2008 is in force in relation to Youth Courts and s 9 of that Act states that in sentencing a juvenile the court must have regard to the principal aim of prevention of offending together with the welfare principle and the purposes of sentencing as set out in CJA 2003, s 142A.

The Crime and Disorder Act 1998 introduced a new range of police and court powers to help to achieve that aim and deliver a faster and more effective youth justice system while at the same time overhauling the management of the agencies working within the system. The Government published a framework document on the principal aim in 1998 that set out a number of key objectives on how it was intended that this aim should be achieved. These were:

- the swift administration of justice so that every young person accused of breaking the law has the matter resolved without delay;
- confronting young offenders with the consequences of their offending, for themselves, their family, their victims, and their

community, and helping them to develop a sense of personal responsibility;

- intervention which tackles the particular factors (personal, family, social, educational or health) that put young persons at risk of offending and which strengthens 'protective factors';
- punishment proportionate to the seriousness and persistence of the offending;
- encouraging reparation to victims by young offenders; and
- reinforcing the responsibilities of parents.

In addition to any other duty that they are subject to it is the duty of all persons carrying out functions in relation to the youth justice system to have regard to the principal aim: CDA 1998, s 37(2).

Youth Justice Board

1.02   The Youth Justice Board was established on 30 September 1998 by CDA 1998, s 41. The Board reports to the Home Secretary and is required to monitor the operation of the youth justice system and advise the Home Secretary on this and set national standards for the provision of youth justice services and custodial accommodation.

CDA1998, s 38(1) places a duty on local authorities to ensure the availability of all youth justice services and chief officers of police, police authorities, probation committees and health authorities within a local authority's area are to co-operate in the discharge by the local authority of their duty.

Every local authority is required to formulate a youth justice plan each year: CDA 1998, s 40.

Youth offending teams

1.03   Under CDA 1998, s 39 local authorities were charged with the creation of youth offending teams (YOTs).These were created in co-operation with other agencies and include:

- (a)   a probation officer;
- (b)   a social worker of a local authority social services department;
- (c)   a police officer;
- (d)   a person nominated by a health authority any part of whose area lies within the local authority's area;

(e) a person nominated by the chief education officer.

Youth Offending Teams were created in all areas in April 1999. In addition to the above objectives the YOTs must conduct their processes in accordance with the Youth Justice Board National Standards. All their work is governed by a policy ensuring it is free from discrimination and subject to monitoring and evaluation.

Unless charged with an offence of homicide juveniles should be tried summarily, that is before magistrates. The courts dealing with their cases are known as Youth Courts and these courts must, in addition to the principal aim, have regard to the welfare of the persons appearing before them (see **1.01** above).

Persons under the age of 18 are known as 'juveniles' or simply as 'youths'. Important divisions of age exist within the 1933 Act and the amending legislation. They are listed below.

Under 10 years

1.04   A child below the age of 10 years is under the age of criminal responsibility and cannot be guilty of any offence in law. (CYPA 1933, s 50) However, a juvenile, whether under the age of 10 or not, may be the subject of care proceedings brought under the Children Act 1989. Care proceedings are civil applications brought by a local authority or the NSPCC, whenever they believe that a court order is needed to ensure the juvenile's proper care and control. Such applications are made to a Family Proceedings Court, together with Child Safety Orders under CDA 1998, s 11 and are therefore outside the scope of this work.

Between 10 and 14 years

1.05   A juvenile within the age group of 10 to 13 inclusive is referred to as a child (CYPA 1933, s 107).

Between 14 and 18 years

1.06   A juvenile who has attained the age of 14 but is under 18 years is referred to as a young person. (CYPA 1933, s 107 as amended by CJA 1991, Sch 8). However, there are specific exceptions where 'young person' means someone who has attained the age of 14 but is under 17 years. These exceptions are referred to at the appropriate parts of the text.

Throughout the text, the description 'juvenile' is used to include both children and young persons, unless it is necessary to differentiate between them.

Aged 16 and 17 years

1.07 Although this age group are not referred specifically to in any legislation, they are set apart from other juveniles in a number of important respects. First, they may attend court without a parent. Second, a number of orders and sentences can only be made in respect of them. Last, in respect of those aged 17 only, they are still treated as adults for the purposes of the Bail Act 1976 and remand hearings. These differences are dealt with fully in the following chapters.

POWERS OF ARREST

1.08 Any person other than a police constable may arrest without a warrant anyone who is in the act of committing an indictable offence or anyone whom he has reasonable grounds for suspecting to be committing such an offence.

When an indictable offence has been committed, any person other than a constable may arrest without a warrant another who is guilty of that offence or anyone whom he has reasonable grounds for suspecting to be guilty of it. (Police and Criminal Evidence Act 1984, s 24A (2) (PACE 1984))

A police officer has wider powers of arrest than an ordinary citizen, in addition to the powers outlined above, he may arrest without a warrant anyone who is about to commit an offence or anyone whom he has reasonable grounds for suspecting to be about to commit an offence.

Further, where a constable has reasonable grounds for suspecting that an offence has been committed, he may arrest without a warrant anyone whom he has reasonable grounds for suspecting to be guilty of the offence. A juvenile should not be arrested or interviewed at his place of education unless this is unavoidable. In this case the principal or his nominee must be informed and agree to any interview (PACE 1984, Code of Practice C11.15, Note for guidance 11D).

The power of summary arrest mentioned above is only exercisable if a constable has reasonable grounds for believing that it is necessary to arrest the person because:

(a) the name of the relevant person is unknown to, and cannot be readily ascertained by, the constable; or

(b) the constable has reasonable grounds for doubting whether a name furnished by the relevant person as his name is his real name;

(c) correspondingly as regards the person's address;

(d) the arrest is necessary to prevent the relevant person:

    (i) causing physical harm to himself or any other person;

    (ii) suffering physical injury;

    (iii) causing loss of or damage to property;

    (iv) committing an offence against public decency (where members of the public going about their business cannot reasonably be expected to avoid the person in question); or

    (v) causing an unlawful obstruction of the highway;

(e) it is necessary to protect a child or other vulnerable person from the relevant person;

(f) in order to allow the prompt and effective investigation of the offence or because of the conduct of the person in question;

(g) it is necessary to prevent a prosecution from being hindered by the disappearance of the person in question; PACE 1984 s 24.

Juveniles involved in criminal: matters are sometimes reported for summons. A summons is a direction in writing to the juvenile to attend the Youth Court on a given day and time and is normally sent to him by post. Where a juvenile is under 16 a parent or guardian should also be summoned. Alternatively there may be a written charge and requisition to attend court (see **3.11**)

REPRESENTING JUVENILE SUSPECTS AT THE POLICE STATION

1.09 PACE 1984 and the Codes of Practice for detention, treatment and questioning of persons by the police apply to both juveniles and adults. The current Codes of Practice came into force on 1 February 2008. The responsibility for the detained person is that of the custody officer, usually a police sergeant appointed by the chief officer of police to a police station designated for the purposes of and suitable for detaining arrested persons.

Code C covers the detention, treatment and questioning of persons by police officers. The provisions for the detention of arrested adults apply equally to juveniles, but extra duties and responsibilities are placed on the police in respect of persons under 17 years of age. It is important to note that, while for most purposes a juvenile is someone under the age of 18, in the police station anyone who appears to be under 17 is to be treated as a juvenile in the absence of clear evidence that they are older. Persons aged 17 or over are to be treated as adults. It is the age that the detained person appears to be that is relevant and not his actual age. Thus if he is over 17 but the evidence available to the custody officer points to him being under that age he is to be treated as a juvenile. Likewise if the police treat as an adult someone who is under 17 but appears to be older they are acting properly (PACE 1984, s 37(15) and Code C1.5).

Any arrested person must be informed by the custody officer of his rights which may be exercised at any time during his detention. Those rights are:

(a) the right to have someone informed of his arrest;
(b) the right to consult privately with a solicitor (the detained person must be told that independent legal advice is available free of charge); and
(c) the right to consult the Codes of Practice (C 3.1).

In addition, where a juvenile suspect is detained the police have a duty to identify specified people and notify them, as soon as is practicable, of the juvenile's arrest (CYPA 1933, s 34). The custody officer must if it is practicable ascertain the person responsible for the juvenile's welfare. That person may be his parent or guardian or if he is in care the care authority or voluntary organisation or any other person who has for the time being assumed responsibility for his welfare. That person must be informed as soon as practicable that the juvenile has been arrested, why he has been arrested, and where he is being detained (C3.13; CYPA 1933, s 34(2), (3) and (4)). This applies even if the offences being investigated are terrorism offences (CYPA 1933, s 34(10)). If it appears that at the time of his arrest the child or young person is being provided with accommodation by or on behalf of the local authority under the Children Act 1989, s 20 the local authority should also be informed of the matters referred to above as soon as it is reasonably practicable (CYPA 1933, s

34(7)). The notes for guidance to the Codes of Practice suggest that if the juvenile is in the care of the local authority or voluntary organisation but is living with his parents or other adults responsible for his welfare then (although there is no legal obligation on the police to inform them) they as well as the authority or organisation should normally be contacted unless suspected of involvement in the offence concerned. Even if a juvenile in care is not living with his parents, consideration is to be given to informing them (Note 3C).

In the case of a juvenile who is known to be subject to a court order under which a person or an organisation is given any degree of statutory responsibility to supervise or otherwise monitor him, reasonable steps must also be taken to notify that person or organisation (the 'responsible officer'). The responsible officer will normally be a member of a Youth Offending Team, apart from where there is a curfew order which requires electronic monitoring when the contractor providing the monitoring will be the responsible officer (C3.14 and CYPA 1933, s 34(7)).

Appropriate adult

1.10   The 'appropriate adult' in the Codes of Practice means:
  (a) parent or guardian or if he is in care the care authority or voluntary organisation;
  (b) a social worker;
  (c) failing either of the above, another responsible adult aged 18 or over who is neither a police officer nor employed by the police.

Local authorities, together with youth offending team managers, have a duty to supply sufficient appropriate adults for their area.

The custody officer must as soon as practicable inform the appropriate adult (who may or may not be the person responsible for the juvenile's welfare) of the grounds for his detention and his whereabouts, and ask the appropriate adult to attend the police station straightaway to see the detained person (C3.15).

Where the detainee is a ward of court the police are required to notify the parent or foster parent with whom the ward is living or other appropriate adult and, if practicable, the reporting officer if one has been appointed. The reporting officer should be invited to attend the interview or nominate a representative to attend on his behalf. A copy of the tape of the interview should be provided to the reporting officer. If the interview has taken place in the absence of the reporting officer he should be notified of it and told of any further interviews that are proposed and invited to attend (*Practice Direction* [2002] 3 All ER 904).

The definition of appropriate adult amounts to a hierarchy. The police in arranging for the attendance of the appropriate adult should start with the parent or guardian and move on to the other categories only if they are not available. So far as category (c) is concerned, in the case of *R v Palmer* [1991] Legal Action 21 it was held that for a 16-year-old detainee, a 17-year-old could not be the appropriate adult because he was under 18 and probably too close in age.

Even when a parent has been present this can lead to difficulties. In *R v Morse* [1991] Crim LR 195 the court said that the juvenile suspect's father was not suitable. He was nearly illiterate, had a low IQ and was probably incapable of appreciating the gravity of the situation. However in *R v W* [1994] Crim LR 130, CA, the Court of Appeal refused to interfere with the finding of the first instance judge that the appellant's mother, who was mentally handicapped and therefore would have needed an appropriate adult herself if she had been arrested, was capable of fulfilling the appropriate adult's role. The court commented that at the time she was acting as appropriate adult she was experiencing a 'lucid interval.'

The notes for guidance to the Codes of Practice (Code C, Note for guidance 1B) make it clear that a person including the parent or guardian of a juvenile may be the appropriate adult unless he is suspected of involvement in the offence, is a victim, is a witness, is involved in the investigation or has received admissions prior to attending at the police station to act as the appropriate adult. In such circumstances it will be desirable for the appropriate adult to be some other person. If the parent of the juvenile is estranged from the juvenile the Notes for Guidance state that he should not be asked to be the appropriate adult if the juvenile expressly and specifically objects to his presence. The determining factor is the attitude of the juvenile and whether he or she expressly and specifically objects. In *DPP v Blake* [1989] 1 WLR 432 a confession was excluded where it had been obtained in the presence of the juvenile's father whom she had specifically rejected in favour of a named social worker who proved to be unavailable. The question of whether the child and parent are estranged is difficult and will eventually be a question of fact for the court to determine.

If a social worker or member of the Youth Offending Team is suspected of involvement, or is a witness, or has received admissions prior to attending at the police station he or she should not be the appropriate adult. (Code C, Note for guidance 1C) A social worker who has called the police should not act as the appropriate adult because the detainee would see him or her as being on the side of the police (*DPP v Morris* (8 October 1990, unreported)).

A solicitor who is present at the police station in a professional capacity should not be the appropriate adult nor should an independent custody visitor (formerly lay visitor) present in that capacity (Code C, Note for guidance 1F).

The Home Office *Guidance for Appropriate Adults* (www.homeoffice.gov.uk/docs/publications/operational-policing/ guidanceapadultcustody.pdf) and Code C para 11.17 state that the appropriate adult's role is:

'To support, advise and assist the detained person particularly during interview;

to observe whether the police are acting properly, fairly and with respect for the rights of the detainee and to tell them if he thinks they are not;

to assist communication between the detainee and the police

to ensure that the detained person understands their rights and that the appropriate adult has a role in protecting their rights.'

The Home Office Guidance specifically states that it is not the appropriate adult's role to advise on the law.

The juvenile should be advised by the custody officer that the appropriate adult is there to advise and assist him and that he may consult with the appropriate adult privately at any time (Code C para 3.18).

Code C para 6.5A indicates that the appropriate adult can ask for advice on behalf of the juvenile. If the juvenile does not wish to have a solicitor but the appropriate adult does the solicitor should then treat the appropriate adult as the client. The solicitor may not force himself onto an unwilling juvenile, nor can the juvenile be forced to see the solicitor.

Code C 11.15 requires the presence of the appropriate adult in the interview and requires the police to explain the appropriate adult's role to him or her. In *H and M v DPP* [1998] Crim LR 653, CA, the Court of Appeal refused to overturn the justices' decision to admit the accused's confession even though the person present in interview whom the court deemed to be the appropriate adult was unaware of that expression and had not known the reason for his presence in the interview. It was also decided in this case that more than one person, for example, both parents, may be present as an appropriate adult. Although there had been a technical failure to follow the Codes of Practice the protection envisaged had been provided.

An interview will not necessarily be deemed inadmissible if an appropriate adult intervenes too much. In *R v Jefferson* [1994] 1 All ER 270, CA, this happened but the detainee's denials were not altered and so the Court of Appeal upheld the decision to admit the evidence. In reviewing such a set of facts now, a court would have regard to art 6 of the ECHR and the effect the evidence would have on the overall fairness of the trial.

The independence of the appropriate adult from the police was underlined in *Leach v Chief Constable of Gloucestershire Constabulary* [1999] 1 All ER 215, CA, where it was held that the police had no duty of care to prevent psychological harm to the appropriate adult.

THE RIGHT TO LEGAL ADVICE

1.11 PACE 1984, s 58 and the Terrorism Act 2000, Sch 8, para 7 gives a right to all persons arrested and held in custody to consult a solicitor in private at any time. This right applies equally to juveniles. If a juvenile wishes to exercise this right the request should be acted upon immediately, even though the appropriate adult has not arrived at the police station(PACE 1984, s 58(4)).

The Code of Practice provides that a detained person who does not know the name of a solicitor should be told of the availability of the local duty solicitor scheme and be provided with a list of such solicitors who are available to provide advice and assistance to detained persons. A duty solicitor should usually be available to provide advice at the police station under the duty solicitor scheme.

If a solicitor is told in the initial telephone call that the suspect is a juvenile, he should speak to him straightaway. In the case of a direct referral from the Criminal Defence Service a duty solicitor must give initial advice on the telephone unless they can advise the client in person without delay. Additionally under the old General Criminal Contract first contact with the client took place within 45 minutes of the solicitor being informed that the client was in custody. This is still good practice in relation to a juvenile client. It is not necessary to wait for the appropriate adult to arrive. Attendance at the police station by the solicitor is required if the client is a juvenile (Part B para 8.2.7). The solicitor representing a juvenile both in the police station and in any subsequent proceedings must not lose sight of the fact that it is the juvenile who is the client and no other person, whether that other person is a parent or social worker. The solicitor should explain this to the appropriate adult at an early stage to reduce the possibility of any misunderstanding later. The Law Society document *Youth Court Guide – Defence Good Practice* (Law Society Criminal Practitioners Newsletter April 2002 available at www.thelawsociety.org.uk), emphasised that the solicitor's primary duty is to the client and that this is the child or young person. No one else whether parent or social worker should be allowed to give instructions. The Law Society's advice makes it clear that instructions should be taken from the juvenile and goes on to say that working with the family and appropriate adult is ancillary but should be approached with respect to their anxiety. Note for Guidance 1E makes it clear that the juvenile detainee has the right to see the solicitor in private. It is often more prudent for the solicitor to see the juvenile in private. If the consultation is to be in the absence of the appropriate adult then steps should be taken by the solicitor to ensure that the appropriate adult understands, particularly if he or she is a parent, what the reasons are for this. If the solicitor speaks to the juvenile alone, he may tell the appropriate adult what was said if the juvenile consents.

The solicitor representing the juvenile in the police station must take steps to be aware of the appropriate adult's attitude to information given in private consultation. The British Association of Social Workers and The Association of Directors of Social Services have both indicated that social workers have a duty to assist in the prevention and detection of crime and if asked they should pass on relevant information to the police. The Department of Health has issued guidance where it contemplates that disclosure will take place if the social worker considers that the juvenile suspect presents a danger to another person or the general public: LAC (88)17. The Law Society Criminal Law Committee has stated that the suspect should be advised in the absence of the appropriate adult about the risk of disclosure and then a decision should be taken by the client about admitting the appropriate adult to the consultations between the lawyer and the client. The Law Society's advice in *Youth Court Cases*

– *Defence Good Practice* is for the solicitor to talk to the juvenile client alone both at the outset and at the various stages of the process.

The solicitor owes a duty of confidentiality to all clients including juveniles. This should be carefully explained to a juvenile client who may well see the solicitor as just another authority figure. The only exception to this is where there is a substantial fear that the juvenile may be in danger of abuse (*The Guide to Professional Conduct of Solicitors*).

If the appropriate adult is already at the police station when information is given to the detained juvenile about his rights then this should be done in the appropriate adult's presence. If the appropriate adult is not present at the police station when the information is given then the information should be repeated to the detainee when the appropriate adult attends (C3.17).

The Law Society Good Practice Guide (*Youth Court Cases – Defence Good Practice*) advises solicitors when dealing with juveniles to have regard to the following:

> 'To start, when taking instructions, by seeking basic details about the client and his circumstances;
>
> to be aware of learning disabilities, ascertain details of school attended and ask if appropriate if anyone helps with their reading;
>
> to take time to prepare the client for interview and to tell him how it will be conducted;
>
> to carefully explain the caution and its consequences;
>
> to consider conducting a practice interview with the client if the advice is to make no comment.'

THE CUSTODY RECORD

1.12   The custody record is a log kept by the custody sergeant recording all that happens to or concerning the detained person whilst in police custody.

In the case of a juvenile detainee the custody officer is to note the following in the custody record:
(a)   details of special action taken in respect of a juvenile detainee under Code C paras 3.12 3.20; (Code C, para 3.24).

    (b) where a juvenile is kept in a cell the reason for this; (Code C, para 8.10).

    (c) the grounds for interviewing a detained juvenile in the absence of the appropriate adult (Code C 11.20).

These are in addition to the many other matters that have to be noted for all detainees.

The appropriate adult has the right to inspect the custody record, as has the detainee and his solicitor.

INTERVIEWS

1.13 A person under 17 years must not be interviewed or asked to provide or sign a written statement in the absence of the appropriate adult. This applies whether the juvenile is suspected of committing an offence or not. The only exception to this is where an officer of the rank of superintendent or above considers that delay will lead to one of the following consequences:

    (a) interference with or harm to evidence connected with an offence or physical harm to other people or serious loss or damage to property; or

    (b) the alerting of other people suspected of having committed an offence but not yet arrested for it; or

    (c) hindering the recovery of property obtained in consequence of the commission of an offence, and a superintendent is satisfied that the interview would not significantly harm the juvenile's physical or mental state (C 11.18).

In those circumstances interviewing may not continue once sufficient information to avert the immediate risk has been obtained. A record has to be made of the grounds for any decision to interview without the appropriate adult and the notes of guidance state that this should only be done in urgent cases of need (Code of Practice C 11.19).

The police are required to inform the appropriate adult present at an interview that he is not expected to act simply as an observer but also to advise the person being questioned; to observe whether the interview is being conducted properly and fairly; and to facilitate communication with the person being interviewed (C 11.17).

Juveniles may only be interviewed at school in exceptional circumstances and only where the principal or his nominee agrees. Every effort should be made to notify either both parents or the other persons responsible for the juvenile's welfare and the appropriate adult (if a different person) that the police want to interview the juvenile and reasonable time should be allowed to enable the appropriate adult to be present at the interview. Where waiting for the appropriate adult would cause unreasonable delay (unless the interviewee is suspected of an offence against the educational establishment), the principal or his nominee can act as the appropriate adult for the purposes of the interview (C 11.16).

The notes for guidance remind the police that although juveniles are often capable of providing reliable evidence they may, without knowing or wishing to do so, be particularly prone in certain circumstances to provide information which is unreliable, misleading, or self incriminating. Special care is therefore to be exercised in questioning juveniles. Because of the risk of unreliable evidence, it is also important to obtain corroboration of any facts admitted whenever possible (C 11C).

If a juvenile is a ward of court, the police can interview him without getting permission from the court, provided they follow the rules for interviewing juveniles. Those having care of the juvenile must notify the court of what has happened at the earliest opportunity (*Re G (minors)* [1990] 2 All ER 633).

Juvenile suspects have the same right to remain silent that adults have. The police must caution the juvenile. The words of the caution are:

> 'You do not have to say anything. But it may harm your defence if you do not mention now something which you later rely on in court. Anything you do say may be given in evidence.'

It is important to ensure that the juvenile understands the meaning of the caution and particular care must be taken to explain it in language that he or she will understand. CJPOA 1994, ss 34, 36 and 37 apply to juveniles and a court may draw proper inferences from a failure to answer questions.

IDENTIFICATION PROCEDURES

1.14 Any procedure involving the participation of a juvenile (whether as a suspect or a witness) must take place in the presence of the appropriate adult. Any procedure requiring information to be given to or sought from a juvenile suspect must be given or sought in the presence of the appropriate adult, and if he has not arrived it must be repeated in his presence when he arrives (D2.14). Thus identification procedures including video identification when the juvenile is present, identification parades, group identifications or confrontations must always take place in the presence of the appropriate adult.

It is generally necessary for a suspect to consent to taking part in a video identification or an identification parade. However, under PACE 1984, s 64A an officer may photograph a detainee at a police station with consent or without if it is withheld or it is not practicable to obtain consent. Code D Note for Guidance 5E gives as one example of impracticability the situation where the parent or guardian cannot be contacted in sufficient time to allow the photograph to be taken. A juvenile suspect's consent is valid only if given in the presence of the appropriate adult and the consent of the parent or guardian is required as well as his own (unless he is under 14 years in which case the consent of the parent or guardian alone is sufficient (D2.12)). For the purposes of D2.12 in the case of a juvenile in the care of the local authority the consent may be given by the authority (see Note D: 2A). However the consent of, for example, a social worker present as appropriate adult will not suffice if the juvenile is not in care. If the only obstacle to an identification procedure is that a juvenile(C:'s parent or guardian refuses consent or reasonable efforts to obtain it have failed the identification officer may arrange a video identification in accordance with Code D Annex A. The parent or guardian who is asked to consent does not have to be at the police station, but they must be given an opportunity to speak to the juvenile detainee and the appropriate adult if they so wish before giving their consent. The consent, if given, must be informed consent (Note D: 2A Annex A para 7).

Video identification parades electronic recording (VIPER) is a speedier process than the old-fashioned method of holding identification parades involving volunteers. A short video film of the suspect with other volunteers of a similar age and appearance is prepared and shown to witnesses. The witness will attend to look at the film with an identification officer and the suspect's legal representative, whose role is to observe the procedure and the manner in which it is conducted. The witness will watch the film at least twice and be asked if they can make a positive identification. The identification officer may then ask some questions for the purposes of clarification.

Where a suspect refuses to take part in a video identification or an identification parade, a group identification can be held or a witness can be shown a moving video made for the purposes of an identification. The suspect should be asked for his consent in the presence of the appropriate adult, but even if he refuses the group identification can still proceed and the video can still be made. The suspect, the appropriate adult and the suspect's solicitor should all be shown the film to enable objections to be made before it is shown to witnesses.

SEARCHES

Initial search

1.15 A search on initial detention at the police station under PACE 1984, s 54 and Code C, section 4 does not have to be carried out in the presence of an appropriate adult. This will normally involve no more than emptying of pockets and rubbing down over clothing, or removal of outer clothing.

Search to establish identity

1.16 A police officer of the rank of inspector or above may authorise a search or examination for the purposes of ascertaining whether a mark would tend to identify the detained person as being involved in the commission of an offence or for the purpose of establishing their identity: PACE 1985, s 54A(1)(a) and(b). Authorisation may only be given where consent has been withheld or it has been impracticable to obtain. In the case of a juvenile this might be applied where the parent or guardian could not be contacted in sufficient time to allow the search, examination or photograph to be carried out.

Strip search

1.17 This is a search involving the removal of more than outer clothing. A strip search should normally be conducted by a police officer of the same sex as the juvenile or take place in the presence of the appropriate adult of the same sex. The search may proceed in the appropriate adult's absence in cases of urgency where there is a risk of serious harm to the person being searched or others. The juvenile may signify that he or she does not wish the appropriate adult present during the search or that he or she wishes an appropriate adult of the opposite sex who is readily available to be present and if this is done the appropriate adult need not be present. This must however be signified in the appropriate adult's presence and must be recorded and signed by the appropriate adult.

Intimate search

1.18 This consists of the examination of the person's bodily orifices other than the mouth. It must only be carried out by medical practitioner or a nurse (Annex A para. 2.4) unless an officer, of at least the rank of inspector, considers it is not practicable, in which case a police officer may carry out the search (Notes A1-A5). Such a search must always be carried out in the presence of the appropriate adult of the same sex. The juvenile may signify that he or she wishes the search to take place without an appropriate adult or in the presence of an appropriate adult of the opposite sex who is readily available. This must however be signified in the appropriate adult's presence and must be recorded and signed by the appropriate adult.

Intimate samples

1.19 An appropriate adult of the same sex must be present during the taking of intimate samples involving the removal of clothing in circumstances likely to lead to embarrassment. The juvenile may signify that he or she wishes this to take place without an appropriate adult or in the presence of an appropriate adult of the opposite sex who is readily available. This must however be signified in the appropriate adult's presence and must be recorded and signed by the appropriate adult.

POLICE DETENTION OF JUVENILES

1.20 A juvenile should not be placed in a police cell unless there is no other secure accommodation available and the custody officer considers that it is not practicable to supervise him if he is not placed in a cell, or the custody officer considers that a cell provides more comfortable accommodation than other secure accommodation within the police station. A juvenile may not be placed in a cell with a detained adult. If a juvenile is placed in a cell the reason must be recorded on the custody record (C 8.8).

All detainees should be visited every hour but juveniles should be visited more often wherever possible (Code C Note for guidance 9B).

AFTER CHARGE

1.21 The custody officer is required by PACE 1984, s 37 to decide whether there is sufficient evidence to charge a detained person, although it is for the Crown Prosecution Service (CPS) to decide whether a suspect should be charged and with what they should be charged. CPS lawyers are available either in police stations or by phone via CPS direct. If the detained person is charged, he must be cautioned, the charge must be read to him and he must be given a written notice showing particulars of the offence with which he is charged. This must include the name of the officer in the case, his police station and the reference number for the case. The charge is to be stated in simple terms but the particulars should also show the precise offence in law with which the defendant is charged. Where a juvenile is charged an appropriate adult must be present and the notice is to be given to the appropriate adult. A record must be kept of anything said at the time of charging.

The general duties of the custody officer, before charge, are set out in PACE 1984, s 37.The custody officer shall order the release of a juvenile from detention either on bail or without bail, unless:

(a)

    (i) his name or address cannot be ascertained or the custody officer has reasonable grounds for doubting whether a name or address furnished by him is his real name or address;

    (ii) the custody officer has reasonable grounds for believing that the person arrested will fail to appear in court to answer bail;

    (iii) in the case of a person arrested for an imprisonable offence the custody officer has reasonable grounds for believing that the detention of the person arrested is necessary to prevent him from committing an offence;

    (iv) in the case of a person arrested for an offence which is not an imprisonable offence, the custody officer has reasonable grounds for believing that the detention of the person arrested is necessary to prevent him causing physical injury to any other person or causing loss or damage to property;

    (v) the custody officer has reasonable grounds for believing that the detention of the person arrested is necessary to prevent

> him interfering with the administration of justice or with the investigation of the offences or of a particular offence; or
>
> (vi) the custody officer has reasonable grounds for believing that the detention of the arrested person is necessary for his own protection;
>
> (b) additionally, an arrested juvenile may be detained if the custody officer has reasonable grounds for believing that he ought to be detained in his own interests (PACE 1984, s 38(1)); or
>
> (c) where drug test procedures are in place a detention of a juvenile between the ages of 14 and 17 may be authorised where it is necessary to enable the sample to be taken: PACE ss 37 and 63B.

'Own interests' is not defined and thus the custody officer has a wide discretion.

In taking the decisions required by (a) and (b) above (except (a)(i) and (vi) and (b)) the custody officer is required to consider whether there are substantial grounds for believing that the defendant, if released on bail, would:

> (a) fail to surrender to custody; or
>
> (b) commit an offence while on bail; or
>
> (c) interfere with witnesses or otherwise obstruct the course of justice, whether in relation to himself or any other person (PACE 1984, s 38(2A)).

Where a custody officer authorises an arrested juvenile to be kept in police detention the custody officer shall ensure that the arrested juvenile is moved to local authority accommodation. The exceptions to this are where the custody officer certifies that:

> (a) by reason of such circumstances as are specified in the certificate, it is impracticable for him to do so; (see *R v Chief Constable of Cambridgeshire, ex p M* [1991] 2 QB 499) or
>
> (b) in the case of the arrested juvenile who has attained the age of 12 years that no secure accommodation is available and that keeping him in other local authority accommodation would not be adequate to protect the public from serious harm from him (PACE 1984, s 38(6)(b)).

R v Chief Constable of Cambridgeshire, ex p M which was decided both before the revision to Code C in April 1991 and before the Criminal Justice Act 1991, is sometimes interpreted to mean that a custody officer would be justified in deciding that the transfer would not be practicable if he believed that the accommodation would not be secure. Home Office Circular 78/1992 'Criminal Justice Act 1991: Detention of Juveniles' states that the construction of s 38(6)(a)

> 'makes it clear that the type of accommodation in which the local authority proposes to place the juvenile is not a factor which the custody officer may take into account in considering whether the transfer is impracticable. In particular the unavailability of local authority secure accommodation does not make the transfer impracticable.'

The circular indicates that 'impracticable' means circumstances where transfer would be physically impossible by reason of, for example, floods, blizzards, or the impossibility despite repeated efforts of contacting the local authority. Code C, note 16D provides that:

> 'Neither a juvenile's behaviour nor the nature of the offence with which he is charged provides grounds for the custody officer to retain him in police custody rather than seek to arrange his transfer to local authority accommodation.'

Where the juvenile is charged with a violent or sexual offence, 'protecting the public from serious harm from him' is to be construed as a reference to protecting members of the public from death or serious personal injury, whether physical or psychological, occasioned by further such offences committed by him (PACE 1984, s 38(6A)).

Where the arrested juvenile is moved to local authority accommodation, it is lawful for any person acting on behalf of the local authority to detain him. (PACE 1984, s 38(6B)) The Children Act 1989, s 21(2) stipulates that every local authority shall receive and provide accommodation for children who are referred under PACE 1984, s 38(6).

The custody officer is under a duty to do everything practicable to ensure that the place of detention for the juvenile is in local authority accommodation and not the police station. In para (b) specific reference is made to taking the lack of secure accommodation into account for young persons who have attained the age of 12 years when deciding whether to transfer them to local authority accommodation. It is submitted that this may not be used as a reason for not so transferring those who are under that age pursuant to para (a).

The certificate under these provisions made in respect of an arrested juvenile shall be produced to the court to which he was first brought.

Although the certificate must be produced to the court, the statute neither provides any sanction for non compliance nor gives the court any powers to act on its non production where the custody officer certifies under s 38(6)(a). Neither the juvenile's unruliness, nor the nature of the offence with which he is charged, provide grounds for the custody officer to fail to arrange this transfer. The requirement to transfer to local authority accommodation applies to a juvenile charged during daytime as it does to a juvenile to be held overnight.

The Police and Criminal Evidence Act 1984, s 39(4) makes it clear that upon such a transfer to local authority accommodation the custody officer's duties cease.

It should be noted that there is no duty to transfer to local authority accommodation where the juvenile has been arrested on a warrant not backed for bail or for breach of bail conditions or breach of remand conditions.

Arrangements should be made for preventing a child or young person under 17 while detained in a police station or being conveyed to or from any criminal court from associating with an adult (not being a relative) who is charged with any offence other than an offence with which the child is jointly charged. Arrangements should also be made to ensure that a girl should be in the care of a woman (CYPA 1933, s 31).

BREACHES OF CODES OF PRACTICE

1.22 A breach of the Codes can lead to evidence obtained as a result of the breach being treated as inadmissible (PACE 1984, ss 76, 76A and 77), or excluded (PACE 1984, ss 78 and 82). A breach of the PACE Codes of Practice may also lead to disciplinary action being taken against the police officer. Such action may only be instigated by the police ie not by a civilian or a solicitor.

CONFESSIONS

1.23 PACE 1984, s 76(2) states that:

'If, in any proceedings where the prosecution proposes to give in evidence a confession made by an accused person, it is represented to the court that the confession was or may have been obtained:

(a) by oppression of the person who made it; or
(b) in consequence of anything said or done which was likely, in the circumstances existing at the time, to render unreliable any confession which might be made by him in consequence thereof,

the court shall not allow the confession to be given in evidence against him except in so far as the prosecution proves to the court beyond reasonable doubt that the confession (notwithstanding that it may be true) was not obtained as aforesaid.'

Section 76A of PACE contains similar provisions to allow a court to exclude the confession of a co-accused sought to be adduced against another in the same proceedings.

'Confession' includes any statement wholly or partly adverse to the person who made it, whether made to a person in authority or not and whether made in words or otherwise (PACE 1984, s 82(1)). 'Oppression' includes torture, inhuman or degrading treatment, and the use or threat of violence (whether or not amounting to torture) (PACE 1984, s 76(8)).

An example of conduct found to be 'unsporting' but not oppressive is the case of *R v Fulling* [1987] QB 426. The facts involved the interviewing of a 34-year-old woman who was questioned 'persistently' about her involvement in an offence of obtaining insurance money by the deception that her home had been burgled. She exercised her right to silence until informed that her lover (also implicated in the offence) had been having an affair, whereupon she became so distressed that (she alleged) she made a statement simply in order to be released from custody. However in *R v Beales* [1991] Crim LR 118 where a defendant was hectored and bullied from first to last, the interview was said to have stepped into the realm of oppression. The Court of Appeal held in *R v Cox* [1991] Crim LR 276 that a trial judge should have excluded a confession that was obtained by oppression, even when the defendant accepted that it was true.

The Court of Appeal held that:
(a) the 1984 Act was not intended to follow the common law. The modern law is to be ascertained by interpreting the Act, not by 'roaming over a vast number of authorities';
(b) the definition in s 76(8) is not all embracing, but is to be extended to cover anything within the ordinary dictionary meaning of the word. The particular definition relied upon was 'exercise of authority or power in a burdensome, harsh, or wrongful manner,

or unjust or cruel treatment, or the imposition of unreasonable or unjust burdens';

(c) oppression implies some impropriety on the part of the interrogator, which leads to the confession. If the defendant would have confessed in any event s 76(2) will not apply. Section 76(2)(b) is potentially wider since it covers not only threats, but also promises. This could apply, for example, where a defendant is offered favourable treatment in return for a confession, such as a promise not to oppose bail. Note, PACE Code C 11.5 also prohibits such behaviour.

The effect of s 76(2) is that in summary proceedings justices should, before the end of the prosecution case:

(a) hold a 'trial within a trial' if it is represented to them by the defence that a confession was, or might have been, obtained by either 'oppression', or in circumstances which might render the confession 'unreliable';

(b) in such a 'trial within a trial' allow the defendant to give evidence confined to the question of admissibility, and the justices will not then be concerned with the truth or otherwise of the confession;

(c) give the defendant a ruling on the admissibility of a confession before or at the end of the prosecution case, in case he should wish to make a submission of no case to answer at the end of the prosecution evidence and ask that the case be dismissed at that point;

(d) not allow the prosecution evidence relating to the obtaining of the confession to be called twice (*R v Liverpool Juvenile Court, ex p R* [1988] 1 QB 1).

It is worth noting that even where a confession is not excluded under s 76(2) it does not prevent it being excluded under s 78(1) on the basis that it would adversely affect the fairness of the proceedings (see **1.24**).

EVIDENCE UNFAIRLY OBTAINED

1.24 The Police and Criminal Evidence Act 1984, s 78 provides that:

(1) In any proceedings the court may refuse to allow evidence on which the prosecution proposes to rely to be given if it appears to the court that, having regard to all the circumstances, including the circumstances in which the evidence was obtained, the

      admission of the evidence would have such an adverse effect on the fairness of the proceedings that the court ought not to admit it.

(2) Nothing in this section shall prejudice any rule of law requiring a court to exclude evidence.

These provisions apply just as much to juveniles as they do to adults.

An example of how the section works can be found in *R v Deacon* [1987] Crim LR 404. Admissions made to the police were ruled inadmissible by the judge on the grounds that the police had wrongly refused the defendant access to his solicitor. It was said that to have allowed the evidence to go before the jury would have had an adverse effect upon the fairness of the trial. Technical breaches of the Code of Practice (defendant not allowed eight hours of continuous rest and failure to record the time the interview ended) weighed little in the decision but nonetheless were to be taken into account. The jury was accordingly directed to acquit the defendant.

However, where the question of unfairness is raised under PACE 1984, s 78 there is no general requirement to conduct a 'trial within a trial' to be held. (*Vel v Owen* [1987] Crim LR 496)

With specific reference to a juvenile court case the Divisional Court in *DC (a juvenile) v DPP* (9 November 1987, unreported) confirmed that there is no obligation upon a magistrates' court to hold a 'trial within a trial' where it is represented to the court that it should use its discretion under PACE 1984, s 78 to exclude evidence of a confession in circumstances where it is not represented that such evidence was or might have been obtained in breach of PACE 1984, s 76(2) or indeed in breach of the ECHR articles: see *Halawa v Federation Against Copyright Theft* [1995] 1 Cr App Rep 21.

Any magistrates' court has power to make a binding ruling before the start of a trial where it believes it to be in the interests of justice to do so: MCA 1980, s 8A (1) and (3).

Such a ruling could include the admission of a confession and would involve representations from both parties. The effect of such a ruling is that it is binding from the time it is made until the case is disposed of: MCA 1980, s 8B(1).

There is power to vary a binding ruling under MCA1980, s 8B(3) and (5), but no application to do so may be made, unless there has been a material change in circumstances or fresh evidence since the ruling was made: *R (on the application of the CPS) v Gloucester Justices* (2008) 172 JP 406.

In general terms no report may be made for a hearing involving a pre-trial binding ruling: MCA 1980 s 8C(1) and (2).

Chapter 2

Prosecution and the constitution of the Court

INTRODUCTION

2.01   The belief that a court appearance by a juvenile will not prevent, and indeed may induce further, offending was encapsulated in the Government's White Paper *Young Offender* published in 1980 where it was stated that:

> 'All the available evidence suggests that juvenile offenders who can be diverted from the criminal justice system at an early age in their offending are less likely to re-offend than those who become involved in judicial proceedings.'

Cautioning as a means of diversion was replaced in the Crime and Disorder Act 1998 by a reprimand and final warnings scheme. In terms of re-offending diversion is as effective as other disposals: Home Office statistics show that four out of five young people aged 14–20 cautioned for a standard list of offences are not re-convicted within two years of the caution. A new conditional caution is introduced by the Criminal Justice and Immigration Act 2008 (see **2.04**).

Diversion means that a juvenile neither has to appear in court nor is he convicted or sentenced. A juvenile who is dealt with in this manner avoids the damaging stigma of criminal proceedings. Broadly, the choices available are to take informal action, to reprimand, to give a final warning, to impose a conditional caution, or to bring proceedings before the Youth Court.

Reprimands and warnings are seen as an early intervention designed to stop offending. The responsibility for decision-making under the final warning scheme rests with the police and the Crown Prosecution Service.

PACE, s 37, as amended by CJA 2003, Sch 2, provides that where a custody officer determines that there is sufficient evidence to charge a person with an offence he shall refer the case to a Crown Prosecutor. The prosecutor then decides whether the juvenile should be charged or offered a reprimand or final warning.

Where a restorative approach or a rehabilitation programme is contemplated the police will involve the youth offending team for assistance in carrying out a prior assessment of the young offender. The assessment is conducted by the youth offending team within 10 working days. The assessment is based upon the 'ASSET' tool and this may involve a visit to the young person, his family and, where relevant, the victim. (See Appendix F) The Home Office guidance specifies the purpose of a prior assessment as being an exploration of the young offender's attitude to intervention and an assessment of the likelihood of his engaging with a rehabilitation or change programme.

REPRIMANDS AND FINAL WARNINGS

Terminology

2.02 *Informal action*: as the overall aim of the final warnings scheme is to end repeat cautioning, the police have a strictly limited discretion to take informal action. Such informal action may comprise of giving advice to a juvenile and his or her parents in circumstances where this is considered to be an effective deterrent to future offending. Usually this will be in cases of minor non-recordable offences or anti-social behaviour which falls short of real criminal activity.

A *reprimand*: will be given to first-time offenders or for less serious offences. A reprimand will usually be delivered by a police officer at a police station. If the reprimand is carried out as part of a restorative approach the victim may be present at a full restorative conference. If a reprimand is given and the victim was not present they must be informed in writing unless they have requested otherwise. Where the offender is under 17, the reprimand must be in the presence of a parent, guardian or other appropriate adult. The full guidance to the police is provided in the Home Office document *Final Warnings Scheme*. See Appendix E or http://www.homeoffice.gov.uk/docs and www.youth-justice-board.gov.uk.

Final warning: is used for offenders who have been reprimanded previously and under the scheme therefore cannot be given a further reprimand. Second-time offenders who have already received a warning cannot receive a reprimand nor should they receive further warning. An exception to this is where the new offence has been committed more than two years since the previous warning and the police officer considers it is not so serious as to require a criminal charge. Although the guidance envisages that a reprimand will be used for first offences and a warning for second offences a police officer must issue a final warning rather than a reprimand if the offence is so serious as to prohibit a reprimand.

In no circumstances, however can a juvenile receive more than two warnings. Following the issue of a warning the youth offending team must be notified so that the further assessment can take place and arrangements made for the young offender to participate in a rehabilitation programme. This may contain some reparative work or individual work with the offender. A record will be maintained detailing the juvenile's attendance and participation.

Under the final warning scheme a juvenile must be assessed as being eligible before either step can be taken. Eligibility consists of five factors:

(a) an offence has been identified, supported by evidence and the juvenile is likely to be charged unless the reprimand or warning is given;

(b) there is evidence against the juvenile sufficient to give a realistic prospect of conviction if a prosecution were commenced;

(c) the juvenile admits the offence. Such an admission must be clear and reliable and cover all the elements of the offence for example dishonesty and a guilty mind where applicable. In *R (On the application of U) v Metropolitan Police Comr* [2002] EWCA 2486 (Admin), [2003] 3 All ER 419, the High Court quashed a final warning given for indecent assault on the basis that the admission had been procured by an inducement and so there had been no informed consent. Guidance to the police however makes it clear that, unlike adult cautions, a juvenile does not 'consent' to a reprimand or warning; the decision rests with the police as to the appropriate disposal (see **12.03** below);

(d) the juvenile has not previously been convicted of an offence either recordable or non-recordable. This of course includes minor road traffic offences such as speeding and can lead to a young person being subject to a final warning for a very minor criminal matter when his only conviction is for a minor road traffic infringement;

(e) it is not in the public interest for the offender to be prosecuted. In assessing the public interest police have regard to the ACPO Gravity Factors. These are reproduced in Appendix E.

In *R (on the application of R) v Durham Constabulary* [2005] UKHL 21, it was held that that the issue of whether the offender consented to a reprimand *or* warning was effectively irrelevant.

Generally, the High Court will not interfere with a decision to prosecute rather than give a warning unless the authorities have departed from the guidelines without rational explanation. In *R (A) v South Yorkshire Police* (2007) 171 JP 465, a case in which an initial mistake in the gravity score was reviewed by the CPS and the decision to prosecute endorsed due to the aggravating features of the offence, the High Court held that this was not manifestly unreasonable.

In *R (on application of the S) v DPP* [2006] All ER (D) 329 (June) the High Court reiterated that it would not interfere unless it could be said that it had not been open to a reasonable prosecutor to decide that a prosecution was in the public interest.

Those advising juveniles at police stations must be aware that the opportunity for a final warning may be lost where a client makes no comment at interview because an admission is required. The prosecution are within their rights to pursue a prosecution and refuse to accept a subsequent admission as a basis for a warning (*R (on the application of F) v DPP* (2004)167 JPN 965). In all cases the views of the victim should be sought and, although the victim's consent to reprimand or warning is not required, it does give the victim an opportunity to express their views on the offence and to be kept informed of the outcome of the case should they so wish.

The venue for delivery of a reprimand or final warning should be suitable, easily accessible and secure, eg a police station or YOT office and should not be carried out in the street or in a person's home. The reprimand or final warning should be delivered by a police officer. If the officer is not a member of the YOT then a representative should be present, as the YOT will carry out any follow up intervention programme.

Any advice given by a defence solicitor on the benefits of a reprimand or a final warning must be balanced against the consequences of agreeing to such an order, for example where it gives rise to registration under the sex offenders register.

The effect of a reprimand or final warning

2.03 The police are required to keep records of reprimands and warnings and these may be cited like convictions in any future criminal proceedings. A reprimand or warning will remain on the Police National Computer for five years or until the offender attains the age of 18, whichever is the later. There is also provision for reports to be made to court on a juvenile's participation in any non-voluntary rehabilitation programme following the issue of final warnings.

A further important consequence is the restriction in the Crime and Disorder Act 1998, s 66 which states that where a person who has been warned under s 65 is convicted of an offence within two years of the warning, a court (including a magistrates' court) shall not impose a conditional discharge unless there are exceptional circumstances relating to the offence or the offender. The court is also required to state its reasons for finding exceptional circumstances.

Conditional cautions

2.04 When fully in force, Sch 19 of the Criminal Justice and Immigration Act 2008 gives the prosecution an additional option of imposing a conditional caution. This is the only caution that may be given to a child or young person. As with all diversions from prosecution the constable involved must consider that there is sufficient evidence to charge the offender with the offence. The same qualifications and restrictions for warnings and reprimands apply (no previous convictions etc) but instead of charging the offender a youth conditional caution may be given.

A youth conditional caution is a caution in respect of an offence committed by the offender to which conditions are attached with which the offender must comply. Any condition attached must have the objective of facilitating the rehabilitation of the offender and/or ensuring that the offender makes reparation for the offence and/or punishing the offender. A financial penalty may be imposed as a condition but only for a prescribed offence and in an amount of no more than £100. Payment of such an order is to a designated officer for a local justice area: CDA 1998, ss 66B and 66C.

Before making a conditional caution the authorised person, who may be the constable, investigating officer or a person authorised by relevant prosecutor, must satisfy five requirements. Those requirements are that:

(1) there is evidence that the offender has committed an offence;

(2) there is sufficient evidence to charge the offender with the offence and that a youth conditional caution should be given in respect of that offence;

(3) the offender admits to the authorised person that he committed the offence;

(4) the authorised person explains the effect of the youth conditional caution to the offender and warns him that failure to comply with any of the conditions attached may result in his being prosecuted for the offence (if the offender is 16 or under this must be done in the presence of an appropriate adult);

(5) the offender signs a document containing details of the offence, his admission, his consent to being given a youth conditional caution and details of the conditions attached to that caution.

If the offender fails, without reasonable excuse, to comply with any of the conditions attached to the youth conditional caution, criminal proceedings may be instituted against him for the offence in question. The document mentioned above may be admissible in such proceedings, and on the commencement of the proceedings the conditional caution ceases to have effect. As with reprimands and warnings, if a person who has been given a conditional caution is convicted of an offence committed within two years of the caution the court so convicting him may not make a conditional discharge in respect of the offence unless it is of the opinion that there are exceptional circumstances relating to the offence or the offender which justify its doing so: CDA 1998, s 66F.

PROSECUTION

2.05   The decision to charge or summons a juvenile in practice rests with the police and the CPS, although a prosecution may be commenced by any person, unless the statute under which the prosecution is brought states otherwise. It is worth noting however, that where the Crown have administered a formal warning and the offender is told that he will not have to go to court, it will be an abuse of process to allow a private prosecution in those circumstances: *Jones v Walley* [2006] All ER (D) 369.

However, as soon as proceedings are instituted, the Crown Prosecution Service is under a duty to take over the conduct of these proceedings. (Prosecution of Offences Act 1985, s 3(2) (POA 1985))

The Director of Public Prosecutions also has the right at any stage to take over the conduct of criminal proceedings if he thinks it appropriate, even though he may be under no duty to do so. (POA 1985, s 6(2))

The Crown Prosecutor may decide during the preliminary stages that the prosecution should be discontinued. Discontinuance has nothing to do with the philosophies behind diversion from prosecution but is based upon a Code of Practice published on behalf of the Director of Public Prosecutions.

The Crown Prosecutor's discretion to discontinue proceedings will therefore be exercised on the basis of such questions as, whether or not the evidence against the defendant is sufficient to provide a realistic prospect of a conviction, whether it is in the public interest to continue the prosecution, the likely penalty, the age of the defendant and the complainant's attitude to the offence. The Crown Prosecution Service 'Code for Crown Prosecutors' (2004) stresses that Crown Prosecutors should not avoid going to court simply because of the juvenile's age. In carrying out the public interest test regard must be given to the gravity factors matrix (Appendix D) and the seriousness of the offence and the offender's past behaviour, all of which may make a prosecution necessary.

Where proceedings are discontinued the Crown Prosecutor will give the defendant notice of his decision and, where the Youth Court is already seized of the case, the court shall also be served with a discontinuance notice. Discontinuance takes effect from the time the discontinuance notice is given. It should be noted that the prosecutor's power to discontinue is in addition to his powers to offer no evidence or withdraw the case, with or without the consent of the court (*R v DPP, ex p Cooke* (1991) 95 Cr App Rep 233).

If the accused wishes the proceedings to continue (where for instance he wishes to clear his name publicly) he must send notice to the court within 35 days of the date when proceedings were discontinued requiring the court to re-list the case.

Once the decision to prosecute has been taken, the police or other informants have a duty to notify the local authority and the probation service of their decision (CYPA 1969, ss 5(8) and 34(2)). In effect this is notification to the youth offending team. In the case of *DPP v Cottier* [1996] 3 All ER 126 it was held that such notification was directory and not mandatory and, as such would not jeopardise proceedings where the prosecution had omitted to make such notification.

Having been so notified, the local authority and probation service via the youth offending team have a duty to provide information to the court as to home surroundings, school record and health and character of the person being prosecuted unless they are of the opinion that it is not necessary to do so (CYPA 1969, s 9). Reports are usually provided by a youth offending team after a conviction has been recorded and a specific request made for a report.

THE YOUTH COURT PANEL

2.06   The general rule under CYPA 1933, s 46 is that no charge against a juvenile may be heard in a magistrates' court other than a Youth Court unless the juvenile is jointly charged with an adult, when the case must be directed in the first instance to the adult court and may be so directed if the juvenile is in some other way connected with an adult's case.

For this reason offenders under 18 are generally dealt with in specially constituted courts of summary jurisdiction called Youth Courts. In the Inner London area there is one combined Youth Court panel; in every other local justice area there must be a Youth Court panel or combined panel approved by the Lord Chief Justice.

The establishment of Youth Court panels is governed by the Youth Courts (Constitution of Committees and Rights to Preside) Rules 2007. Each area must have a Youth Court panel, although it is possible, as indicated above, to have combined panels for two or more local justice areas. The Rules are reproduced in Appendix B.

Each Youth Court must be chaired by a justice who is on the list of approved Youth Court chairman drawn up by the bench training and development committee or the Inner London youth training and development committee. The exception to this rule is made where a chairman who is undergoing training may chair where some illness or emergency arises, so that an approved, qualified chairman is not available (Youth Court (Constitution etc) Rules 2007.

A district judge (magistrates' courts) is qualified to sit as a member of a Youth Court without being a panel member and may sit alone.

The Youth Court panel must meet at least twice a year, but more often if necessary. The panel members must elect a chairman and one or more deputy chairmen of the panel for the following calendar year at their election meeting in the autumn. The election may be at the meeting or by postal ballot.

THE YOUTH COURT

2.07 The Youth Court is a court of summary jurisdiction specially constituted for the purpose of hearing any charge against a child or young person and for the purpose of exercising any other jurisdiction conferred on Youth Courts (CYPA 1933, s 45). It is required to sit as often as necessary for the purpose of exercising any jurisdiction conferred on it (CYPA 1933, s 47(1)). The Youth Court is not an open court, those persons who may be present are:

    (a) members and officers of the court. This category includes the justices, their legal advisor and any members of the court staff;

    (b) parties to the case before the court, their solicitors and counsel, and witnesses and other persons directly concerned in the case. This category includes the parents of the juvenile but not, for example, the juvenile's sisters, brothers, cousins, aunts or uncles; if they wish to be present the justices must specifically consider whether or not to allow this. The court may also be faced with the attendance of a parent's co-habitee who has no implicit right to be present but who may be permitted to remain if the court feels it to be desirable;

    (c) *bona fide* representatives of the press, who are restricted in what they may report Youth Court proceedings, but may not reveal the name, address or school, or include any particulars calculated to lead to the identification of the juvenile, except where the court or the Secretary of State specifically authorises such disclosure to avoid injustice to the juvenile;

    (d) such other persons as the court may specifically authorise to be present (CYPA 1933, ss 47 and 49).

The justices thus have a general discretion as to whom they allow into the Youth Court. Persons whom they specifically authorise to be present will often be trainee solicitors, social work students, trainee YOT workers, and researchers with an interest in the Youth Court. The victims of crime may occasionally wish to sit in on Youth Court proceedings. Unless attending as a witness they have no absolute right to do so although the court should normally accede to a request to be present so long as the victim's motivation in wishing to be present is a proper one. The joint Home Office/Lord Chancellor's department circular *Opening up Youth Court Proceedings* encouraged Youth Courts to exercise this discretion particularly so far as the victim is concerned. The circular made it clear that the court could balance the desirability of allowing the victim into the court against the desirability of doing so where the defendant is very young or where there are a number of charges and therefore a number of victims. It is not desirable for the court to be crowded with such people and the justices must limit the number of visitors to ensure that the purpose of having specially constituted Youth Courts is not defeated.

Arrangements must be made to prevent a juvenile, while waiting before or after attendance in any criminal court, from associating with an adult (not being a relative) who is charged with any offence other than an offence with which the juvenile is charged. This segregation is to prevent the contact of juveniles with adult offenders (CYPA 1933, s 31).

Each Youth Court must be constituted of not more than three justices; it may consist of two justices only, and shall include a man and a woman (unless a district judge is sitting). The rule requiring a mixed court is an important legislative policy in relation to the trial of young offenders. Where a mixed gender bench is not available there is discretion under r 10(3) of the Youth Courts (Constitution etc) Rules 2007 to proceed without there being a mixed tribunal. However before such a discretion is exercised the matter should be aired in open court and the views of the parties invited (*R v Birmingham Justices, ex p F* (1999) 164 JP 523). A district judge may sit alone. Having only two justices is acceptable for dealing with an admission but where the court has to decide the question of guilt or innocence it is desirable to have three justices hearing the case, a point emphasised by both a former Lord Chancellor and Lord Chief Justice. Three justices sitting as a bench have a duty to reach a decision having heard all the evidence and may not order the case to be reheard. If there is reasonable doubt then it is their obligation to acquit him (*R v Bromley Justices, ex p Haymill (Contractors) Ltd* [1984] Crim LR 235).

In the event of two justices failing to agree on a verdict a retrial before a fresh bench would have to be ordered, with the consequential expense and waste of court time (*R v Redbridge Justices, ex p Ram* [1992] QB 384). It would also mean putting the juvenile through the ordeal of a second contested hearing. If no man or woman is available, owing to circumstances unforeseen when the justices were chosen, the court may be constituted without a man or a woman, as the case may be, if the members present do not feel it expedient in the interests of justice to adjourn the case. It is generally undesirable for a Youth Court bench not to consist of both sexes (see above). If at any sitting of a Youth Court a youth court chairman is available a member of the panel who has completed their prescribed youth chairmanship training may sit as chairman under their supervision (r 11 of the Youth Court (Constitution etc) Rules 2007).

It should be noted that a justice is not prevented by the rules relating to Youth Courts from exercising the powers of a single justice. This means that a single justice may hear and determine an application to adjourn and remand in custody or on bail, even though the application relates to a juvenile offender.

WARRANT OF FURTHER DETENTION

2.08   The normal procedure is that an arrested juvenile must be charged within 24 hours or released, unless a police officer of the rank of superintendent or above authorises the detention of a person without charge for up to 36 hours if the investigation is for 'an indictable offence', such as an assault occasioning actual bodily harm. The superintendent must also be satisfied that the detention of the subject is necessary to secure or preserve evidence relating to the offence, or to obtain such evidence by questioning him, and that the investigation is being conducted diligently and expeditiously (PACE 1984, s 42).

Applications may be made by the police to a magistrates' court for an authorisation to detain a suspect for a maximum of a further 72 hours before charge, up to a total of 96 hours (PACE 1984, ss 43 and 44). The time for the purposes of either a superintendent's extension or the application to court is calculated from the 'relevant time', which in most cases will be the point when the arrested person arrives at the police station.

Application to the court

2.09   An application for a warrant of further detention may be made even though no application has been made under s 42 to a superintendent.

This may happen where a superintendent is not available, or where it is obvious that detention for more than 36 hours is going to be necessary, eg in a case requiring forensic examination of evidence.

The application must be made before the expiry of 36 hours after 'the relevant time'. In a case where it is not practicable for the magistrates' court (to which the application will be made) to sit at the expiry of 36 hours after the relevant time, but the court will sit during the six hours following the end of that period, the application may be made before the expiry of that extra six hours.

However, if an application is made after the expiry of the 36-hour period and it appears to the court that it would have been reasonable to make it before the expiry of that period, the court shall dismiss the application (*R v Slough Magistrates' Court, ex p Stirling* [1987] Crim LR 576).

The procedure

2.10   Application to the court should where possible be made within normal court hours because of the difficulties in convening special court sessions. The Code of Practice made under PACE provides that it may be impracticable for courts to sit other than between the hours of 10am and 9pm (Code C15D).

Before a court is convened a number of steps must be taken by the police. An information must be prepared stating:
  (a) the nature of the offence for which the person to whom the application relates has been arrested;
  (b) the general nature of the evidence on which that person was arrested;
  (c) what inquiries relating to the offence have been made by the police and what further inquiries are proposed by them;
  (d) the reason for believing the continued detention of that person to be necessary for the purposes of such further inquiries (PACE 1984, s 43(14)).

The hearing

2.11   The court must be composed of at least two justices who in the case of a juvenile need not be on the Youth Court panel as the application is being made before a charge has been preferred and thus not specifically assigned to a Youth Court under CYPA 1933, s 46.

A district judge may sit alone for these purposes.

The court is not an open court and no persons other than the parties and the court officers should be present. Before the court can hear an application the arrested person must have been given a copy of the written information and must have been brought before the court for the hearing.

If the arrested person is not legally represented but wishes to be so represented, the court must adjourn the hearing to enable him to obtain such representation. He may be kept in police detention during such an adjournment (PACE 1984, s 43).

The application commences when a constable appears before the court and gives evidence on oath or affirmation supported by his written information (*R v Slough Magistrates' Court, ex p Stirling* [1987] Crim LR 576). This is a small but important point because of the provision in PACE 1984, s 43(7) which requires the court to dismiss an application for a warrant of further detention, no matter what the grounds, if it appears to the court that the application could have reasonably been made within the 36-hour period. In such a case, the detained person must be released immediately unless charged.

If the application is in order the court will hear the evidence of the police and also any representations or evidence on behalf of the detained person.

A court's decision to issue a warrant of further detention is based on the court being satisfied that there are reasonable grounds for believing that the further detention of the arrested person is justified. If not so satisfied the court must:

(a) refuse the application; or

(b) adjourn the hearing of it until a time not later than 36 hours after the relevant time.

The detained person may be kept in police custody during the adjournment (PACE 1984, s 43(8), (9)).

If the court refuses the application the person to whom it relates shall forthwith be charged or released either on bail or otherwise. However he need not be released before the expiry of 24 hours after the relevant time, or before the expiry of any longer period for which his continued detention is or has been authorised (PACE 1984, s 42(10)).

If an application is refused no further application may be made unless supported by fresh evidence which has come to light since the refusal (PACE 1984, s 43(17)).

The burden of proof

2.12 It is clearly for the police to satisfy the court that the necessary criteria are fulfilled and many commentators have argued that this must be on the criminal standard of proof, ie beyond reasonable doubt. That standard of proof is used in English criminal law as part of an adversarial system to evaluate two sets of conflicting evidence. In the circumstances of an application for a warrant of further detention there may only be the confirmation of the written information on oath. There is no statutory provision for the detained person to call evidence though in practice it should be allowed.

Further, it appears that the general scheme set up under the statute to review police detention does comply with art 5(3) of the European Convention on Human Rights. The words 'reasonable suspicion' have been interpreted as meaning facts or information which would satisfy an objective observer that the detained person may have committed the offence (*Fox, Campbell and Hartley v United Kingdom* (1990) 13 EHRR 157).

In the Bail Act 1976 similar wording is used: 'The defendant need not be granted bail if the court is satisfied that there are substantial grounds for believing that one of the exceptions in Sch I of the Act applies'. *Re Moles* [1981] Crim LR 170, makes it clear that the strict rules of evidence applicable in a criminal trial are inappropriate when the court's duty is to consider whether substantial grounds for believing a particular state of affairs exist.

Whilst the matter has yet to be tested in the High Court the author's views are that magistrates must make these decisions based on the balance of probabilities. The purpose of PACE 1984, s 43 is to allow the police to secure, preserve, or obtain that very evidence. Alternatively, the words of the statute simply require a judgement as to whether the application is made out or not.

The lack of rules of court may cause other problems to the court in making its decision. The police may wish to submit the detained person's criminal record to the court to assist or support their application for a warrant of further detention. It is submitted that this should not normally be allowed by the court on the basis that such information will be irrelevant to the application and the prejudicial value of the previous convictions will outweigh any probative value they may have. However, it may well be that where an offence is strikingly similar in its method of commission to a recorded offence or offences committed by the detained person then a criminal record may indeed go a long way towards satisfying the justices that detention is necessary to secure or preserve evidence relating to the offence in question. It may be argued that CJA 2003, s 101 allows for evidence of bad character to be admitted in criminal proceedings, however that term was defined in the case of *R v Bradley* ([2005] EWCA Crim 20, 169 JP 73), to include any trial or Newton hearing, so although the point was not specifically argued before the court it seems likely that the statue does not apply to detention applications and that the relevance of such convictions may be the determining factor.

Inferences from silence or a failure to explain evidence may not be drawn by the court as a detention application is not included within the ambit of CJPA 1994, s 34(2) or s37(2).

Length of further detention

2.13 If the court accedes to the police application the warrant must state the time at which it was issued and the length of time for which the person to whom it relates may be detained. The period may be any period the court thinks fit but shall not exceed 36 hours.

If it is proposed to transfer the person to another police area the court is required to have regard to the distance and the time the journey would take (PACE 1984, s 43(12) and (13)).

If an application for further detention is refused in circumstances where the original 24-hour period, or 36-hour period with a superintendent's permission, has not run out then the police may continue to hold the suspect until the expiry of the relevant period. The court also has power to adjourn the hearing until some later stage in the 36-hour period.

If a warrant of further detention is refused or the period authorised in the warrant runs out, the detained person must be charged or released either on bail or not. It is however possible to apply for an extension of the warrant.

Whether a court grants or refuses a warrant of further detention it must give its reasons for doing so. Any warrant extending the time of detention must be proportional to the needs of the police to secure evidence, the seriousness of the offence and the possible consequences of an early release.

Extension of warrant of further detention

2.14 Applications may be made for extensions of the period of detention allowed. Again the application must be on oath and supported by an information containing the matters specified in PACE 1984, s 43(14). The court must be satisfied that there are reasonable grounds for believing that the further detention of the person to whom the application relates is justified (PACE 1984, s 44(1)). The overall period of detention may not exceed 96 hours. No single extension may exceed 36 hours. Where an application for extension is refused the detained person must be charged or released either with or without bail. Where an extension is granted the court is to endorse this on the original warrant and not issue a fresh warrant (PACE 1984, s 44).

A person released at the expiry of a warrant of detention may not be re-arrested without a warrant for the offence or new evidence justifying a further arrest which has come to light since his release. (PACE 1984, s 43(19)).

Chapter 3

Attendance at Court

YOUTH COURT TIME LIMITS

3.01   In the magistrates' courts adults may be dealt with for summary offences (offences which may only be heard in a magistrates' court) or either way offences (which may be heard either in the magistrates' court or in the Crown Court before a judge and jury). Offences, which are triable either way, are not generally subject to a time limit during which they must be brought before the court. However, purely summary proceedings must have the information laid by the prosecution within six months of the date of the commission of the offence or such other time limit as may be expressly provided for in individual statutes (Magistrates Courts Act 1980, s 127 (MCA 1980)). Laying an information is one method by which criminal proceedings are commenced, giving in writing details of the offender and the offence alleged (see **3.09**). It has been decided in the case of *R v Dartford Justices, ex p Dhesi* [1983] 1 AC 328, HL, that an information is laid on the date on which it is received in the office of the clerk to the justices.

Persistent young offenders

3.02   There are strict time limits where a juvenile is in custody. The Prosecution of Offences (Custody Time Limits) Regulations1987 (as amended) provide for a maximum custody time limit of 56 days from a first appearance to the start of trial in relation to summary and either way offences. In this context the term either-way offence includes an indictable offence tried summarily in the Youth Court.

Where a juvenile fits the definition of 'persistent young offender' laid down by the joint Home Office/Lord Chancellor's Department circular

Measuring performance to reduce delays on the Youth Justice System the court has target times within which certain steps should have been taken. For these purposes a 'persistent young offender' is:

'A child or young person sentenced by any court on three or more separate occasions for one or more recordable offence, and within three years of the last sentencing occasion is subsequently arrested or has an information laid against him/her for a further recordable offence.'

The target times in the Youth Court are:
*   Arrest to charge   2 days
*   Charge to first appearance   7 days
*   First appearance to start of trial 28 days
*   Verdict to sentence   14 days.

These are no more than targets and have no sanction attaching to breach.

Delay

3.03 The Prosecution of Offences Act 1985, s 22 provides for restrictions on the period which a person charged with an offence may be remanded in custody. Custody for these purposes includes remands made under CYPA 1969, s 23, to local authority or other accommodation.

The maximum period of a remand to custody is 70 days from first court appearance to the start of trial or committal proceedings. Where, as is usual in the Youth Court, summary trial is appropriate, the time limit is 56 days. A custody time limit may be extended by application. The application may be heard by a court presided over by two lay justices or a district judge (magistrates' courts). Section 22A(3) states that the court shall not grant an extension of the initial stage time limit unless it is satisfied that:
  (a) the need for an extension is due to some good and sufficient cause; and
  (b) the investigation has been conducted and (where applicable) the prosecution has acted with all due diligence and expedition.

Reasons to extend the time limit. In the case of this overall time limit POA 1985, s 22(3) states that the court shall not grant an extension unless it is satisfied that:
  (a) the need for the extension is due to

(i) the illness or absence of the accused, a necessary witness, a judge or a magistrate;

(ii) a postponement which is occasioned by the ordering by the court of two separate trials in the case of two or more accused or two or more offences; or

(iii) some other good or sufficient cause; and

(b) the prosecution has acted with all due diligence and expedition.

The matters to be considered by the court in deciding whether to extend a custody time limit are set out in *R v Crown Court at Manchester, ex p McDonald* [1999] 1 All ER 805.The seriousness of the charge or the need to protect the public will not amount to a good and sufficient cause in itself (*R v Crown Court at Sheffield, ex p Headley* [2000] Crim LR 374). If the prosecution have failed in the early stages to provide primary and initial disclosure to the defence thus delaying the trial date their application for an extension of time will fail (*R v Crown Court at Kingston and Sutton Youth Court, ex p Bell* [2000] All ER (D) 1191).

In *R v Croydon Youth Court, ex p C* [2000] All ER (D) 985 a juvenile trial was listed together with other trials in the Youth Court. It was not given priority in the list and when it transpired that there was insufficient time to hear the complete trial the magistrates decided that there was just and sufficient cause to enable them to extend the time limit under the Prosecution of Offences Act 1985, s 22A(3). On appeal, the High Court decided that the magistrates had addressed themselves to the right issue. Faced with a late start and a disinclination to go part heard, the magistrates' decision to extend the custody time limits was not in any way perverse.

Similarly, where delays are caused by pressure on the court's list, the custody time limits may be extended. In *R (on the application Kalonji) v Wood Green Crown Court* [2007] All ER (D) 283, the judge was held to have acted properly in finding exceptional circumstances, having examined the steps taken to alleviate the listing problems and concluded that they were not systematic.

Where the court extends, or further extends, a time limit the accused may appeal against the decision to the Crown Court, but only if he/she has been charged. There is no right of appeal against an extension applied for by the police before charging the person (POA 1985, s 22A(8)).

So far as the overall time limit is concerned the proceedings shall be stayed where the time limit has expired after the date fixed for the first hearing but before the date fixed for the start of the trial. Where proceedings are stayed POA 1985, s 22B(2) allows for fresh proceedings to be instituted within three months by the laying of an information. If over three months have passed the court must make application to the court that stayed the original proceedings for them to be reinstated. Reinstatement is allowed even if the six-month time limit for the laying of the original information has passed. In *R v Croydon Youth Court* (14 December 2000, unreported) the Divisional Court refused to order a stay of proceedings where abuse of process was argued saying there was no suggestion that a fair trial would be impossible. There is no sanction for exceeding the sentencing time limit.

ATTENDANCE OF THE PARENTS OR GUARDIANS

3.04 Although the juvenile remains responsible for any criminal act committed over the age of criminal responsibility, it is desirable that the parent or guardian should attend court during criminal proceedings for a number of reasons. The court has a duty to consider making a parental bind over and in appropriate circumstances a parenting order. Should the court impose financial penalties it may wish to make the parent responsible for payment. For these reasons and to generally reinforce parental responsibility the Youth Court should make every effort to ensure the attendance of parents.

The law makes a distinction between a child or young person under the age of 16, where the court must require a parent to be present, and a young person of 16 or 17 where they may require the attendance of a parent (CYPA 1933, s 34A). This provision applies during all stages of the proceedings unless and to the extent that the court is satisfied that it would be unreasonable to require such attendance having regard to the circumstances of the case. In some circumstances, it may be obvious to the court that a parent should not be required to attend all stages of the proceedings, for example where the victim of the alleged offence is the juvenile's parent. Less clear is the situation where a parent feels unable to attend court because of pressures brought to bear by employment or the need to care for other younger children in the family. It must be a matter of judgement as to whether this forms part of the circumstances of the case and whether the court would be satisfied that it would be unreasonable in such circumstances to require the attendance of the parent. In order to avoid delay, many courts will wish to send a notice or serve a notice on juveniles at the time they are charged at the police station. Where a juvenile is summoned to court following the laying of an information, a parent may be summoned at the same time in accordance with CYPA 1933, s 34A and Criminal Procedure Rules 2005, r 7.8. A subsequent failure to attend can be enforced by the issue of a warrant (r 7.8). Generally when a parent fails to attend, a letter making clear the court's powers will usually be sufficient to ensure attendance at the next hearing.

The term 'parent' is not defined in the Children and Young Persons Acts. The rules of court however state that parent means the parent who has parental responsibility under the Children Act 1989.

The position of children in care or accommodation provided by the local authority

3.05   The definition of parent or guardian is expanded in CYPA 1933, s 34A(2) to include a local authority where the local authority has parental responsibility for the child or young person in their care or where he is being accommodated by them in the exercise of any functions (particularly those under the Children Act 1989).

Parental responsibility

3.06   Parental responsibility is defined as all the rights, duties, powers, responsibilities and authority which by law a parent of a child has in relation to the child and his property (Children Act 1989, s 3). Therefore, where a child's father and mother were married to each other at the time of his birth, they shall each have parental responsibility for the child. Where they were not so married, then the mother alone shall have parental responsibility although the father may acquire parental responsibility under the provisions of the Children Act 1989, s 2 and since 1 December 2003 where the birth is registered jointly (Children Act 1989, s 4). A local authority has parental responsibility for a child in respect of whom a care order has been made to that authority. The local authority also has the power to determine the extent to which a parent or guardian of a child may meet his parental responsibility for him. A juvenile for whom the local authority have parental responsibility and are looking after, should be accompanied to court by a representative of the social services department who will stand in loco parentis. In such circumstances, it would be unreasonable to require the attendance of the parent unless the child or young person was in fact living with that parent whilst being 'looked after' by the local authority. The lack of the clear definition of 'parent' in any of the pieces of legislation relating to children may leave courts in some difficulty. There is a definition contained in the Family Law Reform Act 1987, s 1(1) which indicates that a parent shall include a father and mother who have not been married to each other. Thus, the father of an illegitimate child would be a parent for these purposes. As indicated the provisions are wide enough to allow for a continuing variation in practice from court to court as to whether or not parents are summoned to attend. Some areas may require only a father or mother to attend, some may require both. In practice, where both parents are available, they should in the case of a young person under the age of 16 years be required to attend court. If they failed to do so, the court would make enquiry into the circumstances of the case to decide whether it would be unreasonable to require such an attendance.

The role of a parent in court

3.07   At the hearing, parents have a vital role to play. It is good practice to involve the parents in the proceedings as much as possible. Following the availability of free professional representation, and the consequent increase in the numbers of solicitors appearing in Youth Courts, it is important that the chairman of the bench or the clerk to the court explain to the parents how proceedings will be conducted, who the parties are and what roles they are expected to play during the hearing. Of course, where a juvenile is not represented then the parent or guardian should be allowed to conduct the case on their behalf. Communication between the chairman, the young offender and his parents, which focuses on the consequences of offending, is to be encouraged. Magistrates should recognise however that some young offenders may be physically/ mentally unable to engage in dialogue or may simply decline to do so. Young people with various learning difficulties may find it hard to follow complex or multi-faceted questions. No adverse inference should be drawn from a failure to engage in this way.

CHARGES, WARRANTS, SUMMONSES AND REQUISITIONS

3.08 Once an initial decision to prosecute has been taken, the next step is to secure the juvenile's attendance at the Youth Court.

Charges

3.09 The current trend is towards charging juveniles to appear before the court rather than summoning them. Guidance from the Home Office indicates a preference towards charging.

Where a juvenile has been arrested for a criminal offence, such as robbery, theft, or assault, he may be charged at the police station and bailed to appear in court at a date and time specified. Alternatively, where the investigation is incomplete, he may be bailed to reappear at a police station without charge.

Under the Bail Act 1976, a person bailed to court is not required to enter into a recognisance (a sum of money that may be forfeited on non-attendance at court). However, bail by the police or by the court does place an obligation upon a person bailed to attend court and failure to attend at the time and place stated without reasonable excuse is an offence punishable with a level five fine, three months' imprisonment or both in the case of an adult convicted summarily (Bail Act 1976, s 6(2) and (7)).

The maximum fine that can be imposed upon a juvenile is limited by virtue of the Magistrates' Courts' Act 1980, s 24. This means that a juvenile offender over the age of 14 could be made subject to a fine up to a maximum of £1,000. In the case of a child found guilty of an offence under the Bail Act, the maximum fine is £250.

Where a juvenile is to be charged with an offence, the procedure is the same as for an adult except that everything should be carried out in the presence of an 'appropriate adult' (PACE 1984, Codes of Practice Code C, para 1.7). 'Appropriate adult' is defined by Code C para 1.7 as:
  (a) his parent or guardian (or, if he is in care, a person representing the care authority or organisation);
  (b) a social worker; or
  (c) failing either of the above, another responsible adult aged 18 or over who is not a police officer or employed by the police.

Further guidance is found in Code C as follows:

C1B. The parent or guardian of a juvenile should not be the appropriate adult if they are suspected of involvement in the offence concerned, a victim, a witness, involved in the investigation or have received admissions. In such circumstances, it will be desirable for the appropriate adult to be some other person. The estranged parent of a juvenile should not be asked to act as the appropriate adult if the juvenile expressly and specifically objects to his presence.

C1C. If a child in care admits an offence to a social worker, or member of a YOT (other than during their period as appropriate adult) another social worker should be appointed in the interest of fairness.

C1E. A detainee should always be given a opportunity to consult privately with a solicitor in the presence of an appropriate adult should they so wish.

C1F. A solicitor or independent custody visitor who is present in that capacity may not act as the appropriate adult.

The rules for the charging of detained persons are found in Code C, para 16which states:

'16.1 When an officer reasonably believes that there is sufficient evidence to provide a realistic prospect of the detainee's conviction, he should without delay (and subject to the following qualification) bring him before the custody officer who shall then be responsible for considering whether or not he should be charged. When a person is detained in respect of more than one offence, it is permissible to delay bringing him before the custody officer until the conditions are satisfied in respect of all the offences. Any resulting action should be taken in the presence of the appropriate adult if the person is a juvenile or mentally ill or mentally vulnerable.

16.1 B Where in compliance with the DPP's charging guidance the custody officer decides that the case should he immediately referred to the CPS to make the charging decision, consultation should take place with a Crown Prosecutor as soon as is reasonably practicable. Where the Crown Prosecutor is unable to make the charging decision on the information available at the time, the detainee may be released without charge and on bail (with conditions if necessary) under PACE 1984 s 37(7)(a). In such circumstances, the detainee should be informed that they are being released to enable the Director of Public Prosecutions to make a decision following consultation, PACE 1984 s 37B(1).

16.2. When a detained person is charged with or informed that he may be prosecuted for an offence, he shall be cautioned.

The caution shall be in the following terms:

> "You do not have to say anything. But it may harm your defence if you do not mention now something which you later rely on in court. Anything you do say may be given in evidence."

Minor deviations do not constitute a breach of this requirement provided that the sense of the caution is preserved. If it appears that the juvenile does not understand what the caution means, the officer who has given it should go on to explain it in his own words.

16.3. At the time the person is charged, he should be given a written notice showing the particulars of the offence with which he is charged and including the name of the officer in the case, and the reference number for the case. So far as possible, the particulars of the charge shall be stated in simple terms but they shall also show the precise offence in law with which he is charged. The notice shall begin with the following words:

> "You are charged with the offence(s) shown below. You do not have to say anything. But it may harm your defence if you do did not mention now something which you later rely on in court. Anything you do say may be given in evidence."

If the person is a juvenile or is mentally ill or mentally vulnerable the notice should be given to the appropriate adult.'

Conditional bail from the police station

3.10   When a custody officer releases a juvenile on bail he may impose conditions on that bail but only when it appears to him necessary to prevent him:

(a) failing to surrender to custody; or
(b) committing an offence whilst on bail; or
(c) interfering with witnesses or otherwise obstructing the course of justice; or,

(d) for his own protection, or, in the case of a juvenile, his welfare or his own interests (Bail Act 1976, s.3A(5)).

A custody officer who imposes conditional bail must give his reasons for doing so; those reasons must be noted in the custody record and a copy given to the juvenile and the appropriate adult. A court may, on application, review bail granted by the custody officer and may remand in custody or bail with the same or more onerous conditions. In either case bail conditions must be reasonable, able to be complied with, proportionate to the need to impose them, clear and enforceable. While it is not possible to set out all permissible conditions, see **7.07** and the criteria set out in the Bail Act 1976 at s 3A.

Summons

3.11   In some cases the police may prefer to require attendance at court of the juvenile and his parents by the issue of a summons. Although in the adult court it is common for summary cases to be dealt with in a defendant's absence, compliance with the Rules of Court make such a procedure unusual in the Youth Court. Instead of a summons the prosecutor may commence proceedings by way of a written charge and a requisition requiring the person to appear before a magistrates' court (CJA 2003, ss 28-31).

In some areas the new procedure for commencing proceedings has been implemented by statutory instrument (SI 2008/1424). The police may institute criminal proceedings against a person by issuing a document (a 'written charge') that charges the person with an offence.

When they issue a written charge, it must at the same time issue a document (a 'requisition') that requires the person to appear before a magistrates' court to answer the written charge.

The written charge and requisition must be served on the person concerned, and a copy of both must be served on the court named in the requisition: CJA 2003, s 29(1) (3).

As a consequence of sub-ss (1) (3), the police in those areas covered by the relevant statutory instrument do not to have the power to lay an information for the purpose of obtaining the issue of a summons under s 1 of the Magistrates' Courts Act 1980 (c 43).

Warrants of arrest

3.12   The issue of a warrant is a serious step for any court to take as it involves a command to the police to arrest the person named in the warrant. (MC Rules 1981, r 96(1)) This means that any constable in possession of the warrant may arrest the offender and bring him before the court. A warrant should not be issued where a summons would be equally effective, except where the charge is of a serious nature. (*O'Brien v Brabner* (1885) 49 JP Jo 227) This case involved what was called 'a trifling assault' by one woman on another and resulted in the defendant being arrested on a Saturday morning and kept in custody until the Monday following. It was stressed that there seemed to be no reason for the justices to have believed that a summons would not have been equally effective in securing the appearance of the accused person and this was really a case for the issue of a summons instead of a warrant.

A warrant of arrest issued by a justice remains in force until it is either executed or withdrawn. (MCA 1980, s 125(1)) Any such warrant must name or otherwise describe the person for whose arrest it is issued and must contain a simple description of the offence charged CPR 2005, r.7.2). Any warrant for the arrest of a person may command that he be brought before the next available court, or that he be arrested and released on bail with a duty to surrender to court on the date and time specified in the warrant.

Warrants with bail

3.13   The Bail Act 1976 allows conditions to be imposed where bail is granted in criminal proceedings. Section 1(1) defines criminal proceedings as including: 'bail grantable in connection with an offence to a person ... for whose arrest for the offence a warrant (endorsed for bail) is being issued'. Therefore, where the court issues a warrant endorsed for bail, it may make conditions which must be complied with by the defendant before and after his release.

Conditions may be imposed:
   (a)   to ensure his attendance, for example the juvenile may be required to reside with his parents until the court appearance;
   (b)   to prevent the commission of further offences, for example the court may require the juvenile to stay indoors between specified times;

(c) to prevent interference with the course of justice, for example a condition that the juvenile does not contact named witnesses in the case;

(d) to ensure co-operation after conviction with the making of any report or inquiries which will assist the court in dealing with him, for example a condition to report to the youth offending team before the court hearing; or

(e) for the defendant's own protection or, in the case of a juvenile, his welfare or his own interests. (Bail Act 1976, s 3(6), MCA 1980, s 117)

Although the insertion of conditions on a warrant endorsed for bail is permissible, it is rare. This is because the court issuing a warrant will not usually have sufficient information to enable it to comply with the Bail Act 1976, s 5(3) which requires the court to give reasons for the imposition of conditions.

Warrant in the first instance

3.14 Instead of instituting proceedings by way of a charge or a summons, the prosecution may ask a justice of the peace to issue a warrant for the arrest of the juvenile. This is called a warrant in the first instance. No warrant shall be issued under this section unless the information is in writing. (MCA 1980, s 1(3)) An example of a warrant in the first instance being issued for a juvenile might be where the juvenile has run away from home and cannot be found for the purpose of serving a summons. MCA 1980, s 1(4) imposes restrictions on the issue of a first instance warrant, 'for the arrest of any person who has attained the age of 18'.

The restrictions are that no warrant shall be issued unless:

(a) the offence to which the warrant relates is an indictable offence or is punishable with imprisonment; or

(b) the person's address is not sufficiently established for a summons to be served on him.

These restrictions do not apply to juveniles. However it is submitted that a magistrate, in exercising a discretion to issue the warrant or not, should apply these restrictions as guidelines in cases where the offender is a juvenile. Where the offence charged is an indictable offence, a warrant in the first instance may be issued at any time notwithstanding that a summons has previously been issued (MCA 1980, s 1(6)).

Warrant for arrest – summons having been served

3.15   Where the juvenile has failed to attend in answer to a summons, the court may issue a warrant for his arrest subject to being satisfied that the summons has been served in accordance with MCR 1981, r 99. Depending on the seriousness of the offence alleged, the court may also cause a letter to be served on the juvenile's parents warning of the court's powers to issue a warrant. Where the court has adjourned the trial after either receiving evidence about the offence or having found the offender guilty, the court shall not issue a warrant unless it thinks it undesirable by reason of the gravity of the offence to continue the trial in the offender's absence (MCA 1980, s 13(5)). This subsection applies equally to adults and juveniles but it will rarely be desirable to proceed in the absence of a juvenile because of the welfare principle in the CYPA 1933, s 44.

In *R (on the application of R) v Thames Youth Court* [2002] All ER (D) 356 (Jul), [2002] Crim LR 977 a youth failed to attend his trial having been arrested and detained by the police on another matter. The High Court quashed a decision to proceed in his absence, saying that where a defendant had not voluntarily absented himself from the trial any conviction was likely to be quashed. The court also commented that where a defendant is a juvenile he or she may not have the same development and understanding as an adult.

It should be noted that MCA 1980, s 13(3) contains similar restrictions on issuing warrants for persons having attained the age of 18, namely that no warrant shall be issued unless:

   (a) the offence to which the warrant relates is punishable with imprisonment; or

   (b) the court, having convicted the accused, proposes to impose a disqualification on him.

It is submitted that although the restrictions do not apply to juveniles they are a good guideline as to the issue of warrants in these circumstances.

Failure to attend by a juvenile who has been bailed

3.16   Where the juvenile has been charged and bailed to court and fails to attend, the court may issue a warrant for his arrest (Bail Act 1976, s 7). The warrant may be without bail or endorsed for bail, with or without conditions. Failure to attend court in answer to bail is an offence punishable with a level 5 fine or three months' imprisonment in the case of an adult (Bail Act 1976, s 6(1), (2) and (7)).

Where a juvenile has been released on bail from a police station with a duty to attend the police station at a later date and fails to attend, a constable may arrest that juvenile without a warrant and take him to the appointed police station. (PACE 1984, s 46A); but see also **3.09** above.

Chapter 4

The Youth Court and Human Rights Act

4.01 The purpose of this chapter is to give the reader an insight into the operation of the Human Rights Act 1998 and to examine some of the areas which practitioners and the courts may come across in their everyday dealings in the Youth Court. Detailed examinations of human rights points cannot be undertaken without reference to European case law and specialist text on the subject.

HISTORY

4.02 The European Convention for the Protection of Human Rights and Fundamental Freedoms was drawn up within the Council of Europe following the Second World War. The Convention was an attempt at collective enforcement of some of the rights stated in the United Nations Universal Declaration of Human Rights 1948. Not only were the numerous rights and freedoms set down in the Convention but it also set up a system of enforcement of the obligations entered into by the various contracting states. The right to petition the European Commission of Human Rights (set up in 1954) was given to individual citizens (see below) and contracting states.

The United Kingdom and UK lawyers were in the forefront of both the drafting and the setting up of the convention but declined to contract in, giving citizens the right to petition the commission until 1966. Until 1998, a violation complaint was dealt with by a two-tier system. First, the matter went before the Commission which decided upon the admissibility of the complaint. If the Commission decided that the complaint was admissible and no settlement had been reached, the matter proceeded before the European Court. This system was changed by Protocol No 11 and in 1998 the newly constituted European Court of Human Rights came into being.

Finally in October 2000 the Human Rights Act 1998 (HRA 1998) came into force in England and Wales.

CONVENTION RIGHTS

4.03   The effect of the HRA 1998 is to require public authorities to deal with individuals in such a way that their rights are protected by the Convention and not breached. It is important to note that individuals cannot act in breach of the Convention, only states or public authorities. The Convention rights are set out conveniently in the table below.

Article no	Subject	Summary
Article 2	Right to life	Protects human life subject to lawful exceptions.
Article 3	Prohibition on torture etc	An absolute prohibition on torture, inhuman or degrading treatment or punishments.
Article 4	Prohibition on slavery and forced labour	An absolute prohibition on slavery and servitude. Forced or compulsory labour is excluded from protection in specified circumstances.
Article 5	Right to liberty and security	Everyone has the right to liberty and security except in limited circumstances. Sets out the rights of a person who is arrested or detained.
Article 6	The right to a fair trial	Lists the requirements of a fair trial, the minimum rights of the accused. Confirms the presumption of innocence.
Article 7	No punishment without law	A prohibition against retrospective criminal legislation.
Article 8	The right to respect for individual private and family life	Protects private and home life and correspondence from unlawful and unnecessary interference.
Article 9	Freedom of, thought conscience and religion	Everyone has the right to freedom of thought, conscience and religion and a qualified right to

		exercise them subject to society's needs.
Article 10	Freedom of expression	Everyone has a qualified right to a freedom of expression, which includes publishing books, articles or leaflets, and the spoken word subject to the needs of society.
Article 11	Freedom of assembly and association	Qualified rights of assembly and free association including for example the right to join a trade union and take part in peaceful demonstrations.
Article 12	The right to marry	Absolute right which includes the founding of a family
Article 14	Prohibition from discrimination within the Convention	A limited right ensuring the enjoyment of Convention rights avoiding discrimination by sex, race, colour, language, religion, political or other opinion national or social origin, association with a national minority, property, birth or status.

The First Protocol

Article 1	Protection of property	A qualified right to peaceful enjoyment of possessions.
Article 2	The right to education	States must respect the rights of parents to ensure education is in line with their religion and philosophy.
Article 3	The right to free elections	States that free elections to the legislature must be held at regular intervals by secret ballot.

The Sixth Protocol

Articles 1 and 2	Abolition of death penalty	An absolute prohibition in peacetime but qualified in time of war.

THE HUMAN RIGHTS ACT 1998

4.04   The HRA 1998 has a two-fold purpose, first to ensure that domestic legislation and its application is compatible with the rights set out in the Convention and secondly to give citizens the right to enforce Convention rights in the domestic courts by providing remedies for breaches. This means that juveniles may rely upon the Convention rights at any point during the youth justice process, from arrest through trial to sentence. The Act itself is a relatively short piece of legislation and an examination of the major sections will help put into context the effect of its provisions.

HRA 1998, s 1 sets out the Convention rights referred to, and s 2 governs the standing of Convention rights. By its provisions the courts must take into account decisions of the European Court of Human Rights, including past opinions of the now defunct Commission of Human Rights. In making a decision upon a point of law the Court must ensure that it is acting lawfully within the terms of Convention law. In doing so, decisions of the European Court of Human Rights must be given precedence over domestic decisions no matter what level they were made at. It should be noted however that where domestic law provides a higher level of protection to the citizen the Act does not require the domestic courts to lower standards to meet any minimum guarantees provided by European jurisprudence.

HRA 1998, s 3 deals with the important topic of interpretation of legislation. The Act states that, so far as is possible, legislation must be read and given effect to in a manner so as to be compatible with the Convention rights whenever it is possible to do so. This section embodies what is referred to as the 'purposive approach', that is to say a requirement that the courts should always aim to interpret legislation so that the objects of the Convention are upheld: namely the protection of rights with minimal interference from the state and proportionate with those objectives. The Youth Court, as with other courts, will treat *primary* legislation slightly differently from *secondary* legislation. Primary legislation refers to Acts of Parliament debated and passed in both the House of Commons and House of Lords. Secondary legislation flows from primary legislation and includes orders, rules, regulations and byelaws. All courts, including the Youth Court, are bound by primary legislation if they are unable to interpret it in a manner which is compatible with the Convention. The Court is not allowed to refuse to enforce primary legislation if it has found it to be incompatible with the Convention. It must work from the premise that the legislation should be read in a manner compatible with the Convention and this may mean reading in or reading out words from the statute. The Court must interpret legislation so as to uphold Convention rights unless it is impossible to do so because the statute itself is clear and unambiguous.

HRA 1998, ss 4-5 deals with declarations of incompatibility. It is clear that the Youth Court will not be bound by a previous construction given to legislation by a higher court if the Youth Court is clear that this construction would lead to a decision incompatible with Convention rights. In the case of secondary legislation if the court finds it incompatible with the Convention the court will interpret those provisions so as to give effect to Convention rights. This may in effect mean ignoring part of the domestic legislation in order to give effect to the Convention rights. An exception to this is the instance where secondary legislation and its primary legislation are closely interdependent with each other that a 'striking down' of the secondary legislation would inevitably compromise the primary legislation. The courts may not strike down primary legislation and so the Act makes provision for a declaration of incompatibility by the High Court.

Where a court finds it impossible to interpret primary legislation compatibly with the Convention it has a duty to follow the legislation giving effect to the will of Parliament. However the High Court may make a declaration of incompatibility. This has the effect of curing the violation or incompatibility by allowing the relevant minister to introduce a fast-track procedure through Parliament amending the legislation and bringing it into line with the Convention. In practice this should be a very rare event.

HRA 1998, s 6 defines a crucial concept within the Act, that is, of a 'public authority'. Under this provision it is unlawful for a public authority to act in a way which is incompatible with a Convention right. This will not apply to actions done as a result of one or more provisions of primary legislation (or provisions made under primary legislation) which could not be read or given effect to in a way that was compatible with Convention rights, so that the authority could not have acted differently.

The definition of a public authority specifically includes a court or tribunal and any person or persons whose functions are of a public nature (excluding either House of Parliament). The Youth Court acts as a public authority as do its legal advisers, police officers and members of youth offending teams. The definition of public authority is consequently wide and potentially complex. The Home Office has provided guidance on specific areas of interest. This can be found on their website: www.homeoffice.gov.uk.

REMEDIES

4.05 It is important to note that whilst HRA 1998, s 6 makes it unlawful for a public authority to act in a way which is incompatible with the Convention this will not give rise to any claim for damages in respect of a judicial act done in good faith (HRA 1998, s 9(3)). So far as the Youth Court is concerned it will normally be the provider of the remedy so long as it acts compatibly with the Convention.

HRA 1998, s 8 provides that in relation to any act of a public authority which the court finds unlawful, it may grant such relief, remedy, or make such order, within its powers as it considers just and appropriate. In relation to criminal proceedings, this may mean excluding evidence, allowing a submission of no case to answer, or a stay of proceedings. An example might be where the court found evidence had been obtained from a child in breach of the Police and Criminal Evidence Act Codes of Practice. The effective remedy here may be to exclude that evidence under PACE 1984, s 78. A potential breach of Article 6 (the right to a fair trial) because the prosecution have failed to provide disclosure may be remedied by the court granting an adjournment with a direction that the appropriate disclosure be given.

A STRUCTURED APPROACH TO HUMAN RIGHTS

4.06 Under the provisions of the Criminal Procedure Rules 2005,before raising a Convention point an advocate should be prepared to identify the nature of the alleged breach, the article of the Convention that is engaged and the remedy sought.

After the court has identified that a Convention right is engaged it must define to which class of article it belongs. *Absolute rights,* including the prohibition against torture, inhuman or degrading treatment, are fundamental rights and where a breach occurs this will be a violation of the Convention regardless of the reason for the breach.

Limited rights are limited in scope by the Convention itself. This means that if a breach of the Convention falls within one of the permitted limitations in the article there will have been no violation. A good example of a limited right is the right to liberty and security guaranteed by Article 5 which states that no person shall be deprived of his liberty save in the following cases and in accordance with a procedure described by law, for example the detention of a minor by lawful order for the purpose of educational supervision, or lawful detention for the purpose of bringing him before the competent legal authority. However if detention falls outside the limitations allowed by the article it is likely that there will have been a violation of the Convention right.

Qualified rights set out in the article conditions or qualifications when a Convention right may be breached. These conditions are as follows:
  (a) The breach is prescribed by national law. Such law must be clear and accessible to the public.
  (b) The breach pursues a legitimate aim. These aims are set out in the qualified rights. For example, the right to a private and family life is qualified where it is necessary in a democratic society to interfere with the right, for example for the prevention of crime or disorder.
  (c) The action taken is proportionate. This essentially means that any breach of a qualified right may be a violation unless the action taken is the least intrusive necessary to fulfil the legitimate aim set out in the article.

Can the violation be avoided?

Primary legislation
  • A court must attempt to interpret the legislation in a way which is compatible with the Convention. If this is not possible, the domestic law must be applied.

Secondary legislation
  • A court must attempt to interpret the legislation in a way that is compatible with the Convention (subject to the effect on primary legislation). If this is not possible, the court must disregard the domestic law and give effect to the Convention right.

Precedent
- A court must attempt to interpret the precedent in a way that is compatible with the Convention. If this is not possible, the court must disregard the domestic law and give effect to the Convention right.

Is a Convention right engaged?
- If no Convention right is engaged, the case must be decided on the basis of domestic law.
- If the Convention is engaged, the relevant Article must be identified

What class of Article is engaged?
- The application of the Convention is dependent upon the class of Article or protocol engaged
  Absolute rights
  - Article 3: prohibition of torture, inhuman or degrading treatment
  - Article 4(1): prohibition of slavery or servitude
  - Article 7: prohibition against punishment without law
  Limited rights
  - Article 2: right to life
  - Article 4(2): prohibition of forced or compulsory labour
  - Article 5: right to liberty
  - Article 6: right to a fair trial
  Qualified Rights
  - Article 8: right to respect for private and family life
  - Article 9: freedom of thought, conscience and religion
  - Article 10: freedom of expression
  su:–Article 11: freedom of assembly and association

Absolute rights
- The threshold is high but if breached for any reason, a violation is established.

Limited rights
- The Articles contain definitive statements of the circumstances, which permit a breach of the right. If the restrictions are not complied with, there has been a violation of the Article.

Qualified rights
- Qualified rights may be breached if: the breach is prescribed by domestic law the law is clear and accessible the breach pursues a

legitimate aim which is set out in the Article the measure is proportional.

HUMAN RIGHTS ISSUES AND YOUNG OFFENDERS

Issues at trial

4.07   The Youth Court is not an open and public court but nevertheless complies with a requirement of Article 6 (the right to a fair trial). This limited right clearly recognises that the press and public may be excluded from all or part of a trial in the interests of, amongst other things, juveniles. However juveniles are not always tried in the Youth Court as proceedings begun by way of a complaint; for example, applications under the Dangerous Dogs Act 1991 and applications for anti-social behaviour orders are not assigned to the Youth Court and must be heard in a magistrates' court.

Some commentators suggested that the anti-social behaviour order was in fact a criminal order as opposed to a civil one. This argument was made on the basis that the European Court will not be bound by domestic jurisdiction and will classify a matter as criminal if there is a substantial criminal sanction available to the court. An example of this is the case of *Benham v United Kingdom* (1996) 22 EHRR 293 involving enforcement of maintenance arrears. It was argued, in the case of the anti-social behaviour order, that an order is capable of imposing a very substantial limitation on the liberty of the individual affected by the order.

The importance of defining whether a matter is civil or criminal is that it will determine whether it is heard in the Youth Court or the magistrates' court. Additionally, the rules of evidence applicable to criminal proceedings would have to be complied with and those proceedings would be subject to the additional protection provided by Article 6 of the European Convention in relation to criminal proceedings. The High Court has decided in the case of *R (on the application of McCann) v Crown Court at Manchester* [2003] 1 AC 787, HL, that, although the court must apply a criminal burden of proof to the first part of the statutory test, an anti-social behaviour order is a matter subject to civil procedures. The court found that there is in fact no punishment involved and that the objective of making an order is not to punish but to protect. Whilst the order impinges on the rights of an individual it does so for the protection of a section of the public who would otherwise be likely to be subjected to conduct of a socially disruptive nature.

It should also be noted that legal representation is available by way of the duty solicitor. Civil legal aid is not available. However, a breach of an order is a criminal offence and legal assistance is therefore normally available under Pt V of the Legal Aid Act 1988.

Following the case of *V v United Kingdom and T v United Kingdom* (1999) 30 EHRR 121 a practice direction was delivered by the Lord Chief Justice entitled 'Trial of Children and Young Persons in the Crown Court'. Although not specifically aimed at the adult magistrates' courts it will be good practice to employ this practice direction when children and young people are tried in the magistrates' court. The practice direction sets out that the trial process should not in itself expose the young person to avoidable intimidation, humiliation or distress. Account must be taken of the age, maturity , intellectual and emotional development, of the defendant. The practice direction also gives advice on the layout of the courtroom, appropriate dress (in the Crown Court), timetabling and the need to explain procedures and involve young people in the trial process at all times. A full copy of the practice direction can be found at www.hmcourts-service.gov.uk/cms/926.htm.

Practical steps that the court may wish to take include: (a) keeping the defendant's level of cognitive functioning in mind; (b) using concise and simple language; (c) having regular breaks; (d) taking additional time to explain court proceedings; (e) being proactive in ensuring the defendant understands the ingredients of the charge; (f) explaining and ensuring the defendant understands the ingredients of the charge; (vii) explaining the possible outcomes and sentences; (h) ensuring that cross-examination is carefully controlled so that questions are short and clear and frustration is minimised.

Both the European Court and the High Court have followed similar reasoning in relation to the requirement to register under the Sex Offenders Act 1997, namely that it is civil in nature and preventative, not punitive. (*Ibbotson v United Kingdom* [1999] Crim LR 153). Nor is the failure to advise that a warning for a sexual offence would result in a requirement to register on the sex offenders registers a breach of Art 6. (*R (R) v Durham Constabulary* [2005] 2 All ER 369)

The right to silence

4.08   The issue as to whether a Youth Court should draw an adverse inference in circumstances where a juvenile has refused to answer questions during police interview is one which affects the overall fairness of the trial process. In *Murray v United Kingdom* (1996) 22 EHRR 29 the European Court considered whether the drawing of adverse inferences following the exercise of the right to silence was a violation of Article 6. The court said that by providing the accused with protection against improper compulsion by the authorities these immunities contributed to avoiding miscarriages of justice and to securing the aims of Article 6. In the *Murray* case guilt was decided by a judge sitting alone who demonstrated by his reasons that careful consideration had been given to the weight given to the adverse inference. Subsequently, the Youth Justice and Criminal Evidence Act 1999 amended ss 34, 36 and 37 of the Criminal Justice and Public Order Act 1994 to prevent adverse inferences being drawn from silence before the defendant receives legal advice.

The matter was further tested in the case of *Condron v United Kingdom* (2000) 31 EHRR 1. The European Court expressed dissatisfaction with the Appeal Court findings that the conviction was safe despite an unsatisfactory direction on the right to silence by the judge. They took the view that the only appropriate test was whether the trial was fair; the safety of the conviction was not the right test:

> 'In the court's opinion, as a matter of fairness, the jury should have been directed that unless it was satisfied that the applicant's silence at the police interview could not sensibly be attributed to their having no answer or none that would stand up to cross-examination, it should not draw an adverse inference.'

In *Condron* it was suggested that the fact that the defendant had been advised to remain silent was a factor that the jury should consider when assessing the validity of the defendant's silence   but it was not the only factor. An assertion that the defendant remained silent on the advice of his solicitor would not carry much weight. However, for the jury to assess the extent to which the solicitor's advice influenced the defendant's actions, the jury would need to have some information about why the solicitor advised silence in the first place.

The Youth Court must apply this judgement and having weighed all the issues and circumstances of the case give very clear reasons if it decides to draw an adverse inference from silence.

Secure accommodation

4.09   The use of secure accommodation when remanding a young person under the Children and Young Person's Act 1969, s 23 makes a useful study when applying the above structured approach. A possible objection might be that Article 3 is engaged (the prohibition against torture, inhuman or degrading treatment). This is an absolute right and as such the courts have set the threshold at a high level. If any ill-treatment or suffering does not reach that minimum level of severity then it falls outside the scope of Article 3. It is unlikely then that the article is engaged at all and, even if it were, s 23 makes provision to allow more vulnerable young men who might fall within the scope of Article 3 to be remanded to secure accommodation rather than a remand centre (and therefore outside the scope of art 3).

It could be argued that Article 8 (the right to private and family life) was engaged by remanding a young person into a secure environment away from their home. Article 8 is a qualified right and as such any breach needs to be described by domestic law which is clear and accessible. In this instance the law is set out clearly and accessibly in CYPA 1969, s 23. Does the breach pursue a legitimate aim, which is set out in the article? In this case one of the qualifications to Article 8 is that:

> 'There shall be no interference by a public authority with the exercise of this right except such as is in accordance with the law and is necessary in a democratic society in the interests of ... public safety ... for the prevention and disorder or crime ..., or for the protection of the rights and freedoms of others.'

Once again the clear purpose of CYPA 1969, s 23 accords with the qualification in Article 8, that is 'to protect the public from serious harm from him.'

The next and probably most obvious breach of the Convention could be Article 5. Article 5 is a limited right in that it sets out and guarantees the right to liberty and security of the person and then provides exceptions or limitations to the right. One of those limitations is 'the detention of a minor by unlawful order ... for the purpose of bringing him before a competent legal authority'. Once again this is clearly within the scope of the domestic legislation.

Another possible breach may be Article 14 of the Convention that prohibits discrimination in the enjoyment of the rights and freedoms set forth in the Convention. The objection here is that Article 5 is used in a discriminatory way as between males and females. This is because 15- and 16-year-old males may be remanded to prison accommodation while females in the same age group will always be held in local authority accommodation. The first question is whether this is an objection of interpretation or of substance. The statute treats males and females in exactly the same way as regards the grounds to restriction of liberty; it is only the accommodation where they are detained which is different. In fact this point was tested in *R (on the application of SR) v Nottingham Magistrates Court* [2001] EWHC Admin 802. The Appeal Court said that given the particular difficulties in providing secure placements for females, legislation which gives them priority to local authority accommodation was legitimate in its aims and a proportionate response to the problem.

The final and most compelling argument is the suggestion that the remand to secure accommodation is a violation of the Convention in that the court, if it decides that the conditions of CYPA 1969, s 23(5) apply, *must* remand a 15- or 16-year-old male to a remand centre or, if none is available, to a prison. As this is primary legislation and is not capable of interpretation in any other way a Youth Court is compelled to follow the legislation. Any further objection would have to be taken by way of case stated to the High Court for a decision as to whether a declaration of incompatibility was required.

Parenting orders and parental bind overs

4.10 Both parental bind overs and parenting orders may be in breach of Article 7 of the Convention if they are not made in clear and specific terms. Article 7 is often paraphrased as meaning that there should be no punishment without law. This encompasses both the prohibitions against retrospective legislation concerning criminal behaviour and a requirement that criminal provisions should be neither vague nor uncertain. In the case of *Hashman and Harrup v United Kingdom* [2000] Crim LR 185 the European Court held that a bind over to be of good behaviour was too imprecise to be complied with and therefore Article 7 was violated. The court did accept however that a bind over to keep the peace was both understandable and enforceable.

The lesson from this case is that parental bind overs, which are aimed at ensuring parents take proper care and exercise proper control over their children, must be clear in their expectations of parents. Parents should know what is expected from them in order to avoid a forfeiture of the recognisance. In the same way parenting orders must be sufficiently clear in their requirements for counselling, guidance etc so that parents are able to comply with the orders.

Parenting orders also impinge upon private and family life as provided for in Article 8. However, Article 8 is a qualified right and as such the state is permitted to intervene in an individual's private and family life so long as that interference is prescribed by law, clear and accessible, necessary in a democratic society and its provisions are proportionate to the harm it seeks to avoid. In *R (M) v Inner London Crown Court* [2003] All ER (D) 104, the High Court held that parental training was necessary in a democratic society and proportionate but the seriousness of the offence would be a relevant factor in the court :'s decision. Although the legislation is both clear and accessible a challenge under Article 6 was not without merit and indeed emphasises that the requirements made should be those which the court considers desirable in the interests of preventing repetition of offending or anti-social behaviour. It will be readily seen that one of the legitimate aims in Article 8 is for the protection from disorder or crime, or the protection of rights and freedoms of others.

It should be clear from this brief analysis that these orders in the Youth Court pertaining to parents should not be in violation of the Convention. However, the court must be careful to follow the statutory provisions, clearly specify the requirements in its orders and give its reasons for doing so.

4.11 A further example of the High Court's approach can be seen in relation to ASBOs in the case of *R (on the application of B) v Greenwich Magistrates' Court and the Commissioner of Police for the Metropolis* [2008] EWHC 2882 (Admin).

Reasons for decisions

4.12 There are many statutory requirements to give reasons in the Youth Court. Examples are where the court imposes a detention and training order or where it orders the removal of press restrictions normally applicable in the court. Such requirements are outlined throughout the text of this work. Article 6(1) states:

'...everyone is entitled to a fair and public hearing within a reasonable time by an independent and impartial tribunal established by law. Judgement shall be pronounced publicly ...'

Essentially, the usual safeguards require the court to give reasons for its decisions. The giving of reasons enables an aggrieved person to understand the decision and make an informed decision on his right to appeal. It also provides an explanation for the public at large and those observing the proceedings in court.

This obligation to give reasons for decisions does not transform the Youth Court nor alter what should be current good practice. In *McKerry v Teesside and Wear Valley Justices* (2000) 164 JP 355 the then Lord Chief Justice Lord Bingham said:

'.... the justices did announce that they were acceding to the request to dispense to the extent to which they did because they considered that the appellant constituted a serious danger to the public and had shown a complete disregard for the law. That was, in my judgement, enough to indicate the basis of the decision...... justices are not obliged to state reasons in the form of a judgement or to give reasons in any elaborate form.'

That is not to say that a reasoned judgement at the end of a trial which covers the major issues in dispute, any legal submissions, and the justices' findings should in any way be discouraged.

The *McKerry* case involved the issue of the partial lifting of the normal reporting restrictions in the Youth Court in respect of a young person aged 15. This is exactly the sort of decision which will require the court to give reasons. The judgement of the Lord Chief Justice was that the reasons of the court depended on both the matter to be decided and the court by which the matter was to be decided. A similar view can be found in the European Court of Human Rights in the case of *Toriga (Ruiz) v Spain* (1994) 19 EHRR 553. The court stated:

'The court reiterates that Article 6(1) obliges the courts to give reasons for their judgements, but cannot be understood as requiring a detailed answer to every argument. The extent to which this duty to give reasons applies may vary according to the nature of the decision.'

Following a trial the reasons should demonstrate that the justices have applied their minds to the ingredients of the offence and the defendant's state of mind so as to be able to inform the defendant in a few sentences why he has been found guilty (*R (on the application of McGowan) v Brent Justices* [2001] EWHC Admin 814).

One area where it is clear that the court will have to give reasons is where there is any suggestion that an inference from the exercise of the right to silence is to be drawn: *Condon v United Kingdom* (2000) 31 EHRR 1.

One other qualifacation is that the courts must not resort to formatted or standard reasons. It is interesting to compare the High Court's criticism of the lower court for pre-preparing bail notices in *R v Mansfield Justices, ex p Sharkey* [1985] QB 613 and subsequent European case law such as *Yagci and Sargin v Turkey* (1995) 20 EHRR 505 in which the European Court disapproved of the use of stereotyped reasons when refusing bail. The Youth Court must be able to demonstrate that each case has been considered on its individual merits and that the reasons given for withholding bail or imposing conditions apply specifically to the facts of the individual case.

In conclusion, the Youth Court like all other tribunals and public authorities must act compatibly with the European Convention on Human rights. In general a rigorous approach to giving reasons for a decision will normally alert the court to any human rights issues. A structured approach to those issues should lead to a successful resolution of the majority of human rights problems.

Chapter 5

Venue of proceedings

ASSIGNMENT

5.01 The Youth Court may only deal with matters that have been specifically assigned to it by virtue of CYPA 1933, s 46, namely: criminal charges (against a child or young person); and applications involving juveniles which are specifically assigned to the Youth Court by rules made under the CYPA 1933, s 46(1).

It is arguable that this section does not exclusively define the jurisdiction of the court but simply assigns certain matters to it. For example applications for secure accommodation under CA 1989, s 25 may be heard by the Youth Court but are not assigned to it by s 46 or by rules. Instead CYPA 1969, s 23 and CJA 1991, s 60(3) rather than s 46 gives the Youth Court jurisdiction.

With certain specific exceptions, the Youth Court hears all criminal charges against juveniles. 'Charge' in this context includes all informations and requisitions laid against juveniles. Broadly speaking, 'informations' and requisitions are laid to commence criminal proceedings and 'complaints' are made to commence civil proceedings.

Applications

5.02 This refers to civil matters, and for the Youth Court to deal with applications they have to be specifically assigned by virtue of rules made pursuant to CYPA 1933, s 46(1).

It is interesting to note that no civil matters have been assigned to the Youth Court. The adult court must still hear other civil applications, usually commenced by the making of a complaint. For example, complaints for binding over (under MCA 1980, s 115), dangerous dog applications (under Dogs Act 1871, s 2) and anti-social behaviour orders under the Crime and Disorder Act 1998 should all be heard before the adult court even though a juvenile is involved.

Again it is arguable that as s 46 does not define the jurisdiction of the court it would be more desirable to hear such cases before the Youth Court. However, the Youth Court is a magistrates' court specially constituted for the purpose of hearing any charge against a child or young person and for the purpose of exercising any other jurisdiction conferred on Youth Courts (CYPA 1933, s 45). Following the wording of s 45 the power to hear proceedings under MCA 1980, s 115 or Dogs Act 1871, s 2 is not 'conferred' on the Youth Court by any statutory provision or by any rules. It would appear therefore that the Youth Court per se would not have jurisdiction to hear such applications. The same argument would apply to breaches of parental bind-overs which are dealt with later.

EXCEPTIONS TO THE RULE THAT JUVENILES BE DEALT WITH IN THE YOUTH COURT

5.03 Although it is desirable for juveniles to be dealt with by the Youth Court, there are occasions when it is in the interests of justice for this rule not to apply. The exceptions deal with situations where adults and juveniles are involved together in criminal activities and are as follows:

(a) where a child or young person and an adult are charged jointly with an offence, a court other than a Youth Court (CYPA 1933, s 46(1) must hear the charge. In *R v Rowlands* [1972] 1 All ER 306, it was held that it was not necessary to use the words 'together' or 'jointly' to make a charge a joint one. Similarly in *R v Peterborough Magistrates' Court, ex p Allgood* (1994) 159 JP 627 it was held that in the case of taking without the owner's consent or aggravated vehicle taking the driver and passengers charged with allowing themselves to be carried are jointly charged;

(b) where a child or young person is charged with an offence, the charge may be heard by a court other than a Youth Court if an adult is charged at the same time with aiding and abetting, causing, procuring, allowing or permitting that offence (CYPA 1933, s 46(1));

(c) where a child or young person is charged with aiding, abetting, causing, procuring, allowing or permitting an offence with which an adult is charged at the same time, the charge may be heard by the adult court (CYPA 1963, s 18);

(d) where a child or young person is charged with an offence arising out of circumstances which are the same as or connected with those giving rise to an offence with which an adult is charged at the same time, the charge may be heard by the adult court (CYPA 1963, s 18);

(e) where a child or young person is brought before an adult court for a remand application that court may deal with the application (CYPA 1933, s 46(2)).

In the case of (a) above the Youth Court clearly still has jurisdiction to hear such charges, or the adult magistrates' court may remit the case to it for trial or sentence: *R v Coventry Justices, ex p M* (1992) 156 JP 809. In (b) to (d) there is discretion as to whether the case starts in the magistrates' court or the Youth Court.

REMITTAL FROM THE ADULT COURT TO THE YOUTH COURT

5.04   The adult court, on finding a juvenile guilty, must remit the case to the Youth Court for the area where the offender habitually resides unless it is satisfied that this would be undesirable. The adult court dealing with a juvenile is limited to imposing a fine, discharge or an order binding over the parent. (PCC(S)A 2000, s 8.)

If the court is required to make a referral order it can do this rather than remitting the defendant (PCC(S)A 2000, s 16). See **8.1**.

The court must send a certificate of remittal to the court to which the juvenile is remitted. The term 'adult court' includes the Crown Court, but in *R v Lewis* (1984) 79 Cr App Rep 94, CA, it was held that it was not always necessary to remit from the Crown Court to the Youth Court for sentence after a finding of guilt. It was held that the effect of the Criminal Justice Act 1982, which aligned the powers of the higher courts and the Youth Courts, meant that the concept of the Youth Court as the only proper forum in which juveniles could be dealt with was now out of place. These powers have been aligned by Courts Act 2003, s 66, which gives Crown and High Court Judges the powers of a district judge (magistrates' court). The Crown Court has to consider whether it would be undesirable to remit to the Youth Court. Reasons for it being undesirable were said to be the risk of unacceptable disparity if co defendants are sentenced in different courts on different occasions, the greater knowledge that the trial judge who has heard all of the evidence would have, the expense of remittal and the avenues of appeal. Appeal can be from the Youth Court to the Crown Court and from the Crown Court to the Court of Appeal (Criminal Division). This decision only applies to the Crown Court and must now be read in the light of CDA 1998, s 51 and Sch 3 (immediate transfer of indictable only cases) dealt with below. Juveniles found guilty by the adult magistrates' court must be remitted unless a fine, discharge or bind-over is appropriate. However see the comment made above in relation to referral orders.

Where a juvenile is before the magistrates' court together with an adult the court may remit the juvenile to the Youth Court for trial in the following circumstances:
- (a) the court proceeds to summary trial of the adult who pleads guilty and the juvenile pleads not guilty;
- (b) the court enquires into the offence as examining justices with a view to deciding if a prima facie case has been made out for sending the adult to the Crown Court for trial, and either sends for trial or discharges the adult, but proceeds to summary trial of the juvenile who pleads not guilty. Again, a certificate of remittal must be sent to the court to which the juvenile is remitted.

R v Tottenham Youth Court ex p Fawzy [1998] 1 All ER 365 makes it clear that in the case of an either way offence the adult court must conduct a mode of trial hearing first before deciding that a remittal is appropriate.

On remitting the juvenile, the adult court may make arrangements for securing his attendance at the Youth Court either by remanding him in custody or releasing him on bail. (MCA 1980, s 29) Where both the adult and the juvenile plead not guilty the adult court will deal with the case.

COMMITTAL TO THE CROWN COURT

5.05 In the case of an adult, certain serious offences may only be dealt with by the Crown Court. Such cases are referred to as being 'indictable only'. Other offences such as theft, assault and burglary are dealt with by either the Crown Court or the magistrates' court at the instance of the court or the adult defendant. These are known as offences 'triable either way'. If an adult and a juvenile are before the adult court together, and the decision is taken that the adult's case must go to the Crown Court, the court may not commit the juvenile for trial unless it is satisfied that it is necessary in the interests of justice (MCA 1980, s 24). Unlike an adult, a juvenile has no right to elect trial by jury in these circumstances. This also applies where the adult's case is sent to the Crown Court under CDA 1998, s 51. The juvenile's case may only be moved directly to the Crown Court where the juvenile is jointly charged with an adult and it is necessary in the interests of justice.

A juvenile must be committed to the Crown Court if charged with homicide, or where all the requirements of the Firearms Act 1968, s 51 are satisfied.

He may also be committed under the 'grave crimes' provisions of the Powers of the Criminal Courts (Sentencing) Act 2000, s 91 or under the 'Dangerousness Provisions' contained in Part 12 of the Criminal Justice Act 2003.

Finally there are provisions to send cases to the Crown Court under s 53 of the Criminal Justice Act 1991(which is subject to repeal by CJA 2003, Sch3(2), para 62(2)) for a range of violent and sexual offences against children. These various provisions are considered below.

Juveniles and adults jointly charged

5.06 Section 24 MCA 1980 applies where the adult and juvenile are jointly charged. The mode of trial for the adult should be considered first. This will only apply where the adult, at the plea before venue stage, either refuses to intimate a plea or pleads not guilty. The criteria applied by the court are different as between the adult and the juvenile. In relation to the adult the court will consider the Sentencing Guidelines Council Guidelines, the National Mode of Trial Guidelines and MCA 1980, ss 18-23. If the adult is directed to the Crown Court or elects to be dealt with by that court the magistrates then move on to consider the juvenile's case. The criterion that the court should consider is whether it is necessary in the interests of justice to commit to the Crown Court. The Code for Crown Prosecutors states that prosecutors making representations on this should bring to the court's attention the following:

    (a) the respective ages of the adult and juvenile;
    (b) the seriousness of the offence;
    (c) the likely plea;
    (d) whether there are outstanding charges against the juvenile in the Youth Court;
    (e) the need to deal with the juvenile expeditiously.

The general policy of the legislature is that young defendants should, where possible, be tried by a Youth Court. Young offenders should not be tried by the Crown Court unless that is clearly necessary (*R (on the application of W) v Southampton Youth* Court [2002] Crim LR 750).

In *Re C (a minor)* (2000) Times, 5 July it was held that neither Article 3 (prohibition of inhuman or degrading treatment or punishment) nor Article 6 (right to a fair trial) precluded the committal of an 11-year-old defendant to the Crown Court under these provisions.

If at plea before venue stage the adult pleads guilty then the court does not have to commit the juvenile to the Crown Court but instead should normally take a plea from the juvenile and remit for trial or sentence. However in the case of a grave crime (see **5.07**) the magistrates' court may still consider whether the charge should be committed as a grave crime under MCA 1980, s 24(1)(a) and PCC(S)A 2000, s 91(3). If the charge is found to be one to which s 91 applies then, if the powers of the adult and youth court respectively are insufficient, the adult may be committed to the Crown Court for sentence and the juvenile committed for trial.

In the old case of *R v Crown Court at Doncaster, ex p Crown Prosecution Service* [1987] Crim LR 395 it was held that when justices were considering whether it was in the interests of justice that a juvenile who was charged jointly with an adult should be sent to the Crown Court it was necessary that they both appeared before the court at the same time (but see *R v Coventry City Magistrates, ex p M* (below)). Once that decision had been taken it was not necessary that they should appear together in subsequent committal proceedings. The facts of this case were that on 19 March 1986 the defendant, then aged 16, appeared before the Doncaster justices charged with offences of burglary together with six other defendants. His co-defendants included two juveniles and four adults. On that day the justices considered the mode of trial. They decided that the adults should go to the Crown Court and, having heard representations from both sides, decided that it was in the interests of justice for the juveniles also to be committed to the Crown Court for trial. They then adjourned for the committal proceedings to take place. On 30 April they committed all of the defendants except one juvenile who had been arrested for other offences. He was committed to the Crown Court the next day. The Crown Court judge declined to deal with the defendant who had been committed subsequently and referred his case back to the justices. The Divisional Court overturned the judge's ruling, saying that what mattered was that the juveniles and the adults should appear together at the mode of trial stage.

In the case of *R v Coventry City Magistrates, ex p M* [1992] Crim LR 810 it was held that a juvenile court (now Youth Court) could commit a juvenile to be tried at the Crown Court with an adult with whom he had been jointly charged pursuant to MCA 1980, s 24(1)(b) when the adult had already been committed for trial by a different bench, as it was not a requirement of the section that the adult should be before the court at the same time the juvenile was committed. In this case the juvenile was charged with aiding and abetting rape. The court considered *R v Doncaster Crown Court* but found that it was not correct to interpret that case, as saying that both juvenile and adult defendant had to appear together at the mode of trial stage.

Where the court decides that it is in the interests of justice to commit the juvenile for trial, it may also commit him for trial for any other indictable offence with which he is charged at the same time if that other offence arises out of circumstances which are the same as or connected with those giving rise to the joint offence (MCA 1980, s 24). For example, if an adult and a juvenile are charged jointly with an offence of robbery, and the juvenile is also alleged to have stolen a motor vehicle when escaping from the scene of the crime, that charge can also be committed to the Crown Court for trial as it arises out of the same circumstances as the joint charge of robbery.

Where a magistrates' court, including the Youth Court, commits a person to the Crown Court for trial for an either way offence or a number of such offences, it may also commit him for trial for any summary offence with which he is charged and which in the case of an adult is punishable with imprisonment or involves disqualification from driving and arises out of circumstances which appear to the court to be the same as or connected with those giving rise to the offence, or one of the offences, triable either way (CJA 1988, s 41). This does not apply in respect of a defendant committed for trial charged only with an offence triable only on indictment (*R v Miall* [1992] QB 836, CA). If the defendant is convicted of the either way offence in the Crown Court then the court may sentence him for the summary offence if he pleads guilty to it. The Crown Court is limited to the powers which the magistrates would have had for that offence.

Where the offence committed to the Crown Court is one which in the case of an adult is only triable on indictment then a purely summary offence of taking a motor vehicle without the owner's consent, driving whilst disqualified, common assault or criminal damage may be included in the indictment at the Crown Court. This may only happen if the charge is founded on the same facts or evidence as the indictable offence or is part of a series of offences of the same or similar character as the indictable offence. The facts of the summary offence must be disclosed in the statements upon which the indictable offence was committed to the Crown Court (CJA 1988, s 40).

GRAVE CRIMES

5.07   For certain very serious offences the charges against juveniles aged 10 to 17 years inclusive may be committed to the Crown Court for trial even where no adult offender is involved. MCA 1980, s 24(1) states that a juvenile shall be tried summarily unless the adult and juvenile are jointly charged and the court considers it necessary in the interests of justice to commit the juvenile with the adult to the Crown Court. The court may also commit to the Crown Court for trial if it considers that the offence is one for which the Crown Court judge may wish to order long-term detention under PCC(S)A 2000, s 91(3). The sentence under s 91 may be for any period up to the maximum for the offence. An example would be 14 years for burglary. The Crown Court may exercise its power under s 91 to order long-term detention only where it is of the opinion that none of the other methods in which the case may legally be dealt with is suitable. The order made by the Crown Court is for the offender to be detained in such place and on such conditions as the Secretary of State may direct. The juvenile could be held in any suitable accommodation as is felt appropriate from an ordinary local authority children's home to a prison. This is at the discretion of the Home Secretary. This discretion is illustrated by the case of *R v Secretary of*

State for the Home Department, ex p J [1999] 01 LS Gaz 23, CA. The juvenile had been placed in a Young Offender Institution and it was argued that he should have been placed in a care establishment. It was held that in deciding upon the appropriate place of detention for an offender under s 91 the Secretary of State is bound to have regard to the welfare of the individual. He is also to take account of the need for punishment and the need to maintain confidence in the criminal justice system. He is also entitled to have regard to the finite number of places in childcare establishments.

The court fixes the term of the order but the offender may be released by the parole board.

The power under s 91 to order long-term detention applies to juveniles from 10 to 17 inclusive. The provisions apply to:
  (a) all offences which in the case of an adult carry a maximum term of imprisonment of 14 years or more;
  (b) various forms of sexual assault of either male or female including, an offence under s 3 (sexual assault), s 13 (child sex offences committed by children or young persons), s 25 (sexual activity with a child family member) or s 26 (inciting a child family member to engage in sexual activity) of the Sexual Offences Act 2003;
  (c) firearms offences under s 5(1) and (1A) which carry a maximum of 10 years' imprisonment, a minimum of three years for defendants aged 16 but under 18 (Firearms Act 1968, s 51A as inserted by Criminal Justice Act 2003, s 287).

Some of the more common examples of offences punishable by 14 years or more are:
  (a) arson (criminal damage by fire); (Criminal Damage Act 1971, s 1);
  (b) aggravated burglary (burglary with a weapon of offence, firearm, imitation firearm or explosive); (Theft Act 1968, s 10);
  (c) blackmail (demanding money with menaces) (Theft Act 1968, s 21);
  (d) burglary, including burglary with intent to commit rape, inflict injury on any person, attempt to inflict serious bodily harm therein or unlawfully damage the building or steal anything in the building (but excluding non dwelling house burglary which carries a maximum term of 10 years' imprisonment) (Theft Act 1968, s 9);

(e) handling stolen goods (Theft Act 1968, s 22);
(f) rape, assault by penetration and assault by penetration (Sexual Offences Act 2003, s 2);
(g) robbery (Theft Act 1968, s 8);
(h) assault with intent to rob (Theft Act 1968, s 8(2));
(i) sexual activity with a child (Sexual Offences Act 2003, s 9);
(j) wounding with intent to do grievous bodily harm or causing grievous bodily harm with intent (Offences Against the Person Act 1861, s 18);
(k) production of class A or B drugs (MDA 1971, s 4(2));
(l) supplying class A, B or C drugs (MDA 1971, s 4(3));
(m) possessing class A or B drugs with intent to supply (MDA 1971, s 5(3));
(n) cultivating cannabis (MDA, s 6(2));
(o) possession of firearm with intent to endanger life (Firearms Act 1968, s 16);
(p) causing death by dangerous driving, causing death by careless driving whilst intoxicated , causing death by aggravated vehicle-taking (Maximum penalties increased by CJA 2003, s 285).

The above list is not exhaustive.

The test to be applied by the magistrates in determining whether a defendant should be committed to the Crown Court suggests that children under 15 should be tried in the Youth Court and at mode of trial the magistrates must ask themselves whether there is a real prospect that the defendant whose case they are considering might require a sentence of, or in excess of, two years or whether, although the sentence might be less than two years there is some unusual feature of the case that justifies declining jurisdiction bearing in mind that the absence of a power to impose a detention and training order because the defendant is under 15 is not an unusual feature.

Questions such as the age of the witnesses or the desirability of disposing of the matter as rapidly as possible cannot weigh against the clear words of s 24(1). In *R v Devizes Youth Court, ex p A* (2000) 164 JP 340, Art 6 (the right to a fair trial) was specifically considered in this context and it was held that the question of whether the Crown Court was a suitable venue for trials concerning juveniles was not relevant to the venue decision under MCA 1980, s 24 and PCC(S)A 2000, s 91.

The higher courts have sometimes criticised the magistrates for accepting jurisdiction rather than committing for trial under s 91. In *R v North*

Hampshire Youth Court, ex p DPP (2000) 164 JP 377 two 15-year-old girls were charged with wounding with intent contrary to OAPA 1861, s 18. This was an attack on another 15-year-old involving punching, hitting, and stamping causing three wounds to the ear and scalp that required stitches, a broken tooth, swollen lips, swollen and bruised eyes and swelling and bruising to the head, face, forearms, back and abdomen. The Divisional Court quashed the Youth Court's decision to retain jurisdiction saying it ought to have committed the juveniles to the Crown Court.

Equally, the High Court has been critical of magistrates sending inappropriate cases to the Crown Court. The Justices' Clerks' Society issued guidance to its members in August 2006 at the request of Thomas LJ. Some examples of recent case law will serve to illustrate the types of cases that are or are not appropriate to be treated as grave crimes.

Robbery. The decision of a Youth Court to decline jurisdiction on robbery offences that included the production of a weapon or force being used and injury to a victim were held not to be manifestly wrong on judicial review by the High Court. Such offences fell within level 2 of the Sentencing Guidelines Council's Guidelines on robbery; the recommended starting point for such offences was three years detention rising to six years. Additionally, the guidelines state that justices can take account of aggravating features so as to treat the offences as being on a higher level thus reflecting an increased severity in sentence: *C v Croydon Youth Court* [2006] EWHC 2627 (Admin).

Sexual offences. In *R (on the application of G) v Burnley Magistrates Court* [2007] EWHC 1033 (Admin), G and four co-accused sexually assaulted a 13-year-old girl at a party. Having followed her to the toilet they fondled her breast and a vibrator was inserted into her vagina. G was the youngest of the defendants at the age of 13, the others being 14 years old. He was of previous good character. Charged under s 13 of the Sexual Offences Act 2003 magistrates committed the matter to the Crown Court as a grave crime. The Divisional Court said that the Youth Court's decision had been erroneous and should be quashed. Whilst the incident in question was unpleasant and reprehensible it lasted for a relatively short period of time. As G and his co-accused were of previous good character and aged between 13 and 14 at the time of the alleged offence there was no real prospect of sentences in excess of two years' detention being imposed.

Following the Sexual Offences Act 2003 the definition of rape was widened and a Protocol has been issued by the Senior Presiding Judge dealing with 'Rape cases in the Youth Court'. Although historically the position was that the Youth Court should never accept jurisdiction in a rape case (*R v Billam*), recent authorities have suggested that in the case of very young defendants it may be appropriate to accept jurisdiction (*R (on the application of B) v The Richmond on Thames Youth Court* [2006] EWHC 95). The determination of venue is still governed by MCA 1980, s 24 (see below **5.08**). When considering whether the Youth Court should retain jurisdiction in a rape case, the court will need to consider the suitability of the Youth Court as a venue and the desirability of the case being heard by a circuit judge authorised to try serious sexual cases. If jurisdiction is retained a request should be made to the regional listing coordinator for an authorised circuit judge to sit as a district judge at the Youth Court (Courts Act 2003, s 66). The justices' clerk for the region should be consulted and kept informed of all developments.

The previous guideline case on the imposition of long-term detention under s 91 (*R (on the application of W) v Southampton Youth Court* [2002] Crim LR 750) has been refined in the case of *R (H, A and O) v Southampton Youth Court* [2004] EWHC 2912 (Admin), 169 JP 37 by Leveson J, and approved in *R (on the application of the CPS) v Redbridge Youth Court* [2005] EWHC 1390 Admin. He sets out the position in the Youth Court as follows;

(a) The general policy of the legislature is that those who are under 18 years of age and in particular children under 15 years of age should, wherever possible, be tried in the Youth Court. It is that court that is best designed to meet their specific needs. A trial in the Crown Court with the inevitably greater formality and greatly increased number of people involved (including a jury and the public) should be reserved for the most serious cases.

(b) It is further policy of the legislature that, generally speaking, first-time offenders aged 12 to 14 and all offenders less than 12 years should not be detained in custody and decisions as to jurisdiction should have regard to the fact that the exceptional power to detain for grave offences should not be used to water down that general principle. Those under 15 years will rarely attract a period of detention and, even more rarely, those who are under 12.

(c) In each case the court should ask itself whether there is a real prospect, having regard to his or her age, that this defendant whose case they are considering might require a sentence of, or in excess of, two years or, alternatively, whether, although the sentence might be less than two years, there is some unusual feature of the case that justifies declining jurisdiction, bearing in mind that the absence of a power to impose a detention and training order because the defendant is under 15 is not an unusual feature.

Once a juvenile has been committed to the Crown Court under the provisions of s 91 PCC(s)A 2000 the restrictions concerning DTOs do not apply. In *R v Jenkins-Rowe and Glover* [2000] Crim LR 1022 a 14-year-old was sentenced to long-term detention under s 91. It was argued that he was not a persistent offender for the purpose of making a detention and training order and therefore should not have received long-term detention. The Court of Appeal rejected this argument saying that the provisions relating to detention and training orders did not affect long-term detention. Thus if a defendant under 15 is committed for trial under s 91 because the youth court believes the offending deserves two years or more the Crown Court is not restrained from passing a long-term detention sentence regardless of whether that sentence is more or less than two years by the fact that he is not a persistent offender.

Procedure in potentially grave crime cases

5.08 It follows from the above that the magistrates have to make a decision as to venue. This decision has to be made after hearing representations. There is no requirement to hear evidence (*R v South Hackney Juvenile Court, ex p RB (a minor) and CB (a minor)* (1983) 77 Cr App Rep 294).

Additional principles have been set out in the case of *R (W) v Brent Youth Court and CPS (Interested Party); R (B) v Richmond-upon-Thames Youth Court and CPS (interested party)* [2006] All ER (D) 34 :

(a) The principles already set out *R (H, A and O) v Southampton Youth Court* (2004) should be applied.
(b) The Youth Court should expect to be assisted by both its legal advisor and the advocates.
(c) In order to make a satisfactory decision, the court must have all the necessary information before it namely:
   (i) the factual allegation (which must be assumed to be true, unless manifestly not so), it being the duty of the advocates

> to ensure that the summary is both scrupulously fair and balanced;
>
> (ii) any undisputed mitigation, including any indication of an intention to plead guilty;
>
> (iii) the defendant's previous record (if any and if relevant). The most recent case on whether previous convictions can be taken into account at a grave crime mode of trial is *R (Tullet) v Medway Magistrates' Court* [2003] EWHC Admin 2279, 167 JP 541.
>
> In that case a juvenile aged 17 appeared before the court charged with a dwelling house burglary, described as an opportunistic, daytime walk-in burglary of unlocked premises. He had five previous convictions for dwelling house burglaries. The court held that taking previous convictions into account was justifiable;
>
> (iv) the correct approach as set out in the authorities; and
>
> (v) any relevant sentencing guidelines. Where there are no guidelines from the Sentencing Guidelines Council, any relevant published advice by the Sentencing Advisory Panel, provided that the court recognises that such advice does not carry legal force.

Where several defendants are charged together, the position of each of them is to be considered separately. It should be noted that when brought into force CJA 2003, Sch 3 amends MCA 1980, s 19 to allow for the citing of previous convictions in the venue decision in the adult court. The schedule also introduces a new plea before venue provision (MCA 1980, ss 24A-D) in the Youth Court.

There is also some debate over whether the court which has to consider venue in relation to potentially grave crimes has to look at each offence individually or whether it is able to aggregate the seriousness of a number of offences charged at the same time thus pushing all of the offences into the grave crime bracket. The orthodox view is that each offence should be considered individually and s 91 refers to 'the offence.' It is at least arguable that this is an illogical approach. It is established that at the sentencing stage the persistence of offending aggravates the sentence (*R v Simmons* (1995) 16 Cr App Rep (S) 801, CA). The grave crime procedure is a sentencing prediction and nothing more. Why should it not be possible to look at the totality of all of the offences charged together? This point has never been considered judicially. It was argued in *R v Hammersmith Juvenile Court, ex p O* (1987) 86 Cr App Rep 343 but the court chose not to rule on it.

PCC(S)A 2000, s 76, includes a sentence passed under PCC(S)A 2000, s 91 within the definition of 'custodial sentence'. This means that the criteria laid down in s 79 of the Act apply. Before the Crown Court can pass a sentence under s 91 it has to be of the opinion that:

    (a) the offence, or the combination of the offence and one other offence associated with it, was so serious that only a custodial sentence can be justified for the offence; or

    (b) where the offence is a violent or sexual offence, that only a custodial sentence would be adequate to protect the public from serious harm from the defendant. (PCC(S)A 2000, s 79(2))

Thus it is submitted that an adult court or a Youth Court, when determining whether an offence falls to be committed to the Crown Court as a grave crime, must also have regard to these provisions. The Crime and Disorder Act 1998, s 47(6) amends the Magistrates' Courts Act 1980. This now provides that, where a Youth Court commits a child or young person for trial at the Crown Court for a grave crime under s 24 it may also commit him for trial at the same time for any related indictable offence. The CDA 1998 removed the presumption that cases which are not committed to the court for trial should be postponed until after the more serious matter has been dealt with. This reversed the decision in *R v Khan* (1994) 158 JP 760, CA.

There is no statutory procedure laid down for grave crimes mode of trial. It is incumbent upon the prosecutor and the legal advisor to bring to the attention of the bench that a matter is potentially one to which the grave crime provisions could apply so that the court may consider the matter. Where a crime is not classified as a grave crime but still meets the criteria in the dangerous offender provisions outlined below, a young offender may still be committed to the Crown Court if an extended sentence detention for life or public protection sentence is required.

REVIEWING THE MODE OF TRIAL DECISION

5.09   One problem that has arisen is whether a court may change its decision to proceed summarily or to commit to the Crown Court.

Where the court has decided to try the case summarily it may change the decision 'at any time before the conclusion of the evidence for the prosecution'. Similarly, where the justices have determined trial at the Crown Court they may decide that the case is more suitable for summary trial while considering whether to commit to the Crown Court (MCA 1980, s 25).

Before a guilty plea

In *R v Newham Juvenile Court, ex p F (a minor)* [1986] 3 All ER 17, a 16-year-old appeared before the magistrates charged with robbery and possessing a firearm. The magistrates decided to proceed summarily. No plea was taken and the case was adjourned. The defendant then appeared before a differently constituted bench which purported to change the decision of the first bench and commit the defendant for trial to the Crown Court. It was held that the court had power to review its mode of trial decision right up to the time of the start of the committal proceedings or summary trial if there had been a change of circumstances since the original decision was made. However, a fresh charge of a purely indictable nature does not constitute a change in circumstances (*R v St Helens Magistrates' Court, ex p Critchley* [1988] Crim LR 311). In this case the court did not consider any new factors. Had the court actually taken denials and commenced the summary trial then it could have reverted to committal proceedings. In practice the court may only change the mode of trial decision if there are fresh matters put to it before plea or where a denied hearing or committal proceedings have started.

In *R v Hammersmith Juvenile Court, ex p O* [1987] Crim LR 639, the juvenile defendant appeared before the court charged with two offences of burglary. Summary trial was agreed and not guilty pleas were entered. The case was adjourned until another date. On the later date the defendant faced a further charge of attempted robbery. The court, deciding that the trial on the earlier matters had not begun and that in any event details of the applicant's character were now available, reconsidered the question of venue. It was decided that the burglaries and the robbery should be transferred to the Crown Court as being grave crimes. It was held on appeal that the trial on the burglary charge had been started when the plea was entered. On the later date the court had no jurisdiction to change the decision as to mode of trial except under the provisions of MCA 1980, s 25(5). It was further said that the criminal record should not have been taken into account in determining venue. Had the court waited until it had started the trial it could have changed its decision by virtue of MCA 1980, s 25(5).

After a guilty plea

In *R v Herefordshire Youth Court, ex p J* (1998) 142 Sol Jo LB 150. The defendant appeared in the Youth Court charged with indecent assault on a girl aged three. The defendant pleaded guilty and the prosecutor outlined the facts. The solicitor for the defendant requested an adjournment for pre-sentence reports. The clerk then raised the issue of whether, as the offence was one to which s 91 could apply, the court should consider grave crimes mode of trial. Eventually the magistrates purported to treat the guilty plea as void. The Divisional Court remitted the case to the justices (with a direction to sentence the juvenile) ruling that the entering of the guilty plea was mode of trial and the court therefore had to sentence the defendant. In the case of *H v Balham Youth Court* [2003] EWHC 3267 (Admin), it was held that a court may not change the mode of trial decision until it has commenced the summary trial or has started the committal hearing. Where it has started the committal hearing it has power to revert to summary trial. However there is no power to change the mode of trial decision whether or not new material arises. In *R (on the application of DPP) v Camberwell Green Youth Court* [2003] EWHC 3217 (Admin) it was held that MCA 1980, s 25 provides explicitly for the circumstances in which a change can take place and it is not permissible to read into the Act a power to change mode of trial decisions in other circumstances.

In *R (on the application of R) Manchester City Youth Court* [2006] All ER (D) 66 a 15-year-old defendant of previous good character was charged with one offence of burglary of a dwelling and he admitted his guilt. The magistrates however declined jurisdiction although both prosecution and defence represented the summary trial. At the committal proceedings it was argued that the court should revert to summary trial, this application was refused on the grounds that the court would effectively be sitting in appeal on the decision of the first court. The High Court, reviewing the decision, said that there was no real possibility of two years' detention and the court should have accepted jurisdiction. They pointed to s 25(5) and (7) MCA 1980, which permits examining magistrates to inquire into the case and to consider whether the case should be tried summarily; such a decision was not fettered by the previous court's ruling.

Such circumstances led to confusion in *R (on the application of D) v Sheffield Youth Court* [2008] EWHC 601 Admin. A juvenile was charged with eight counts of supplying class 'A' drugs and three of offering to supply class 'A' drugs. He appeared in an adult court jointly charged and entered guilty pleas. The case was remitted to the Youth Court where the Crown Prosecution Service asked the proceedings to be re-opened under s 142 MCA 1980 and declared nullity as the adult court had failed to consider venue under s 24(1) MCA 1980. The juvenile appealed against the granting of that application and the High Court, whilst accepting that the adult court had a duty to consider s 24(1) before taking pleas, held that the failure to do so did not permit a reopening under s 142 of the Act.

Committal to the Crown Court

5.10　Juveniles may be committed to the Crown Court for trial not only in the case of a grave crime under s 91 but also where involved jointly with an adult being committed to the Crown Court or being sent there under CDA 1998, s 51 or where charged with homicide. Committal proceedings may take place in the adult magistrates' court where jointly charged or in the Youth Court for grave crimes, dangerousness or homicide.

At the committal proceedings the court determines whether there is sufficient evidence to commit to the Crown Court for trial. They may not commit unless there is a case to answer (a 'prima facie' case.)

The evidence which the court considers in order to make this decision may only be in the form of written statements. It is not permitted to call witnesses. Where the defendant is represented by a solicitor the witness statements must be served on that solicitor and if s/he considers that the statements disclose a 'prima facie' case the defendant may be committed without consideration of the evidence (MCA1980, s 6(2)).

Where the defendant is not legally represented or his solicitor does not agree to a committal without consideration of the evidence the court must inquire into the offence. This committal will take the form of the statements being read out or summarised to the court and the court considering legal submissions (MCA 1980, s 6(1)).

If the juvenile is not represented at committal stage the committal must be by way of consideration of the evidence. The court is under a duty to assist the juvenile and allow his parents to conduct the case on his behalf.

Transfer for trial

5.11 If a person is charged with a sexual offence or an offence involving violence or cruelty to a child then at the instance of the prosecution the charges can be transferred to the Crown Court without committal proceedings. To do this the DPP or a Crown Prosecutor acting under his authority must be of the opinion that there is sufficient evidence for the matter to be committed, that a child victim or witness is involved and that for the purpose of avoiding any prejudice to the welfare of the child the case should be taken over and proceeded with without delay to the Crown Court (CJA 1991, s 53(1)) subject to repeal by CJA 2003, Sch3(2), para 62(2).

Similar provisions exist for serious and complex fraud cases under CJA 1987, s 4.

A child for these purposes is someone under 17 for sexual offences and under 14 for any other offence.

On the case being transferred the magistrates may remand in custody or on bail.

Dangerous offenders

5.12 Sentences for dangerous offenders are passed by the Crown Court but are relevant to the Magistrates' Court in that a person convicted of certain offences before the Magistrates' Court or Youth Court may be assessed as 'dangerous' and then committed to the Crown Court for a longer sentence to be ordered.

To qualify for any of these sentences:
  (a) the offender must have committed a 'specified offence or serious specified offence'; and
  (b) the court must be of the opinion that there is a significant risk to members of the public of serious harm caused by the commission of further specified offences by the offender: CJA 2003, s 226. A specified offence is one listed in Sch 15 of the Act. The schedule contains lists of violent offences in Part 1 and sexual offences in Part 2. Where a specified offence is punishable with at least 10 years' imprisonment in the case of an adult it is classified as a 'serious offence'; and

(c) another criterion introduced by the Criminal Justice and Immigration Act 2008 that has to be satisfied before the imposition of a sentence of imprisonment for public protection, is that the offence must merit at least two years of actual time served in custody before a public protection sentence can be imposed; and

(d) even if a court finds the offender is dangerous, the imposition of a sentence of public protection is not mandatory.

'Serious harm' means 'death or serious personal injury, whether physical or psychological.'

Making the assessment

5.13 Section 229(2) of the Act, as amended, details how the court is to assess whether there is a significant risk to members of the public of serious harm occasioned by the commission of further specified offences and the factors which the court can take into account in assessing whether the offender is dangerous

The court:
(a) **must** take into account all such information as is available to it about the nature and circumstances of the offence,
(b) **may** take into account any information which is before it about any pattern of behaviour of which the offence forms part, and
(c) **may** take into account any information about the offender which is before it.

Significant risk

5.14 Significant risk is not defined in the statute and is therefore a matter for the court to assess in each individual case.

The Court of Appeal in *R v Lang* [2006] 2 All ER 410 set out a detailed list of considerations to be borne in mind when the court is assessing significant risk. These include:
(a) The fact that *significant* has a higher threshold than a mere possibility of occurrence, and could be taken as meaning 'noteworthy, of considerable amount or importance'.

(b) In assessing the risk of further offences being committed the court had to take into account the nature and seriousness of the instant offence; the defendant's history of offending, including not just this kind offence, but its circumstances and the sentences passed (details of which the prosecution had to have available); information in relation to the defendant's social and economic circumstances including his accommodation, education, associations and relationships, together with his attitude towards offending and supervision that will be derived, largely, from antecedents, pre-sentence reports and medical reports.

(c) A serious specified offence does not necessarily mean there is a significant risk of serious harm. Robbery is a serious offence, but can be committed in a variety of ways many of which do not give rise to a significant risk of serious harm. The court must guard against making assumptions. A pre-sentence report should usually be obtained before a sentence is passed based upon a significant risk of harm.

(d) Where a specified offence is not serious, there would be comparatively few cases in which a risk of serious harm could properly be regarded as significant.

(e) As to whether the defendant demonstrated any pattern of offending, repetitive violent or sexual offending at a relatively low level without serious harm will not in itself give rise to a significant risk of serious harm in future.

(f) It is necessary to bear in mind in relation to offenders under 18 that within a short period of time they will be adults and they may change and develop. Their level of maturity may be highly pertinent when assessing their future conduct and whether it might give rise to a significant risk of serious harm.

Although there is no presumption of dangerousness even where there are previous convictions for specified offences, it is important that previous convictions are considered by the court. Equally, it is not a prerequisite to a finding of dangerousness that the offender should be an individual with previous convictions; a man of good character could qualify for an indeterminate sentence of public protection: *R v Johnson, A-G's Reference (No 64 of 2006)* [2007] All ER 1237.

When considering 'a pattern of behaviour' and 'information about the offender' the court may also take into account any previous acquittals and complaints which were not pursued or prosecuted: *R v Considine and Davis* [2007] EWCA Crim 1166.

Further consideration to the issue was given in *R v Johnson, A-G's Reference (No 64 of 2006)* [2007]1 All ER 1237. Looking at a number of specific issues surrounding the dangerousness provisions, the Appeal Court concluded by stating that it will not normally interfere with the conclusions reached by a sentencer who has accurately identified the relevant principles, and applied his mind to the relevant facts.

If an offender is convicted of a specified offence the court will need to assess whether they pose a significant risk to members of the public of serious harm that may be occasioned by the commission by the offender of further specified offences. If the court considers that the offender does pose such a risk, following his conviction in the Youth Court, in that he satisfies the criteria under CJA 2003, s 226 or s 228 they must commit him to the Crown Court, in custody or on bail, to be sentenced: PCC(S)A 2000 s 3A.

The Crown Court has a range of powers including detention for life or detention for the public protection under CJA 2003, s 226 and extended sentences under CJA 2003, s 228, referred to as sentences for public protection.

Section 51A of the Crime and Disorder Act (inserted by CJA 2003, Sch 3) requires the court to send an offender charged with a specified offence who appears to the court to be liable for a sentence under s 226(3) or 228(2), if convicted, forthwith to the Crown Court for trial. Note that PCC(S)A 2000 ss 3A–3B are not in force as of 1 October 2008, but s 3C is, thus giving rise to this power. The power to remand on bail or in custody is contained in CDA 1998, s 52.

Procedural considerations on jurisdiction

5.15 As a consequence of the above legislation, some of which is 'manifestly inconsistent', it is important that the Youth Court adopts a standard procedure and is careful to identify cases to which either the grave crimes or the dangerousness provisions apply. Further guidance can be found in Part Four — Venue for Trial (Youths) of the Sentencing Guidelines Council guidelines. When para 9 of Sch 3 CJA 2003 is brought into force, s 24(1) MCA 1980 will become subject to the provisions of s 51A CDA 1998. Some grave crimes are not specified offences within the meaning of Sch 15 of the Criminal Justice Act 2003 and many specified offences are not grave crimes. In such circumstances the individual statutes will need to be considered as appropriate.

Where however a juvenile is charged with an offence that is both a specified offence and capable of being a grave crime the court must bear in mind the following factors considered in *CPS v South East Surrey Youth Court* [2005] EWHC 2929 (Admin):

(a) the policy of the legislature is that those under 18 should, wherever possible, be tried in a Youth Court, which is best designed to meet the needs of juvenile offenders.

(b) where a non-serious specified offences is charged, and assessment of dangerousness will not be appropriate until after a finding of guilt has been made. At that stage, if the dangerousness criteria are met, following receipt of an appropriate pre-sentence report, the defendant can be committed to Crown Court for sentence as a dangerous offender,

(c) if it is appropriate to consider the dangerousness provisions at the outset of the case, a defendant can be sent to the Crown Court for trial immediately, if it is in the interests of the youth to be tried on indictment s 51A(3)(d) CDA 1998. However, it is unlikely that the court will be in a position to make this decision in the absence of a formal risk assessment undertaken by the Youth Offending Team;

(d) in the case of a joint charge with an adult the magistrates must assess the need for a joint trial against the presumption that the Youth Court trial will be most appropriate;

(e) where the defendant is not deemed dangerous the court should go on to consider whether grave crimes provisions apply; if they do he can then be committed the trial to the Crown Court.

When neither the dangerousness nor the grave crime provisions apply the court will proceed to a summary trial in the Youth Court.

It must be remembered that there is no general power to commit to the Crown Court for sentence in the Youth Court, the only exception being committal to sentence under s 3 PCC (S)A 2000 where the dangerousness provisions apply.

Homicide

5.16 A juvenile charged with an offence of homicide must be committed to the Crown Court for trial. Homicide is not a specified violent offence; therefore until s 51A(3)(a) is brought into force these cases will have to be dealt with by the usual committal process under MCA 1980, s 6 or CDA 1998, s 51 if jointly charged with an adult.

Homicide means any offence of unlawful killing, for example murder, manslaughter, infanticide, child destruction.

Such offences will be brought before the Youth Court in the first instance unless the juvenile is jointly charged with an adult and committed to the Crown Court for trial under CDA 1998, s 51.

Remittal to the Youth Court

5.17   Where any court finds a juvenile guilty of an offence other than homicide, it may (and if not a youth court shall) remit the case to a Youth Court where the offender habitually resides or if committed or sent for trial to a Youth Court in the place where he was committed to the Crown Court, unless it is undesirable to do so. That court may then deal with him in any way in which it might have dealt with him if he had been tried and found guilty by that court. The court remitting the juvenile is empowered to bail the juvenile or remand him in custody. It must send a certificate to the clerk of the other Youth Court setting out the nature of the offence and stating that the offender has been found guilty and has been remitted for the purpose of being dealt with (PCC(S)A 2000, s 8).

In *R v Allen and Lambert* (1999) 163 JP 841, CA, the defendants had been committed to the Crown Court on charges of arson, burglary and attempted burglary under the 'grave crimes' provisions. The arson charge was dismissed and guilty pleas entered to the burglary charges, which were then remitted by the Crown Court to the Youth Court for sentence. The Youth Court then purported to commit back to the Crown Court for sentence on all matters.

On appeal, it was held that the power of remittal gives the Youth Court authority to deal with the defendant in any way that it might have dealt with him having been tried and found guilty by that court. This included committal for sentence (when available) but not committal for trial. It was also said that where justices found offences to be grave crimes and committed them to the Crown Court it was undesirable for the Crown Court to exercise its power to remit to the Youth Court for sentence. This judgment follows the judgement in *R v Lewis* (1984) 79 Cr App Rep 94.

Where any case is remitted, the offender has the same right of appeal against any order of the court to which the case is remitted as if he had been found guilty by that court, but has no right of appeal against the order of remission.

5.18   The court to which the juvenile is remitted for sentence may allow a change of plea from guilty to not guilty (*R v Stratford Youth Court, ex p Conde* [1997] 1 WLR 113). It is doubted whether there is power to remit back to the original court that remitted for sentence. There seems little point in remitting a 17-year-old to the adult court after conviction, for even though he attains the age of 18, detention in a young offender institution will not be available to the court as he was not 18 at the time of conviction.

Remittal to the adult court

5.19   PCC(S)A 2000, ss 9 and 10 provides the Youth Court with a discretionary power to remit a juvenile to an adult magistrates' court in the same area. This power arises once the juvenile reaches the age of 18 and the remittal may be for trial or for sentence. The intention of the legislation is to permit the courts to ensure that young people are dealt with in the most appropriate way, according to their majority, attitude and offending history, whilst avoiding unnecessary delay. There is no power to appeal such a remittal. The remitting court simply adjourns proceedings and applies the provisions of the Bail Act 1976 as normally operated. There would appear to be no reason why the adult court should not remit to another adult court under PCC(S)A 2000, s 10 should this prove necessary. In *R (on the application of Denny) v Acton Justices (DPP, interested party)* [2004] All ER 961 it was held that the Youth Court has no power to remit a person who becomes 18 during the proceedings to the adult court for sentence for a purely indictable offence.

Dangerousness

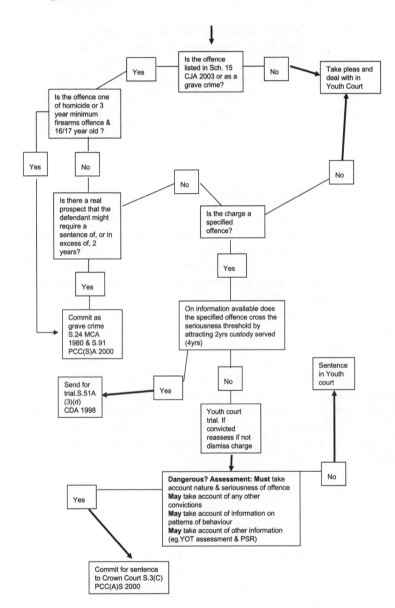

Chapter 6

The Youth Court hearing

PROCEDURE

6.01 The Youth Court is a magistrates' court specially constituted and recognised as such in the Children and Young Persons Act 1933, s 45 as amended. Its procedures at the hearing are also governed by the Children and Young Persons Act 1933 and by the Magistrates' Courts' (Children and Young Persons) Rules 1992 and the Criminal Procedure Rules 2005.

There are restrictions on the persons who may be present in the Youth Court and these are dealt with at **2.07**.

Press reporting

6.02 By virtue of s 49 of the Children & Young Persons Act 1933 no newspaper may publish a report of any matter, including the name, address, school or any other educational establishment, place of work or any still or moving picture if it is likely to lead members of the public to identify a juvenile as someone concerned in proceedings. This does not mean that the court can protect the name of a dead child: *R v Central Criminal Court, ex p Crook and Goodwin* [1995] 1 All ER 537, CA. The court has power to waive this restriction where it is necessary to do so in order to avoid injustice to the juvenile, for example where the interests of justice would be served in publishing details to encourage witnesses to come forward.

The court may also dispense with the restrictions in respect of a juvenile who is unlawfully at large in order to secure his apprehension if he has been charged with or convicted of:
  (a) a violent offence;
  (b) a sexual offence;

(c) an offence punishable with 14 years' imprisonment or more in the case of a person aged 21 or over.

The power may be exercised by a single justice but only on the application of the DPP and only after notice has been given to any legal representative of the juvenile (CPYA 1933, s 49(8)).

Additionally, the court may of its own motion dispense with all or part of the restrictions applying to a juvenile who has been convicted of an offence if it is satisfied it is in the public interest to do so. (CYPA 1933, s 49(4A)) The court may not exercise this power without affording the parties an opportunity to make representations. In *McKerry v Teesside and Wear Valley Justices* (2000) 164 JP 355, Bingham LJ said that the court had to be satisfied that it was in the public interest to dispense with reporting restrictions and that would very rarely be the case.

An adult magistrates' court or Crown Court dealing with a juvenile or before whom a juvenile witness appears may make an order in proceedings under CYPA 1933, s 39. This restricts the press as if the court were a Youth Court. If this is done, the chairman of the court should make an announcement in open court so that the restriction may be made effective. If no warning is given the press are free to publish such details as they wish. An example of such proceedings would be a local authority complaint for an anti-social behaviour order. Such a complaint is not assigned to the Youth Court and would therefore involve the child or young person appearing before an adult magistrates' court. In such circumstances the court must weigh the legitimate interest of the public in receiving fair and accurate reports of persons alleged to have been involved in anti-social behaviour within the community against the need to protect the young person and show proper regard for his welfare. The case law surrounding this area is dealt with at **14.23.** Article 10 of the European Convention guarantees the right to freedom of expression. However the article also recognises that such a freedom carries with it duties and responsibilities, which may be subject to restrictions or penalties prescribed by law and necessary in a democratic society amongst other things for the protection of the rights of others. In this instance the other rights to be balanced are the juvenile's right to private and family life and possibly the rights of the victim or victims who may not welcome publicity. Additional factors highlighted for consideration in *McKerry* were the importance of the principle that justice should be administered in public, that great weight is given to the welfare of youths in court proceedings and on no account should publicity be used as a punishment. Any person who publishes any matter in contravention of s 39 shall, on summary conviction, be liable on each offence to a fine not exceeding level 5. However, when a juvenile attains the age of 18 reporting restrictions will fall away (*DPP v Todd* [2003] EWHC 240 (Admin)).

Unlike orders under s 49, an order under s 39 may only be imposed where there is good reason. A member of the press who is aggrieved by the making of a s 39 order should go back to the court which made the order if the media were not afforded the opportunity to make representations or there has been a material change in circumstances. Alternatively, a defendant or the press may make an appeal against the order (or the withholding or discharging of the order) by proceedings for judicial review in the Divisional Court (*R v Lee* [1993] 1 WLR 103, CA).

The position is further complicated where the Youth Court makes an anti-social behaviour order as an ancillary order in criminal proceedings: CDA 1988, s 1C. Section 49 of the 1933 Act is disapplied by CDA 1988, s 1C(9C) ,although CYPA 1933, s 39 will still give the court discretion to apply press restrictions in such cases. When Sch 2 of the YJCEA 1999 is brought into force a new sub-s (3) will restrict the application of that section to civil proceedings only.

Sections 44 45 and 47 48 of the Youth Justice and Criminal Evidence Act 1999 (YJCEA 1999) cannot be brought into force without an order which will be subject to affirmative resolution by both Houses of Parliament. When in force it will extend the restrictions on the reporting or publishing of information that could lead to the identification of a juvenile involved in criminal proceedings. The restrictions would apply from the beginning of a criminal investigation. Section 46 (which came into force on 7 October 2004) empowers the court to impose similar reporting restrictions on the identification of other witnesses who may be vulnerable to intimidation. Any such restrictions imposed could be lifted at the request of the witness where the court or a single justice was satisfied it was necessary in the interests of justice to do so. Applications are subject to r 16 of the CPR 2005.

Also in force are YJCEA 1999 s 49, which creates new offences for breaching any restrictions, and s 50, which provides statutory defences.

TRIAL IN THE YOUTH COURT

Criminal proceedings

6.03 The proceedings begin with the court, usually through its legal advisor, identifying the juvenile, ascertaining his age and whether or not a parent accompanies him. A parent or guardian of a juvenile under the age of 16 years is required to be in court. A parent of 16- and 17-year-old youths may be required to attend (CYPA 1933, s 34A). The charge and the nature of the proceedings are then explained to the child or young person in simple language suitable to his age and understanding (Criminal Procedure Rules 2005, r.38.3). Relevant extracts of the Rules are reproduced at Appendix C.

For example, a charge of theft involving an appropriation and a dishonest intention permanently to deprive the owner of the property might be explained to a 14-year-old thus: 'The police say you stole a pedal cycle, that means that it did not belong to you, that you were going to keep it as your own, and you knew that it was wrong to do that. Do you understand?'

In the case of *R v Blandford Justices, ex p G (infant)* [1967] 1 QB 82, which involved a 15-year-old charged with the theft of jewellery, it was said that although it would be good sense and desirable to ensure that the legal elements of the charge are explained, the rule does not impose a duty on the court to give a detailed or elaborate explanation of the legal constituents of the charge.

If the court is satisfied that the juvenile understands the charge he should be asked if he pleads guilty or not guilty to the charge (CPR 2005, r 38.4). Every effort should be made to ensure that the plea entered by a juvenile is unqualified. In *R v Blandford Justices*, above, the plea entered before the magistrates was equivocal, that is to say the juvenile admitted the offence and then went on to say she intended to replace the jewellery. The court failed to take the proper course of entering a 'not guilty' plea on the juvenile's behalf on hearing the evidence. The conviction was subsequently quashed in the High Court.

Not guilty trial

6.04 Where a not guilty plea is entered, this will involve the witnesses being called to give evidence. On the basis of that evidence the magistrates must decide if the case has been proved beyond reasonable doubt.

If the juvenile fails to attend his trial the court may proceed in the absence of the accused but shall not do so if it considers that there is an acceptable reason for his failure to appear (MCA 1980, s 11 as amended by CJ&IA 2008, s 54).

After each prosecution witness has given his evidence in chief, the defence solicitor is given the opportunity to cross-examine. If the juvenile is unrepresented, the court shall allow the parent to assist the juvenile in his cross-examination (CPR 2005, r 38.5(3)). If the juvenile makes assertions such as 'I did this' or, 'he did that', the court shall then put to the witness such questions as it thinks necessary on behalf of the juvenile. It may, for this purpose, question the juvenile in order to bring out or clear up any point arising from any such assertion. This is a function which may be carried out by an experienced chairman, but it may be delegated to the legal advisor, thus avoiding the justices entering the arena. In *Simms v Moore* [1970] 3 All ER 1, a case in which the legal advisor assisted an unrepresented party in examination of witnesses, Lord Parker CJ said:

'Where, however, the unrepresented party, whoever he may be, is not competent, through a lack of knowledge of court procedure or rules of evidence or otherwise, to examine the witnesses properly, the court can at its discretion permit the clerk [*sic*] to do so. Fortunately, this is a relatively rare occurrence as most juveniles will be represented in a not guilty trial.'

This is now embodied in the Practice Direction: Role of the legal advisor in court.

At the conclusion of the prosecution case the magistrates must decide whether or not the prosecution has made out a prima facie case which the juvenile should be called on to answer. The High Court has provided guidance as to the circumstances in which the court may rule there is no case to answer:

'How then should the judge approach a submission of "no case"? If there is no evidence that the crime alleged has been committed by the defendant, there is no difficulty. The judge will of course stop the case. The difficulty arises where there is some evidence but it is of a tenuous character, for example because of inherent weakness or vagueness or because it is inconsistent with other evidence. (a) Where the judge comes to the conclusion that the Crown's evidence, taken at its highest, is such that a jury properly directed could not properly convict on it, it is his duty, on a submission being made, to stop the case. (b) Where however the Crown's evidence is such that its strength or weakness depends on the view to be taken of a witness's reliability, or other matters which are generally speaking within the province of the jury and where on one possible view of the facts there *is* evidence on which a jury could properly come to the conclusion that the defendant is guilty, then the judge should allow the matter to be tried by the jury.' (*R v Galbraith* [1981] 2 All ER 1060, CA, per Lord Lane).

Although revoked, the former direction remains good advice to magistrates, namely that, apart from these two situations (above) a tribunal should not in general be called on to reach a decision as to conviction or acquittal until the whole of the evidence which either side wishes to tender has been placed before it. If, however, a submission is made that there is no case to answer, the decision should depend not so much on whether the adjudicating tribunal (if compelled to do so) would at that stage convict or acquit but on whether the evidence is such that a reasonable tribunal might convict. If a reasonable tribunal might convict on the evidence so far laid before it, there is a case to answer.' (Per Lord Parker CJ, *Practice Note* [1962] 1 All ER 448).

The court may of its own motion find that there is no case for the juvenile to answer. However, it is more common for a juvenile's solicitor to make a submission of no case to answer, and where this is done the prosecution should be afforded an opportunity to reply to the submission (*R v Barking and Dagenham Justices, ex p DPP* [1995] Crim LR 953).

Occasionally, a juvenile may ask to change his plea from guilty to not guilty. In such circumstances the court has discretion to exercise. This discretion must be exercised reasonably, taking account of the circumstances of the case and the legal advice received by the juvenile (*R (on the application of S) v Sheffield Youth Court* [2000] All ER (D) 2373). The Criminal Procedure Rules (r 37.6) require any application to change a plea of guilty to be in writing and sets out the information required for the application.

Where the court finds that there is a case to answer the juvenile must be told that he may address the court or that he may give evidence (CPR 2005, r 38.6). The juvenile and his parents should be told that he has the right to remain silent or to give sworn evidence, and to call any witnesses they may have. The juvenile and his parent should also be told that if he refuses to answer any questions the court may draw such inferences as appear proper from his failure (CJ & POA 1994, s 35). The choice and its effect should be explained in clear and simple language. This section does not prevent a defendant from addressing the court on the admissibility of evidence, making a submission of no case to answer or making a closing speech.

The circumstances in which evidence can be given in the absence of a juvenile or his parent or guardian are set out in MC (C&YP) Rules 1992 r19 (1) & (2):

(a) Where the evidence likely to be given is such that in the opinion of the court it is in the interests of the relevant minor that the whole, or any part, of the evidence should not be given in his presence, then, unless he is conducting his own case, the court may hear the whole or part of the evidence, as it thinks appropriate, in his absence; but any evidence relating to his character or conduct shall be heard in his presence.

(b) If the court is satisfied that it is appropriate so to do, it may require a parent or guardian of the relevant minor to withdraw from the court while the relevant minor gives evidence or makes a statement; but the court shall inform the person so excluded of the substance of any allegations made against him by the relevant minor: MC (C&YP) Rules 1992, r 19 (1) and (2). The rules are reproduced at Appendix A.

The onus is on the prosecution to prove its case beyond reasonable doubt, not for the defendant to prove his innocence. A conviction may never be reached on the basis of inferences from silence alone ((CJ & POA 1994, s 38(3)).

Whether the juvenile gives evidence or not, he may call witnesses to assist his defence and, if he is not represented, and has difficulty framing questions, the court should assist him by putting relevant questions to the witness. This function might properly be assigned to the legal advisor. It is a matter of considerable importance that the legal advisor should be proficient in putting the juvenile's story to the witnesses and testing the strength of the prosecution case. Note, however, the case of *Hobby v Hobby* [1954] 2 All ER 395, in which Sachs J said:

'Both parties were represented at the trial by solicitors. Accordingly, neither of them was in need of assistance as to how to present the case to court. Both parties were entitled, within the limits of relevancy and reasonableness, so to conduct their case as seemed best to their legal representatives in court. In those circumstances a justices' clerk is no more entitled to step into the arena and conduct a litigant's case for him than is a justice himself. Indeed, it is important in the interests of justice that the clerk should not give even the appearance of seeking himself to conduct the case of either party or to limit the way in which that case is conducted.'

PROCEDURE AFTER A FINDING OF GUILT

6.05 Where the juvenile admits the charge or he is found guilty, a number of procedural points should be borne in mind. The following are found in CPR 2005, r 41.

(1) The juvenile and his parent or guardian if present shall be given the opportunity of making a statement. The opportunity should be given even where the juvenile is legally represented, although in this case it is preferable that the advocate be asked if he feels that his client or the parents would like to say anything to the court.

It is of importance that the juvenile and the parent be made aware that the court is prepared to hear them while still observing the propriety of affording the advocate his proper role. Many functions may be delegated to the legal advisor but it is preferable that the chairman conducts communication with the juvenile and his parents, after a finding of guilt. It is worth noting that legal representatives speak on behalf of the juvenile and not the parents. Nevertheless, the court should attempt to engage with the young person in an attempt to address his attitude to offending and the consequences of his offending behaviour.

Effective communication at this level is an art requiring considerable skill and clarity of expression.

(2) The court shall take into consideration information as to the juvenile's general conduct. This may include previous findings of guilt and warnings or reprimands previously administered by the police.

Where previous findings of guilt are to be placed before the court they should be shown to and agreed by the juvenile and his parent or guardian. The juvenile's legal representative may indicate the acceptance of previous findings of guilt.

Where previous findings of guilt are disputed then they must be proved by the prosecution either by producing the court register or an extract thereof certified by the court to be a true extract, or by producing a record of the previous findings and by proving the identity of the offender to be the same as that of the person appearing in the antecedent record to have been found guilty.

(3) The court shall also consider information as to home surroundings, school record and medical history of the juvenile such as is necessary to deal with the case in his best interests. This refers particularly to reports provided by the youth offending team (YOT). Legally the school and the probation service or the local authority social services department have a duty to supply information under CPYA 1969, s 9. It is now usual for most of the relevant information to be contained in a pre-sentence report prepared by the YOT.

PRE-SENTENCE REPORTS

6.06 A pre-sentence report (PSR) means a report in writing which contains information as to such matters prescribed by rules and prepared with a view to assisting the court in determining the most suitable method of dealing with an offender. (CJA 2003, s 158) National Standards provided by the Youth Justice Board prescribe that pre-sentence reports must be produced within 15 working days of request. A report for a persistent young offender must be produced within 10 working days of a request. A persistent young offender is defined for these purposes as a juvenile who had been dealt with by the courts on three or more occasions, and commits another offence within three years of last appearing before a court.

A written pre-sentence report must conform to standard headings so that the sentencer will have the sources of information, offence analysis (including what is known about the impact of the offence on any victim), and an assessment of the offender's awareness of the consequences of his offending upon himself his family and any victim. The report should also contain an offender assessment together with an assessment of risk to the community, which should include the risk of re-offending. Finally the report should have a conclusion. In making that conclusion and in considering possible proposals, the report writer should have particular regard to the individual's maturity where it has an influence on offending or the risk of re-offending. In the case of 16- and 17-year-olds the report writer should consider which sentence available to the Youth Court is most suitable to the individual offender.

Not all sentences require a full risk assessment and a full PSR. A specific sentence report can be prepared quickly for less serious offending where the court has indicated a disposal such as a reparation order. (See **8.07**)

Any written report of a probation officer, local authority or medical practitioner may be received and considered by the court without being read aloud and, if the court considers it necessary in the interests of the juvenile, it may require him or his parent or guardian, if present, to withdraw from the court.

In criminal cases the court shall arrange for copies of any written report before the court to be made available to:

(a) the legal representative, if any, of the relevant minor;

(b) any parent or guardian of the relevant minor who is present at the hearing; and

(c) the relevant minor, except where the court otherwise directs on the ground that it appears to it impracticable to disclose the report having regard to his age and understanding or undesirable to do so having regard to potential serious harm which might thereby be suffered by him.

In any case in which the relevant minor is not legally represented and where a report, which has not been made available to him, has been considered without being read aloud or where he or his parent or guardian has been required to withdraw from the court in pursuance of then:

(a) the relevant minor shall be told the substance of any part of the information given to the court bearing on his character or conduct which the court considers to be material to the manner in which the case should be dealt with unless it appears to it impracticable so to do having regard to his age and understanding; and

(b) the parent or guardian of the relevant minor, if present, shall be told the substance of any part of such information which the court considers to be material as aforesaid and which has reference to his character or conduct or to the character, conduct, home surroundings or health of the relevant minors, and if such a person, having been told the substance of any part of such information, desires to produce further evidence with reference thereto, the court, if it thinks the further evidence would be material, shall adjourn the proceedings for the production thereof and shall, if necessary in the case of a report, require the attendance at the adjourned hearing of the person who made: CPR 2005 r 44(3) (4).

A court may receive an oral pre-sentence report except in circumstances where it is required by a court in relation to the passing of a discretionary custodial sentence, in which case it must be in writing: CJA 2003, s.158(1A).

MC(CYPA) Rules 1992, r 21 deals with non-criminal applications such as applications to detain a child in secure accommodation. The Children Act 1989, s 25 goes further, to provide that:

'(1) The court shall arrange for copies of any written report before the court to be made available, so far as practicable before the hearing, to—
(a) the applicant;
(b) the legal representative, if any, of the relevant minor,
(c) the parent or guardian of the relevant minor, and
(d) the relevant minor, except where the court otherwise directs on the ground that it appears to it impracticable to disclose the report having regard to his age and understanding or undesirable to do so having regard to potential serious harm which might thereby be suffered by him.'

Any written report may be received and considered by the court without being read aloud.

In *R v Kirkham* [1968] Crim LR 210, the Court of Appeal stated that reports should be received by the court before any statement in mitigation. The case is as relevant to the Youth Court as to adult courts, and the practice has advantages in that it precludes the necessity for the advocate to go into detail about home background, schooling or personal factors as these should be dealt with fully in the pre-sentence reports.

The CJA 2003, s 159 sets out the statutory position. It states that the court shall give a copy of the report to the offender or his legal representative and to the prosecutor. If the offender is under 18 and not represented, a copy of the report need not be given to him but shall be given to his parent or guardian if present in court. Similar rules apply to other reports such as reports to enable an action plan order or reparation order to be made.

The MC (C&YP) Rules 1992, r 22(1) states:

'Before finally disposing of the case the court shall in simple language inform the relevant minor, any person conducting the case on his behalf, and his parent or guardian, if present, of the manner in which it proposes to deal with the case and allow any of those persons so informed to make representations; but the relevant minor shall not be informed as aforesaid if the court considers it undesirable or, having regard to his age and understanding, impracticable so to inform him.'

Again, the need for clear and easily understandable language on the part of the chairman is important. The court at this stage is making a proposal to the juvenile and his parents about the disposal of the case. Opportunity must therefore be given to the parties to comment on that proposal and the court must consider those representations before making a final order (CPR.2005, r 44(2)).

On sentencing r 44(2) states that on making any order, the court shall, in simple language, suitable to his age and understanding, explain to the relevant minor the general nature and effect of the order unless it appears to it impracticable so to do having regard to his age and understanding and shall give such an explanation to the relevant minor's parent or guardian, if present.

Chapter 7

Adjournments and remands

7.01 A magistrates' court may at any time whether before or after beginning to try an information in a criminal case adjourn the matter, and may do so when only composed of a single justice (MCA 1980, s 10(1)). If the juvenile appears in response to a summons or requisition the case can be adjourned, for example to enable the juvenile or his parents to obtain legal representation or to a trial date for witnesses to attend. When granting an adjournment the court may fix the time and place when the hearing is to resume, or leave the time and place to be determined later. The court cannot resume the hearing unless it is satisfied that the parties have had adequate notice (MCA 1980, s 10(2)). If the parties have attended court, notice should be given in court in a clear and unequivocal manner. If they have not attended court, a notice of adjournment should be sent to the address on the summons in accordance with MC Rules 1981, r 99.

The overriding objective in the Criminal Procedure Rules 2005 (see Appendix C for extracts) is that criminal cases be dealt with justly. This involves all aspects of adjournments and case management and includes:

    (a) acquitting the innocent and convicting the guilty;

    (b) dealing with the prosecution and the defence fairly;

    (c) recognising the rights of a defendant, particularly those under Art 6 of the European Convention on Human Rights;

    (d) respecting the interests of witnesses, victims and jurors and keeping them informed of the progress of the case;

    (e) dealing with the case efficiently and expeditiously;

    (f) ensuring that appropriate information is available to the court when bail and sentence are considered; and dealing with the case in ways that take into account the gravity of the offence alleged, the complexity of what is in issue, the severity of the consequences for the defendant and others affected, and the needs of other cases (CPR 2005, r 1).

Each party must actively assist the court in fulfilling its duty under r 3.2, with or without a direction; and apply for a direction if needed to further the overriding objective. Rule 3.2 places a duty on the court to actively manage the case. This includes the early identification of the real issues, achieving certainty as to what must be done, by whom, and when and in particular by the early setting of a timetable for the progress of the case. The court must also make any direction appropriate to the needs of that case as early as possible and monitor the progress of the case and compliance with directions (CPR 2005, rr 3.2 and 3.3).

At every hearing, if a case cannot be concluded there and then the court must give directions so that it can be concluded at the next hearing or as soon as possible after that. The court must, where relevant, if the defendant is absent, decide whether to proceed. It must take the defendant's plea (unless already done) or if no plea can be taken then find out whether the defendant is likely to plead guilty or not guilty and set, follow, or revise a timetable for the progress of the case, which may include a timetable for any hearing including the trial.

The court must, in giving directions, ensure continuity in relation to the court and to the parties' representative where that is appropriate and practicable; and. where a direction has not been complied with, find out why, identify who was responsible, and take appropriate action (CPR 2005, r 3.8).

REMANDS

7.02 When adjourning the hearing of a criminal case, the court may remand the defendant. (MCA 1980, s 10(4)) Where the juvenile appears on a criminal charge and has been bailed to attend court, then the court will remand the juvenile, either on bail or in custody, and in either case the remand must be to a fixed date. Where a person is remanded in custody before a finding of guilt, it must not, subject to exceptions dealt with below, be for more than eight clear days, and where he is remanded on bail the court may remand him for a longer period if both parties agree (MCA 1980, s 128(6)). A court may remand in custody for more than eight clear days if it has previously remanded him in custody for the same offence and he is before the court. However it has to have given the parties an opportunity to make representations and must have set a date on which it expects the next stage in the proceedings to take place. This remand may not exceed 28 days (MCA 1980, s 128A). If the defendant is present and consents he may be remanded in custody for up to 28 days. This will apply, for example, where he is being remanded for the first time or the court is not able to set a date for the next stage. If the court is satisfied that any person who has been remanded is unable by reason of illness or accident to appear or be brought before the court at the expiration of the period of remand the court may remand him for a further time in his absence (MCA 1980, s 129). The court must have been given solid grounds on which to form a reliable opinion. (*R v Liverpool City Justices, ex p Grogan* (1990) 155 JP 450)

Remands for reports

7.03 After a finding of guilt the court may adjourn for the purpose of enabling inquiries to be made or of determining the best method of dealing with the offender. After the finding of guilt but before making any order, the court may adjourn for a maximum of four weeks, unless the offender is remanded in custody when the maximum is three weeks. (MCA 1980, s 10) The four-week time limit on the remand period when the court requires reports on bail is discretionary and not mandatory (*R v Manchester City Justices, ex p Miley and Dynan* (1977) 141 JP Jo 248). Consequently failures by the court to comply with the time limit will not the affect the validity of the proceedings. Where a case is adjourned for inquiries or a report, the defendant need not be granted bail if it appears to the court that it would be impracticable to complete the inquiries or make the report without keeping the defendant in custody (Bail Act 1976, Sch 1, para 7). Reports in this context may include pre-sentence, specific sentence, school, medical, psychological or psychiatric reports.

When remanding to local authority accommodation after a finding of guilt, the court is limited to a remand of three weeks.

It must be emphasised that the power to adjourn after a finding of guilt must be exercised judicially and for a proper purpose. Courts must not therefore remand after a finding of guilt purely for punitive purposes. In *R v Toynbee Hall Juvenile Court Justices, ex p Joseph* [1939] 3 All ER 16, the Divisional Court quashed the remand of a juvenile found guilty of riding on the railway without paying the fare. The juvenile court's chairman gave the reasons for the remand saying that 'the boy was a liar and had to learn not to defraud the railway company... and that for his own good the boy ought to go to a remand home'.

Custody time limits

7.04 The Prosecution of Offences (Custody Time Limits) Regulations 1987 are regulations made by the Secretary of State under the power granted to him by POA 1985, ss 22 and 29.

A time limit is set for the time spent in custody between the accused's first appearance and commencement of summary trial, namely 56 days. Between the accused's first appearance and committal to the Crown Court it is 70 days. A uniform 112 days is allowed from committal to the Crown Court until arraignment.

The regulations apply in Youth Courts by virtue of the definition of 'custody' inserted into POA 1985, s 22 by CJA 1988, Sch 11 namely that it includes local authority accommodation to which a person is remanded or committed by virtue of CYPA 1969, s 23.

The regulations, which only apply to indictable and either way offences, reflect the general rights of the detained person under Art 5(3) ECHR. As Lord Bingham said in *R v Manchester Crown Court, ex p McDonald* [1999] Cr App R 409: 'Everyone arrested or detained (for trial) shall be entitled to trial within a reasonable time or to release pending trial.' Where the prosecution fails to commence trial or committal to the Crown Court within the time limit set, the accused is automatically entitled to bail. If the time limit is unlikely to be adhered to the prosecution may apply for an extension of the limit. This application must be made before the expiry date and may only be granted where the court is satisfied that there is good and sufficient cause for doing so and that the prosecution has acted with all due diligence and expedition. Either way offences include those which must be tried summarily in the Youth Court by virtue of CYPA 1969, s 45 (*R v Stratford Youth Court, ex p S* [1998] 1 WLR 1758).

The Regulations provide that an application to extend may be made orally or in writing. Although not a requirement of reg 7, it is good practice to give the grounds for the application in the notice (~*R v Central Criminal Court, ex p Marrota Crown* Office Digest 13).The prosecution is required to give written notice of its intention to apply not less than five days beforehand in the Crown Court and not less than two days beforehand in a magistrates' court The requirement to give notice is directory and not mandatory however; failure to give notice will be a factor for the court in considering whether the prosecution has acted with all due diligence and expedition. The accused may waive his right to notice and the court (if satisfied that it is not practicable in all the circumstances for the prosecution to give the notice required) may abridge the period.

Procedure regarding appeals against a court's decision to extend a custody time limit can be found in CPR 2005, r 20.

In *R v Sheffield Justices, ex p Turner* [1991] 2 QB 472, it was held that a defendant was unlawfully detained in custody after the expiry of the 70-day remand time limit. However, that did not prevent the justices committing him in custody for trial at the Crown Court as that was a fresh stage in proceedings and a different time limit applied.

POLICE BAIL

7.05 The police may require an arrested person to return to the police station and may bail that person to do so (PACE 1984, s 47(3)(b)).

On charging a defendant with an offence the police may grant bail to attend court: PACE 1984, s 47(3)(a). A charged person has the right to bail unless exceptions set out in the schedule to the Bail Act 1976 are satisfied: these are dealt with in the next section. If the custody sergeant grants bail with conditions the defendant should be given a record of those conditions. The sergeant may impose any conditions that a court could impose except a condition listed in s 3A including a condition of residence in a probation hostel: Bail Act 1976, s 3A(5). The custody sergeant may vary such conditions at any time before the first court appearance (Bail Act 1976, s 3A(4)).

BAIL – THE GENERAL PRINCIPLES

7.06 A juvenile aged 17 years is treated as an adult for the purposes of the Bail Act 1976. However, in cases involving allegations of criminal damage MCA 1980, s 22 requires the court to determine in the mode of trial hearing for defendants aged 18 and above whether the value of the offence of criminal damage exceeds £5,000. If the value is accepted as less than £5,000 the case is to be tried summarily and will fall under Part 1A Bail Act 1976. 17-year-olds, although subject to the Bail Act, are not covered by the mode of trial provisions. In order to enable the court to determine if the bail decision on a 17-year-old defendant charged with an offence of criminal damage is to be made under Part 1A, the court is required to consider whether the value of any offence of criminal damage is less than £5,000 (Bail Act 1976, s 9A). In such a case the charge will be subject to Bail Act 1976, Part 1A (see **7.13** below).

A juvenile has a general right to unconditional bail. It is perhaps worth noting that the restrictions on granting bail to adults charged with offences carrying life imprisonment (para 2A of Part 1 of Sch 1 to the 1976 Act) do not apply to under 18 year olds. However in such circumstances in the youth court the court shall give particular weight to the fact that the defendant was on bail in criminal proceedings on the date of the offence.

Bail under the Bail Act 1976 does not involve a recognisance or surety when it is unconditional. Bail by the police either to report back to the police station or to attend court may have conditions attached to it.

Unconditional bail imposes a duty on the offender to surrender to custody at a time and place appointed, which may be either the police station or the court. Failure to surrender without reasonable excuse is an offence in itself punishable in the case of an adult convicted summarily by three months' imprisonment or a level 5 fine (Bail Act 1976, s 6(7)). Even surrendering late to the court provides the court with discretion whether or not to put a Bail Act charge (*R v Scott* [2007] All ER (D) 191). A juvenile who fails to surrender to custody could be made subject to any of the orders available to the court or a fine not exceeding £1000 (£250 in the case of a child). Custody, however, is not available (see **7.09**).

Bail may be subject to conditions or may be refused if certain criteria set out in the Bail Act 1976 are satisfied.

Bail conditions

7.07 The court or custody sergeant may impose conditions on bail where it appears to be necessary to ensure that an offender:
  (a) surrenders to custody;
  (b) does not commit an offence while on bail;
  (c) does not interfere with witnesses or otherwise obstruct the course of justice;
  (ca) for his own protection or, if he is a child or young person, for his own welfare or in his own interests,

The court may additionally impose conditions to ensure that an offender:

(d) makes himself available for the purpose of enabling inquiries or a report to be made to assist the court in dealing with him for the offence;

(e) to secure that before the time appointed for him to surrender to custody, he attends an interview with an authorised advocate or authorised litigator, as defined by s 119(1) of the Courts and Legal Services Act 1990.

He may be required to comply with such conditions as are imposed either before or after release on bail (Bail Act 1976, s 3(6)).

Where a court or custody sergeant imposes conditions of bail, reasons must be stated and a record of the decision kept. A copy of that note must be given to the person in relation to whom the decision was taken (Bail Act 1976, s 5(4)).

Conditions, imposed by the police or the court, may be as follows:

(a) to ensure attendance at court. The most common conditions imposed under this exception to unconditional bail are:

   (i) to report to a police station at times specified by the court during the adjournment period. This is an unpopular condition with police forces due to manpower and administrative difficulties;

   (ii) residence at an address specified by the court. In the case of a juvenile this is usually his parents' address. However, situations can arise where the court imposes a condition of residence at the address of a relative for example, where the juvenile is estranged from his immediate family;

   (iii) that sureties be provided. This involves persons agreeing to secure the attendance of the juvenile at court by pledging a sum of money that may be forfeit if they fail to ensure that attendance. No money is actually deposited with the court. The court must be satisfied, however, that any person standing surety has the financial resources to pay the amount set by the court in the event of non attendance by the juvenile and the subsequent forfeiture of the monies: *R v Birmingham Crown Court, ex p Rashid Ali* (1998) 163 JP 145. The court, in considering the suitability of a person to stand surety, may also have regard to his character and any previous convictions, and his proximity to the person for whom he is to be surety. Proximity in this sense may mean either geographically or in terms of kinship;

    (b) to prevent the commission of offences. The most common conditions imposed are:

        (i)   of curfew: that the juvenile remains indoors between specified hours. Usually this involves the hours of darkness;

        (ii) not to associate with co-accused. This embraces the case where offenders are alleged to have acted in unison in the commission of an offence and it is believed that if they associate they will commit further offences;

        (iii) not to contact the complainant. This is sometimes imposed where the charge is, for example, one of assault and there is still bad feeling between the parties;

    (c) to prevent interference with witnesses or the obstruction of the course of justice. The most common condition is not to contact prosecution witnesses where the court fears that the offender may attempt to prevent these witnesses giving evidence;

    (d) to ensure the availability of the offender if necessary for the purpose of enabling inquiries if a report is to be made to assist the court in dealing with him for the offence. This condition may be worded to involve co operation with a doctor, probation officer or social worker where the court believes he would otherwise be uncooperative;

    (e) to ensure he attends for interview with a solicitor before the next hearing.

These last two conditions, (d) and (e), may only be imposed by a court and if the police feel an electronic monitoring condition, residence at a hostel or medical reports in a murder case are required then the case must go before a court for such conditions to be attached.

An offender may be required to comply with such conditions as are imposed either before or after release on bail. For example, the offender may be remanded into local authority accommodation until suitable sureties are found. In addition, a parent may stand surety for his child to ensure that the juvenile shall comply with any conditions imposed on him under sub-ss (6), (6ZAA) or (6A) as mentioned above. The parent may only stand surety to guarantee those conditions to which he consents, and the sum shall not exceed £50. If the young person is likely to attain the age of 17 years before the date fixed for his surrender to custody a parent may not stand surety to ensure compliance with conditions. (Bail Act 1976, s 3(7))

Although it is rare in the context of the Youth Court, if it appears that the juvenile is unlikely to surrender to custody, he may be required to give security for his surrender to custody. The security may be given by him or on his behalf. This involves the deposit of a sum of money with the appropriate officer.

Before imposing conditions on bail, the court or custody sergeant must be satisfied that there is a genuine need for each condition imposed and that they are both precise and workable. For example, in a case of theft from a city store the justices may be tempted to impose a condition that the juvenile stays away from the city centre to prevent the commission of further offences. Objections to this condition are that the city centre is not identifiable, the offender's solicitor may have his office in the city centre and the Youth Court itself may be situated near the main shopping centre. In human rights terms bail conditions should be proportionate to the mischief which they aim to prevent.

Electronic monitoring of conditions of remand

7.08 A juvenile aged between 12 and 16 may be made the subject of a remand condition that he or she is subjected to electronic tagging (Bail Act 1976, s 3(6ZAA)). The criteria to be satisfied are:

(a) he or she is been charged with or convicted of a violent or sexual offence or an offence punishable in the case of an adult with 14 years' imprisonment or more; or

(b) he or she is charged with or has been convicted of one or more imprisonable offences which together with any other imprisonable offences of which he or she has been convicted of in any proceedings:
   (i) amount to, or
   (ii) would, if he or she was convicted of the offences with which he or she is charged, amount
   to a recent history of repeatedly committing imprisonable offences whilst remanded on bail or while remanded to local authority accommodation.

The court has to have been notified by the that electronic monitoring arrangements are available and the youth offending team must have notified the court that in its opinion the imposition of such a condition will be suitable in that defendant's case (Bail Act 1976, s 3AA(4) and (5); CYPA 1969, ss 23(7) and 23AA). 17-year-olds are again treated similarly; however the court must also be satisfied that the offender would not be granted bail without the requirements (Bail Act 1976, s 3AB).

A defendant may be made the subject of a condition that he or she complies with the terms of an intensive supervision and surveillance programme. Such a programme involves 25 hours supervision per week and additional surveillance and can be combined with a condition of electronic monitoring. The youth must previously have received at least one youth rehabilitation order or custodial penalty in the past. The Youth Justice Board also makes this condition available where a youth is charged with an offence that is sufficiently serious that an adult could be sentenced to 14 years' custody or more (see **7.15**).

Failure to surrender and breaching bail conditions

7.09   If a defendant, who has been released on bail, fails without reasonable excuse to surrender to the custody of the court he is guilty of an offence (Bail Act 1976, s 6(1)). Alternatively, if the defendant, having had a reasonable excuse for failing to surrender to custody at the appointed time, fails to surrender to custody as soon after the appointed time as is reasonably practicable he is also guilty of a criminal offence (Bail Act 1976, s 6(2)). Such an offence is punishable in the case of an adult with a fine not exceeding level 5 or imprisonment not exceeding three months. It would appear that custody is not available for this offence in the Youth Court as the minimum detention and training order sentence available is four months: see *Pye v Leeds Youth Court* [2006] EWHC 2527 (Admin).

Such an offence is only triable in the court at which proceedings are to be heard in respect of which bail has been granted. The case will normally be heard immediately in accordance with the Practice Direction (Criminal Consolidated) 2004 and not adjourned until the end of the substantive hearing.

Where the bail in question was granted by a police officer, proceedings for failure to surrender should be started by a charge or the laying of an information within six months of the time of the commission of the relevant offence or an information laid no later than three months from the occurrence of the first of the events below to occur after the commission of the relevant offence.

Those events are—:
  (a)   the person surrenders to custody at the appointed place;
  (b)   the person is arrested, or attends at a police station, in connection with the relevant offence or the offence for which he was granted bail;

(c) the person appears or is brought before a court in connection with the relevant offence or the offence for which he was granted bail (Bail Act 1976, s 6(12)-(14)).

Where the bail was granted by a court, the court may initiate proceedings following an express invitation by the prosecutor. The prosecutor must consider that proceedings are appropriate in all the circumstances (Practice Direction (Criminal Consolidated) 2004 Part 1.13.9).

Breach of bail conditions is not a criminal offence. It does however give a constable having reasonable grounds for believing that the person is likely to break or has broken the bail condition a power of arrest. Following arrest the defendant must be brought before a magistrates' court except where he was arrested within 24 hours of the time appointed for him to surrender to custody to a particular court. In such a case he must be brought as soon as practicable, and in any event within 24 hours after his arrest, before a justice of the peace for the area in which he was due to appear.

The 24-hour period shall not be taken to include Christmas Day, Good Friday or any Sunday. Detention, solely for a breach of bail conditions, beyond the 24-hour time limit may be an unlawful imprisonment. A defendant need not be granted bail if he is arrested under s 7 of the Bail Act 1976 and the court is satisfied that there are substantial grounds for believing that he will fail to surrender, interfere with witnesses or commit offences.

Procedure on breach of bail conditions

7.10 Non compliance with bail conditions is not in itself an offence, but a person released on bail may be arrested without warrant and brought before the court:

(a) if a constable has reasonable grounds for believing that that person is not likely to surrender to custody; or

(b) if a constable has reasonable grounds for believing that that person is likely to break any of the conditions of his bail or has reasonable grounds for suspecting that that person has broken any of these conditions; or

(c) in a case where that person was released on bail with one or more surety or sureties, if a surety notifies a constable in writing that that person is unlikely to surrender to custody and that for that reason the surety wishes to be relieved of his obligations as a surety. (Bail Act 1976, s 7(3))

A person arrested in breach of bail conditions may be remanded in custody on the grounds specified in the Bail Act or he may be released on the same or amended conditions.

Proceedings under the Bail Act 1976, s 7(5) can be held before a single justice. Where an allegation that a defendant is in breach of his bail conditions is denied there is no power to adjourn the case and a decision must be taken on the occasion when the defendant is produced to the court (*R v Liverpool City Magistrates' Court, ex p DPP* [1993] QB 233). In R (on the application of Culley) v Crown Court sitting at Dorchester [2007] EWHC 109 (Admin), it was made clear that once the 24-hour limit had elapsed the court no longer had jurisdiction to deal with the matter. It followed that everything done after the expiration of the 24-hour period was ultra vires and unlawful. Courts therefore need to be vigilant to ensure that breach of bail applications are concluded within the 24-hour period.

Where a defendant does not accept an alleged breach of bail condition, it is unnecessary to have a hearing in which evidence on oath is called. Section 7 provides:

> 'a simple and expeditious procedure for dealing with the situation where a constable believes that a person bailed is unlikely to surrender to custody or alternatively, that a person bailed is likely to breach a condition of his bail, or has broken a condition of his bail.'

The structure of s 7 clearly contemplates the constable who has arrested the person bailed bringing him before the justice of the peace and stating his grounds for believing that the defendant has broken a condition of his bail. That may well involve the giving of 'hearsay evidence'. No doubt the justice of the peace will in fairness give the defendant an opportunity to respond to what the constable is saying. The justice will then either form one of the opinions set out in sub-s (5) and, if he does so, go on to decide whether to remand the defendant in custody or on bail on the same or more stringent conditions; or, if the justice feels unable to form one of the opinions set out in the subsection, he will order the defendant to be remanded on bail on the same terms as were originally imposed (*R v Liverpool City Magistrates, ex p DPP* [1993] QB 233).

The effect of the Human Rights Convention on the procedure set down by the High Court in the Liverpool case was reviewed in *R (on the application of the DPP) v Havering Magistrates Court* [2001] 3 All ER 977. The court held that Article 6 had no direct relevance where justices where exercising their judgment on whether or not to commit a person to custody following a breach of bail conditions.

The court said that it was clear that Article 5 did have direct relevance. Where a decision was taken to deprive somebody of his liberty that should only be done after he had been given a fair opportunity to answer the basis upon which such an order was sought. In testing whether or not such an opportunity had been given, it was essential to bear in mind the nature and purpose of the proceedings in question. To this end the procedures set out in domestic law were entirely compatible with the requirements of the article. The fact of a breach of conditions was evidence of a relevant risk arising, but it was no more than one of the factors that the justices had to consider in exercising their discretion.

The court had to ensure that the defendant had a full and fair opportunity to comment on, and answer, any material before the court. If that included oral evidence from a prosecution witness the accused had to be given an opportunity to cross-examine. Similarly, if he also wished to give oral evidence he should be entitled to do so.

The fact that, under domestic law there is no power to adjourn the hearing once a defendant has been brought before the court under the Bail Act 1976, s 7(4), does not result in a breach of Article 5. A person arrested under s 7(4) must be dealt by the court and released on bail or remanded in custody (*R v Teesside Magistrates' Court ,ex p Ellison* 165 JP 355).

If any person who is bailed fails to attend at the time and place appointed, the court may issue a warrant for his arrest (Bail Act 1976, s 7(1)).

Reconsideration of bail on application of the prosecution

7.11   Where a magistrates' court (including a Youth Court) or a constable has granted bail for an indictable or either way offence the prosecutor may apply to:
  (a) vary the conditions of bail;

   (b) impose conditions in respect of bail which has been granted
       unconditionally;
   (c) withhold bail.

These provisions do not apply to bail granted by a constable to return to
a police station under PACE, s 37 (as amended by CJA 2003, Sch 2).

Such an application may only be made where it is based on information
in the hands of the prosecutor, which was not available to the court or
constable when the decision was taken. Procedural requirements under r
19 of the CPR 2005 must be complied with including provision for notice,
statements and a 72-hour time limit. Where the decision of the court is
to withhold bail from the person to whom it was originally granted it
must, if that person is before the court, remand him in custody. If he is
not before the court it must order him to surrender himself forthwith
into the custody of the court. When he surrenders himself the court
must remand him in custody. If he fails to surrender he may be arrested
without warrant and must then be taken before a justice of the peace for
the petty sessions area in which he was arrested as soon as practicable
and in any case within 24 hours (Bail Act 1976, s 5B).

Prosecution right of appeal

7.12   Where bail is granted to a person charged with an offence
punishable in the case of an adult with imprisonment the prosecution
may appeal to a Crown Court judge. They may only appeal if they made
representations against the granting of bail. The prosecution must give
oral notice at the end of the remand proceedings and written notice within
two hours. The bailed person is then kept in custody/local authority care
until the appeal is heard and the hearing must be commenced within 48
hours from the date on which the notice was given. (Bail Amendment
Act 1993 s.1)

REFUSAL OF BAIL

7.13   Every person who appears or is brought before a court accused
of an offence has the general right to bail (Bail Act 1976, s 4). No person
may be remanded in custody unless the court finds that one or more of
the specific exceptions found in the Bail Act 1976, Sch 1 applies. In the
context of the European Convention on Human Rights Article 5(3)

requires that a person charged with an offence be released pending trial unless the prosecution can show that there are *relevant and sufficient* reasons to justifying his continued detention. The role of the court in considering bail is to examine all the facts both for and against the existence of a genuine public interest requirement justifying departure from the presumption of individual liberty.

In the case of imprisonable offences, the following reasons may justify refusal of bail:

(1)

    (a) there are substantial grounds for believing that the defendant if released on bail would:

        (i)   fail to surrender; or

        (ii) commit fresh offences; or

        (iii) interfere with witnesses or obstruct justice;

    (b)

        (i)   the offence is an indictable offence or an offence triable either way; and

        (ii) it appears to the court that he was on bail in criminal proceedings on the date of the offence the court will be required to give particular weight to this factor (Bail Act 1976, Sch 1, para 2A as amended by CJA 2003, s 14)

    (c) the court is satisfied that the defendant should be kept in custody for his own protection, or

    (ca) if he is a child or young person his own welfare or in his own interests;

    (d) the defendant is a serving prisoner;

    (e) the court is satisfied that it has not been practicable to obtain sufficient information for the purpose of making a bail decision for want of time since the institution of proceedings against him;

    (f) the defendant having been released on bail in, or in connection with, the proceedings for the offence he has been arrested for being in breach of conditions of that bail;

    (g) where his case is adjourned for inquiries or a report and it appears that it would be impracticable to complete the inquiries or complete the report without keeping the defendant in custody;

In the case of a summary only offences punishable with imprisonment and criminal damage cases where the value is less than £5,000, Part 1A of the Bail Act 1976 (as amended by s 52 & Sch.12 CJIA 2008) contains more restrictive grounds for withholding bail with effect from 14 July 2008. In such circumstances bail may be withheld if:

(a) it appears to the court that, having been previously granted bail in criminal proceedings, he has failed to surrender to custody in accordance with his obligations under the grant of bail and the court believes, in view of that failure, that the defendant, if released on bail (whether subject to conditions or not), would fail to surrender to custody;

(b) it appears to the court that the defendant was on bail in criminal proceedings on the date of the offence and the court is satisfied that there are substantial grounds for believing that the defendant, if released on bail (whether subject to conditions or not), would commit an offence while on bail;

(c) there are substantial grounds for believing that the defendant, if released on bail (whether subject to conditions or not), would commit an offence while on bail by engaging in conduct that would, or would be likely to, cause physical or mental injury to any person other than the defendant; or any person other than the defendant to fear physical or mental injury;

(d) the defendant should be kept in custody for his own protection or, if he is a child or young person, for his own welfare;

(f) he is in custody in pursuance of a sentence of a court or a sentence imposed by an officer under the Armed Forces Act 2006;

(g) having been released on bail in or in connection with the proceedings for the offence, he has been arrested in pursuance of s 7 of this Act and the court is satisfied that there are substantial grounds for believing that the defendant, if released on bail (whether subject to conditions or not) would fail to surrender to custody, commit an offence while on bail or interfere with witnesses or otherwise obstruct the course of justice (whether in relation to himself or any other person);

(h) it has not been practicable to obtain sufficient information for the purpose of making a bail decision for want of time since the institution of the proceedings.

In the case of non-imprisonable offences, the following reasons apply:

(a) it appears to the court that, having been previously been granted bail in criminal proceedings, the defendant has failed to surrender to custody and the court believes, in view of that failure, that the defendant would fail to attend;

(b) the court is satisfied that the defendant should be kept in custody for his own protection or, if he is a child or young person, for his own welfare;

(c) the defendant is in custody in pursuance of the sentence of the court or of any authority acting under any of the armed services Acts: ie the Army Act 1955, the Air Force Act 1955 and the Naval Discipline Act 1957;

(d) having been released on bail or in connection with the proceedings for the offence, the defendant has been arrested as being in breach of of the conditions of his bail and the court is satisfied that there are substantial grounds for believing that the defendant, if released on bail (whether subject to conditions or not) would fail to surrender to custody, commit an offence on bail or interfere with witnesses or otherwise obstruct the course of justice (whether in relation to himself or any other person). (Bail Act 1976, Sch 1).

When withholding bail the court must give reasons, include a note of those reasons in the court register and give a copy of that note to the defendant (Bail Act 1976, s 5).

In deciding whether to grant or refuse bail the court is required to have regard to such of the following considerations as appear to it to be relevant:

(a) the nature and seriousness of the offence, or default (and the probable method of dealing with the defendant for it);

(b) the character, antecedents, associations, and community ties of the defendant;

(c) the defendant's record in respect to the fulfilment of his obligations under previous grants of bail in criminal proceedings;

(d) (except in the case of a defendant whose case is adjourned for inquiries or a report) the strength of the evidence of his having committed the offence or having defaulted, as well as any other things which appear to be relevant (Bail Act 1976, Sch 1, Pt 1, para 9).

The above provisions apply strictly in the Youth Court as they do in the adult court. At each remand hearing, the court, before it may remand in custody, must be satisfied that there are substantial grounds for believing one or more of the exceptions to the general right to bail apply, and that there are adequate reasons to support that finding. Having found the an exception to bail and the supporting reasons, the court should then consider whether or not the imposition of conditions would achieve the same objective as a remand in custody.

REFUSAL OF BAIL IN THE YOUTH COURT

7.14 Where a court remands a child or young person charged or convicted of one or more offences or commits him for trial and refuses him bail the remand is to local authority accommodation(CYPA 1969, s 23(1)). In this context 'young person' means someone who has attained 14 years and is under 17 years. The period of remand before conviction is for a maximum of eight days (the remand in absence procedure does not apply to juveniles), if the remand is after conviction the maximum period is three weeks. When remanded to local authority accommodation the juvenile will live wherever the social services department direct and this can include a residential children's home, remand foster placements or the juvenile living at home or with other members of his or her family. The remanding court must designate the local authority that is to receive the defendant as the local authority in whose area it appears to the court that he resides, or the offence or one of the offences was committed. In the case of a young person being looked after by a local authority it will be that local authority.

It is important to note that a remand to the care of the local authority does not confer parental responsibility on the authority. This may have ramifications when the court decides issues as to who pays a compensation order (*North Yorkshire County Council v Selby Youth Court Justices* [1994] 1 All ER 991).

On remanding a person to local authority accommodation the court may require the defendant to comply with conditions as if he had been granted bail. These conditions could include conditions of electronic tagging or intensive supervision and surveillance programmes (see **7.15**). If such conditions are imposed the court is required to explain to the defendant in open court why those conditions are imposed. Those reasons are to be specified in the warrant of commitment and in the court register. If a court remands a person to local authority accommodation it may impose requirements on that authority for securing compliance with the conditions or stipulations that he may not be placed with a named person. The court may only impose such conditions and requirements after consultation with the local authority. The court has no power to direct that a child or young person who was remanded to local authority accommodation reside at a specific place. (*Cleveland County Council v DPP* (1994) 93 LGR 596)

If the court wished to impose an electronic tagging condition it must ensure that the criteria are satisfied. A juvenile aged 12 or over may be made the subject of a condition that he or she is subjected to electronic tagging (Bail Act 1976, s 3(6ZAA). The criteria to be satisfied are:

(a) he or she is been charged with or convicted of a violent or sexual offence or an offence punishable in the case of an adult with 14 years' imprisonment or more; or

(b) he or she is charged with or has been convicted of one or more imprisonable offences which together with any other imprisonable offences of which he or she has been convicted of in any proceedings:
  (i) amount to, or
  (ii) would, if he or she was convicted of the offences with which he or she is charged, amount

to a recent history of repeatedly committing imprisonable offences whilst remanded on bail or while remanded to local authority accommodation.

The court has to have been notified that electronic monitoring arrangements are available in their local justice area and the youth offending team must have notified the court that in its opinion the imposition of such a condition will be suitable in that defendanti:'s case (Bail Act 1976, s 3AA(4) and (5); CYPA 1969, ss 23(7) and 23AA).

Intensive supervision and surveillance and local authority remand

7.15 A defendant may be made the subject of a condition of a remand to local authority accommodation that he or she complies with the terms of an intensive supervision and surveillance programme. Such a programme involves 25 hours supervision per week and additional surveillance and can be combined with a condition of electronic monitoring. The Youth Justice Board only make this condition available to the court if the defendant satisfies the Board's criteria. The youth has to have previously been charged or warned or convicted of offences on four or more separate dates within the previous 12 months. Only offences committed on separate dates will be counted. Multiple or unrelated offences sentenced on the same date count as one offence. The youth must previously have received at least one community rehabilitation order or custodial penalty at any time. The Youth Justice Board also makes this condition available where a youth is charged with an offence that is sufficiently serious that an adult could be sentenced to 14 years or more.

The police have power to arrest a juvenile who breaches a condition of his remand to local authority accommodation (CYPA 1969, s 23A). Breach of such conditions is not an offence in itself but may trigger an application for a remand to secure accommodation.

The court may impose conditions on a defendant remanded to local authority accommodation on application by the local authority and where it does so may impose requirements on the local authority for securing compliance with conditions. The court may vary or revoke such conditions on the application of the local authority or the defendant.

This should not be confused with the common bail condition to reside as directed by the local authority. Such a condition does not remand a juvenile into local authority accommodation.

SECURE ACCOMMODATION

7.16   Where a juvenile is looked after by a local authority the authority may keep that person in secure accommodation for up to 72 hours in any period of 28 consecutive days (Children (Secure Accommodation) Regulations 1991, reg 10). Apart from this power the local authority has to have an order of the court to keep the juvenile in secure accommodation for a maximum period of 28 days. The local authority may apply for permission to accommodate the juvenile securely under CA 1989, s 25 or the court may remand the juvenile directly to secure accommodation. The maximum period for which a court could make a secure accommodation order of a juvenile who has been remanded to local authority accommodation is the period of the remand.

Application for secure accommodation order

7.17   A local authority may apply to the court for an authority to use secure accommodation for the purpose of restricting the liberty of a child whom they are looking after. Applications are made under the Children Act 1989. They are excluded from the definition of specified proceedings by virtue of the Family Proceedings Courts (Children Act 1989) Rules 1991, r 2(2). Such applications can be made either to a Youth Court or a magistrates' court by virtue of the CJA 1991, s 60(3) in the case of children who are remanded into local authority accommodation under CYPA 1969, s 23. If the remand order was made by the Crown Court the application should be made to the Family Proceedings Court.

If the Youth Court made the remand then any secure accommodation application should be made to that court. If the remand order was made in the adult magistrates' court, perhaps by virtue of the young person being jointly charged with an adult, then the application for secure accommodation should be made to that court.

Where a juvenile has been remanded into local authority accommodation by a Youth Court sitting outside that authority's boundary the local Youth Court has jurisdiction to hear an application by the authority for a secure accommodation order (*Liverpool City Council v B* [1995] 1 WLR 505).

Generally a juvenile may not be placed in secure accommodation unless it appears to the court that:
  (a) he has a history of absconding and is likely to abscond from any other accommodation;
  (b) if he absconds, he is likely to suffer significant harm; or
  (c) if he is kept in any other accommodation he is likely to injure himself or other persons (Children Act 1989, s 25(1) and (3))

One previous instance of absconding is sufficient for there to be a 'history of absconding' (*R v Calder Justices, ex p C (a minor)* (4 May 1993, unreported)).

In the case of a juvenile who is either:
  (a) charged with or convicted of an offence punishable in the case of a person of 21 or over with 14 years' imprisonment or more;
  (b) charged with or convicted of an offence of violence,
the criteria is modified to allow the court to allow detention in secure accommodation if it appears that any other accommodation is inappropriate because:
  (a) the juvenile is likely to abscond from other such accommodation; or
  (b) the juvenile is likely to injure himself or other persons if he is kept in such other accommodation (Children (Secure Accommodation) Regulations 1991, reg 6).

In *Re G (a child) (secure accommodation order)* [2001] 3 FCR 47, it was held that where a child had previously been remanded to local authority accommodation and had not committed a further offence, the conditions in regulation 6 had not been met but the Youth Court could nevertheless make a secure accommodation order if it was satisfied under section 25(3) that all the criteria of section 25(1) were met and indeed it was required to do so.

In this context the words 'convicted of' has been held not only to apply to the present proceedings but also to any such offences of which the juvenile has on previous occasions been convicted (*Re C* (22 October 1993, unreported, CO 2974/93)).

The local authority may apply for a secure accommodation order for a juvenile whom it is looking after and who is residing in its accommodation. Thus in *Re C* [1994] 2 FCR 1153 the family proceedings court had jurisdiction to make a secure accommodation order for a girl who had been bailed with a condition to reside as directed by the social services and was being accommodated in local authority accommodation.

In *Re M (a minor)* [1995] Fam 108, CA, it was held that it is the duty of the court to put itself in the position of a reasonable local authority and consider first, whether the criteria were satisfied and secondly, whether it would be in accordance with the local authority's duty under Children Act 1989, s 22(3) to safeguard and promote the welfare of the child by placing him or her in secure accommodation. Although the welfare of the child was a relevant consideration it could not be a paramount one as the local authority was permitted to exercise its powers in relation to the child to protect members of the public from serious injury.

A child under 13 may not be placed in secure accommodation without the prior approval of the Secretary of State (Children (Secure Accommodation) Regulations 1991, reg 4). Such approval may be sought through the Department of Health duty service.

Procedure at the hearing

7.18 The hearing of an application for secure accommodation is as if it were by way of complaint and the Magistrates' Courts Act 1980, ss 56 and 57 apply. This means that if at the time of the hearing or the adjourned hearing the relevant minor appears but the complainant local authority fails to appear, the court may dismiss their application or if evidence has been received on a previous occasion it may proceed in the absence of the applicant. Where neither the applicant nor the juvenile appears the court has power to dismiss the application.

Where the court proceeds with the application the procedure and order of evidence and speeches is governed by the Magistrates' Courts Act 1980, s 53 and MCR 1981, r 14. This means that the applicant may address the court outlining the application and will then call evidence in support of the application. At the conclusion of the evidence for the applicant the juvenile may address the court whether or not he afterwards calls evidence. At the conclusion of any evidence on behalf of the juvenile the applicant may call evidence to rebut that evidence. Either party may then, with the leave of the court, address the court a second time. Where the court grants leave to one party it must not refuse leave to the other. The parent or guardian of the juvenile is also entitled by the Magistrates' Courts (Children and Young Persons) Rules 1992 to make representations to the court and shall be allowed to do so at any such stage after the conclusion of the evidence at the hearing as the court considers appropriate (r 15).

As these are civil proceedings the provisions of the Civil Evidence Act 1995 governing the admissibility of hearsay evidence may apply.

Before the hearing commences the court must inform the juvenile of the general nature of the proceedings and of the grounds on which they are brought. Such an explanation should be made in terms suitable to the juvenile's age and understanding. If for any reason the court is unable to give such an explanation to the juvenile because of his absence, age or lack or understanding then the court must inform the parent or guardian present at the hearing giving a similar explanation as it would to the juvenile himself.

A court may not make an order for secure accommodation in the case of a juvenile who is not legally represented unless he has failed, refused to apply or had public funding withdrawn. Most juveniles will have the benefit of legal representation in applications for secure accommodation but where this is not the case the court must allow his parent or guardian to conduct the case on his behalf. If the court thinks it appropriate and subject to any request by the juvenile himself it may allow a relative of his or some other responsible person to conduct the case on his behalf. One of the reasons that it is preferable the juvenile should be legally represented is that the court has power under r 19 to hear evidence in the absence of the relevant minor or to require his parent or guardian to withdraw. This should only be done where the court is of the opinion that it is in the interests of the relevant minor that the evidence should be received but without him being present or in the case of the parent or guardian that it is appropriate that they withdraw when certain evidence is heard. The court must however hear evidence relating to the character or conduct of the juvenile in his presence and if a parent or guardian is excluded then the court must inform that person of the substance of any allegations made against him by the relevant minor.

Oral evidence need not be adduced by either party if they agree that statements filed will constitute the evidence (*Re AS (secure accommodation order)*) [1999] 1 FLR 103. If at the end of the applicant's case the court is satisfied that there is sufficient evidence upon which a reasonable tribunal could find the application proved, then it must tell the juvenile or the person conducting the case on his behalf of his right to give evidence or make a statement and call witnesses.

If having heard the juvenile's case the court finds the matter proved it should so announce and go on to consider its disposal of the application. Before finally disposing of the case the court must inform the relevant minor, any person conducting the case on his behalf and his parent or guardian if present of the manner in which it proposes to deal with the case. This should be done in simple language and those persons informed should be allowed to make representations. The only exception to the court explaining its proposals to the relevant minor are if the court considers it undesirable for some reason or having regard to his age and understanding it feels it would be impracticable to inform him. Having heard any such representations on its proposal the court must then make its order and shall in simple language suitable to the age and understanding explain to the juvenile the general nature and effect of the order. Again the court may dispense with this explanation if it appears impracticable to do so having regard to the age and understanding of the juvenile. The court must in any case give such an explanation to the relevant minor's parent or guardian if they are present in court (Magistrates' Courts (Children and Young Persons) Rules 1992, r 17.

Court ordered remands direct to secure accommodation (12- to 14-year-old boys and 12- to 16-year-old girls)

7.19 Courts may remand certain juvenile offenders direct to local authority secure accommodation (also known as a remand to local authority accommodation with a security requirement.) These provisions apply to any 12-, 13-, or 14-year-old boy and to any 15- or 16-year-old girl. The provisions for 15- and 16-year-old boys are slightly different and are dealt with later.

The court may remand juveniles in these age groups to local authority secure accommodation if the following criteria are satisfied:

(a) the juvenile is charged with, or has been convicted of, a violent or sexual offence or an offence punishable in the case of a person aged 21 or older with 14 years or more imprisonment;

(b) the juvenile is charged with or has been convicted of one or more imprisonable offences which together with any other imprisonable offences of which he or she has been convicted in any proceedings:

　(i)　amount to; or

　(ii)　would, if he or she were convicted of the offences with which he or she is charged, amount to

a recent history of repeatedly committing imprisonable offences while remanded on bail or to local authority accommodation;

(c) and in either case the court is of the opinion after considering all of the options for the remand of the person, that only remanding to local authority secure accommodation would be adequate to protect the public from serious harm from him or her or to prevent the commission by him or her of imprisonable offences (CYPA 1969, s 23(5)).

PCC(S)A 2000, s 161 indicates that in relation to sexual and violent offences 'serious harm' means death and/or serious physical or psychological injury occasioned by further such offences committed by the young person. Serious harm is not defined in relation to other offences. However, the definition for sexual and violent offences gives an indication of the gravity of the harm to which the public would need to be exposed from a juvenile in other circumstances before the test was likely to be satisfied.

The court has to be of the opinion that remanding the juvenile to local authority accommodation would be the only adequate way to protect the public from serious harm from the juvenile or would prevent the commission by him or her of imprisonable offences. The court has to consider this question specifically and separately from (a) or (b) above.

In the criteria the words 'convicted of' have been held not only to apply to the present proceedings but also to any such offences that the juvenile has on previous occasions been convicted of (*Re C* (22 October 1993, unreported, CO 2974/93)).

It should also be noted that in (b) above 'imprisonable offence' is not limited to those punishable by 14 years' imprisonment or exclusively to violent or sexual offences.

In considering a remand to secure accommodation the local authority, probation service or youth offending team must be consulted by the court (CYPA 1969, s 23(4)).

When a court remands a juvenile to local authority accommodation, unless that juvenile is a male aged 15 or 16, the local authority is under a duty to place that juvenile in such accommodation (CYPA 1969, s 23(4)).

Remands direct to secure accommodation (vulnerable 15- and 16-year-old boys)

7.20 The criteria to be satisfied are:
  (a) the defendant is charged with or has been convicted of a violent or sexual offence or an offence punishable in the case of a person aged 21 or over with 14 years' imprisonment or more; or
  (b) the defendant is charged with or has been convicted of one or more imprisonable offences which together with any other imprisonable offences of which he or she has been convicted in any proceedings:
    (i) amount to; or
    (ii) would, if he or she were convicted of the offences with which he or she is charged, amount to;
    a recent history of repeatedly committing imprisonable offences while remanded on bail or to local authority accommodation;
  (c) and in either case the court is of the opinion after considering all of the options for the remand of the person, that only remanding to local authority secure accommodation would be adequate to protect the public from serious harm from him or to prevent the

commission by him or her of imprisonable offences; (CYPA 1969, s 23(5)).

(d) the court is of the opinion and declares that by reason of his physical or emotional immaturity or a propensity of his to harm himself it would be undesirable for him to be remanded to a remand centre or prison (CYPA 1969, s 23(5A)).

In the absence of a declaration of vulnerability the remand will be to prison accommodation, see **7.22** below. The Home Office guidance suggests that it is the duty of the local authority to draw these matters to the attention of the court. (*Implementation Guidance: Court-ordered Secure Remands*) It may be necessary for the defendant to be remanded to prison accommodation for a short period for the assessment to be carried out;

(e) the court may only remand a male of this age directly to local authority secure accommodation if it has consulted with the local authority and it is satisfied that secure accommodation place is available for him.

The court has to be of the opinion that remanding the juvenile to local authority or direct to secure accommodation would be the only adequate way to protect the public from serious harm from the juvenile or to prevent the commission by him or her of imprisonable offences. The court has to consider these questions specifically and separately. The seriousness of the offence is not of itself necessarily sufficient justification for such a remand. The court may however infer from his previous convictions that the public is at risk of serious harm from him having regard to the nature of the offences or the manner in which he committed them. A series of offences may not be aggregated so as to render serious such harm as may be caused by them (*R v Croydon Youth Court, ex p G (a minor)* (1995) Times, 3 May).

In the above criteria the words 'convicted of' have been held not only to apply to the present proceedings but also to any such offences that the juvenile has on previous occasions been convicted of (*Re C* (22 October 1993, unreported, CO 2974/93). 'History of absconding' has been held to mean at least one previous occasion of absconding. (*R v Calder Justices, ex p C* (4 May 1993, unreported)) It is likely therefore that 'recent history of repeatedly committing imprisonable offences' should be interpreted in the same way. What is 'recent' will be a matter for the court to determine on the facts of each case.

Legal representation

7.21 The Youth Court may not exercise the power to remand directly to local authority secure accommodation in respect of an unrepresented juvenile unless:

(a) he was granted a right to representation funded by the Legal Services Commission as part of the Criminal Defence Service but the right was withdrawn because of his conduct or he is financially ineligible; or

(b) having been informed of his right to apply for such representation and having the opportunity to do so, he refused or failed to apply. (CYPA 1969, s 23(4A) as amended by the Access to Justice Act 1999, Sch 4).

Where the court declares that a person falls within the criteria to be remanded to secure accommodation it is under a duty to state in open court that it is of the opinion that the criteria apply and explain to the defendant in ordinary language why it is of that opinion. These reasons have to be specified in the commitment warrant and in the court register (CYPA 1969, s 23(6)).

REMANDS TO REMAND CENTRES OR PRISONS

7.22 Where a child or young person (ie under 17) charged with or convicted of one or more offences is not released on bail, the court must remand him to local authority accommodation unless:

(a) he is a male of 15 years or older, and

(b) the defendant is charged with or has been convicted of a violent or sexual offence or an offence punishable in the case of a person aged 21 or over with 14 years' imprisonment or more; or

(c) the defendant is charged with or has been convicted of one or more imprisonable offences which together with any other imprisonable offences of which he or she has been convicted in any proceedings, amount to or would if he or she were convicted of the offences with which he or she is charged amount to a recent history of repeatedly committing imprisonable offences while remanded on bail or to local authority accommodation;

(d) and in either case the court is of the opinion after considering all of the options for the remand of the person, that only remanding to a remand centre, prison or local authority secure accommodation would be adequate to protect the public from serious harm from him or to prevent the commission by him or her of imprisonable offences (CYPA 1969, s 23(5)).

The court has to be of the opinion that remanding the juvenile to a remand centre or prison would be the only adequate way to protect the public from serious harm from him. The court has to consider this question specifically and separately from (a) or (b) above. The seriousness of the offence is not of itself necessarily sufficient justification for such a remand (*R v Croydon Youth Court, ex p G (a minor)* (1995) Times, 3 May).

Before a court makes such a finding, it must consult with a probation officer, a social worker of a local authority social service department, or a member of the youth offending team. In these circumstances, the remand is to a remand centre if the court has been notified that a remand centre is available, but if it has not been so notified to a prison.

As stated above the words 'convicted of' have been held not only to apply to the present proceedings but also to any such offences that the juvenile has on previous occasions been convicted of. (*Re C* (22 October 1993, unreported, CO 2974/93) 'History of absconding' means at least one previous occasion of absconding (*R v Calder Justices, ex p C* (4 May 1993, unreported)).

The Youth Court may not exercise the power to remand to a remand centre or prison in respect of an unrepresented juvenile unless either:
  (a) he was granted a right to representation funded by the Legal Services Commission as part of the Criminal Defence Service but the right was withdrawn because of his conduct or he is financially ineligible; or
  (b) having been informed of his right to apply for such representation and having the opportunity to do so, he refused or failed to apply (CYPA 1969, s 23(4A).

Where the court declares that a person falls within the criteria to be remanded to a remand centre or prison it is under a duty to state in open court that it is of the opinion that the criteria apply and explain to the defendant in ordinary language why it is of that opinion. These reasons have to be specified in the commitment warrant and in the court register (CYPA 1969, s 23(6)).

Where a person is remanded to local authority accommodation the local authority may apply to the court for him to be remanded to a remand centre or prison. This may only be done if the criteria referred to above are satisfied.

In *R (on the application of SR) v Nottingham Magistrates' Court* [2001] EWHC Admin 802, (2001) 166 JP 132, this provision for 15- and 16-year-old males to be remanded to prison accommodation rather than local authority secure accommodation was held to be justifiable discrimination pursuant to Art 14.

REMANDS TO POLICE CUSTODY

7.23 On refusing bail the court may remand to police custody for a period of up to 24 hours if the defendant is 16 or younger. If he or she is 17 the remand to police custody may be for up to three days. Such a remand may only be ordered if it is necessary for the purpose of making enquiries for other offences. The defendant should be brought back before the court as soon as the need for the remand has been satisfied. If a defendant needs to be remanded for a short period, for any other reason, then the remand will be to local authority accommodation or prison accommodation dependent upon the appropriate criteria being satisfied. The court must be satisfied that the exceptions to the right to bail are satisfied (MCA 1980, s 128(7) and (8)).

It should not forgotten that the court retains the power to impose 'bail conditions' when making a remand to local authority care with or without a security requirement: see **7.07** above.

Youth Court remands flowchart

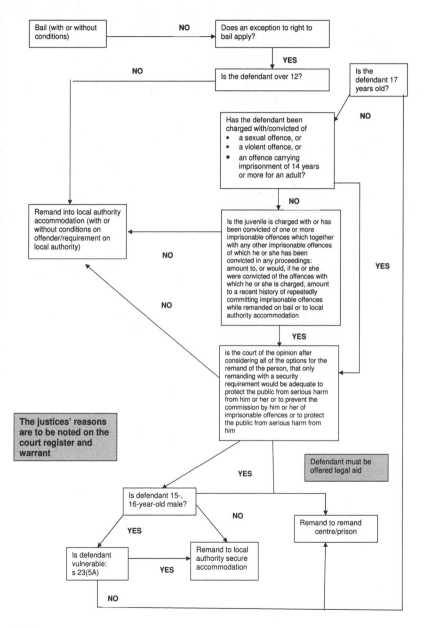

7.24

7.25

Youth Court Remands Availability

	Prison M	Prison F	Police cells M	Police cells F	Local authority security requirement M	Local authority security requirement F	Requirements imposed on local authority M	Requirements imposed on local authority F	Local authority accommodation with conditions M	Local authority accommodation with conditions F	Local authority accommodation M	Local authority accommodation F	Bail cond M	Bail cond F	Bail uncond M	Bail uncond F
10-13	✗	✗	✓	✓	■	■	✓	✓	✓	✓	✓	✓	✓	✓	✓	✓
14	✗	✗	✓	✓	✓	✓	✓	✓	✓	✓	✓	✓	✓	✓	✓	✓
15	⊙	✗	✓	✓	⊙	✓	✓	✓	✓	✓	✓	✓	✓	✓	✓	✓
16	⊙	✗	✓	✓	⊙	✓	✓	✓	✓	✓	✓	✓	✓	✓	✓	✓
17	✓	✓	✓	✓	✗	✗	✗	✗	✗	✗	✗	✗	✓	✓	✓	✓

■ 12 years or under only with the consent of the Secretary of State.
✓ Available.
✗ Not available.
⊙ Prison/remand centre unless vulnerable (CYPA) 1969 s 25(5)(a) then LA secure accommodation.

Chapter 8

Referral orders, deferment of sentence discharges, reparation orders, and financial orders

REFERRAL ORDERS

8.01   Where a defendant under the age of 18 years appears for sentence before a Youth Court or adult magistrates' court the court *must* make a referral order if:

(a) the offence is imprisonable;

(b) the offence or offences are not ones for which the sentence is fixed by law;

(c) the defendant pleaded guilty to the offence and any connected offence;

(d) the court is not proposing to impose a custodial sentence or make a hospital order, to grant an absolute discharge for the offence or any connected offence;

(e) the defendant has never been convicted by a court in the United Kingdom of any other offence.

Where a defendant under the age of 18 years appears for sentence before a Youth Court or adult magistrates' court the court *may* make a referral order if:

(a) the offence or offences are not ones for which the sentence is fixed by law;

(b) the court is not proposing to impose a custodial sentence or make a hospital order, or to grant an absolute discharge;

(c) the defendant has pleaded guilty to one but not all the (connected) offences for which he is to be sentenced or the defendant has pleaded guilty to a non-imprisonable offence and does not therefore satisfy the compulsory conditions and either:

(i) the defendant has never been convicted by a court in the United Kingdom of any other offence, other than mentioned in (c) above; or

(ii) the defendant has been dealt with by a UK court for an offence other than 'the offence and any connected offence' on only one previous occasion, but was not referred to a youth offender panel on that occasion; the youth offending team or probation officer recommend that the offender is suitable for referral to a youth offender panel; and the court considers there are exceptional circumstances that justify ordering the offender to be so referred.

The Youth Court must specify the length of the order during which time the offender will have contact with the Panel. This must be not fewer than 3 and not more than 12 months and will be assessed on the basis of the seriousness of the offence.

Where the court makes a referral order it must *not* make a sentence that consists of or includes youth rehabilitation order, impose a fine, grant a conditional discharge or make a reparation order for that offence. The court may not bind over a parent or the young offender (CJA 2003, s 324) but may make a parenting order and a referral order on the same offence (CJA 2003, Sch 34). A referral order may be accompanied by ancillary orders such as costs and compensation.

The order requires the offender to attend meetings with the Youth Offender Panel. The Panel will comprise at least one member of the youth offending team and at least two lay people who are not members of the youth offending team. The court must order the offender's parents or guardian to attend meetings where the offender is under 16 years of age and may do so in the case of a 16-17-year-old. Whatever the offender's age the court shall not order attendance by the parent if the court is satisfied that it would be unreasonable to do so or to an extent which the court is satisfied would be unreasonable. The parent or guardian will normally be required to attend at least the first meeting. The court may order the parent or guardian to attend the meetings of the panel, in his or her absence in which case the court is required to send a notice to such a person. As indicated above, the court may make a parenting order at the same time as making a referral order. Before it does so it must however consider a report by a probation officer, social worker or a member of the youth offending team. Where the parent or guardian has been ordered to attend panel meetings and no parenting order has been made the panel may refer him or her to the Youth Court which shall then cause the parent to appear before it. The Youth Court may make a parenting order if it is satisfied that the parent or guardian failed without reasonable excuse to comply with the requirement to attend and that a parenting order would be desirable in the interests of preventing the commission of further offences by the youth (see also Parenting Orders below).

At the first meeting the Panel will reach an agreement with the youth on a programme aimed at preventing re-offending by the offender. The Panel can tailor the programme to the offender and the offending. The court is required to send to the Panel a statement of the offence for which the defendant has been made the subject of the referral order. Often a copy of the prosecution statements will be sent to the Panel. Defence advocates need to be alive to this and ensure that the statement from the court reflects any basis of plea.

The role of the Youth Offender Panels is outside the scope of this work but following a referral they will meet with the offender and devise programmes, participation and reparation in an attempt to address offending behaviour. Once the contract has been agreed the compliance period for the referral order begins.

After the contract has taken effect circumstances may arise (including the offender is making good progress under the contract) so that it appears to the youth offender panel to be in the interests of justice for the referral order to be revoked. In such circumstances the panel may refer the offender back to the Youth Court requesting it to revoke the order or alternatively to revoke the order and deal with the offender for the offence in respect of which the original order was made.

If the Youth Court decides not to exercise its power to revoke the referral order the youth offender panel may not make a further application in the following three months except with the consent of the appropriate court (PCC(S)A 2000, s 27A).

Once a youth offender contract, for less than 12 months, has taken effect the panel may refer the offender back to the appropriate court requesting it to extend the length of the order. This can be done at any time so long as the period of the order has not ended and the request for the extension is not in excess of three months. The panel shall make the referral by sending a report to the appropriate court explaining the circumstances that have arisen since the contract took effect and why the offender is being referred back to it for an extension of the period. If the offender is under 18 at the time of the referral back to court he will appear in a Youth Court; otherwise he will appear in a magistrates' court.

If the referral order is to be extended, the offender must appear before the court, the contract must be in force and any extension must not extend the order beyond the maximum 12 months. In determining whether to grant an extension the court shall have regard to the extent of the offender's compliance with the terms of the contract (PCC(S)A 2000, Sch1, para 9ZB-9ZE).

BREACH OF THE ORDER AND THE COMMISSION OF OFFENCES

8.02   The court may revoke the original order and re-sentence the juvenile if he or she has been referred back to the court by the panel, because of breach of the contract, or commission of a further offence whilst subject to the referral. The court must have regard to the circumstances of the referral back to the court and where the contract has taken effect between the offender and the panel the extent of his or her compliance with the contract. If the court sentences for a further offence this has the effect of automatically revoking the referral order without an application being made.

If the youth committed another offence before the referral order was made it may make an order extending the compliance period if the order was less than 12 months in length, up to the 12-month maximum.

If the youth commits an offence after the referral order is made the court may extend the period of the order if it is satisfied, on the report of the youth offender panel, that there are exceptional circumstances. Again the total compliance period must not exceed 12 months (PCC(S)A 2000, Sch 1, para 11).

DEFERMENT OF SENTENCE

8.03   A deferment of sentence is strictly speaking not a sentence at all. The court may, after a finding of guilt, defer dealing with the offender for the purpose of enabling it to have regard, in determining the method of disposal, to his conduct (including, where appropriate, the making by him of reparation for his offence) or to any change in his circumstances. Such a deferment may be for a period not exceeding six months. The date must be fixed by the court at the point of deferment and the case adjourned without the imposition of bail upon the offender (Powers of Criminal Courts (Sentencing) Act 2000, s 1(1), as substituted by CJA 2003, Sch 23). This power is exercisable only if the juvenile consents, and for these purposes he should be asked in open court for his consent. He or she must also undertake to comply with any requirements as to his conduct during the period of deferment that the court considers it appropriate to impose (PCC(S)A 2000, s 1(3)(b) as inserted by CJA 2003, Sch 23). Furthermore, the court should be satisfied, having regard to the nature of the offence and the character and circumstances of the offender that it would be in the interests of justice to exercise this power.

The requirements as to his conduct may include reparative and other activities. The court can include requirements as to the defendant's residence. If the defendant is to undertake requirements the court may appoint a supervisor to monitor his or her compliance with the requirements. The supervisor must consent to acting and must also provide the court with such information as it requires about the defendant's compliance. If the offender fails to comply with the requirements he or she may be returned to court before the end of the period of deferment. The defendant may then be sentenced for the original offence. The court may issue a summons or warrant to ensure his or her attendance.

Should the offender commit a further offence during the period of deferment, the court which deals with that further offence may also deal with the deferred sentence, unless the deferred sentence was imposed by the Crown Court (see below). Where the court deals with the offender because of breach of requirements or because he has committed a further offence it has the same powers of sentence that it had when it decided to defer sentence. The court may not defer sentence if the compulsory referral conditions are satisfied.

It can be seen from the drafting of the statute and from the possible ramifications of a deferred sentence that this is not an order that the court will impose lightly. It is an option that should be used in very limited circumstances and reserved for the offender whose circumstances suggest a positive likelihood of altering his behaviour in any way clearly specified by the court.

The principles set out on deferment of sentence have been reinforced in the case of *R v George* [1984] 3 All ER 13, CA. Deferment of sentence should not be adopted without careful consideration of whether the sentencer's intentions could not best be achieved by other means. If deferment is decided upon, care must be taken to avoid the risk of misunderstanding and a risk of injustice when the defendant returns to court. Where the court has deferred sentence it must give a copy of the order deferring sentence and setting out the requirements to the offender and any person appointed as supervisor.

As a matter of principle, a substantial custodial sentence is said not to be appropriate after a deferment where the report on conduct and circumstances given to the court is not unfavourable. In many cases an order of conditional discharge can be as effective as deferring sentence.

Deferring sentence should be reserved for those cases in which the justices have reason to believe that the juvenile's lifestyle will change constructively over the period of deferment. The Sentencing Guidelines Council makes it clear that the court should, impose specific and measurable conditions that do not involve a serious restriction on liberty, give a clear indication of the type of sentence it would have imposed if it had decided not to defer and ensure that the offender understands the consequences of failure to comply with the court's wishes during the deferment period. For these reasons, it is recommended that the justices deferring sentence should return to make the final order.

If the juvenile is found guilty of any offence during the period of deferment the court, which deferred sentence on him, may deal with him for the deferred matter before the term of deferment expires. If the court that makes a finding of guilt for the subsequent events is the same court which deferred sentence then it may deal with both the deferred matter and the new offence. However, if the subsequent offence is dealt with by another Youth Court, that court may deal with the deferred matter as well as the new offence. Note, however, that this power is not exercisable by the Youth Court if the court that deferred passing sentence was the Crown Court. Where a court dealing with a subsequent offence, deals with another court's deferred sentence, it is not required to obtain that court's consent. As a matter of practice, inquiry should be made of the other court for details of the deferment.

ABSOLUTE DISCHARGE

8.04   Where the court convicts a juvenile of an offence and it is of the opinion, having regard to the circumstances (including the nature of the offence and the character of the offender), that it is inexpedient to inflict punishment, it may discharge the defendant absolutely (PCC(S)A 2000, s 12(1)(a)). This power is generally reserved for cases where the defendant has committed a crime in law but can be said to be morally blameless.

An absolute discharge may also be applicable where a juvenile is being made subject to a custodial order and has other offences for which a custodial sentence would either not be lawful or would be inappropriate. In such circumstances the court may impose an absolute discharge, although some courts prefer to record no separate penalty for the offences not subject to the custodial order. Either course of action is preferable to the imposition of a financial penalty, which could be considered oppressive in addition to a custodial order.

CONDITIONAL DISCHARGE

8.05   This is an order discharging the offender on the condition that he commits no further offence during a specified period not exceeding three years. If he is found guilty of a subsequent offence during the period of the conditional discharge he may be dealt with not only for that offence but also for the original offence for which he was conditionally discharged. As in the case of an absolute discharge the court should be of the opinion that it would not be expedient to inflict punishment, having regard to the nature and circumstances of the offence and the character of the offender.

When making an order for conditional discharge, the court is required to explain the effect of the order to the juvenile in ordinary language (PCC(S)A 2000, s 12(4)). Note that this explanation will no longer be necessary when CJA 2003, Sch 32, para 93 is in force. For this reason an order of conditional discharge may not be made in the juvenilee:'s absence, whereas an order of absolute discharge may be made in the defendant's absence. The court may delegate the explanation of a conditional discharge to a defendant's advocate. However, the case of *R v Wehner* [1977] 3 All ER 553, CA, makes it clear that the better practice is face-to-face communication from the magistrate to the defendant, thus ensuring that the juvenile before them has fully understood the order made.

The effect of a conditional discharge is that it is not deemed to be a conviction for any purpose other than the purpose of the proceedings in which the order is made and any subsequent breach of the order (PCC(S)A 2000, s 12(4)).

Unless there are exceptional circumstances the court may not impose a conditional discharge for an offence committed within two years of a final warning. The exceptional circumstances must be related directly to the offence or the offender and the court must explain its reasons for believing there are exceptional circumstances (CDA 1998, s 66).

As noted elsewhere, a conditional discharge may not normally be imposed at the same time as a referral order, nor may it be given as a penalty for a breach of an anti-social behaviour order.

BREACH OF CONDITIONAL DISCHARGE

8.06 Where it is proved to the satisfaction of the court which made the order for conditional discharge that the juvenile subject to the order has been found guilty of an offence committed during the relevant period, the court may deal with him for the offence for which the order was made in any manner in which it could deal with him if he had just been found guilty by that court of that offence. If the juvenile subject to a conditional discharge is found guilty by another magistrates' court or Youth Court of any offence during the relevant period, that court may, with the consent of the court which made the order, deal with him for the original offence as if it had just found him guilty of that offence (subject to restrictions imposed on an adult court by PCC(S)A 2000, s 8).

If a juvenile attains the age of 18 and is then found guilty of an offence committed during the currency of a conditional discharge made by the Youth Court, the Youth Court has jurisdiction to enforce his attendance and deal with him for the original offence. Where an offender attains the age of 18, and appears before a magistrates' court in breach of a conditional discharge made in the Youth Court in respect of an offence triable only on indictment in the case of an adult, the powers of the magistrates' court to deal with the breach are exercisable as if the offence were an offence triable either way that had been tried summarily (PCC(S)A 2000, s 13(9)).

The Youth Court may issue a summons or warrant for the purposes of enforcing attendance. Before issuing a summons an information must be laid and where a warrant is issued that information must be in writing and substantiated on oath (PCC(S)A 2000, s 13(3)).

The correct procedure for dealing with an offender found guilty of an offence during the operational period of a conditional discharge is to put the alleged breach to the offender and ask him if it is admitted or denied. If it is denied the court must determine whether a further offence has been committed within the terms of the section. The admission or denial should be entered on the court register along with the adjudication when the case is finally dealt with. An obligation is placed on the prosecution to relate to the court the details of the original offence so that the court may deal with that offence in a fair and effective manner.

REPARATION ORDERS

8.07 A reparation order is a disposal requiring a young offender to make reparation to the victim of the offence or to the community at large. This is reparation other than the payment of compensation and may cover a variety of activities from simply writing a letter of apology to carrying out work to assist the local community.

There is a statutory presumption that the court will make such a reparation order if it has power to do so. If it does not make a reparation order it must give its reasons (PCC(S)2000, s 73(8)).

A reparation order may only be made if the court has been notified by the Secretary of State that arrangements for implementing such orders are available. The court shall not make a reparation order if it proposes:
    (a) to pass on him a custodial sentence; or
    (b) to make a youth rehabilitation order, or a referral order.

The court may not make a reparation order where a youth rehabilitation order is in force in respect of the offender, unless when it makes a reparation order it revokes the youth rehabilitation order. See **CHAPTER 11** for revocation powers.

Before it makes an order the court is required to obtain a report by a probation officer, social worker, or member of a youth offending team indicating:
    (a) the type of work that is suitable for the offender; and
    (b) the attitude of the victim.

The order shall not require the offender to work for more than 24 hours in aggregate and must be completed within three months. The requirements of the order shall, so far as is practicable, avoid conflict with the offender's religious beliefs and any community order to which he is subject. It may not interfere with schooling or work.

Before it makes the order the court shall explain the effect of the order, the consequences of breach and that it has power to review the order on the application of either the offender or the responsible officer.

FINES

8.08 One common order made in dealing with criminal offences in the Youth Court is the fine. In the Youth Court (or adult court) where an offender under the age of 14 is fined, the maximum fine available is £250. (MCA 1980, ss 24(4) and 36(2)) When a juvenile over the age of 14 and under the age of 18 is fined in the Youth Court (or adult court), the maximum fine available is £1,000. (MCA 1980, ss 24(3) and 36(1)) There is no statutory maximum fine in respect of a juvenile who is sentenced before the Crown Court, although when dealing with an appeal or breach of a conditional discharge imposed by a lower court the lower courts' maxima apply.

General considerations

The basic principle of fines imposition is that the court must ensure that the financial penalty imposed reflects and is commensurate with the seriousness of the offence being punished. The aim is for the fine to have an equal impact on offenders with different financial circumstances. It may be a hardship but should not force the offender below a reasonable 'subsistence' level. The court will therefore go through its normal assessment of mitigating and aggravating factors to assess the gravity of the offence, and then proceed to look at the offender's financial circumstances and ability to pay the fine. The court has a duty to take into account the financial circumstances of the offender in so far as they are known or appear to the court. Normally a fine should be of an amount that is capable of being paid within 12 months. In the Youth Court the offender will usually be before the court and a means enquiry can take place. (CJA 2003, ss 162 and 164)

This requirement, to take the offender's financial circumstances into account in setting the amount of the fine, also applies to compensation orders and to the financial circumstances of a parent or guardian who is ordered to pay a fine on behalf of their child (see **8.09**). If a parent or guardian is not before the court, the court has power to make an order requiring them to provide the court with a statement of means within a period specified. The court has the power to make such a determination as it thinks fit of the financial circumstances of an offender where he has been convicted in absence, or in the case of a parent or guardian who has been ordered to pay the fine on behalf of the young offender when they fail to comply with the order to give a statement of financial circumstances.

It is worth noting that where the court has made a determination of financial circumstances in the absence of sufficient information, it may at a subsequent means enquiry remit all or part of the fine if as a result of its enquiry it finds that the original fine was disproportionate to the actual means of the offender.

If the court orders the juvenile to pay the fine then it is likely to be a fairly small fine repayable from pocket money or a part-time job, or if the offender is in the 16- or 17-year-old bracket, from wages if the offender is working. The parents, however, will pay the majority of financial penalties in the Youth Court.

PARENTAL RESPONSIBILITY FOR FINANCIAL PENALTIES

8.09 The courts have for many years had an obligation, now consolidated under PCC(S)A 2000, s 137, to order fines, etc to be paid by parents where this is thought to be appropriate. Section 137(3) is worded so that in the case of an offender who is under 16 years the court must order the parent or guardian to pay the fine unless it would be unreasonable in the circumstances of the case so to do, or the parent or guardian cannot be found. In the case of the youth appearing in the Youth Court, ie the 16- and 17-year-old, the court has a power to order the parent or guardian to pay the fine rather than a duty to do so.

Provided a parent has been given the opportunity to attend court, an order for payment may be made against him in his absence. If the parent is present he must be given the opportunity to make representations as to whether he should be responsible for the payment of the financial penalty.

It may be said to be unreasonable, having regard to the circumstances of the case, to order the parent or guardian to pay a financial order where he/she satisfies the court either that he/she did not have charge or control of the juvenile at the time the offence was committed, or that he/she had not conduced to the commission of the offence by neglect or failure to exercise due care or control over the juvenile.

In *TA v DPP* [1997] 1 Cr App Rep (S) 1, a 16-year-old girl was accommodated in a local authority children's home under a voluntary arrangement. There was no care order in force. She kicked a police car and subsequently pleaded guilty to criminal damage. She was given a conditional discharge and ordered to pay £30 costs. Her mother was made responsible for payment of £100 compensation. The Divisional Court set this order aside saying it was unreasonable bearing in mind that the mother had had no opportunity to prevent her committing the offence as the girl was not living with her. The requirement to inquire into whether it would be reasonable to make the parent pay financial penalties and the need to give the parent the opportunity to be heard before making such an order were again underlined in *R v J-B* [2004] EWCA Crim 14, [2004] 2 Cr App Rep (S) 211, CA. In this case the Court of Appeal held that it would be unreasonable to order a parent to pay where it was impossible to identify any fault on the part of the parent or guardian or anything done by him that may have caused the defendant to commit the offence. The court should not order the parent or guardian to pay a fine without considering his/her means (*Lenihen v West Yorkshire Metropolitan Police* (1981) 3 Cr App Rep (S) 42). Nor should the court rely on assertions made about the parent's attitude to the offending and to the prevention of that offending made in pre-sentence reports without checking the truthfulness of those comments with the parent (*R v Crown Court at Sheffield, ex p Clarkson* (1986) 8 Cr App Rep (S) 454).

Approach to the assessment of fines

8.10   The Sentencing Guidelines Council sets out guidance in its Definitive Sentencing Guidelines for Magistrates' Courts in an attempt aims to establish a clear, consistent and principled approach to the assessment of fines. Unfortunately these apply to adults only. It is impossible to anticipate every situation that may be encountered and in each case the court will need to exercise its judgement to ensure that the fine properly reflects the seriousness of the offence and takes into account the financial circumstances of the offender.

Victims surcharge

8.11 Whenever a court imposes a fine in respect of an offence committed after 1 April 2007, it must order the offender to pay a surcharge of £15. Where the offender is of adequate means, the court must not reduce the fine to allow for imposition of the surcharge. Where the offender does not have sufficient means to pay the total financial penalty considered appropriate by the court, the order of priority is compensation, surcharge, fine, costs.

Further guidance is set out in *Guidance on Victims' Surcharge* issued by the Justices' Clerks' Society on their website www.jc-society.co.uk.

LOCAL AUTHORITY RESPONSIBILITY FOR FINES, COSTS AND COMPENSATION

8.12 Section 137 also makes local authorities responsible for the payment of fines, etc for offenders under the age of 18 where they have parental responsibility for them, and they are in their care, or are being provided with accommodation by the authority in the exercise of any functions, in particular those under the Children Act 1989. The legislation was considered in *North Yorkshire County Council v Selby Youth Court Justices* [1994] 1 All ER 991. This was a case concerning a compensation order made against a local authority. It was held that an order made under CYPA 1969, s 23, remanding a young person to local authority accommodation did not confer parental responsibility on the local authority. Thus a local authority cannot be ordered to pay fines, costs or compensation in relation to a juvenile remanded to its care.

In *D (a minor) v DPP* [1995] Crim LR 748, it was held that where a local authority was found to have done everything that it reasonably and properly could to protect the public from a young person in its care who was guilty of a criminal offence it would be unreasonable and unjust that it should be ordered to pay a compensation order. It followed from this case that if the local authority had breached a statutory duty then a compensation order could be made against it. This point was taken in i:*Bedfordshire County Council v DPP* [1995] Crim LR 962, where the council was ordered to pay compensation because it failed to check adequately on the juvenile's whereabouts. The sentencing court did not find that such checks would have prevented the offending. The Divisional Court held that to make a compensation order against the local authority the court must be satisfied of a causal link between the failure by the local authority and the offending. In *Marlowe Child and Family Services Ltd v DPP* [1998] Crim LR 594, where a local authority placed a juvenile with a company that specialised in looking after difficult children, the court could not make the company responsible for paying a compensation order because the company was not a guardian.

For the purpose of assessment of any such financial penalty in respect of the local authority, it will be fixed by reference solely to the circumstances and the seriousness of the offence. If the young person in local authority accommodation is ordered to pay the fine, it is the offender's means, and not those of the local authority, which are to be assessed for the purpose of the fine.

Chapter 9

Youth community rehabilitation orders and sentences

GENERAL CONSIDERATIONS

9.01   The process of sentencing young people who appear before a Youth Court has never been a simple one. The difficulties in the past were largely rooted in the failure to implement the Children and Young Persons Act 1969 in its entirety which would have resulted in a largely welfare-based system. Legislation has continued to amend and alter the sentencing process in the Youth Court and courts have continued to adapt and to apply the legislative imperative. Despite this there remains on the statute book an important consideration or duty which the court is bound to discharge namely:

> 'Every court in dealing with a child or young person who is brought before it, either as an offender or otherwise, shall have regard to the welfare of the child or young person, and shall in a proper case take steps for removing him from undesirable surroundings, and for securing that proper provision is made for his education and training' (CYPA 1933, s 44, as amended). This general welfare principle must be considered having regard to the principal aim of the youth justice system and the specified purposes of sentencing which are discussed below.'

The Criminal Justice Act 1991 brought to the Youth Court a new philosophy of sentencing. The Act seeks (now embodied in the Criminal Justice Act 2003) to ensure proportionality of sentencing so that the severity of the sentence should reflect the seriousness of the offence committed. Sentencing is seen in terms of a graduated restriction upon the offender's liberty such restriction increasing with the seriousness of the offence.

This new legislative framework gives a clear and graduated approach to sentencing. It starts with fines and discharges at the lower end of the seriousness scale moving through to community penalties where the offence is '*serious enough*' to merit such a sentence and finally to custodial alternatives in cases where the offending is '*so serious that neither a community penalty nor a fine be justified for the offence*'. The community sentence in the Youth Court is known as a 'Youth Rehabilitation Order'.

The Crime and Disorder Act 1998 introduced yet another layer to the sentencing principles to be applied in the Youth Court. The principal aim is in s 37 of the aforementioned Act. It reads:

'(1) It shall be the principal aim of the youth justice system to prevent offending by children and young persons.

(2) In addition to any other duty to which they are subject, it shall be the duty of all persons and bodies carrying out functions in relation to the youth justice system to have regard to that aim.'

This is clearly not a paramount duty of the court but it must influence its considerations, and is a guiding principle for those writing reports to assist sentencers. The purposes of sentencing are set out in CJA 2003, s 142A with respect to juveniles. This reiterates that the court must have regard to the principal aim of the youth justice system in accordance with the welfare principle and the purposes of sentencing. Those purposes are set out as:

(a) the punishment of offenders,
(b) the reform and rehabilitation of offenders,
(c) the protection of the public, and
(d) the making of reparation by offenders to persons as affected by their offences.

Magistrates will also have regard to the guidelines issued by the Sentencing Guidelines Council, some of which have specific reference to young offenders. Although the legal restrictions and requirements are dealt with in detail in the following section, a few general considerations are noted here to put the concept of the community sentence into its proper context. A community sentence or order stands in its own right and should reflect the seriousness of the offence for which it is imposed. A community sentence is not imposed as an alternative to custody. Sentencers, however, must be aware when passing sentence for the original offence that breach of the order may result in custody.

General considerations before making a youth rehabilitation order

9.02 A court shall not pass a youth rehabilitation order on an offender unless it is of the opinion that the offence, or the combination of the offence and one or more offences associated with it, was serious enough to warrant that sentence. The order and requirements forming the sentence must be the most suitable for the offender and the restrictions which they impose upon the offender's liberty must be such as in the opinion of the court are commensurate with the seriousness of the offence, or the combination of the offence and the other offences associated with it. In reaching this opinion, the court must take into account all information about the circumstances of the offence including any aggravating or mitigating factors, the offenders' culpability and any harm the offence caused or may have caused. The court should also take account of all relevant information about the offender which will include previous findings of guilt: CJA 2003, s 148. Previous convictions are treated as an aggravating factor depending on the nature of the offence and the time elapsed between offences. Offences committed whilst on bail are aggravated by that factor. Before making the order, the court must obtain and consider information about the offender's family circumstances and the likely effect of such an order on those circumstances.

When deciding on the restrictions on liberty imposed by a community sentence the court may have regard to any period the offender has spent in custody in connection with the offence. This includes remands to local authority care, with or without a security requirement (CJA 2003, s 149).

A rare exception to the usual requirement of an offence being serious enough for a community sentence is found in CJA 2003, s 151. It states that where a person is over the age of 16 when convicted of an offence not punishable with imprisonment (which would not normally be considered serious enough for a community order) the court may, if it considers it to be in the interests of justice, impose one, if the offender has three or more convictions dealt with by a fine since attaining the age of 16 (CJA 2003, s 151(1A)). This section was *not* brought in to force in April 2005 but has been amended by the CJ&IA 2008.

REPORTS

9.03   Pre-sentence reports must be obtained before the court makes a youth rehabilitation order in order that it can be satisfied that the restriction on liberty imposed is commensurate with the seriousness of the offending, and that requirements are the most suitable for the offender. Before preparing a report the youth offending team will complete an ASSET report form, a copy of which is reproduced at Appendix F.

The court need not have a pre-sentence report if in the circumstances of the case the court is of the opinion that it is unnecessary to obtain one (CJA 2003, s 156(4)). In the case of a juvenile, the court shall not form this opinion unless there was a previous pre-sentence report obtained in respect of the offender and the court has had regard to information contained in that report or the most recent report (CJA 2003, s 156(5)). In practice such a report should be current so as to deal with any significant changes that may have occurred in the young person's life.

The purpose of a pre-sentence report in relation to a youth rehabilitation order is to give the court information as to the suitability of the offender for one or more of the available requirements and create an order that will be most likely to address the offending behaviour. The failure of the court to obtain a pre-sentence report in the required case will not invalidate the court's order, but in the case of an appeal a report must be obtained and considered at the appeal hearing. The appellate court does not have to obtain a report if it is of the opinion that the Youth Court was justified in forming the opinion that it was unnecessary to obtain one or, although the Youth Court was not justified in forming that opinion, in the circumstances of the case at the time it is before the court, it is unnecessary to obtain such a report (CJA 2003, s 156(7)). In any event an appellate court would have to obtain a report or have regard to an existing report before forming the opinion in sub-s (7) (CJA 2003, s 156(8)).

Pre-sentence reports must comply with the requirements set out in the National Standards for the Supervision of Offenders in the Community. These requirements prescribe that the report shall contain an introduction, an offence analysis, relevant information about the offender, the risk to the public of re-offending and a conclusion. A report may be received in an oral form unless the court is considering passing a custodial sentence.

Other reports

9.04 Reparation orders require a report to be prepared but this need not be a pre-sentence report complying with National Standards and may take the form of a short form or expedited report which can be prepared more quickly. A short form or expedited report in relation to a reparation order must include the type of reparative activity suitable for the offender and the attitude of the victim (PCC(S)A 2000, s 73(5)).

A copy of any report should be given to the offender or his lawyer and the prosecutor. If the offender is under 18 and not represented he does not have to be given a copy of the report. The court may order that the report may not be disclosed to the juvenile if it considers disclosure is impracticable having regard to his age and understanding or undesirable having regard to the risk of harm which might thereby be suffered by the juvenile. (See Children Act 1989, s 31 for a definition.) The parent or guardian (if present) is always entitled to see the report (CJA 2003, s 159(2) and Magistrates Courts (Children and Young Persons) Rules 1992). 'Parent', in this context, means local authority if the child is in care or being accommodated by the local authority. If the court makes a youth rehabilitation order it may also make ancillary orders such as endorsement of driving licence, disqualification from driving, compensation orders and orders as to costs.

Where a person aged 14 years or more is convicted of an offence and the court is considering a community sentence, it may require the offender to provide a sample for the purposes of ascertaining whether the offender has any specified class A drug in his body (CJA 2003, s 161(1)).

If the offender is under 17 the sample must be provided in the presence of an appropriate adult. A failure to provide a sample, without reasonable excuse may result in a fine not exceeding level 4. Section 161 of the CJA 2003 was not brought into force as at October 2008.

GENERAL REQUIREMENTS ON MAKING A YOUTH REHABILITATION ORDER

9.05 Before making an order, imposing two or more requirements, or making two or more youth rehabilitation orders in respect of associated offences, the court must consider whether, in the circumstances of the case, the requirements to be imposed are compatible with each other.

The court must ensure, as far as is practicable, that any requirements imposed in the order avoid conflicting with the offender's religious beliefs. Nor should requirements interfere with the offender's ability to attend work, school or other educational establishment.

In terms of its length a youth rehabilitation order must specify a date, not more than three years after the date on which the order takes effect, by which time all the requirements in it must have been complied with.

The order normally takes effect on the day after the order is made. However, if a detention and training order is in force in respect of the offender at the time it makes the order it may order that it takes effect at the expiry of the term of the detention and training order or when the period of supervision begins following release from custody of the detention and training centre.

The court is not permitted to make a youth rehabilitation order when another youth rehabilitation order or a reparation order is already in force, unless it first revokes those earlier orders.

Concurrent and consecutive orders

9.06 Where an offender is convicted of two or more associated offences the court may make two or more youth rehabilitation orders; where it does so it must direct in relation to requirements of the same kind whether those requirements are to be concurrent or consecutive to each other. Fostering requirements may not be directed to run consecutively. Where the court directs that two or more requirements of the same kind are to run consecutively, the number of hours, days or months specified in the order may run one after another, so long as the aggregate number does not exceed the maximum that may be specified in relation to any one of them.

Additional requirements

9.07 A court may only make an order for any youth rehabilitation order with intensive supervision and surveillance requirement or a youth rehabilitation order with a fostering requirement if:

(a) the court is dealing with the offender for an offence that is punishable with imprisonment,
(b) the court is of the opinion that the offence, or the combination of the offence and one or more offences associated with it, was so serious that, but for these provisions, a custodial sentence would be appropriate (or, if the offender was aged under 12 at the time of conviction, would be appropriate if the offender had been aged 12), and
(c) if the offender was aged under 15 at the time of conviction, the court is of the opinion that the offender is a persistent offender (CJ&IA 2008, s1(3)(a) (b)).

A court may not include a local authority residence requirement or a fostering requirement in a youth rehabilitation order in respect of an offender unless the offender was legally represented at the relevant time in court, or either:
(a) the offender was granted a right to representation funded by the Legal Services Commission as part of the Criminal Defence Service for the purposes of the proceedings but the right was withdrawn because of the offender's conduct; or
(b) the offender has been informed of the right to apply for such representation for the purposes of the proceedings and has had the opportunity to do so, but nevertheless refused or failed to apply.

These provisions are the same as the custody threshold requirements.

An electronic monitoring requirement may be added at the court's discretion but must be added where the court makes either a curfew or an exclusion requirement as part of its youth rehabilitation order.

THE YOUTH REHABILITATION ORDER REQUIREMENTS

9.08 The general statutory restriction and requirements that have to be met before passing a community order are set out above **9.09**. Set out below are the permissible requirements and the restrictions pertaining to each requirement that may be found in the CA & IA 2008, Sch 1, Pt 1.

Permissible requirements

9.09 The following requirements may be attached to a youth rehabilitation order. As stated above the details are found in Sch 1 of the Act and the relevant paragraph of the schedule is in brackets next to each of the requirements:

(a) an activity requirement (paras 6 8),

(b) a supervision requirement (para 9),

(c) in a case where the offender is aged 16 or 17 at the time of the conviction, an unpaid work requirement (see para 10),

(d) a programme requirement (para 11),

(e) an attendance centre requirement (para 12),

(f) a prohibited activity requirement (para 13),

(g) a curfew requirement (para 14),

(h) an exclusion requirement (para 15),

(i) a residence requirement (para 16),

(j) a local authority residence requirement (paras 17 and 19),

(k) a youth rehabilitation order with fostering requirement (paras 4,18 and 19),

(l) a mental health treatment requirement (paras 20 and 21),

(m) a drug treatment/drug testing requirement (paras 22 and 23),

(n) an intoxicating substance treatment requirement (para 24),

(o) an education requirement (para 25),

(p) an electronic monitoring requirement (see para26), and

(q) a youth rehabilitation order with intensive supervision and surveillance (para 2).

(a) Activity requirement

9.10 An activity requirement means that the offender must do any or all of the following:

(a) participate, on such number of days as may be specified in the order, in activities at the place or places specified by presenting himself at the place specified or to a specified person in accordance with instructions given by the responsible officer and comply with instructions given by, or under the authority of, the person in charge of that activity;

(b) participate in activity, or activities, specified in the order on such number of days so specified;

(c) participate in one or more residential exercises for a continuous period or periods comprising such number of days as specified;

(d) engage in activities in accordance with instructions of the responsible officer on such number of days as may be specified.

Where the order requires the offender to participate in a residential exercise, it must specify a place or an activity. Such a requirement may last for a period of no more than seven days and require him to:

(a) present himself at the beginning of that period to a person or persons specified in the instructions at a place or places so specified and reside there for that period; or

(b) participate for that period in activities specified in the instructions.

A requirement to participate in a residential exercise may not be given except with the consent of a parent or guardian of the offender.

The specified activities may consist of or include reparation, for example contact between the offender and victims affected by his offending behaviour as part of specified activities or as directed by the responsible officer.

A court may not include an activity requirement in a relevant order unless it has consulted either an officer of a local probation board or a member of a youth offending team, and it is satisfied that the activities to be specified in the order can be made under arrangements that exist in the local justice area in which the offender resides and that it is feasible to secure compliance with those requirements.

A court may not include an activity requirement in a relevant order if compliance with that requirement would involve the co-operation of a person other than the offender and the offender's responsible officer, unless that other person consents to its inclusion.

The aggregate of the number of days specified must not exceed 90 unless the 'custody' criteria are satisfied (see **9.07**) as set down in CJ & IA 2008, s1(4)(a)-(c) when the number of days permitted doubles to 180 days.

(b) Supervision requirement

9.11 A supervision requirement is a requirement that, during the relevant period, the offender must attend appointments with the responsible officer or another person determined by the responsible officer, at such time and place as may be determined by the officer. The purpose for which a supervision requirement may be imposed is that of promoting the offender's rehabilitation.

For these purposes the 'relevant period' means the period for which the community order remains in force.

(c) Unpaid work requirement

9.12 This is a requirement that the offender must perform unpaid work in accordance with the number of hours specified in the order, at such times as he is instructed by the responsible officer. Unless revoked, a requirement imposing an unpaid work condition remains in force until the offender has worked under it for the number of hours specified in it.

The work required to be performed under an unpaid work requirement in a youth rehabilitation order ordinarily must be completed in a period of 12 months.

The number of hours that a person may be required to work under an unpaid work requirement must be specified in the relevant order and must be in the aggregate:

(a) not less than 40, and

(b) not more than 240.

The court may not impose an unpaid work requirement in respect of an offender unless, after hearing (if the courts thinks necessary) from an appropriate officer, the court is satisfied that the offender is a suitable person to perform work under such a requirement.

The court must also be satisfied that provision for the offender to work under this requirement can be made under arrangements that exist in the local justice area in which the offender resides.

Where the court makes orders in respect of two or more offences of which the offender has been convicted on the same occasion and includes unpaid work requirements in each of them, the court may direct that the hours of work specified in any of those requirements is to be concurrent or consecutive. However the total number of hours must not exceed the maximum of 240 hours.

(d) Programme requirement

9.13 This requirement involves the offender's participation in a systematic set of activities specified in the order, on such number of days as may be specified. The court may not include a programme requirement in the youth rehabilitation order unless:

(a) the programme that the court proposes to specify in the order has been recommended to the it as being suitable for the offender by an officer of a local probation board or by a member of a youth offending team or an officer of a provider of probation services, and

(b) the court is satisfied that the programme is available at the place proposed to be specified.

A court may not include a programme requirement in the youth rehabilitation order if compliance with that requirement would involve the co-operation of a person other than the offender and the offender's responsible officer, unless that other person consents to its inclusion.

A requirement to attend a programme operates to require the offender:

(a) in accordance with instructions given by the responsible officer, to participate in the programme at the place specified in the order on the number of days specified in the order, and

(b) while at that place, to comply with instructions given by, or under the authority of, the person in charge of the programme.

(e) Attendance centre requirement

9.14   An attendance centre requirement is a requirement to attend at an attendance centre for any period on any occasion at the beginning of the period and, during that period, to engage in occupations, or receive instruction, under the supervision of and in accordance with instructions given by, or under the authority of, the officer in charge of the centre.

The aggregate number of hours for which the offender may be required to attend at an attendance centre will depend on the age of the offender:

(a) if the offender is aged 16 or over at the time of conviction, the hours must be:
  (i) not less than 12, and
  (ii) not more than 36.

(b) if the offender is aged 14 or over but under 16 at the time of conviction, the hours must be:
  (i) not less than 12, and
  (ii) not more than 24.

(c) if the offender is aged under 14 at the time of conviction, must not be more than 12.

A court may not include an attendance centre requirement in a youth rehabilitation order unless it has been notified by the Secretary of State that an attendance centre is available for persons of the offender's description, and provision can be made at the centre for the offender.

Not all areas have an attendance centre in their locality. Some areas have access to a centre but only use it for older offenders particularly if it is geographically remote from the juvenile's home. The statute requires that the court is satisfied that the attendance centre proposed to be specified is reasonably accessible to the offender, having regard to the means of access available to the offender and any other circumstances.

The first time at which the offender is required to attend at the attendance centre is a time notified to the offender by the responsible officer. The subsequent hours are to be fixed by the officer in charge of the centre in accordance with arrangements made by the responsible officer, having regard to the offender's circumstances. An offender may not be required to attend at the centre on more than one occasion on any day, or for more than three hours on any occasion.

(f) A prohibited activity requirement

9.15 This means a requirement that the offender must refrain from participating in activities specified in the order:
  (a) on a day or days so specified; or
  (b) during a period so specified.

A court may not include a prohibited activity requirement in a relevant order unless it has consulted either an officer of a local probation board (a provider of probation services) or a member of a youth offending team.

The statute provides that one of the requirements that may be included in an order is that the offender does not possess, use or carry a firearm within the meaning of the Firearms Act 1968.

(g) Curfew requirement

9.16 A curfew requirement is a requirement that the offender must remain, for periods specified in the relevant order, at a place so specified. It may specify different places or different periods for different days, but may not specify periods which amount to fewer than two hours or more than 12 hours in any one day.

The order may not exceed a period of six months beginning with the day on which it first takes effect. The court must also make an electronic monitoring requirement (see **9.28**) unless the court considers it inappropriate to do so in the particular circumstances of the case or the court is prevented from including an electronic monitoring requirement because the requirements of para 26 of Sch 1 cannot be met, for example it is not practicable to secure the co-operation of a person other than the offender. Before making a relevant order imposing a curfew requirement, the court must obtain and consider information about the place proposed to be specified in the order (including information as to the attitude of persons likely to be affected by the enforced presence there of the offender).

(h) Exclusion requirement

9.17 An exclusion requirement is a provision prohibiting the offender from entering a place named in the order for a specified period of not more than three months. An exclusion requirement:

  (a) may provide for the prohibition to operate only during the periods specified in the order; and

  (b) may specify different places or areas for different periods or days.

The court must also make an electronic monitoring requirement (see **9.28**) unless the court considers it inappropriate to do so in the particular circumstances of the case or the court is prevented from including an electronic monitoring requirement because the requirements of para 26 of Sch 1 cannot be met, for example it is not practicable to secure the co-operation of a person other than the offender.

(i) Residence requirement

9.18 This requirement is only applicable to offenders aged 16 or over at the time of conviction.

The requirement means that, during a period specified in the relevant order, the offender must reside with an individual or at a place specified in the order. If the court wishes to specify residence with an individual, that individual has to consent to the requirement.

If the order makes specific provision for it, a residence requirement does not prohibit the offender from residing, with the prior approval of the responsible officer, at a place other than that specified in the order.

Before making a youth rehabilitation order containing a residence requirement, the court must consider the home surroundings of the offender.

A court may not specify a hostel or other institution as the place where an offender must reside, except on the recommendation of an officer of a local probation board, or provider of probation services, a local authority social worker or a member of a youth offending team.

(j) Local authority residence requirement

9.19 The imposition of this requirement means that, during the period specified in the order, the offender must reside in accommodation provided by or on behalf of a local authority specified in the order.

A court may not include a local authority residence requirement in a youth rehabilitation order made in respect of an offence unless it is satisfied that the behaviour that constituted the offence was due to a significant extent to the circumstances in which the offender was living, and that the imposition of that requirement will assist in the offender's rehabilitation.

A court may not include a local authority residence requirement in a youth rehabilitation order unless it has consulted the local authority and a parent or guardian of the offender (unless it is impracticable to consult such a person) and the local authority that is to receive the offender. A youth rehabilitation order that imposes a local authority residence requirement may also stipulate that the offender is not to reside with a person specified in the order.

The order must specify the local authority in whose area the offender resides or is to reside.

Any period specified in the order as a period for which the offender must reside in accommodation provided by or on behalf of a local authority must not be longer than six months, and must not include any period after the offender has reached the age of 18.

9.20   A court may not include a local authority residence requirement in a youth rehabilitation order in respect of an offender unless the offender was legally represented at the relevant time in court, or either:

- (a) the offender was granted a right to representation funded by the Legal Services Commission as part of the Criminal Defence Service for the purposes of the proceedings but the right was withdrawn because of the offender's conduct, or
- (b) the offender has been informed of the right to apply for such representation for the purposes of the proceedings and has had the opportunity to do so, but nevertheless refused or failed to apply.

It is worth noting that a local authority has power to place an offender with a local authority foster parent where a local authority residence requirement is imposed (CJ&IA 2008, Sch 2, Pt 2, para.18(6)).

(k) Fostering requirement

9.21   A fostering requirement means a requirement that, for a period specified in the order, the offender must reside with a local authority foster parent.

A period specified in a youth rehabilitation order as a period for which the offender must reside with a local authority foster parent must end no later than the end of the period of 12 months beginning with the date on which the requirement first has effect but must not include any period after the offender has reached the age of 18. An 18-month period may be substituted following breach proceedings (CJ&IA 2008, Sch2, paras 6(9), 8(9) and 16(2)).

If at any time during that time the responsible officer notifies the offender that no suitable local authority foster parent is available, and that the responsible officer has applied or proposes to apply under for the revocation or amendment of the order, the fostering requirement is, until the determination of that application, to be taken as requiring the offender to reside in accommodation provided by or on behalf of a local authority.

A youth rehabilitation order that imposes a fostering requirement must specify the local authority that is to place the offender with a local authority foster parent under s 23(2)(a) of the Children Act 1989.

The authority so specified must be the local authority in whose area the offender resides or is to reside.

A court may not include a fostering requirement in a youth rehabilitation order unless the court has been notified by the Secretary of State that arrangements for implementing such a requirement are available in the area of the local authority that is to place the offender with a local authority foster parent.

Pre-conditions to imposing fostering requirement

9.22 A court may only make an order for any youth rehabilitation order with a fostering requirement if :
  (a) the court is dealing with the offender for an offence that is punishable with imprisonment,
  (b) the court is of the opinion that the offence, or the combination of the offence and one or more offences associated with it, was so serious that, but for these provisions, a custodial sentence would be appropriate (or, if the offender was aged under 12 at the time of conviction, would be appropriate if the offender had been aged 12), and
  (c) if the offender was aged under 15 at the time of conviction, the court is of the opinion that the offender is a persistent offender (CJ&IA 2008, s1 (3)(a) (b) and (4)).

The court may not include a fostering requirement in a youth rehabilitation order in respect of an offender unless he was legally represented at the relevant time in court, or either,
  (a) the offender was granted a right to representation funded by the Legal Services Commission as part of the Criminal Defence Service for the purposes of the proceedings but the right was withdrawn because of the offender's conduct, or
  (b) he has been informed of the right to apply for such representation for the purposes of the proceedings and has had the opportunity to do so, but nevertheless refused or failed to apply.

(l) Mental health treatment requirement

9.23 This requires the offender to submit, during periods specified in the order, to treatment by or under the direction of a registered medical practitioner or a chartered psychologist (or both, for different periods) with a view to the improvement of the offender's mental condition.

The treatment required must be one of the following kinds of treatment as may be specified in the relevant order:

(a) treatment as a resident patient in an independent hospital or care home within the meaning of the Care Standards Act 2000 or a hospital within the meaning of the Mental Health Act 1983, but not in hospital premises where high security psychiatric services within the meaning of that Act are provided;

(b) treatment as a non-resident patient at such institution or place as may be specified in the order;

(c) treatment by or under the direction of such registered medical practitioner or chartered psychologist (or both) as may be so specified;

but the nature of the treatment may not to be specified in the order except as mentioned in (a), (b) or (c) above.

A court may not include a mental health treatment requirement in an order unless:

(a) the court is satisfied, on the evidence of a registered medical practitioner approved for the purposes of s 12 of the Mental Health Act 1983, that the mental condition of the offender:
   (i) is such as requires and may be susceptible to treatment, but
   (ii) is not such as to warrant the making of a hospital order or guardianship order within the meaning of that Act;

(b) the court is also satisfied that arrangements have been or can be made for the treatment intended to be specified in the order (including arrangements for the reception of the offender where he is to be required to submit to treatment as a resident patient); and

(c) the offender has expressed his willingness to comply with such a requirement.

While the offender is under treatment as a resident patient in pursuance of a mental health requirement, his responsible officer shall carry out the supervision of the offender to such extent only as may be necessary for the purpose of the revocation or amendment of the order.

The evidence of a registered medical practitioner may be in writing or oral in accordance with s 54(2) and (3) of the Mental Health Act 1983 with respect to proof for the purposes of sub-s (3)(a) of an offender's mental condition just as they have effect with respect to proof of an offender's mental condition for the purposes of s 37(2)(a) of that Act.

Mental health treatment at place other than that specified in order

9.24   Where the medical practitioner or chartered psychologist, treating the offender in pursuance of a mental health treatment requirement, is of the opinion that part of the treatment can be better or more conveniently given in or at an institution or place that:

(a) is not specified in the relevant order; and

(b) is one in or at which the treatment of the offender will be given by or under the direction of a registered medical practitioner or chartered psychologist;

he may, with the consent of the offender, make arrangements for him to be treated accordingly.

These arrangements may provide for the offender to receive part of his treatment as a resident patient in an institution or place notwithstanding that the institution or place is not one that could have been specified for that purpose in the relevant order.

Where any such arrangements are made for the treatment of an offender the medical practitioner or chartered psychologist by whom the arrangements are made shall give notice in writing to the offender's responsible officer giving details of the place and the treatment provided as it is deemed to be treatment to which the offender is required to submit to in pursuance of the order.

Detailed consideration to the mentally ill juvenile is given in Chapter 15.

(m) Drug treatment requirement

9.25   A drug rehabilitation requirement means a requirement that during a period specified in the order the offender must submit to treatment by or under the direction of a specified person having the necessary qualifications or experience with a view to the reduction or elimination of the offender's dependency on or propensity to misuse drugs.

During that period, he may be required to provide samples for the purpose of ascertaining whether he has any drug in his body (a drug-testing requirement) (CJ&IA 2008, Sch 2, para 23(1)).

A drug-testing requirement may not be made unless the court has been notified that arrangements for implementing drug-testing requirement are in force in the local justice area in which the offender resides. This additional requirement may only be imposed as part of a drug treatment requirement and the offender must express his willingness to comply with it.

Where it is imposed the court must specify that each month the minimum numbers of occasions on which samples are to be provided. They may also specify times at which, and circumstances in which, the responsible officer or treatment provider may require samples and descriptions of the samples that may be so required.

A court may not impose a drug treatment requirement unless:
  (a) it is satisfied that:
      (i)   the offender is dependent on, or has a propensity to misuse, drugs; and
      (ii) his dependency or propensity is such as requires and may be susceptible to treatment;
  (b) it is also satisfied that arrangements have been or can be made for the treatment intended to be specified in the order (including arrangements for the reception of the offender where he is to be required to submit to treatment as a resident),
  (c) the requirement has been recommended to the court as being suitable for the offender either by an officer of a local probation board (or provider of probation services) or by a member of a youth offending team, and
  (d) the offender expresses his willingness to comply with the requirement.

The treatment and testing period is the period specified in the youth rehabilitation order and will be treatment as a resident in such institution or place as may be specified in the order, or treatment at a non-resident place, as may be so specified.

A youth rehabilitation order imposing a drug rehabilitation requirement must provide that the results of tests carried out on any samples provided by the offender in pursuance of the requirement to a person other than the responsible officer are to be communicated to the responsible officer.

(n) Intoxicating substance treatment requirement

9.26 This is a requirement that the offender submits during a specified period or periods to treatment by or under the direction of a specified person having the necessary qualifications or experience with a view to the reduction or elimination of the offender's dependency on or propensity to misuse intoxicating substances.

Intoxicating substances are defined as alcohol or any other substance or product (other than a drug) which is, or the fumes of which are, capable of being inhaled or otherwise used for the purpose of causing intoxication.

Before making an order the court must be satisfied that arrangements have been or can be made for the treatment intended and the requirement must have been recommended to the court as suitable for the offender by member of the youth offending team, an officer of the local probation board or a provider for probation services. The court may not impose an intoxicating substances treatment requirement in respect of an offender unless it is satisfied that he is dependent or has a propensity to misuse intoxicating substances, and his dependency is such as requires and may be susceptible to treatment.

Arrangements must be made for the treatment intended to be specified in the order (including arrangements for the reception of the offender where he is to be required to submit to treatment as a resident).

A court may not impose an intoxicating substance treatment requirement unless the offender expresses his willingness to comply with its requirements.

The treatment required by an intoxicating substance treatment requirement for a specified period must be:
  (a) treatment as a resident in such institution or place as may be specified in the order;
  (b) treatment as a non-resident in or at such institution or place, and at such intervals, as may be so specified; but the nature of the treatment shall not be specified in the order except as mentioned in para (a), (b) above.

(o) Education requirement

9.27 This is a requirement that the offender must comply, during a period or periods specified in the order, with approved education arrangements. These may be arrangements made for the offender's education by his parent or guardian and approved by the local education authority specified in the order. The authority should be the local education authority for the area in which the offender resides.

Before the court can include an education requirement in a youth rehabilitation order it must have consulted with the local education authority and be satisfied that arrangements exist for the offender to receive sufficient full-time education suitable for his age, ability, aptitude and special educational needs (if any).

The court must also be satisfied that the inclusion of the education requirement is necessary for securing the good conduct of the offender or for preventing the commission of further offences.

Any period specified in the youth rehabilitation order as a period during which the offender must comply with approved education arrangements must not include a period after the offender has ceased to be of compulsory school age.

(p) Electronic monitoring requirement

9.28 This requirement must be added to a curfew or exclusion requirement and may be added to other requirements. It entails the offender being 'tagged' with an electronic monitoring device that monitors his whereabouts during the hours specified in the order. As outlined above this requirement must be attached where the court makes a curfew or exclusion requirement.

Before making the order the court must have been notified that arrangements for electronic monitoring of offences are available in the local justice area proposed to be specified in the order and they must include provision in the order for making a person responsible for the monitoring.

The period of monitoring of the offender's compliance with other requirements will be for a period specified in the order or determined by the responsible officer in accordance with the order.

Consequently, where an electronic monitoring requirement is to take effect, determined by the responsible officer, he must, before beginning that period, notify the offender, the person responsible for monitoring and any other person without whose cooperation it will not be practicable to secure that the monitoring takes place. The consent of any such person is required and the requirement may not be included in the order without that consent.

(q) Intensive supervision and surveillance

9.29   A court may only make an order for any youth rehabilitation order with intensive supervision and surveillance or a youth rehabilitation order with fostering if:

- (a)   the court is dealing with the offender for an offence that is punishable with imprisonment,
- (b)   the court is of the opinion that the offence, or the combination of the offence and one or more offences associated with it, was so serious that, but for these provisions, a custodial sentence would be appropriate (or, if the offender was aged under 12 at the time of conviction, would be appropriate if the offender had been aged 12), and
- (c)   if the offender was aged under 15 at the time of conviction, the court is of the opinion that the offender is a persistent offender (CJ&IA 2008, s 1(3)(a) and (b)).

This requirement allows the court to make an extended activity requirement of no more than 180 days. If the court decides to make an extended activity requirement they must also impose a supervision requirement and a curfew requirement with electronic monitoring.

This order is known as an intensive supervision and surveillance requirement. It may also include one or more of the other requirements (with the exception of a fostering requirement) outlined above subject to its being proportionate to the seriousness of the offence.

The restrictions outlined above do not apply if the offender has failed to comply with an order for pre-sentence drug testing under s 161(2) of the Criminal Justice Act 2003.

The court is under an obligation to send copies of a youth rehabilitation order made to the offender and other person involved with the order in accordance with CJ&IA 2008 Sch.2 para.24.

For a quick reference guide to orders see Appendix H.

Chapter 10

Custodial orders

10.01   In the context of the Youth Court, a custodial sentence means a detention and training order ... The detention and training order replaced secure training orders and detention in the young offenders' institution in the Youth Court in April 2000. Detention in a young offenders institute is still available for 18- to 21-year-olds in the magistrates' court. The Crown Court dealing with a young offender may also pass detention under PCC(S)A 2000, s 91 or a sentence of custody for life under ss 90-95 of the Powers of Criminal Courts (Sentencing) Act 2000 (PCC(S)A 2000) and CJA 2003, s 226(3) or detention for public protection or an extended sentence under s 228.

Detention in a detention and training centre is available in the Youth Court up to a maximum length of 24 months. This gives the Youth Court concurrent jurisdiction with the Crown Court outside its powers related to grave crimes and dangerous offenders. The order is available for both males and females between the ages of 12 to 17. This power is not available for 10- and 11-year-olds. Additionally, in the case of a child or young person aged 12 but under 15 years the court must be of the opinion that he or she is a persistent offender in order to pass such a sentence.

PERMITTED TERMS OF DETENTION AND TRAINING ORDER

10.02   The order is a two-part sentence, the first half being a period of detention and training served in youth secure detention accommodation, the second half being a period under supervision in the community. The court is restricted by statute to the term of the order which may be for 4, 6, 8, 10, 12, 18 or 24 months. In the case of *R v Shar* [2007] EWCA Crim 186 it was suggested that these terms are only administratively convenient and a 15 months' sentence was upheld has not being wrong in principle. Note however the term of a detention and training order may not exceed the maximum term of imprisonment that the Crown Court (in the case of an offender aged 21 or over) may impose for the offence (PCC(S)A 2000, s 101(2)). Concurrent and consecutive orders may be made where more than one principal offence is involved so long as the overall term does not exceed the 24 months maximum. In effect this means that if the court made consecutive orders for 6 months and 8 months a total of 14 months can be lawfully imposed even though it is not within one of the specified terms for a single period. (*R v Norris* [2000] 2 Cr App Rep (S) 105, CA) It also means that terms less than four months cannot be imposed consecutively so as to aggregate to four months (*R v Ganley* [2001] 1 Cr App Rep (S) 60, CA). Section 133 of the Magistrates' Courts Act 1980 limits the maximum period of imprisonment or detention in a young offenders' institution that magistrates may impose. This section does not apply to detention and training orders. A Youth Court can therefore impose consecutive orders for summary offences to an aggregate that exceeds six months. If the offences are purely summary with a maximum of six months each they may be made consecutive to each other to achieve a total sentence of more than six months. The overall total period of detention and training of 24 months may however not be exceeded (*C v DPP* [2001] Crim LR 670). A court is not permitted to make a detention and training order consecutive to a long-term detention order under PCC(S)A 2000, s 91 (*R v Kent Youth Court, ex p Kingwell* [1999] 1 Cr App Rep (S) 263).

It is also wrong in principle to impose a greater sentence in the Youth Court than is possible in the adult court for a single offence. Consequently a juvenile found guilty of criminal damage to a value of less than £5,000 is not liable to a custodial sentence as the minimum period of a DTO is four months (*Pye v Leeds Youth Court* [2006] EWHC 2527 (Admin)). The same principle will also apply to offences such as motor vehicle interference, failure to surrender to bail and obstructing a police constable in the execution of his duty.

RESTRICTIONS ON THE PASSING OF CUSTODIAL SENTENCES

10.03 The following restrictions apply before the court may make an order of detention and training:

(a) The court may not make an order for detention and training in respect of a person who is not legally represented unless;

  (i) he was granted a right to representation funded by the Legal Services Commission as part of the Criminal Defence Service but the right was withdrawn because of his conduct, or

  (ii) because he is financially ineligible; or

  (iii) having been informed of his right to apply for such representation and had the opportunity of doing so, he refused or failed to apply. (PCC(S)A 2000, s 83(3))

  A person is treated as being legally represented if a solicitor or counsel represented him after a finding of guilt and before sentence (PCC(S)A 2000, s 83(4)).

(b) The court may not pass a custodial sentence on the offender unless it is of the opinion:

  (i) that the offence or the combination of the offence and one or more offences associated with it, was so serious that neither a fine alone nor a community order can be justified for the offence CJA 2003, s 152(2); and

  (ii) nothing in (a) above shall prevent the court from passing a custodial sentence on an offender who refuses to express his willingness to comply with a requirement in a community sentence order which is proposed by the court and requires that consent (CJA 2003, s 152(2) and (3)). Essentially this second statement relates to a CRO with a requirement for intoxicating substance treatment, a drug treatment requirement or a mental health treatment requirement; or

  (iii) he fails to comply with an order for pre-sentence drugs testing (CJA 2003, s 152(3)) to provide samples.

(c) Before forming the above views about an offence the court must obtain and consider a pre-sentence report (CJA 2003, s 156(3). The only exception to this is where the offender is under the age of 18, and the court is of the opinion that a pre-sentence report is unnecessary because it has had regard to a pre-existing PSR or, where there are more than one, the most recent. (CJA 2003, s 156(4), (5)) This will apply, of course, in the Crown Court and in the Youth Court where, despite the fact that an offence may be triable only on indictment in the case of an adult, it will be tried summarily in the Youth Court if the provisions of PCC(S)A 2000, s 91 do not apply. The statute envisages courts receiving pre-sentence reports in all cases where a custodial order is being considered. In the case of an offence triable on indictment which by its very nature is so serious as to make custody look inevitable, courts have, in the past, proceeded without a pre-sentence report; however, even this will be rare in practice. In *R v Massheder* (1983) 5 Cr App Rep (S) 442, the appellant, who was aged 15, pleaded guilty to an offence of arson which involved deliberately starting a fire in a lift shaft at Kennett House, Southwark. Over £5,000 worth of damage was done. The judge passed a sentence of 18 months' detention under CYPA 1933, s 53(2) and did so without the benefit of a report. He gave two reasons for not having obtained a report namely:

(i) there was no report available due to a industrial dispute in the social services department of whom the report had been requested; and

(ii) the offence was very serious and beyond anything in the nature of a community sentence.

In substituting a supervision order for two years, the Court of Appeal said that a report was necessary in a case of this nature and that indeed that had been recognised by the judge at the first instance when he had made the initial request of the social services department. In the exceptional circumstances of a court not obtaining a pre-sentence report, it would be good practice for the court to give its reasons as to why it was unnecessary to obtain a pre-sentence report (a failure to give such reasons would in any event breach Article 6 of the Human Rights Convention). See also *R (on the application of Rees) v Feltham Justices* [2001] Crim LR 47.

As stated above the court may form an opinion that it is unnecessary to obtain pre-sentence report but only:

(i) if a previous pre-sentence report obtained in respect of the offender is available; and

(ii) the court has had regard to the information contained in that report, or if there is more than one report the most recent.

(d) Before forming the opinion that the offence is so serious that only a custodial sentence can be passed the court must take into account all information about the circumstances of the offence including any aggravating or mitigating factors as are available to it. In the case of a violent or sexual offence the court may also take into account any information about the offender which is before it. In the event of a custodial sentence being passed without the benefit of a pre-sentence report, the sentence will not be invalidated by the failure of the court to comply with the statute. However, on appeal to the Crown Court from the Youth Court the appellate court must obtain a pre-sentence report if one was not previously obtained and must give due consideration to that report (CJA 2003, s 156(6))*). Transitional provisions allow for a report prepared prior to the 2003 Act to be used after 4 April 2005.*

(e) A pre-sentence report for a juvenile facing a custodial sentence must be in a written format (CJA 2003, s 158(1B)).

When a detention and training order is likely, it is important that the youth offending team officer writing the pre-sentence report contacts the Youth Justice Board Secure Accommodation Clearing House to make a provisional booking for a placement. It is recommended that this is done as soon as the core ASSET (Youth Justice Board assessment) profile has been completed by the YOT which may indicate the likelihood of a custodial sentence. (See Appendix F)

The Youth Court itself should ensure that the agency providing prisoner transport is notified as soon as the court has made its decision.

THE LENGTH OF SENTENCE

10.04   A custodial sentence shall be for such a term:

(a) as in the opinion of the court is commensurate with the seriousness of the offence, or the combination of the offence and other offences associated with it; or

(b) where the offence is of a violent or sexual offence, for such longer term as in the opinion of the court is necessary to protect the public from serious harm from the offender.

In both cases the maximum term of 24 months may not be breached (PCC(S)A 2000, s 80(2)).

Therefore a court may only pass a detention and training order for a term longer than is commensurate with the seriousness of the offence, or the combination of the offence and other offences associated with it where it is of the opinion that the offence is of a violent or sexual nature and that the public need protection from serious harm from the offender. If it reaches this opinion, it must give its reasons in open court and explain to the offender in ordinary language why the sentence is for such a term (CJA 2003, s 174(1) and (2)).

In determining the length of a detention and training order the court must take into account any period for which the offender has been remanded in custody in connection with the offence or in the case of multiple offences the total period he has been remanded in custody in connection with any of those offences (PCC(S)A 2000, s 101(8)). For these purposes, remand in custody is defined as including time spent in police detention, a remand prison accommodation, a remand under the Mental Health Act and remands to local authority accommodation where the young person is placed and held in secure accommodation and or time remanded on bail with an electronically monitored curfew of at least nine hours per day. Time spent on remand to local authority accommodation, where the placement is not a secure one, is eliminated from the court considerations in determining the length of sentence (PCC(S)A 2000, s 101(11)). Time spent on remand in custody is not subsequently offset against the term set by the court. This is an important consideration which can lead to potential injustice where it is overlooked (*R v Cassidy* (2000) Times, 13 October)). It is worth noting that CJA 2003, ss 240-242 do not apply to detention and training orders.

It has also been made clear by the appellate courts that whilst time spent on remand is not automatically deducted from the period to be imposed it has to be taken into account by the court (*R v Ganley* [2001] 1 Cr App Rep (S) 60, CA). However the requirement to take remand time into account does not require the court to reflect that time inevitably in some specific way in the sentence passed. It does not provide for a one-to-one discount. In *R v Inner London Youth Court, ex p I* [2000] All ER (D) 612 the defendant had spent less than 24 hours in custody. It was held that the court was entitled to find that the time could make no difference to the sentence passed. The sentence was a four-month detention and training order. It was argued unsuccessfully that the 24 hours spent in custody should have been taken account of so that the court would be looking at a sentence of less than four months and not be able to pass a detention and training order. The case makes it clear that the requirement in the Act to 'take into account remand time' does not mean that there will be an automatic discount. The court may however be persuaded to adjust the length of DTO where the time spent on remand has been 'considerable'. In *R v B* [2000] Crim LR 870, *ex p I* was cited with approval. The Court of Appeal repeated that the requirement to take time on remand into account did not provide for a one-to-one discount. The reason given was that the periods to which a court was entitled to sentence by way of a DTO were specified in blocks and reducing a sentence by precisely the time spent on remand would be inconsistent with that provision *R v Inner London Crown Court, ex p N and S* [2000] Crim LR 871 reiterates these points.

In *R v Fieldhouse and Watts* [2000] Crim LR 1020 the Court of Appeal illustrated how the court might take periods on remand into account depending on the length of order being considered. The court took as an example the case of a defendant who had served four weeks on remand. This would be the equivalent of a two-month term. The court is likely to take such a period into account in different ways depending on the period of DTO it had in mind. If that period was four months a non-custodial sentence is likely. If the period was 6, 8, 10 or 12 months then 4, 6, 8, and 10 months respectively might be appropriate. However for 18- or 24-month sentences the court may well conclude that no reduction could properly be made.

The difficulties of this provision are illustrated in *R v Eagles* [2006] EWCA 2368 where the Court of Appeal indicated that a 17-year-old who had spent 88 days on a remand should have been given 176 days credit against his 12 months DTO sentence to properly reflect the nature of that sentence. As a consequence, the Court of Appeal substituted a six-month sentence, this being the nearest permissible period, having given full credit for the time spent on remand.

If a court is considering making a detention and training order it is good practice for it to indicate its intention in open court so that it may hear any representations from the defence and be informed of any time spent on remand. In most cases the court would expect to direct that the whole period of remand would count towards the sentence. Where the court found that it was not just to do so, it must say so and state what the circumstances were that led it to that opinion bearing in mind the statutory requirement to state in open court the reasons for and the effect of the court sentence (*R v Barber* [2006] All ER (D) 240; *R v Haringey Youth Court, ex p A* (2000) Times, 30 May).

As stated above, the court must be alert to a juvenile who has been subject to a qualifying curfew condition whilst on bail as this *must* be taken into account when the period of the DTO is fixed. Consequently where the offender has been on bail with a curfew condition and electronic monitoring with a requirement to remain at a specified place for at least nine hours in any given day, then half the time he has been on bail with that curfew condition must count as time served unless the court considers it just in all circumstances not to give such a direction. In the latter case the court can order that a lesser period should count towards the sentence.

EARLY AND LATE RELEASE

10.05   As previously stated the first half of a detention and training order will normally be spent in detention and the second half under supervision in the community. Offenders should be made aware however that there is provision for early or late release depending on their behaviour and progress whilst in detention. There is no early or late release for sentences between 4 and 6 months but for sentences between 8 and 12 months release may be one month before or one month after the halfway point. For sentences between 18 and 24 months release maybe one or two months before or all after the halfway point. Early release may be authorised by the Home Secretary whilst delay beyond the halfway point can be authorised by the Youth Court on application on behalf of the Home Secretary. There is a mechanism for appeal against a decision not to release early or a decision to apply for a delayed release. The Secretary of State may release an offender at any time if he is satisfied that exceptional circumstances exist which justifies the offender's justify his release on compassionate grounds.

The provisions for early release on home detention curfew (tagging) pursuant to s 34A of the Criminal Justice Act 1991 as amended, do not apply to offenders under the age of 18. This should be borne in mind particularly in the Crown Court when sentencing adult and juvenile co-defendants. (*R v D* [2000] All ER (D) 295)

PERSISTENT OFFENDER (UNDER 15 YEARS OLD)

10.06   Whilst there is no statutory definition for the term 'persistent offender', the legislation provides that in the case of a child or young person under the age of 15 years at time of conviction (and 12 years or more) the court must be of the opinion that he is a persistent offender before it can pass a detention and training order. In *R v Smith* [2000]

Crim LR 613, a 14-year-old pleaded guilty in the Crown Court to a count of robbery, one of possessing an offensive weapon and one of false imprisonment. Originally sentenced to three years' long-term detention an appeal was lodged with the Court of Appeal. The court took the view that a detention and training order was appropriate and that as the defendant had committed a series of crimes over a period of two days this qualified him for the category of persistent offender even though he had no previous convictions. In *R v Charlton* [2000] 2 Cr App Rep (S) 102, CA, a 14-year-old was sentenced to a 12 months' detention and training order for two groups of offences of burglary and taking without consent. The Court of Appeal upheld the sentence noting that the Government's definition of persistent young offender referred to for the purposes of fast-track arrangements did not apply and indeed predated the Crime and Disorder Act 1998. The sentencing judge had based his decision on the evidence before him in the individual case and the Court of Appeal refused to interfere with that finding.

In *R v D* [2000] All ER (D) 1496 the Court of Appeal suggested that an offender with no previous convictions may still be classed as a persistent offender. However, the offence involved was one of affray and the defendant had a caution, previous convictions for handling stolen goods, and was awaiting sentence for riding on a stolen motorcycle. This led the court to say that the different nature of the earlier offending meant that the defendant could not properly be regarded as a persistent offender.

The case of *R v D* [2000] Crim LR 867 establishes that the sentencing court is entitled to have regard to previous cautions when deciding whether an offender is a persistent offender. The defendant had three previous cautions. The court said a caution could only be given if there was sufficient evidence to warrant a prosecution and the offender admitted the offence. The court was therefore entitled to take them into account in deciding whether the defendant was a persistent offender.

In the case of *R v LM* [2003] Crim LR 205 the court held that where a defendant crossed a relevant age threshold between the date of commission of the offence and the date of conviction the starting point should be the sentence the defendant was likely to receive if he had been sentenced at the time of the commission of the offence. In this case the offender had been 14 at the time of the commission of the offence and therefore could not have received a detention and training order unless he had been a persistent offender. He was not a persistent offender and therefore a custodial sentence was not appropriate or available: the court substituted an 18-month supervision order. This approach was first followed by the Court of Appeal in *R v Ghafoor* [2003] 1 Cr App Rep (S) 428, CA, where an offender was 17 at the time of commission and 18 at the time of sentence. The court held that he should have been sentenced by reference to his age at the time of commission of the offence and a detention and training order was substituted for a four-and-a-half-year young offender institute sentence. However in *R v T* (unreported, 17 August 2004), another Court of Appeal case, it was held that PCC(S)A 2000, s 100(2)(a) was clear in that it stipulated a defendant convicted after they became 15 could be made the subject of a detention and training order and did not need to be a persistent offender.

Consequently, a defendant under the age of 15 who is not a 'persistent offender', and will therefore, not qualify for a detention and training order if convicted, should not normally be committed to the Crown Court for trial with a view to a term of detention under s 91 PCC(S)A 2000, unless, in the event of conviction, he is likely to receive a detention term in excess of two years (*R (on the application of M) v Waltham Forest Youth Court* [2002] EWHC 1252 Admin).

MENTALLY DISORDERED OFFENDERS

10.07 The subject of the mentally disordered juvenile is dealt with more fully in Chapter 15 but it should be noted at this point that before passing a custodial sentence on an offender who is or appears to be mentally disordered, the court must consider any information before it which relates to his mental condition such as a medical report or pre-sentence report and must consider the likely effect of a custodial sentence on his mental condition and on any treatment which may be available for it (CJA 2003, s 157).

THE SERIOUSNESS OF THE OFFENCE

10.08 The first restriction mentioned above (see **10.04**) is that the court shall not pass a custodial sentence unless it is of the opinion that the offence, or the combination of the offence and one or more offences associated with it, was so serious that neither a fine nor a community order can be justified for the offence. The principle here is that a number of offences tried together will generally make the offending more serious. An 'associated offence' is defined as an offence for which the offender is sentenced at the same time as he is sentenced for an offence of which he is convicted in the same proceedings or it may be a matter which the offender wishes the court to take into consideration when sentencing him for the offence of which he has been convicted.

Some commentators have referred to this restriction as the 'custody threshold' over which the court must step before being able to impose a custodial sentence. In assessing seriousness, the court should take into account any aggravating factors and also any circumstances mitigating the offender's sentence.

When considering possible mitigation the court must decide consider at what stage in proceedings the offender indicated his intention to plead guilty and the circumstances in which this indication was given. An early guilty plea or admission should normally lead to a substantial reduction in sentence and where this happens the court must state in open court that it has imposed a less severe punishment by virtue of the plea (CJA 2003, s 144). Details can be found in the Sentencing Guidelines publication *Reduction in Sentence for a Guilty Plea* @ www.sentencing-guidelines.gov.uk.

In the case of an offender convicted of a number of offences, the length of the sentence should be mitigated by applying the 'totality' principle. This effectively means bundling all the offences together and taking an overview of their collective seriousness rather than sentencing each individually and adding their seriousness together. Having assessed the seriousness of the offence in that light, the court is then still able to mitigate that sentence by taking into account any such matters as in the opinion of the court are relevant in the mitigation of sentence including previous good character.

The court is, however, empowered to take into account aggravating factors of an offence which are disclosed by the circumstances of other offences committed by the offender (this may include previous offending or any failure by the defendant to respond to previous sentences). The court may take those factors into account for the purpose of forming an opinion as to the seriousness of the offence (CJA 2003, s 143(2)) and the court must by statute treat the fact that an offence was committed while the offender was on bail as an aggravating factor (CJA 2003, s 143(3)).

Seriousness is not an absolute concept and courts will continue to look to the Sentencing Guidelines Council and the Court of Appeal for guidance as to the sort of aggravating factors that make individual offences serious. In considering seriousness they must consider the offender's culpability in committing the offence and any harm the offence caused, was intended to cause or might foreseeably have caused (CJA 2003, s 143(1)). A study of previous decisions gives some idea of the sort of features which will make offences more serious than others and take them over the custody threshold. The offender's previous record of offending may or may not be relevant to the seriousness of the offence. Certainly an offender with a good character or a few minor convictions is entitled to use this is a mitigating factor in all but the most serious of crimes.

The offender who repeatedly re-offends can, however, expect no mitigation based on his previous record.

Where the previous convictions reveal something in the way in which they were committed they may aggravate the seriousness of the current offence. For example if their history shows a pattern of offending which convinces the sentencer that the court is dealing with a 'professional burglar ' or a juvenile consistently targets picks on elderly victims these will represent aggravating factors when assessing the seriousness of the current offence of dishonesty. Indeed such cases may fall within the mandatory minimum sentencing scheme for those convicted of three or more offences of burglary.

In *R v Osborne* (1990) 12 Cr App Rep (S) 55, CA, the case involved an appellant who had pleaded guilty to what was then reckless driving and driving with excess alcohol. The aggravating features included a consumption of four pints of lager, driving through a housing estate at high speed, mounting the pavement and hitting two lampposts. This was followed by a police chase at speeds of 60-70 mph and the appellant concealing himself to avoid arrest. The Court of Appeal said that it was correct to hold this offence as being so serious that a non-custodial sentence could not be justified.

Another example of a case where aggravating features were held to make the offence so serious as to justify a custodial sentence is that of *R v KB* (2000) 164 JP 714. A 12-year-old pleaded guilty to five sexual offences against two other boys. Reports suggested that his upbringing and childhood had produced a need for long-term support and therapy. Whilst on remand within a local authority residential care centre he was said to have made progress during his 11-month stay. The judge held that although a continuation of the remand placement would be a suitable method of treating the appellant, it would not deal with the seriousness of the offences which called for an immediate custodial sentence. A sentence of four years' detention (under what was then s 53 of the Children and Young Persons Act 1933) was upheld. However, in *R v W* [1999] 1 Cr App Rep (S) 488, CA, an eight-month detention order was reduced to an eight-month supervision order for a 13-year-old boy convicted of indecent assault on a 12-year-old girl. The assault consisted of touching the girl's private parts against her will and simulated sex by lying on top of her. In view of the slight age difference and the young age of the defendant the appeal was allowed.

Offences of arson with intent to endanger life have always been treated very seriously by the courts and will nearly always be treated as a grave crime under the provisions of PCC(S)A 2000, s 91. Arson in itself (criminal damage by fire) will not necessarily merit a custodial sentence as stated in *R v Dewberry and Stone* (1985) 7 Cr App Rep (S) 202, CA, in which a young man with no previous court appearances was convicted of setting fire to a coat in a school room causing £200 worth of damage. The Court of Appeal said that whilst arson was a very serious offence, the range of criminality was vast and the offence to which the appellant pleaded guilty came in the lower range of cases of arson and did not merit a custodial sentence. Dewberry's co-defendant, Stone, was convicted of a further count of arson resulting in damage of some £67,000. Both offences were committed after the appellant had consumed vodka. The court said that in cases of arson, attention should be focused on the intention with which the acts were done rather than the consequences which resulted. The aggravating feature in this case was that the appellant had gone to the school on a second occasion and started a fire deliberately making that offence so serious that a non-custodial sentence could not be justified.

Criminal damage itself may be so serious as to merit a custodial sentence. In *R v George* (1992) 14 Cr App Rep (S) 12, CA, a 16-year-old pleaded guilty to damaging a church at night to the value of £33,000. He had four previous offences, the last of which was the criminal damage. The Court of Appeal described this as a quite disgraceful offence, which merited 12 months' detention. This was reduced to 10 months on the basis of a discount for a guilty plea.

Offences of violence may fulfil the seriousness criteria. Again, this will depend on the aggravating features in the offending. In *R v Beddoes* (1990) 12 Cr App Rep (S) 363, CA, the appellant pleaded guilty to an offence of violent disorder. He was involved in a fight when a large group of young men attacked a group of soldiers with snooker cues and glasses. Two people were hospitalised as a result of the incident. The defendant received a custodial sentence on the basis of the seriousness of the offence. An offence of violence, however, which on the bare facts may fit the seriousness criteria, may nevertheless be subject to mitigating factors which will allow the court to pass a community sentence.

Offences of robbery are subject to a definitive set of guidelines from the Sentencing Guidelines Council and include specific guidance with regard to young offenders. Depending upon the nature of the aggravating circumstances the guidelines set out a sentencing range that stretches from a community order to six years' detention. The guidelines should be used in all cases involving robbery.

Burglary of a dwelling house will usually be so serious that a non-custodial sentence cannot be justified, although of course the discretion to impose a community penalty remains with the court. In *R v Winson and Poole* [1998] 1 Cr App Rep (S) 239, CA, a 15-year-old and a 13-year-old entered a dwelling house by an unlocked rear door and stole theft and cash. A sentence of 12 months' detention was reduced to nine months on appeal bearing in mind the guidelines laid down in the case of *R v Brewster* [1998] 1 Cr App Rep (S) 181, CA.

The general restrictions in CJA 2003, s 152 do not apply to sentences fixed by law, or to dangerous offenders. In the case of adults they do not apply to third-time drug traffickers and burglars of dwelling houses.

Where relevant a sexual offence means an offence under the Sexual Offences Act 2003 except ss 52 or 71 (causing or controlling prostitution and offences in a public lavatory).

The definition does not include an offence under ss 30, 31 or 33-36 of the 1956 Act, and offences related to living off immoral earnings and brothel-keeping. Nor does the definition included child abduction, or indecent exposure.

REASONS FOR IMPOSING A CUSTODIAL SENTENCE

10.09   Where a court passes a custodial sentence, then it is under a duty to state in open court that it is of the opinion that one or both of the above criteria apply and why it is of that opinion. The court must explain to the offender in open court and in ordinary language why it is passing a custodial sentence on him and its reasons must be recorded in the court register and on the warrant of commitment (CJA 2003, s 147).

When giving its reasons the court must include a statement that it is of the opinion that a sentence consisting of or including a youth rehabilitation order with intensive supervision and surveillance or fostering cannot be justified for the offence, together with its reasons for reaching that opinion (CJA 2003, s 174 (4B)).

Giving reasons in open court is a pre-requisite of Art 6 of the European Convention on Human Rights and is embodied in the Criminal Justice Act 2003, s 174, which requires the court to give reasons for and explain the effect of its sentence. Should a particular sentence fall outside the guidelines as set out by the Sentencing Guidelines Council, or in general terms the court imposes a sentence that might be unexpected, the reasons for this departure from normal sentencing need to be dealt with in the court's reasons. Similarly, when different types of sentence are imposed on defendants jointly charged there may again be a need for the court to give fuller reasons than normal. A structured approach to the sentencing decision in the Youth Court carried out in consultation by the magistrates and their legal advisor will generally provide sound reasons that can be given in open court.

REFUSAL TO EXPRESS A WILLINGNESS TO AGREE TO A REQUIREMENT IN A COMMUNITY SENTENCE

10.10   This other criterion outlined above means that an offence that would not have otherwise fallen within the custody bracket may still result in a custodial sentence. Indeed, where custody is imposed due to the lack of an agreement to a requirement in any specified community sentence, the court does not have to justify its passing of such a sentence. Nor is it required to obtain a pre-sentence report although it must still explain to the offender in ordinary language why it is passing a custodial sentence and record its reasons. In most cases a PSR will have been obtained in order to facilitate the making of the intended community sentence.

There are a number of community rehabilitation order sentence requirements that need an offender's agreement, namely an order with the requirement of treatment for intoxicating substance treatment, a drug treatment requirement, an alcohol dependency requirement, supervision orders with a requirement for psychiatric treatment or a mental health treatment order or, a failure to comply with an order for pre-sentence drugs testing.

drug rehabilitation requirement. Two points need to be considered. First, the offender should have a clear understanding of his choice as to whether or not to agree to the sentence proposed. In *R v Marquis* [1974] 2 All ER 1216, CA, it was said that a suggestion that a custodial sentence was the only alternative, when in fact this was not the case, could invalidate the consent given by the defendant. However, in *R v Barnett* (1986) 8 Cr App Rep (S) 200, CA, the point was made that where custody is a realistic alternative to the community sentence proffered, the offender's knowledge that this is so does not negate his consent to the making of a community sentence. The relevance of these cases is somewhat diminished as community sentences are now sentences in their own right commensurate with the seriousness of the offence.

Furthermore, the offender may have reason for not wishing to agree to specific community sentence requirements but this does not make a custodial order a foregone conclusion. The court has other community sentences requirements that may be equally appropriate to meet the seriousness of the offence and the needs of the offender and its overall aim to prevent further offending.

SUPERVISION AFTER RELEASE

10.11   The aim of the detention and training order is that it should be constructive and linked to the work to be done by the youth offending team during the custodial part of the sentence. The youth offending team must appoint a supervising officer who will meet with the detainee, his parents or carer. A training plan will be drawn up to meet the young offender's needs with respect to education, health and accommodation. In this way it is anticipated that release back into the community subject to supervision will be part of a process rather than an abrupt change from custody to community.

Supervision will generally be carried out by the youth offending team. The offender will be issued a supervision notice before release giving him details of the supervision. Under national standards, minimum levels of contact are set including the fact that the offender must be seen on the day of release and the supervising officer must make a home visit within five working days of that release. Thereafter contact must be twice-weekly during the first three months and then at least once every 10 working days for the duration of the order. The supervision notice may include a requirement to comply with an intensive supervision and surveillance programme.

In breach of supervision and further offending

10.12 Where a breach of supervision requirement is alleged an information will usually be laid in the local justice area where the juvenile lives. Where the detention and training order was imposed by the Crown Court an information should be laid in the local justice area where the offender lives. The court will issue a summons and has the power to issue a warrant where necessary if the information is in writing and upon oath (PCC(S)A 2000, s 104(1)). At the hearing the supervising officer will present evidence to the court about the alleged breach and the juvenile will have an opportunity to challenge that evidence. If having heard evidence from both sides the Youth Court is satisfied that there has been a failure to comply with the supervision requirement of the detention and training order it may direct that the juvenile be returned to detention for a period of up to three months or for the remainder of the order (where this is less than three months). Alternatively the court may impose a fine not exceeding level 3 (£250 for a child) and direct that supervision of the offender should continue for the remainder of the term of the order: see *H v Doncaster Youth Court* [2008] All ER (D) 194 (Nov).

If the juvenile is convicted of a further offence (punishable with imprisonment, in the case of a person aged 21 or over) during the supervised period, in addition to any other sentence it imposes a court can order detention in custody for a period not greater than that from the date of the commission of the offence to the end of the detention and training order. Any such sentence may be ordered to be served concurrently or consecutively to any sentence imposed for a new offence. For the purpose of calculation, an offence committed during or over a period of time is treated as having been committed on the last of those days (PCC(S)A 2000, s 105(4)).

Chapter 11

Breach, revocation and amendment of youth rehabilitation orders and reparation orders

11.01   The Criminal Justice and Immigration Act 2008, Sch 2 contains the relevant provisions dealing with youth rehabilitation order breaches. Reparation orders, although not community sentences, are dealt with later in this chapter.

BREACH OF A REQUIREMENT

11.02   Before any breach proceedings are taken the responsible officer has a duty to issue an initial warning to the offender.

If the responsible officer is of the opinion that the offender has failed without reasonable excuse to comply with any of the requirements of a community order, the officer must give him a warning unless:

 (a) the offender has within the previous 12 months been given a warning in relation to a failure to comply with any of the requirements of the order, or

 (b) during the period of a first warning he has been given another warning in respect of the failure to comply with the order, and

 (c) the responsible officer is of the opinion that, during that warned period, the offender has again failed without reasonable excuse to comply with the order.

A warning must:

 (a) describe the circumstances of the failure,

 (b) state that the failure is unacceptable, and

 (c) inform the offender that, if within the next 12 months (or if it is a second warning during the period of that warning) he again fails to comply with any requirement of the order, he will be liable to be brought before a court.

Breach of order after warning

11.03   If the responsible officer has given the warning as described above and there is a subsequent failure, without reasonable excuse, to comply with the order the officer must cause an information to be laid before a justice of the peace in respect of that failure unless he is of the opinion that there are exceptional circumstances that justify not laying the information. In relation to a youth rehabilitation order made by the Crown Court that does not include a direction that any failure to comply with the requirements of the order is to be dealt with by a magistrates' court, the reference to a justice of the peace is to be read as a reference to the Crown Court (see **11.07**).

If during the lifetime of an order, the responsible officer lays an information before a justice of the peace stating that the offender has, without reasonable excuse, failed to comply with any one of the requirements of the order, that justice may issue a summons. If the information is in writing and on oath, a warrant may be issued for the offender's arrest. This will bring the offender before the court for the local justice area concerned. If the offender fails to appear in answer to the summons the court may issue a warrant for his arrest.

If the offender is aged under 18 the appropriate court will be the Youth Court in the relevant local justice area and if he is aged 18 or over the appropriate court will be an adult magistrates' court.

PROCEDURAL MATTERS

11.04   On amending or revoking a youth rehabilitation order, the proper officer of the court must give copies of the order to the responsible officer and the offender (or his parent or guardian if he is under 14 years). Where the offender is or was required by the order to reside in a different local justice area copies of the amending order must be provided to the local probation board acting for that area and the magistrates' court acting for that area. Any other person affected by the order being revoked or amended must also receive a copy.

Breach of requirement of order

Breach, revocation and amendment of youth rehabilitation order s Breach proceedings

11.05 If at any time while a relevant order is in force in respect of an offender it appears on information to a justice of the peace acting for the local justice area concerned that the offender has failed to comply with any of the requirements of the order, the justice may:
  (a) issue a summons requiring the offender to appear at the place and time specified in it; or
  (b) if the information is in writing and on oath, issue a warrant for his arrest.

Any summons or warrant issued shall direct the offender to appear or be brought:
  (a) in the case of any relevant order which was made by the Crown Court that does not include a direction that any failure to comply with any of the requirements of the order be dealt with by the magistrates' court, before the Crown Court; and
  (b) in the case of a relevant order that is not an order to which paragraph (a) above applies, before a magistrates' court acting for the local justice area concerned.

If the responsible officer lays an information before a justice of the peace, during the lifetime of an order, stating that the offender has, without reasonable excuse, failed to comply with any one of the requirements of the order, that justice may issue a summons. If the information is in writing and on oath, a warrant may be issued for the offender's arrest. This will bring the offender before the court for the local justice area concerned.

If the offender is aged 18 or over breach proceedings will commence in a magistrates court other than the Youth Court. Offenders under the aged 18 will appear before the Youth Court.

Where a summons issued above requires an offender to appear before the Crown Court and the offender does not appear in answer to the summons, the Crown Court may issue a further summons requiring the offender to appear at the place and time specified in it. If the offender does not appear in answer to that summons, the Crown Court may issue a warrant for the arrest of the offender (CJ&IA 2008, Sch 2, para 5).

Powers of Youth or magistrates' court

11.06   If it is proved to the satisfaction of a Youth Court or magistrates' court before which an offender appears that he has failed without reasonable excuse to comply with any of the requirements of the relevant order, the court may deal with the offender in respect of the failure in one of the following ways (and must deal with him in one of those ways if the relevant order is in force):

(a)   by fining the offender an amount not exceeding £250 if he is under 14 or an amount not exceeding £1,000 in any other case;

(b)   by amending the youth rehabilitation order requirements so as to add to or substitute any requirement already imposed by the order. However, this may not include an extended activity requirement or fostering requirement if the order does not already include such a requirement. Where the original order included a fostering requirement and this is substituted by a new fostering requirement the order may run for 18 months (as opposed to the original 12) beginning with the date on which the original requirement first took effect;

(c)   where the relevant order was made by a Youth Court or magistrates' court, by dealing with him, for the offence in respect of which the order was made, in any way in which he could have been dealt with for that offence by the court that made the order if the order had not been made.

Any requirement imposed under (b) above must be capable of being complied with before the date specified under CJ&IA 2008, Sch 1, para 32(2) and not more than three years after the order first took effect. In addition, where the original order does not contain an unpaid work requirement and the court imposes such requirement the minimum number of hours and that may be imposed is reduced to 20 from the normal 40.

As always when dealing with the original offence (c) above) the court shall take into account the extent to which the offender has complied with the requirements of the relevant order. In such circumstances the court must revoke the original order if it is still in force. In the case of an offender who has wilfully and persistently failed to comply with those requirements, and the court is dealing with him under (c) above, the court may impose a youth rehabilitation order with an intensive supervision and surveillance requirement without regard to the fact that the court is not dealing with the offender for an offence that is punishable with imprisonment nor need it form the opinion that the offence is so serious that it would (but for the restrictions) merit a custodial sentence. Furthermore, where the court does make such an order and the original offence was not punishable with imprisonment in any subsequent breach the court is taken to have had power to deal with the offender for that offence by making a detention and training order for a term not exceeding four months (CJ&IA 2008, Sch 2, paras 12-14).

An offender is not to be treated as having failed to comply with an order in respect of a mental health treatment requirement, a drug treatment requirement or, an intoxicating substance treatment requirement, solely on the ground that the offender had refused to undergo any surgical, electrical or other treatment required by that requirement if, in the opinion of the court, the refusal was reasonable having regard to all the circumstances.

If in dealing with the offender by way of re-sentencing (paragraph (c) above) and the order is a youth rehabilitation order with intensive supervision and surveillance requirements and the original offence was punishable with imprisonment, the court may impose a custodial sentence, notwithstanding anything contained in the general restrictions on imposing discretionary custodial sentences under Criminal Justice Act 2003, s 152(2) (CJ&IA 2008, Sch 2, para 14).

Crown Court orders

11.07   Where a relevant order was made by the Crown Court and a Youth or magistrates' court has power to deal with the offender, it may instead commit him to custody or release him on bail until he can be brought or appear before the Crown Court.

A Youth or magistrates' court that deals with an offender as above shall send to the Crown Court:
  (a) a certificate signed by a justice of the peace certifying that the offender has failed to comply with the requirements of the relevant order in the respect specified in the certificate; and
  (b) such other particulars of the case as may be desirable; and a certificate purporting to be so signed shall be admissible as evidence of the failure before the Crown Court.

The Crown Court has similar powers to the Youth Court in dealing with breaches; however, in proceedings before the Crown Court any question whether the offender has failed to comply with the requirements of the relevant order is determined by the court and not by the verdict of a jury.

Commission of further offences

11.08 An offender who is convicted of a further offence while an original order (which is either made by the Youth Court or the Crown Court, but contains a direction that breaches may be dealt with in the Youth Court), is in force in respect of him, the convicting court may revoke that order. Where it does revoke the order, it may deal with the offender, for the offence in respect of which the order was made, in any way in which it could have dealt with him for that offence had it been the convicting court. If the court deals with him in this manner it must take into account the extent to which the offender has complied with the order.

The court may not revoke and re-sentence the offender unless it considers it would be in the interests of justice to do so, having regard to circumstances that have arisen since the youth rehabilitation order was made.

Where the Crown Court orders that the Youth Court is authorised to deal with breach proceedings, the Youth Court may nonetheless commit the offender back to the Crown Court in custody or on bail to be dealt with by the judge.

Revocation of order with or without re-sentencing: powers of magistrates' court

11.09 Where a relevant order made by a Youth or magistrates' court is in force in respect of any offender and, on the application of the offender or the responsible officer, it appears to the appropriate Youth or magistrates' court that, having regard to circumstances that have arisen since the order was made, it would be in the interests of justice for the order to be revoked, or for the offender to be dealt with in some other way for the offence in respect of which the order was made, the appropriate court may:
  (a) revoke the order; or

(b) revoke the order, and deal with the offender for the offence in respect of which the order was made, in any way in which he could have been dealt with for that offence by the court which made the order if the order had not been made.

Circumstances that may lead to a revocation include the offender making good progress or responding satisfactorily to supervision order treatment as the case may be.

If the offender is under 18 when the application is made it will be dealt with by the Youth Court and, if he is over 18 at that time, a magistrates' court for the local justice area.

Where an application to revoke an order is dismissed, then during the period of three months beginning with the date on which it was dismissed no further application may be made except with the consent of the appropriate court (CJ&IA 2008, Sch 2, Part 3, para 11(7)).

In dealing with an offender for the original offence, a court shall take into account the extent to which the offender has complied with the requirements of the relevant order. A person so sentenced may appeal to the Crown Court against that sentence.

Where a Youth or magistrates' court proposes to exercise its powers under this paragraph otherwise than on the application of the offender, it shall summon him to appear before the court and, if he does not appear in answer to the summons, may issue a warrant for his arrest.

No application may be made by the offender while an appeal against the relevant order is pending.

Amendment of orders

Amendment by reason of change of residence

11.10   At any time while the order is in force, a Youth or magistrates' court acting for the local justice area concerned is satisfied that the offender proposes to change, or has changed, his residence from that area to another area, the court may (and on the application of the responsible officer, must) amend the relevant order by substituting the other local justice area for the area specified in the order.

Amendment of requirements of order

11.11   A Youth or magistrates' court acting for the local justice area .concerned may, on the application of an eligible person, amend an order by cancelling or inserting any of the requirements in the order (either in addition to or in substitution for any of its requirements) that the court could include if it were then making the order.

In either case where the original order contains a specific area requirement (for example a curfew requirement) or a programme requirement, the court must not make an amendment that would prevent the offender from complying with that requirement. In such circumstances the court must substitute a similar requirement within the new area.

Where the court replaces a requirement with a new requirement, the new requirement must be capable of being complied with before the end of the order. In the case of a fostering requirement that substitutes the original fostering requirement it may run for a period of 18 months beginning with the date on which the original requirement first had effect.

An order containing an unpaid work requirement may on the application of the offender or the responsible officer be amended to extend the period of 12 months during which time the order must be completed, if it would be in the interests of justice to do so having regard to circumstances that have arisen since the order was made.

Treatment requirements

11.12   The court may not impose a treatment requirement such as mental health treatment, drug treatment or drug testing by way of amendment unless the offender has expressed willingness to comply with the requirement. If an offender fails to express willingness to comply with such a requirement the court may revoke the youth rehabilitation requirement and deal with the offender for the original offence in respect of which the order was made in any way the court could have dealt with the offender for that offence. If such circumstances arise the court must take into account the extent to which the offender has complied with the order.

Procedural requirements

11.13 The procedural requirements for summonses and warrants are required to be followed unless the application is only cancelling a requirement of an order, reducing the period of any requirement, or substituting a new local justice area or a new place for the one specified in a relevant order.

BREACH OF REPARATION ORDERS

National standards

11.14 The manner in which all of these orders are managed by youth offending teams is governed by the National Standards for Youth Justice. Any unexplained missed appointments must be followed up with a visit, telephone call or a letter within one working day. If there is no acceptable reason for the missed appointment or there are other causes for concern, follow-up action with either a formal warning or a breach must be taken. Breach action must be initiated within 10 working days of the most recent failure to comply if the offender has received more than two formal warnings during the first 12 weeks of the order. After the first 12 weeks, an offender can only receive one formal warning before breach proceedings are taken.

Disclosure

11.15 In order to ensure a fair trial in accordance with Art 6 of the European Convention, youth offending teams should provide full disclosure of the circumstances surrounding the breach by way of a written statement or statements to the defendant or his legal representative.

Breach proceedings

11.16 Whilst a, reparation order is in force for a juvenile who has not yet attained the age of 18, the responsible officer may make application to the court seeking to prove that the offender has failed to comply with the order. In such a case, where the court is satisfied of the failure to comply, it may fine the offender an amount not exceeding £1,000 (£250 in the case of a child). Any fine imposed shall be deemed to be a sum adjudged to be paid by conviction.

In the case of a reparation order, where the offender is 18, the appropriate court in such circumstances will be the Youth Court.

Where the order was made in a Youth Court any breach may be dealt with by revoking the order and dealing with the offender for the original offence. The court has the powers that it would have had where it was dealing with the offence at the time the offender was originally sentenced.

Where the order was made by the Crown Court, a Youth Court may commit the offender in custody or release him on bail to appear before the Crown Court. The court should also send particulars of the offender's failure to the Crown Court in a certificate signed by justice of the peace to the Crown Court. The Crown Court may deal with the offender for the original offence in any way in which it could have dealt with him for that offence had it not made the order, and if it does so it should revoke the reparation if it is still in force.

Ensuring the attendance of the offender at court

11.17   Where the supervising or responsible officer commences breach proceedings he will normally do so by issuing a summons to the offender. However, where the application is substantiated on oath a warrant with or without bail may be issued and this can include circumstances where a summons cannot be served usually because the offender has left his address or has absconded. In such circumstances the youth offending team manager must ensure that the police are given all the relevant information about the possible whereabouts of the offender. If a warrant is issued and a juvenile is arrested he must normally be brought before a Youth Court for the relevant local justice area. If no Youth Court is sitting the person having custody of the offender may arrange for his detention in a place of safety for up to 72 hours starting from the time of arrest. A place of safety will usually be local authority accommodation although this may include a police station. The juvenile must be brought before a Youth Court within that period. Where he is brought before a Youth Court other than the appropriate court, the Youth Court may direct his release or remand him to local authority accommodation. If the offender is aged 17 or over the remand should be to a remand centre if availability has been notified or alternatively prison accommodation. The schedule makes no mention of a power to bail either with or without conditions. As magistrates' courts have no powers outside those provided by statute it seems unlikely that they could claim to act under a common law power.

There is power to remand, or further remand, to local authority accommodation where the application is for revocation or amendment of the orders. No such powers are mentioned where there is a need to further remand in breach proceedings. A further remand to custody in such circumstances may not be lawful and as such would violate Article 5 of the European Convention on Human Rights. This sets out that no person shall be deprived of his liberty save in accordance with a procedure prescribed by law and limited by the terms of the article. The court's alternatives would appear to be a remand on bail, despite the lack of an express power, or a reliance on MCA 1980, s 55(5) which provides a general power to remand, in cases commenced by complaint or application, following an arrest under a warrant. (Note this section will be repealed by the Criminal Justice and Courts Services Act 2000, Sch 7 when in force.)

Variation or revocation of reparation orders

11.18   On the application of an appropriate officer or of the offender a court may vary or revoke a reparation order, any requirements made under PCC(S)A 2000, Sch 8, para 5 or s 73. Variation includes reference to cancelling any requirement or inserting, as an additional or substitute requirement, any provision which could have been included in the order if the court had then power to make it and were exercising that power.

On varying or discharging a reparation order, the court must send a copy to the supervised person, and if the supervised person is a child, to his parent or guardian. The supervisor and local authority must also receive a copy.

Repeat applications

11.19   In the case of reparation order where the application for revocation has been dismissed, no further application may be made except with the consent of the appropriate court.

Chapter 12

Additional powers and ancillary orders in the Youth Court

INTRODUCTION

12.01   In addition to the range of disposals considered in Chapters 8-10, there are many other orders available to the court that may be imposed at the same time. Some of these orders are in respect of parents, some are ancillary orders that are primarily intended for use in the adult court, but have a role to play in the Youth Court.

Due to their complexity and dual nature Anti-social behaviour orders are dealt with in Chapter 14.

BINDING OVER ORDERS

12.02   A binding over order is a measure of preventive justice, by which the person entering into the order agrees to be of good behaviour or, in the case of parents, agrees to ensure the good behaviour of their child. When the order is made the court fixes the duration of the order, which is at the court's discretion, and also a sum of money, called a recognisance, which may be forfeited if the order is not complied with during the period fixed. In all cases involving a bind over the court must follow directions in the Criminal Consolidated Practice Direction Part III, 31 [2007] All ER (D) 520 (Mar).

Parents and guardians

12.03   Where a juvenile is found guilty of an offence, the court may, as a preventive measure, and with the consent of the parent or guardian, bind over the parent or guardian. The recognisance may not exceed the sum of £1,000 for a period not exceeding three years or until the juvenile attains the age of 18 years, whichever is the shorter. The terms of the bind over are:

(a) to take proper control of and exercise control over the offender; and

(b) where a youth rehabilitation order has been passed to ensure that the offender complies with the requirements of that sentence.

The Practice Direction requires that the court specifies the actions which the parent or guardian is to take. Under PCC(S)A 2000, s 150, when a child or young person under 16 years is convicted of an offence the court is under a duty to bind over the parent or guardian if it is satisfied, having regard to the circumstances of the case, that it would be desirable in the interests of preventing the commission by him of further offences. Where it decides not to bind the parent or guardian over the court is required to state in open court why it is not satisfied that it would be so desirable. If the parent or guardian refuses to consent and the court considers that refusal unreasonable, the court may fine the parent or guardian up to £1,000.

In fixing the amount of the recognisance the court is required to take into account the means of the parent or guardian and reduce or increase the amount accordingly (PCC(S)A 2000, s 150(7)). Care should be exercised to involve parents in the proceedings and the court should perhaps consider explaining its obligation to bind over parents before it goes on to consider the substantive order of the court. Before the court makes an order binding over the parents, they should be given an opportunity of representations as to why they should not enter into a recognisance if such reasons exist. The parent may wish to be represented by a solicitor in these circumstances.

The court may revoke an order under s 150 on the application of the parent or guardian if it appears to be in the interests of justice to do so, having regard to any change of circumstances since the order was made.

A parent or guardian may appeal to the Crown Court against an order made under s 150.

The juvenile

12.04 The juvenile offender may be bound over to keep the peace by way of complaint under MCA 1980, s 115 for a specific incident.

Alternatively, the justices may use their powers to bind over under the Justices of the Peace Act 1361. This is not by reason of any offence having been committed but as a measure of preventive justice where the juvenile's conduct amounts to a breach of the peace involving violence or an imminent threat of violence or that there is a real risk of violence in the future. Such violence may be perpetrated by the individual who will be subject to the order or by a third party as a natural consequence of the individualhï:'s conduct. This is also known as a common law bind over (Consolidated Practice Direction Part III.31.2.).

The two provisions are quite separate, as stated in *R v Aubrey-Fletcher, ex p Thompson* [1969] 2 All ER 846. In this case a magistrates' court used its common law powers to bind over and the High Court on appeal held that this case was not a bind over under MCA 1980, s 115. In such cases there must be a complaint and the complaint must be adjudged to be true, in other words the case must be heard out completely. An order under the Act of 1361 can be made at any time during the proceedings.

A complaint under MCA 1980, s 115, is not a matter assigned to the Youth Court by CYPA 1933, s 46, and should therefore be heard in an adult magistrates' court. The only way in which a juvenile may be bound over in the Youth Court is by virtue of the court's common law powers. In such circumstances it should be stressed that the person to be bound over must consent to the binding-over order. Where an adult is concerned, the court may commit that person to prison until he consents to be bound over. (MCA 1980, s 115(3)) In the case of a juvenile, imprisonment is not available to the court and therefore the court has no sanction to enforce consent to a binding over order. This point arose in the case of *Veater v Glennan* [1981] 2 All ER 304, where the police made a complaint for a binding-over order against six juveniles aged 14 and 15 years. At the hearing the juveniles admitted disorderly behaviour but refused to consent to being bound over in the sum of £100 to keep the peace for one year. The magistrates took the view that they had no sanction to compel a binding over, nor could they impose a unilateral obligation to be bound over. The High Court agreed that this was the case (but see also *R v Crown Court at Lincoln, ex p Jude* [1997] 3 All ER 737).

Any bind over should avoid the terms 'to be of good behaviour' as this has been held to be too imprecise to be enforceable (*Hashman and Harrup v United Kingdom* [2000] Crim LR 185).

Although a juvenile may not be imprisoned for refusing to consent to a binding-over order, the court still has the power to bind him over if he consents. This was decided in *Conlan v Oxford* (1983) 79 Cr App Rep 157, where the juvenile (youth) court had declined to bind over a juvenile because there was no sanction to enforce its order in the event of a refusal. Goff LJ held that this was incorrect and that the court did have the power to bind a juvenile over despite the absence of an enforcement sanction.

Estreatment of a recognisance

12.05 Where the power to bind over has been utilised, the juvenile having consented to be bound over, the recognisance may be forfeited on complaint to the court (MCA 1980, s 120). This will usually occur where there is an offence committed or a breach of the peace during the currency of the binding-over order. The hearing of a complaint alleging breach of a binding-over order is not a matter assigned by CYPA 1933, s 46 to the Youth Court and should thus be heard by the adult court. See Chapter 5 for further argument as to the jurisdiction of the Youth Court to hear such complaints. Where the complaint is denied the hearing will proceed by hearing the evidence of the complainant and of the juvenile. The court will decide whether the case is proved. The complaint may be admitted, thus rendering evidence unnecessary (*Berkhamsted RDC v Duerdin-Dutton* [1964] Crim LR 307) but the Practice Direction requires that representations are still heard. If contested, the court should be satisfied beyond reasonable doubt of the matters complained of before a binding over order may be imposed. Where the procedure has been commenced on complaint, the burden of proof rests on the complainant. In all other circumstances, the burden of proof rests upon the prosecution (Consolidated Practice Direction Part III, 31.8).Proceedings on complaint to forfeit a recognisance may result in the estreatment of the whole or part of the recognisance, and an additional order as to costs. Where the parent is the subject of the bind over he may be subject to proceeding to forfeit the recognisance by virtue of PCC(S)A 2000, s 150(3) and MCA 1980, s 120.

There is no statutory authority as to who commences a complaint to estreat a parental bind over should they fail to keep proper control over their child. However, whilst it is clearly inappropriate for the court to lay such a complaint where a juvenile offends, the police at the time of charge are in a position to do so both legally and practically. In the normal course of events the re-offending and its surrounding circumstances will be sufficient to enable the magistrates (in an adult court) to decide whether or not the complaint is proved, but see the remarks above.

PARENTING ORDERS

12.06   A parenting order is made against a parent or guardian of a child or young person.

Where a young person under the age of 16 is convicted of an offence the court must make a parenting order if satisfied that a parenting order would be desirable in the interests of preventing the commission of any further offence by the child or young person.

If it is not so satisfied, the court must state its reasons in open court, that a parenting order would not be desirable in the interests of preventing the commission of any further offence by the child or young person.

The Youth Court will make a parenting order against the parent or guardian of a child or young person:
- (a) where the juvenile has been convicted of an offence, or
- (b) where a court makes or deals with a failure to comply with a child safety order, or
- (c) where a court makes an anti-social behaviour order or sexual offences prevention order in respect of the juvenile, or
- (d) where a parental compensation order is made in relation to the child's behaviour, or
- (e) where a conviction is recorded for failure to ensure regular school attendance or comply with the school attendance order, or
- (f) where a referral order has been made or where a parent is referred back to court by a Youth Offender Panel after failing to attend panel meetings.

The prohibition on the making of a parenting order and a referral order for the same offence was removed by s 324 and Sch 34 or the Criminal Justice Act 2003.

This means that parenting orders may be made by all criminal courts: ie Youth Court, magistrates' court and Crown Court. They may also be made by a Family Proceedings Court and a magistrates' court exercising its civil jurisdiction.

The parenting order is made by the court of its own motion. The consent of a parent/guardian is not required although many courts recognise the importance of the willing participation of the parents in a parenting order. The order will last for a period not exceeding 12 months, and must require the parent or guardian to comply with requirements that the court considers desirable in the interests of preventing the commission of further offences. (Where the order was made in non-Youth Court proceedings the requirements are those which the court considers desirable to prevent the behaviour which led to the making of a particular order.)

The order must include a requirement to attend a parenting programme for a period not exceeding three months. All orders must include this unless the parent has previously received a parenting order. The court fixes the length of the parenting programme but must allow sufficient time for assessing parents and any work needed to prepare the parents for the programme.

Additional requirements

12.07 The court may wish to impose additional requirements to ensure or encourage the parent to prevent undesirable or offending behaviour. Such requirements may include making sure the juvenile is indoors between certain hours and ensuring that the juvenile is accompanied to school. There may be further requirements that the juvenile attends a programme or course to address relevant problems, eg anger management or drug or alcohol misuse; that the juvenile avoids contact with disruptive and possibly older children and that the juvenile avoids unsupervised visits to certain places, eg shopping centres. Another common requirement is that the juvenile does not have contact with named co-defendants. Any such requirements shall, so far as practicable, avoid any conflict with a parent's religious beliefs and any interference with the times, if any, in which he normally works or attends an educational establishment (CDA 1998, s 9). As breach is a criminal offence the requirements must be clear so that the parents or guardians know exactly what is required of them.

The parenting order may include a residential course if two conditions are satisfied. These are that the attendance by the parent or guardian on such a course where the court is satisfied that it is likely to be more effective than he or she attending a non-residential course in preventing the child or young person from re-offending, and that likely interference with family life is proportionate.

A parenting order must specify a responsible officer. This will often be a member of the youth offending team but it may be a social worker, a probation officer, or a person nominated by the chief education officer such as an education welfare officer.

Variation

12.08   During the operational period of a parenting order the court that made it may, on application of the responsible officer or the parent, make an order discharging or varying the parenting order. This includes cancelling or inserting any provision within the court's existing powers. When application to discharge an order is dismissed no further application for its discharge shall be made by any person except with the consent of the court which made the order.

Breach

12.09   If the parent fails without reasonable excuse to comply with any requirement included in the order or specified in directions given by the responsible officer, he shall be liable on summary conviction to a fine not exceeding level 3. The prosecution of a parent for breach of a parenting order will take place in the magistrates' court and is conducted by the Crown Prosecution Service.

DEPRIVATION ORDERS AND FORFEITURE

Deprivation

12.10   Where a juvenile is found guilty of an offence, the court by or before which he is found guilty may make an order depriving the offender of his rights to certain property (PCC(S)A 2000, s 143). The court must be satisfied that the property in his possession or under his control at the time of his apprehension was:
   (a)   used for the purpose of committing or facilitating the commission of any offence; or
   (b)   was intended by him to be used for that purpose.

An order may also be made depriving an offender of property where the offence or an offence taken into consideration consists of unlawful possession of property which:

    (a) has been lawfully seized from him; or

    (b) was in his possession or under his control at the time when he was apprehended for the offence of which he has been convicted or when a summons in respect of that offence was issued.

An example of this provision's most common use is the confiscation of keys used in the course of theft of cars or tools used in the course of burglary.

Where the court makes an order of conditional or absolute discharge under PCC(S)A 2000, s 12, a deprivation order may still be made, as such an order is deemed to be a conviction for the purposes of the proceedings in which it is made (PCC(S)A 2000, s 12(7)).

Forfeiture

12.11   Orders of forfeiture are rare in the Youth Court because of the nature of the offences from which the statutory powers of forfeiture arise. Where the statute gives a court a power of forfeiture, it may order property to be confiscated and either sold or destroyed as appropriate. For example, drugs found in a person's possession may be subject to a forfeiture order made under the Misuse of Drugs Act 1971, s 27. Another of the more common offences seen in the Youth Court is the possession of a knife, bladed article or weapon. Where such a case is proved the court may order the forfeiture of the knife or other article (Knives Act 1997, s 6 and Prevention of Crime Act 1953).

Perhaps the most common offences of all in the Youth Court where the question of forfeiture arises are those involving the possession of air weapons by juveniles. There is a general power to confiscate a firearm under the Firearms Act 1968, s 52, if the court has made a custodial order. Specific offences in relation to air weapons are those under s 22(4) of the 1968 Act (possession of an air weapon or ammunition by a minor under the age of 17 years). There is power on a finding of guilt to order confiscation by virtue of the Firearms Act 1968, Sch 6.

Effect of an order

12.12   The effect of a forfeiture order is to deprive the offender of his rights to property. The court may direct the property to be sold or disposed of in any other manner, for example by its destruction. The proceeds of sale of items forfeited are treated as a fine and sent to the Home Office, to be applied to public funds. The effect of a deprivation order is to deprive the offender of his rights (if any) to the property, and the property will be taken into the possession of the police (PCC(S)A 2000, s 143(3)). Subsequent claims to ownership of the property can be dealt with either by the civil courts or by an application under the Police (Property) Act 1897, s 1, to the magistrates' court.

RESTITUTION ORDERS

12.13   PCC(S)A 2000, s 148, provides for the making of restitution orders. Although orders for the restitution of goods against juveniles are rare, such an order may be made if the court is satisfied on the facts of the case, either having heard evidence during the trial or from documentary evidence. The court must have found the offender guilty:

- (a) of an offence involving goods which have been stolen, whether or not stealing is the gist of his offence; or
- (b) of any other offence and an offence under (a) above is taken into consideration.

The powers of the court in these circumstances are:

- (a) to order anyone having possession or control of the goods to restore them to any person entitled to recover them from him; or
- (b) on the application of a person entitled to recover from the person convicted any other goods, being the proceeds of any disposal or realisation of the whole or part of them, the court may order those other goods to be delivered or transferred to the applicant; or
- (c) the court may order that a sum not exceeding the value of the goods shall be paid out of the money of the person convicted which was taken out of his possession on his apprehension, to any person who, if those goods were in the possession of the person convicted, would be entitled to recover them from him.

Orders under both (b) and (c) may be made at the same time, provided that a victim does not receive more than the value of the original goods.

A restitution order may be made notwithstanding the fact that sentence is deferred in all other respects.

COMPENSATION ORDERS

12.14   The criminal courts often deal with offences that result in the victim suffering loss in some form or another. Magistrates are given power to award compensation to be paid by the offender either at their own discretion or on the application of the prosecution. The power to award compensation is contained in PCC(S)A 2000, s 130, and by virtue of this provision the court may order the offender, after finding him guilty, to pay compensation:

> 'for any personal injury, loss or damage resulting from that offence or any other offence which is taken into consideration by the court in determining sentence or to make payments for funeral expenses or bereavement in respect of a death resulting from any such offence, other than a death due to an accident arising out of the presence of a motor vehicle on a road.'

If personal injury loss or damage arises out of an accident caused by the presence of a motor vehicle on a road, a compensation order may be made (see below).

If the court does not make a compensation order it is required to give reasons on passing sentence.

A compensation order may be made instead of, or in addition to, dealing with the offender in any other way.

The amount of compensation which the court may order is limited to £5,000 for each offence. Where compensation is ordered for offences taken into consideration the court is still limited to a total compensation order of £5,000 for each offence that has actually been charged.

For example, an offender is charged with and admits three offences of theft and also asks the magistrates to take into consideration 20 other matters. Compensation is applied for on both the offences and the matters taken into consideration. A total of £300 is awarded as compensation on the offence charged, and therefore the court is limited to awarding compensation in total of £15,000, less the £300 awarded, that is £14,700, on the matters taken into consideration (PCC(S)A 2000, s 131).

The court must be satisfied that the injury loss or damage which occurred is attributable to the offence in respect of which a compensation order is made.

A compensation order may only be made in respect of injury, loss or damage that was due to a road traffic accident involving the presence of a motor vehicle on a road, if:

(a) it is in respect of damage which is treated as resulting from an offence under the Theft Act 1968, eg TWOC; or

(b) it is in respect of injury, loss or damage as respects that the offender is uninsured in relation to the use of the vehicle; and compensation is not payable under the agreement between the Secretary of State and the Motor Insurers' Bureau. The current limit payable is £300 as at October 2008.

A compensation order is to be of such amount as the court considers appropriate having regard to any evidence and to any representations that are made by or on behalf of the accused or the prosecutor (PCC(S)A 2000, s 130(4)). This subsection contemplates that the court can make assessments and approximations where the evidence is scanty or incomplete and then makes an order which is deemed 'appropriate.'

Where the basis for making any compensation order is challenged, the court must consider evidence and cannot act merely on representations. The position prior to the passing of the Criminal Justice Act 1982 was that before awarding compensation the court had to be satisfied that the amount to be ordered was either agreed or proved. In *R v Vivian* [1979] 1 All ER 48, CA, £209 compensation was claimed for damage done to a car. It was asserted that the estimate was excessive because the damaged car was very old and had defects before the collision. The judge, without hearing any evidence on this disputed point and without hearing detailed representations, made a compensation order of £100. This was quashed on appeal. The Court of Appeal said that as there was neither agreement on nor proof of the amount which the owner of the damaged car was entitled to claim, a compensation order ought not to have been made. The words 'considers appropriate' in PCC(S)A 2000, s 131 are rather vague, but although there is no mention of a standard of proof it is submitted that the magistrates must at least be satisfied on the balance of probabilities that a particular amount is appropriate before making an order.

In *R v Horsham Justices, ex p Richards* [1985] 2 All ER 1114, a compensation order was made by the justices. The application had been contested and the court made the order after hearing representations but without receiving any evidence. Neill LJ held that this approach was wrong and that the court had no jurisdiction to make a compensation order without receiving evidence where there were real issues raised as to whether the claimants had suffered any, and if so what, loss.

In *R v Miller* [1976] Crim LR 694, CA, the principles to be followed in making orders for compensation were considered. This was a case in which a defendant was convicted of theft of £6,100 from his employer. He was sentenced to 18 months' imprisonment and ordered to pay £6,100 compensation. The defendant obtained employment after his release from prison but could only offer payments of £5 per week. The following points extracted from the judgment in *Miller* are still of relevance when considering the making of a compensation order, both in the adult and Youth Court:

- An order should only be made where the legal position is quite clear.
- Regard must be had to the defendant's means.
- The order must be precise, relate to an offence, and specify the amount and the instalments, if there is to be payment by instalments.
- The order must not be oppressive.
- There may be good moral grounds for making an order including payment by instalments to remind the defendant of the evil he has done.
- The order must be realistic.

In considering the amount of compensation, the court must have regard to the means of the juvenile's parents or, if appropriate, the means of the juvenile himself. It is the duty of the court to order that any compensation awarded be paid by the parents of the juvenile unless the court is satisfied that the parent or guardian cannot be found or that it would be unreasonable, having regard to the circumstances of the case, to make such an order. (PCC(S)A 2000, s 137) However, see below in relation to juveniles of 16 years or older and those accommodated in local authority accommodation.

In *R v Scott* (1986) Times, 2 April, it was held that the compensation awarded to be paid should not be such that it would take an excessive period of time to pay. However in *R v Olliver and Olliver* [1989] Crim LR 387, CA, it was stated that there was no reason in principle why an order should not be paid over two or three years. This case was decided on its particular facts and many Youth Courts prefer to work to a 12-month maximum period.

Where the court considers it appropriate both to impose a fine, a victim surcharge (see **12.15**) and a compensation order, but the offender has insufficient means to pay all the orders,, the compensation order must be given preference by the court (PCC(S)A 2000, s 130(12)). Thus, if the court considers that the offence should attract, for example, a £80 fine and also wishes to impose a compensation order of £60, if the offender's means are limited to the extent that the court considers the offender can only pay £80 in total they should make a compensation order of £60 order the victim surcharge of £15 and reduce the fine to £5 so that the compensation can be paid. See below for principles in respect of costs.

Where the offence involved is one contrary to the Theft Act 1968 and the property involved is recovered in a damaged condition, then the court may order compensation for all the damage caused while out of the owner's possession, however and by whomsoever it was caused (PCC(S)A 2000, s 130(5)).

A victim's civil remedies remain the same whether a compensation order is made or not. However, any subsequent award will be reduced by any sum already awarded in criminal proceedings.

Where the juvenile has attained the age of 16 the court has a power rather than a duty to order the parent to pay (PCC(S)A 2000, s 137(3)).

In relation to a child or young person for whom the local authority have parental responsibility and who is in their care, or is provided with accommodation by them, references to parent or guardian are to be construed as references to the local authority. Parental responsibility can only be acquired by a local authority where it is expressly conferred by statute, for example under a care order or emergency protection order made under the Children Act 1989. Consequently, where a juvenile had been remanded to the local authority under the provisions of CYPA 1969, s 23, this did not give parental responsibility and therefore a compensation order could not be made against the local authority in these circumstances. (*North Yorkshire County Council v Selby Youth Court Justices* [1994] 1 All ER 991) See also Chapter 8 for a discussion of the power to order local authorities to pay financial orders.

The court is permitted to find that it would be unreasonable to make such an order having regard to the circumstances of the case. What would be regarded as 'unreasonable' by the courts remains to be seen. It is suggested that before a compensation order is made against a local authority, that authority should be given the opportunity of making representations. (*Bedfordshire County Council v DPP* [1996] 1 Cr App Rep (S) 322) When making a compensation order the court is required to have regard to the offender's means. Where the parent or guardian is ordered to pay, it is the means of the parent or guardian which must be taken into account. (PCC(S)A 2000, s 138) An order against the local authority is not restricted by the offender's means. (PCC(S)A 2000, s 138(2))

Victim surcharge

12.15   For offences committed on or after 1 April 2007 there is a duty on the court to impose a surcharge of £15 whenever they order an offender to pay a fine. This is a mandatory provision. The revenue from the imposition of victim surcharges goes towards assisting victims and witness services throughout England and Wales.

Only one surcharge is required to be ordered on any occasion when the sentence or sentences imposed by the court includes a fine. The court is required to take the offender's means into account and a fine should not be reduced in favour of a surcharge unless the offender has insufficient means to pay the fine.

Where a court is faced with imposing multiple financial orders a priority must be followed. Preference must be given to compensation followed by the victim surcharge followed by a fine and costs. In a situation where the juvenile has insufficient means to pay the court may find that it can only make a compensation order. The same order of priority applies for payment of sums outstanding.

COSTS

12.16   A magistrates' court convicting any person of an offence may make such order as to costs to be paid by the accused as it considers 'just and reasonable' (Prosecution of Offences Act 1985, s 18). However, where any fine imposed is £5 or less, no order for costs may be made unless in the particular circumstances of the case the court considers it right to do so. If the juvenile himself is ordered to pay the costs the amount may not exceed the amount of any fine imposed on the same occasion (POA 1985, s 18(5)). As with all monetary orders in the Youth Court, PCC(S)A 2000, s 137 places a duty on the court to order the parent or guardian to pay costs awarded unless he/she cannot be found or it would be unreasonable in the circumstances of the case to order him/her to do so. Where the juvenile has attained 16 years of age the court has a power rather than a duty to order the parent to pay and where the juvenile is accommodated by a local authority that authority could be ordered to pay (see earlier discussion re compensation orders at **12.14**). Whoever is ordered to pay the amount the order ought to be such that the defendant or parent is able to pay it off within one year. (*R v Nottingham Magistrates' Court, ex p Fohmann* (1986) 151 JP 49; and see *R v Northallerton Magistrates' Court, ex p Dove* [2000] 1 Cr App Rep (S) 136).

A Youth Court may order costs to be paid out of central funds in favour of a defendant in three situations:
  (a) where any information charging a person with an offence is not proceeded with;
  (b) where a defendant is discharged at committal proceedings;
  (c) where any information is dismissed at summary trial (POA 1985, s 16).
  This is known as a defendant's costs order.

Normally a defendant should expect that costs will be awarded from central funds if he falls within one of these three categories (*R v Birmingham Juvenile Court, ex p H* (1992) 156 JP 445). The court should only refuse to make such an order if it has positive reasons for doing so. This might be appropriate where the defendant by his own conduct has brought suspicion on himself and has misled the court. However a court should not deny a defendant his costs order where it would undermine the presumption of innocence in the ECHR (*R v South West Surrey Magistrates' Court, ex p James* [2000] Crim LR 690 and *Practice Direction* [2004] 93 Cr App Rep 89).

If the Crown Prosecution Service has served a notice of discontinuance pursuant to POA 1985, s.23, there is no need for a defendant to attend court simply to obtain an award of costs. An application for costs may be made in writing and then considered by the court on the paperwork before it. Home Office Circular, the 13/1986, indicates that there should be a presumption in the defendant's favour so that he does not suffer financially due to a decision of the prosecution to discontinue proceedings. This was confirmed in the case of *DPP v Denning* [1991] 2 QB 532.

In many cases a defendants' costs order will not be requested as those costs are already covered by a representation order.

The court may award the costs of the prosecution from central funds in any proceedings that are purely indictable or triable either way in the case of an adult. However, no order may be made for prosecution costs from central funds in favour of a public authority. 'Public authority' includes a police force, the Crown Prosecution Service or any other local or national government department (POA 1985, s 17).

The courts may now order costs against a defendant for breach of a community sentence (or suspended sentence) under the Criminal Justice Act 2003 following an amendment to reg 14 Costs in Criminal Cases (General) Regulations 1986 (Costs in Criminal Cases (General) (Amendment) Regulations 2008, SI 2008/2448).

DISQUALIFICATION AND ENDORSEMENT OF DRIVING LICENCES

12.17 Under the Road Traffic Acts, a juvenile under 17 years cannot hold a licence to drive a motor car, additionally a juvenile under 16 years cannot hold a licence to drive a motor cycle. Nevertheless, if a juvenile appears before the court charged with an offence which carries obligatory endorsement, the court is required to order that particulars of the finding of guilt be endorsed on any driving licence held by the defendant along with the number of penalty points awarded, unless the defendant is on that occasion disqualified from driving, when particulars of the disqualification must be endorsed on the driving licence. Where a person is convicted of more than one endorsable offence and these offences were committed on the same occasion, the court only endorses the licence with the number of points for the offence which carries the highest number of points (Road Traffic Offenders Act 1988, s 28(4)). The court has discretion to determine that s 28(4) shall not apply, but if it does so determine the reasons must be stated in open court and recorded in the court register. Thus, if someone is convicted of speeding and careless driving on the same occasion the court could impose three points for the speeding and five for the careless driving. Normally only the highest number, in this example five, would be endorsed but if the court determines that RTOA 1988, s 28(4) should not apply it could endorse eight points.

The meaning of 'same occasion' for these purposes was clarified in *Johnson v Finbow* [1983] 1 WLR 879, where two offences of failing to stop after an accident and failing to report an accident were held on appeal to have been committed on the same occasion.

If a defendant does not hold a driving licence then the order of endorsement and penalty points should still be made, as it operates as an order that any licence he may hold or subsequently obtains should be so endorsed until he becomes entitled under s 45(5) of the Road Traffic Offenders Act 1988 to have a licence issued to him free from these particulars (RTOA 1988, s 45(1)).

Although endorsement, and in some cases disqualification, is obligatory, the statute allows the court a limited discretion to find 'special reasons' not to endorse or disqualify the defendant.

In *R v Wickins* (1958) 42 Cr App Rep 236, the Court of Criminal Appeal prescribed four requirements that a 'special reason' must fulfil:
  (a) it must be a mitigating or extenuating circumstance;
  (b) it must not amount in law to a defence to the charge;
  (c) it must be directly connected with the commission of the offence;
  (d) the matter must be one which the court ought properly to take into consideration when imposing punishment.

The concept was further reviewed and summarised in *DPP v O'Connor* [1992] RTR 66, which also emphasised that is was a two-stage process, first determining whether there are special reasons and then asking whether it is a case where in its discretion the court ought not to endorse or disqualify for the full period.

A simple example of a possible special reason might be where a juvenile had been actively misled by a parent into believing he was insured to drive. However, it is worth noting that, special reasons may not be found in a case of aggravated vehicle taking (Theft Act 1968, s 12A) on the basis that the defendant was not the driver.

Most offences carrying penalty points and an endorsement gives the magistrates a discretionary power to disqualify the offender from driving if the offence is thought to be a serious one of its kind. Offences of theft, or attempted theft, of a motor vehicle, taking a motor vehicle without the owner's consent, allowing oneself to be carried in a vehicle so taken and going equipped, carry a discretionary disqualification only. Some offences such as causing death by dangerous driving, dangerous driving, causing death by careless driving while driving under the influence of drink or drugs, driving with excess alcohol, failure to provide a specimen and aggravated vehicle taking, carry an obligatory disqualification for a minimum period set by statute. For some of these offences the disqualification period may be reduced if the offender attends a course approved by the Secretary of State (RTOA 1988, s 34A).

In addition, if an offender comes within what is often called the 'totting up' system he must be disqualified for a minimum period of six months in the absence of mitigating circumstances. To fall within the totting-up provisions of RTOA 1988, s 35, the offender must have accumulated 12 points within a three-year period prior to the present offence. If he has a previous disqualification on his present driving record imposed within three years of the commission of the present offence, the minimum period of totting up disqualification must be 12 months and, if there are two more relevant disqualifications, the minimum period is two years' disqualification.

A previous disqualification may only be taken into account for this purpose if it was for a fixed period of 56 days or more.

If an offender has accumulated sufficient points to be liable to disqualification he may plead mitigating circumstances amounting to exceptional hardship and ask the court not to disqualify him or to reduce the period of disqualification (RTOA 1988, s 35(1)). If such mitigating circumstances have been successfully pleaded and taken into account by a court on an occasion within a three-year period preceding the conviction for the present offence, they may not be used again (RTOA 1988, s 35(4)(b)).

In *R v Thomas* [1983] 3 All ER 756, CA, it was held that grounds for mitigating the normal circumstances of the conviction within RTOA 1988, s 35 are constituted by the principle of sentencing policy that a long period of disqualification in addition to a custodial sentence may well be counter-productive and thus contrary to the public interest if imposed on a young offender incapable of leaving motor vehicles alone, so that it extends for a substantial period after his release from custody. Accordingly, the court may impose less than the minimum period defined in s 35(2).

Newly qualified drivers are subject to a probationary period of two years beginning on the day on which a test of competence to drive is passed. If a person is convicted of (or accepts a fixed penalty or conditional offer for) an endorsable offence during this period with six or more penalty points being endorsed, the Secretary of State will revoke the driving licence and may not issue a full licence until a further driving test has been passed (Road Traffic (New Drivers) Act 1995). It may be appropriate for a court to impose a short disqualification for some offences thus avoiding the imposition of points (*R v Edmunds* [2000] 2 Cr App Rep (S) 62, CA).

Interim disqualification

12.18 In certain circumstances the court may order an interim disqualification. This only applies to offences which carry disqualification, and may only last for a maximum of six months. Normally the interim disqualification will last until the defendant is sentenced. This power is available on committal to the Crown Court to be dealt with (PCC(S)A 2000, s 6), where a magistrates' court remits to another magistrates' court (PCC(S)A 2000, s 10), where a court defers sentence and on adjournment after conviction and before sentence (RTOA 1988, s 26). This power is not specifically applied to remittal from the adult court to the Youth Court, although it is arguable that this is an adjournment after conviction and before sentence.

Principles applicable to disqualification

12.19 It will be relatively rare to consider disqualifying a juvenile offender, but when disqualification is considered courts may have regard to the following principles:

(a) A disqualification for life will rarely be appropriate. In *R v Buckley* [1994] Crim LR 387, CA, such a disqualification was upheld in a serious case of reckless driving where the defendant's record included 20 offences for taking vehicles without consent, 21 for driving whilst disqualified and five for what was then, reckless driving. The offender was also sentenced to five years in custody.

(b) Extremely long periods of disqualification should be avoided if at all possible. In *R v Baptista* (2 May 1975, unreported), a defendant convicted of driving with excess alcohol was disqualified for 20 years. Kenneth Jones J expressed disapproval of long disqualifications such as this, saying that the court must balance the danger to the public represented by the defendant against the frustration he would feel in connection with obtaining possible future employment.

(c) The effect of disqualification on the offender's prospects of obtaining employment in the future may be considered. This applies particularly in the case of juveniles who are about to leave school and start to look for work. In *R v Aspden* [1975] RTR 456, a defendant was disqualified for two-and-a-half years. On appeal this was reduced to 12 months, James LJ stating that this was because of the effect that a long period of disqualification would have on the defendant's employment.

(d) Imposing a period of disqualification that would extend for a substantial period after release from custody can be counter-productive and should be avoided (*R v A* [2006] EWCA Crim 2382).

A defendant who has been disqualified from driving may apply for that disqualification to be lifted. There are, however, the following restrictions on how soon after the imposition of the disqualification the defendant may apply:

(a) if the disqualification is for less than four years he may apply after two years;

(b) if the disqualification is for more than four years but less than 10 years he may apply after one half of the period;

(c) in any other case he may apply after five years (RTOA 1988, s 42(3)).

In fixing the period of disqualification the magistrates should avoid reference to the above provisions. In the case of *R v Lobby* (1975, unreported) James LJ severely criticised a judge who had taken these provisions into account when disqualifying a person for four years and then alluded to the fact that he could apply for his licence to be restored to him after two years.

Disqualification for any offence

12.20 The court has power to disqualify a defendant from driving for any offence instead of or in addition to dealing with him in any other way. (PCC(S)A 2000, s 146) Certain non-endorsable offences – kerb crawling, unlawful tipping and unlawful off-road driving – recommend themselves for such a penalty, although these are offences rarely seen in the Youth Court.

ENFORCEMENT OF FINANCIAL ORDERS

12.21   Financial orders include fines, compensation, and costs. Where the parent has been required to pay any sum ordered by the Youth Court but fails to do so, the subsequent enforcement of that order is a matter for the adult court. In a case involving the imposition of a financial order upon a juvenile, if the court has satisfied itself that the parent or guardian cannot be found, or that it would be unreasonable to make an order for payment against the parents having regard to the circumstances of the case, the juvenile himself shall be ordered to pay (PCC(S)A 2000, s 137). If, having been ordered to pay, the juvenile then fails so to do, the court must initially enforce the order against the juvenile himself.

The Children and Young Persons Act 1933, s 46 states that '… no charge against a child or young person, and no application whereof the hearing is by rules made under this section assigned to Youth Courts, shall be heard by a court of summary jurisdiction which is not a Youth Court.' Clearly, enforcement of monetary orders is not a matter specifically assigned to the Youth Court, and as such it may be argued that the proceedings should be in the adult court. Welfare considerations should be borne in mind. In addition it may be argued that a 'charge' preferred against a juvenile and the subsequent fine enforcement is part of the same proceedings.

The case of *Evans v Macklen* [1976] Crim LR 120, supports this argument. A defendant was convicted of an offence in her absence and a warrant issued for her arrest. She was arrested by a constable who was not in possession of the warrant at the time. The MCA 1980, s 125(3) states: 'A warrant to arrest a person charged with an offence may be executed by a constable notwithstanding that it is not in his possession at the time.' It was submitted, on appeal, that the defendant was not 'charged with an offence'. The Divisional Court held that the words in this section could be construed as referring to a person 'who had been charged with an offence' in the sense that an information had been laid, and the arrest was therefore lawful.

A juvenile who has defaulted on payment of a monetary order is in a similar position. At some stage in the proceedings he has been 'charged with an offence' and therefore may be dealt with by the Youth Court.

At the time of making an order against the juvenile the court may require the money to be paid straightaway within a certain specified period of time, eg 28 days, or by instalments (MCA 1980, s 75). Where the court has ordered payment by instalments and the juvenile defaults in the payment of any one instalment, he may be treated as being in default of the whole sum still outstanding. When a juvenile falls into default the court may issue a summons, or a warrant with or without bail for his arrest. The considerations on issuing warrants and summonses are dealt with in Chapter 2. Where a warrant with bail is issued, the bail is not bail as in criminal proceedings pursuant to the Bail Act 1976. Instead the person bailed has to enter into a recognisance fixed by the court which may be forfeited if he fails to attend the hearing.

The hearing

12.22   The purpose of requiring the juvenile's attendance at court is to hold an inquiry into his means. Normally the court will require the defaulter to take the oath before he is questioned about his non-payment. Not every case of default is a case of wilful refusal and the following line of questioning will often assist the court in establishing the reasons for non-payment:

(a) Can you explain why these monies have not been paid?

(b) What is your income? Is that from a job, pocket money or other means?

(c) Do you have any other source of income or any savings?

(d) Do you pay rent or board to your parents? How much is that each week?

(e) Have you any additional outgoing for household or personal necessities?

(f) Do you have any other payments to make, for example to a mail order catalogue?

(g) Do you have any other fines or court orders to pay?

Before the hearing the court will require a defaulter to complete a statement of means form.

The court has a wide range of powers in dealing with the juvenile defaulter. These are explained below.

Further time to pay

12.23   A magistrates' court which, after a finding of guilt, orders fines, compensation or costs to be paid may allow further time for payment or allow payment by instalments (MCA 1980, s 75(1)). The court subsequently may allow further time to pay, order payment by instalments or, if payment by instalments has already been permitted, vary such instalments (MCA 1980, s 85A). The court may adjourn and fix a further hearing to review payment.

Means inquiry

12.24 Where the court has dispensed with immediate payment and allowed time to pay or payment by instalments under MCA 1980, s 75(1), it has power, either then or later, to fix a day on which (if any instalment which has fallen due remains unpaid, or if the whole was to be paid by that date and any part remains unpaid) the offender must appear before the court for a fine default hearing and a means inquiry (MCA 1980, s 86(1)). This power is particularly useful and effective if the justices imposing the original financial order are able to return on that date fixed for the subsequent means inquiry and thereby monitor their order.

Remission

12.25 The court has the power on inquiring into a defaulter's means to remit the whole or part of the fine, if having regard to any change in his circumstances since it was imposed the court thinks it just to do so (MCA 1980, s 85). Although unusual in the Youth Court, there is also a power to remit a fine where it is imposed in the offender's absence where he later shows that his means were less than those taken in to account by the court (CJA 2003, s 165).

The court may not remit any other sum adjudged to be paid on conviction whether as a pecuniary penalty, forfeiture, or compensation. Compensation may be reviewed under the procedure found in the PCC(S)A 2000, s 133.

ORDER AGAINST THE PARENTS

Binding over against parents

12.26 The court may make an order requiring the defaulter's parent or guardian to enter into a recognisance to ensure that the defaulter pays the outstanding sum. The court must have the parent's consent to make this order. Such an order may not be made unless the court is satisfied that the defaulter has, or has had since the date on which the sum was ordered, the means to pay the sum or any instalment of it on which he has defaulted, and refuses or neglects or has refused or has neglected to pay it (MCA 1980, s 81(1)(a)).

The court may make an order directing that the parent should take over the payment of the fine. The court must be satisfied that in all the circumstances it is reasonable to make this order (MCA 1980, s 81(1)(b)). The parent must be given the opportunity to make representations but if the parent has been required to attend and has failed so to do this order may be made in the parent's absence (MCA 1980, s 81(5)). The court shall not make this order unless it is satisfied that the defaulter has, or has had since the date on which the sum in question was adjudged to be paid, the means to pay the sum or any instalment of it on which he has defaulted and refuses or neglects or, as the case may be, has refused or neglected to pay it (MCA 1980, s 81(4)). The court must also have considered or tried all other methods of enforcing payment and be satisfied that they are inappropriate or unsuccessful.

Once the parent has been made responsible for his child's fine it is then enforced against him as if it were his own fine, in the adult court (MCA 1980, s 81(7)).

Money payment supervision order

12.27 At the time of imposing a fine, or when dealing with a subsequent default, the court may make a juvenile defaulter the subject of a money payment supervision order. By this means the court orders the defaulter to be placed under the supervision of any person that the court may appoint. Normally the court would appoint either a social worker or a probation officer, but it may appoint any person whom it believes would be an appropriate supervisor. Some magistrates' courts employ a person specifically designated as a fine enforcement officer, and such a person will be an appropriate supervisor for the purposes of MCA 1980, s 88(1). It is the duty of the appointed supervisor to advise and befriend the offender with a view to inducing him to pay the sum adjudged to be paid. Where the court is contemplating the possibility of making a money payment supervision order to either the probation or social services, it is desirable that they request a means inquiry report from the relevant agency in order to ascertain the likely success of such an order. When a money payment supervision order has been made the court is required to consider a report about the offender's conduct and means before making any other order in respect of him (MCA 1980, s 88(6)). The order will last as long as there is an amount outstanding or until the court discharges it.

It should be noted that the function of a money payment supervision order is confined to the payment of monies and does not fulfil the same functions as a supervision order. It should however be considered on a default to pay (see *R v Exeter City Justices, ex p Sugar* (1992) 157 JP 766).

Distress warrants

12.28   Where default is made in paying a sum that has been adjudged to be paid after a finding of guilt, the court may issue a distress warrant (MCA 1980, s 76). This warrant authorises the bailiffs to seize goods which are then sold, the money realised being applied towards the fine. The bailiffs are entitled to seize goods to pay their costs. It would only be appropriate to issue distress warrants against juveniles in rare cases, as juveniles are unlikely to have sufficient goods. It was held in *R v German* (1891) 56 JP 358, that magistrates have a discretion to issue or refuse to issue a distress warrant, and are not bound to issue such a warrant if they are not satisfied that there would be sufficient goods to distrain upon. In this case a magistrates' court had imposed fines for non-attendance of children at school. The order was that the children would attend school or the parents would pay fines. The children did not attend school, fines were imposed, and the school board officer applied for distress warrants to enforce payments, but was not in a position to satisfy the justices that there were any goods to distrain upon. Accordingly, the justices refused to issue distress warrants. For the above reasons the issue of a distress warrants against a juvenile is a very rare occurrence, even though the court must consider them (*R v Norwich Magistrates' Court, ex p Lilly* (1987) 151 JP 689).

Attachment of earnings order

12.29   If the juvenile defaulter is in employment, the court may make an order to his employer requiring him to take an amount out of the defaulter's wages periodically and forward that sum to the court. Such an order may only be made when the court has first conducted a means enquiry, and it must take into account the defendant's income and his outgoing. The court will fix a 'normal deduction rate' and a 'protected earnings rate.' The normal deduction rate is the amount to be deducted by the employer every week. The protected earnings rate is the level below which the defendant's earnings must not fall, and if his income falls below this rate no deduction may be made. The experience of many courts is that attachment of earnings orders are not appropriate or successful where the fine is small, or where the defendant does not have a good work record with the same firm over a long period.

The school leaving age at present is 16. This means that few juveniles are likely to be in employment.

Deductions from income support

12.30   CJA 1991, s 24, provides that regulations may be made empowering the court to apply to the Secretary of State to deduct sums from income support to pay a fine, compensation or costs. No one appearing before a Youth Court as an offender will be entitled to receive income support.

Youth default orders

12.31   Where a sum adjudged to be paid is outstanding and the court would have had power to issue a commitment warrant (were it not for the restrictions contained in the Powers of the Criminal Courts (Sentencing) Act 2000), then instead of using its powers under MCA 1980 it may make a default order. The court must have held a means enquiry in the defendant's presence (MCA 1980, s 81(3)).

In making the youth default order the court may attach an attendance centre requirement (in the case of a 16 or 17-year-old an unpaid work requirement), and the order may include an electronic monitoring requirement (CJ&IA 2008, Sch1, Pt 2), as if the court had just made a community rehabilitation order.

The court has power to postpone the making of the order on such conditions as it deems fit, for example that the young person repays the outstanding sum at a weekly amount.

Revocation or amendment of a youth default order is treated in the same manner as if the court had made a community rehabilitation order.

A youth default order will cease to exist when payment has been made in full and the number of hours or days outstanding will be reduced proportionately by part payment.

Attendance centre requirement

12.32 The court must have been notified by the Secretary of State that an attendance centre is available for the reception of persons of his description, and that the centre specified is reasonably accessible to the defaulter. The considerations to which the court may have regard are the age of the juvenile, the distance between his home and the attendance centre and the availability of and cost of transport. Any attendance at the centre must not interfere with school or work hours. If the court decides that the defaulter is suitable for an attendance centre order, the aggregate number of hours must not be more than the number specified in Table 'A' below. If the offender is under 14 the aggregate number of hours shall not exceed the number specified in Table 'B' below.

Table 'A'

Amount	Number of hours
An amount not exceeding £250	8
An amount exceeding £250 but not exceeding £500	14
An amount exceeding £500	24

Table 'B'

Amount	Number of hours
An amount not exceeding £250	8
An amount exceeding £250 but not exceeding £500	10
An amount exceeding £500	12

Where an offender has been ordered to attend at an attendance centre and then pays the whole sum, the order ceases to have any effect. If he makes a part payment, the number of hours is reduced proportionately

(CJ&IA 2008, s 39(7) (b)). For example, where the defaulter has been made subject to a 12 hours' attendance centre order for the non-payment of a £120 fine; he attends the centre for a total of two hours and then pays £50 towards the total amount: this has the effect of reducing the number of hours by seven-twelfths of the original order, thus leaving five hours to be completed or the remaining £50 to be paid.

Unpaid work requirement

12.33   As with community rehabilitation orders as a sentence for an offence these orders only apply to juveniles aged 16 or older. The minimum period of unpaid work in relation to default is 20 hours (CJ&IA 2008, Sch7, para 2(2))). The court must have held a means enquiry in the defendant's presence. The maximum number of hours will depend on the amount in default and are shown in Table 'C' below.

Table 'C'

Amount outstanding	Number of hours
not exceeding £200:	40
exceeding 200 but not exceeding £500:	60
exceeding £500:	100

Where the offender has been ordered to perform unpaid work and then pays the whole sum the order ceases to have effect. If he makes a part payment the number of hours is reduced proportionately.

A court may not make this order unless notified that arrangements for implementation have been made in their area and not revoked.

Curfew orders

12.34   These are only available where the juvenile has attained the age of 16. (Crime (Sentences) Act 1997, s 35(1) and (2), which is subject to repeal by CJA 2003, s 303). No person may be made subject to a curfew order unless in the case of an adult, imprisonment would have been appropriate. Therefore the court must be satisfied that the default is due to the offender's wilful refusal or culpable neglect. The court must have held a means enquiry in the defendant's presence. The maximum periods of curfew are set out in Table 'D' below.

Table 'D'

Amount outstanding	*Number of days*
not exceeding £200	20
exceeding £200 but not exceeding £500	30
exceeding £500 but not exceeding £1000	60
exceeding £1000 but not exceeding £2500	90
exceeding £2500	180

If he makes a part payment the number of days is reduced proportionately.

This order requires notification by the Secretary of State that it is in force for a particular area before it may be used.

Chapter 13

Common problems in the Youth Court

EVIDENCE

13.01 Witnesses in a court of law normally give evidence after taking the oath or affirmation. This is known as sworn evidence. However, this is not always the case where juveniles are involved. Children under 14 years will not be asked to take the oath but will give unsworn evidence. Young persons aged 14 and above will normally give sworn evidence or evidence on affirmation just as would an adult witness in an adult court (Youth Justice and Criminal Evidence Act 1999, s 55).

Competence is a concept involving a person's ability to appreciate the requirement to understand questions put to them and give answers to questions which can be understood, that is to be able to give evidence in an intelligible manner. In the Youth Court this will depend on the age and maturity of the child witness. There is no longer any rule of law requiring such evidence to be corroborated by other evidence once the court has adjudged that a child is competent to give testimony.

The effect of the legislation is to set a basic rule that all persons (whatever their age) are competent to give evidence in criminal proceedings (YJCEA 1999, s 53). This section sets out two exceptions to this rule. The first exception is that the defendant is only competent as a witness for the defence and not the prosecution. The second exception is that a witness will not be competent to give evidence if it appears to the court that he is not able to understand questions put to him and give answers to them which can be understood. If a witness over the age of 14 is able to communicate intelligently he will be presumed competent unless the issue is raised. If the issue is raised it is for the party calling the witness to satisfy the court that, on the balance of probabilities, the witness is competent to give evidence. Once raised, any questioning of the witness must be done by the court and not the parties and the issue is one to be determined by the court which may receive expert evidence. Any question of competence with regard to a prosecution witness should be decided at the beginning of the trial (*R v Yacob*(1981) 72 Cr App R 313, CA).

In *R v MacPherson* [2005] EWCA Crim 3605 the Court of Appeal made the following additional observations in allowing the evidence of a five-year-old child to be admitted. They emphasised that the test of competence in the 1999 Act was whether the witness could understand questions and give answers that could be understood. Clearly an infant who could communicate only in baby language with its mother would not ordinarily be competent. However the complainant in the present case could speak and understand English with strangers and was competent. Questions of credibility and reliability were not relevant to the issue of competence. Those matters went to the weight of the evidence, and might be considered, when appropriate at the end of the prosecution case by way of submission of no case to answer. A child should not be found incompetent as a witness on the basis of age alone.

If a witness gives unsworn evidence where he should have given evidence on oath it shall not by itself be grounds for an appeal (YJCEA 1999, s 56). If a person gives unsworn evidence in criminal proceedings under this legislation which is wilfully false, he may be guilty of a summary offence, punishable, in the case of an adult, with imprisonment for a term not exceeding six months or a fine not exceeding £1,000 or both (£250 in the case of a person under the age of 14).

In normal circumstances, a witness who is competent to give testimony is also compellable. In the context of a Youth Court, this means that a witness summons may be issued under MCA 1980, s 97 to secure the presence of a child who is a witness in the proceedings. In *Re P (minor: compellability as witness)* [1991] 2 All ER 65, the Court of Appeal, in a case involving a child who was a party in care proceedings, stated that s 97 was applicable to a child (even if they were a party to the proceedings). However, Lady Justice Butler-Sloss said that the section was an inappropriate vehicle for securing the attendance of a child in proceedings where she was a witness and had made serious allegations of sexual abuse against her stepfather, when it was he who was applying for the summons under s 97 of the Magistrates Courts Act 1980. Her Ladyship went on to say that, reading the section as a whole, if the court considered at the time of an application for a summons that for reasons of the welfare of the child, the child should not be called as a witness, then it would be inappropriate to issue a summons. It may well be that this decision must be read in the knowledge of the availability of special measures for witnesses; see **13.23** below.

In the conduct of a criminal trial, it is for the criminal court (that is a judge in the Crown Court or magistrates in a Youth Court) to consider whether or not a ward of court should be called as a witness in those proceedings rather than the decision being made by the wardship judge. However, application for leave to interview the child is necessary and the rules and practice directions relating to applications in respect of wards of court apply in such circumstances (*Re R (a minor) (wardship: witness in criminal proceedings)* [1991] Fam 56).

It will remain good practice for a court receiving evidence from children under the age of 14 to enquire about their understanding of questions put to them, and whether in the opinion of the court they are possessed of sufficient intelligence to give answers to the questions which can be understood. The current legal position now reflects the view of the Criminal Law Commission in their *Eleventh Report* (Cmnd No 4991) which recommended that children below 14 should always give unsworn evidence and children of 14 and above should always give evidence on oath, whilst leaving with the court a discretion to exclude from consideration any evidence of a witness under 14 years of age where it appears to the court that the witness is incapable of giving intelligible testimony.

THE OATH

13.02   The oath taken by a juvenile witness when giving evidence, and by adults in the Youth Court, is different from that normally administered in a magistrates' court. The oath reads: 'I promise before Almighty God to tell the truth, the whole truth and nothing but the truth' (CYPA 1963, s 23).

The taking of the oath in the Youth Court should be treated as a serious matter but not made an ordeal, especially for young children. Every effort should be made to find out, for example, if the witness can read before he comes into court so that the oath may be repeated after a court officer without embarrassment. Holy books from different religions, and not just the New Testament, should be available.

If any person wishes to affirm, he may do so for whatever reason, and without any need to explain his reason (Oaths Act 1978, s 5(1)).

The provisions of the Oaths Act 1978, s 1, are directory only, so that where, for example, a witness fails to hold the New Testament in his hand, the evidence is still admissible. In the case of *R v Chapman* [1980] Crim LR 42, CA, a juvenile witness took the oath without taking the New Testament in his hand as required. When this was brought to the judge's attention, he directed the jury to treat the boy's evidence as an unsworn statement and (as the law stood then) in need of corroboration. On appeal, the Court of Appeal held that the failure to comply with the technical requirements of the Oaths Act 1978 did not necessarily invalidate the taking of the oath.

SPECIAL MEASURES FOR VULNERABLE OR INTIMIDATED WITNESSES

13.03 Many victims and witnesses find coming to court to give evidence both stressful and frightening. The Youth Justice and Criminal Evidence Act 1999 seeks to assist such witnesses in giving the best evidence they can to the court. Part II of the Act provides a definition of a vulnerable or intimidated witness and a test to determine eligibility for special measures provision. Most importantly in this context are special provisions for child witnesses. The Act also provides a mandatory prohibition on cross-examination by defendants in person of complainants in sexual cases and a certain child witnesses. See ss 34-37.

A Youth Court may make a special measures direction in respect of any witness if the quality of the evidence is likely to be diminished by reason of fear or distress on the part of the witness in connection with testifying in the proceedings. More importantly, a witness will be eligible for assistance if he is under 17 at the time of hearing or the quality of evidence is likely to be diminished by reason of a mental disorder impairment of intelligence or physical disability. The quality of a witness's evidence is defined in terms of its completeness, coherence and accuracy (YJCEA 1999, s 16).

By s 17(4) the court must treat a sexual complainant as an eligible witness unless the witness expresses the wish not to be treated as one.

It should be noted that the Act also applies to defendants as well as both defence and prosecution witnesses. Section 33A of the Youth Justice and Criminal Evidence Act 1999 provides for the use of video link evidence and by the defendant if he is under 18 years of age and the following criteria are met:

(a) the defendant's ability to participate effectively in the proceedings as a witness giving oral evidence in court is compromised by his level of intellectual ability or social functioning; and

(b) the use of a live link would enable him to participate more effectively in the proceedings as a witness (whether by improving the quality of his evidence or otherwise); and

(c) it is in the interests of justice for the defendant to give evidence through a live link.

If the court gives a direction for a live link to be used the defendant may not give oral evidence before the court otherwise than through that live link whilst the direction remains in force. The court must give its reasons when granting, refusing or discharging a live link direction.

Where a court is concerned that a defendant is particularly vulnerable they must make use of their inherent jurisdiction to ensure a fair trial: *(Practice Direction) Crown Court: trial of children and young persons* [2000] 1 Cr App Rep 483.

Provisions for child witnesses in need of special protection

13.04   Child witnesses who are classed as being in need of special protection are deemed eligible for special measures without the court having to be satisfied of the test set out in YJCEA 1999, s 17. Children giving evidence in sexual offence cases and, more commonly in the youth court, children giving evidence in cases involving offences of violence are in need of special protection and subject to a strong presumption that special measures will apply. This means they will have a video-recorded statement admitted as to their evidence in chief, if one has been prepared, or they may give evidence via a live TV link. In sexual cases children will be cross-examined on video unless they say they do not want the facility and in the violent category children will be cross-examined via a live TV link.

Other child witnesses who are not deemed to be in need of special protection may also be subject to special measures unless the court considers that those measures will not maximise the quality of their evidence.

The leading case of *R (on the application of D) v Camberwell Youth Court* [2005] UKHL 4, confirms that YJCEA 1999, s 21(3) and (5) has a near mandatory effect so that children in need of special protection must give their evidence by video (if one exists) and then give their evidence on the live TV link. The court has little option but to make a special measures direction in such cases and will depart from that only in exceptional circumstances where it is clear that there has been a material change and the court certifies that it is in the interests of justice to do so. The court also held that these provisions do not breach Article 6 of the ECHR. Witnesses have rights and are entitled to protection. There is nothing in the fair trial provisions which prohibit a vulnerable witness from being allowed to give evidence in a way different to the accused.

In *R (on the application of H) v Thames Youth Court* [2002] All ER (D) 121 (Aug), the defendant, a 13-year-old, was charged with robbery of another 13-year-old who he punched to the ground. The Youth Court directed evidence in chief to be by video recording and that the witness be cross-examined by live TV link. On appeal against the direction it was held that, although there was no direct evidence of the victim's state of mind the court could infer from the circumstances of the case that the witness would feel intimidated should he appear to give evidence at the trial.

Procedural considerations

13.05 Applications for the use of special measures are made under the Criminal Procedure Rules 2005 Part 29. Although applications can be made by either the prosecution or the defence, defence applications are rarer.

A special measure may not be taken by a court unless the Secretary of State has made the measure available to the court in which proceedings will take place. The special measures, which may be available, are as follows:

(a) screening the witness from the accused. The screen used must not prevent the witness from being seen and being able to see the magistrates, the legal representatives and any interpreter or other person appointed to assist the witness. It will be good practice for the court's legal adviser to remind the magistrates that no adverse inference should be drawn merely from the fact that the screen has been permitted to ensure the quality of the witness's evidence (*R v T* [2000] All ER (D) 1805). Section 32 covers the position of a trial on indictment with a jury;

(b) allowing the witness to give evidence via a live video link. Such links are available in Crown Court venues and in magistrates' court centres throughout England and Wales. Youth Courts are equipped to deal with evidence through a television link but, where a Youth Court gives leave for such evidence to be given and suitable facilities for receiving the evidence are not available at any courthouse in which the court can lawfully sit, then the court may sit for the purposes of the whole or part of those proceedings at any place in which such facilities are available and which has been appointed for the purpose by the justices acting for the local justice area for which that court acts;

(c) in sexual cases or cases involving intimidation clearing the public from the court while the witness testifies. Clearing the court will not include the accused, legal representatives, interpreters and at least one media representative;

(d) the wearing of wigs and gowns may be dispensed with in the Crown Court;

(e) a video recording of an interview of the witness may be admitted as evidence in chief of that witness and the court must consider, having regard to all the circumstances, that it is in the interests of justice for the recording or part of it should be admitted or not;

(f) cross-examination and re-examination of the witness may be videotaped in advance of the trial. This direction would mean that all the evidence of a child could be given and recorded pre-trial. Any such recording must be made in the hearing and sight of the magistrates, legal representatives and the accused must be able to hear and see any such examination and communicate with his legal representatives(YJCEA 1999, s 28);

(g) using an interpreter or other intermediary for the purpose of examining the witness; it is worth noting that in cases where the defendant can speak English but the parent/guardian does not the court may make arrangements for an interpreter to attend the Youth Court to interpret for the parent/guardian. The Costs in Criminal Cases (in General) Regulations 1986 provides authority for a court to pay for an interpreter required by a parent or guardian of the youth when the court considers the expense properly incurred.

    (h)   allowing the witness to use an aid to communication such as a signboard.

A party to the proceedings may make an application for the court to give a direction or the court may raise the issue of its own motion. The first step is for the court to determine that the witness is eligible. The court must examine whether any of the special measures available (or a combination of them) would be likely to improve the quality of the evidence given by the witness. In deciding whether to make a special measures direction the court must take into account all the circumstances of the case, any views expressed by the witness and whether the measure or measures proposed might tend to inhibit evidence being effectively tested by a party to the proceedings.

The application must be in writing using the prescribed form (CPR 2005, r 29.1(1)). Part A of the form must be completed for all applications and, where the application is for evidence to be given by TV link, Part B must also be completed. Part C is used for video-recorded evidence and Part D for the use of an intermediary.

Where the applicant proposes to tender only part of the video recording of an interview with a witness, the application must also be accompanied by those parts of the interview which it is not proposed to tender in evidence and by a statement of the circumstances in which such video recordings were made giving all the details outlined above.

Any application should be made within 28 days after the date on which the defendant first appeared and was brought before a court on information for the offence; but that period may be extended before or after it expires on application in writing specifying the grounds of the application CPR 2005 (r.29.1(14).

Any party who receives a copy of the application must within 14 days of service of that notice notify the applicant and the appropriate officer of the court in writing stating if he:

    (a)   disputes that the witness is eligible for assistance by virtue of s 16 or 17 of the 1999 Act,

    (b)   disputes that any of the special measures available would be likely to improve the quality of evidence given by the witness or that such measures (or a combination of them) would be likely to maximise the quality of that evidence, and

    (c)   opposes the granting of a special measures direction.

Where the application relates to the admission of a video recording, a party who receives a recording must provide the information required by rule 29.7(7) (see below).

After the expiry of 14 days from receipt of the application the court will determine whether the application may be dealt with without a hearing, or at a hearing at which the applicant and such other party or parties as the court may direct can be represented. The appropriate officer of the court shall notify the applicant and where necessary any other parties of the time and place of any such hearing. After the hearing the court shall within three days notify the parties of the decision (CPR 2005, r 29.1(13)).

If the court is satisfied that the applicant was unable to make an application in time under r 29.1 it may entertain an application orally at the trial or indeed may raise the issue of special measures of its own motion (r.29.3).

A copy of an application must be sent to the appropriate officer in the Youth Court and all other parties to the proceedings. The proper officer of the court must be in receipt of the application within 28 days of the date on which the defendant first appears before the court charged with the offence or within 14 days of the defendant entering a not guilty plea to the charges (r 29.1). Such a time-limit may be extended on application to a single justice (r 29.2). The rules then provide 14 days for the other parties to serve a notice of opposition to the application. Where no such notice is served, a direction for special measures may be given without a court hearing. However, where the court is aware the direction will be opposed a hearing must be held.

Where leave to use videotape evidence is given the procedure at the trial is relatively straightforward if somewhat restrictive. The child witness must be called by the party tendering the video evidence, but that witness may only be examined in chief on any matter which, in the opinion of the court, has not been dealt adequately with in his recorded testimony (YJCEA 1999, s 27(5)). Where video-recorded evidence is produced by the defence, the rules of advanced disclosure that apply to the prosecution do not come into effect and any such video may be served on the prosecution at the end of their case (r 29.7).

Where the application for special measures direction includes a video recording of an interview of a witness that is to be admitted as evidence in chief, the application must be accompanied by the video recording that is to be tended in evidence (r 29.7). Various other procedural matters are dealt with in r 29.7, including the need for the defendant to be identified by name together with the offence with which he is charged. The witness in respect of whom the application is made must also be identified by name and date of birth and a statement must be included giving the date on which the video recording was made, at what point in the recording an oath was administered, and a statement by the applicant that the witnesses are either available for cross-examination or unavailable for cross-examination and the parties have agreed that there is no need for the witness to be cross-examined. The applicant's statement should also disclose the circumstances in which the video recording was made and the date on which it was disclosed to the other party. Various other technical details are required and parties seeking to produce evidence in chief by way of video must comply closely with the rules to ensure that the equipment and the procedures are bona fide.

Rule 29.8 deals with expert evidence in connection with any application connected with a special measures direction. The party who proposes to produce such evidence must furnish the other party with the statement in writing of any finding or opinion that he proposes to produce, not less than 14 days before the trial date. These provisions may be rendered obsolete by the new disclosure regime under the CJA 2003.

The court has power to discharge or vary the special measures direction and, where the court has previously refused an application, it may be renewed if there's a material change in circumstances (r 29.5). Whenever it makes a direction varying or refusing an application for directions the justices must give their reasons for so doing and those reasons must be entered in the register of proceedings.

It should be noted that these provisions only apply in the criminal jurisdiction. Civil applications for anti-social behaviour orders and complaints under the dangerous dog legislation will not qualify for the use of special measures.

Sexual offences

13.06   Certain sexual offences in the Youth Court may be designated as grave crimes in accordance with PCC(S)A 2000, s 91. One such offence is the crime of rape or sexual penetration. The Sexual Offences Act 1993 abolished the presumption of the criminal law that a boy under the age of

14 was incapable of sexual intercourse. Consequently if the prosecution can prove that penile penetration took place without the consent of the victim, a juvenile above the age of 10 years may be convicted of rape. It follows that a juvenile may also be convicted of assault by penetration and sexual assault. Note, however, that child sex offences (Sexual Offences Act 2003, ss 9-15) although primarily aimed at adults, may be charged in the case of a juvenile offender by virtue of SOA 2003, s 13. The SOA 2003 makes special provision for young offenders found guilty of certain sexual offences, namely those in the 'ostensibly consensual' category. The maximum penalty is reduced to five years' custody in the case of a juvenile instead of 14 years. An alternative in such a case, where the ages of the parties are close and the acts were consensual, would be to draw the matter to the attention of the local authority with a view to care proceedings being commenced.

The age of the offender will also be significant in deciding venue and in the sentencing exercise in relation to non-consensual offences, where no special sentencing provisions have been provided for in the legislation. Its significance is particularly acute in relation to the strict liability offences such as 'rape of a child under 13', where the maximum penalty is life imprisonment, especially if an offender is very young and the disparity in age between the offender and the victim is very small.

Section 44(1) of the Children and Young Persons Act 1933 provides that every court dealing with a child or young person, as an offender or otherwise 'shall have regard to the welfare of the child or young person'. The youth and immaturity of an offender must always be potential mitigating factors for the courts to take into account when passing sentence. However, where the facts of a case are particularly serious, the youth of the offender will not necessarily mitigate the appropriate sentence.

This means that, although rape is likely to trigger the grave crimes procedure, the SGC's guidelines on sexual offences mean that some serious sexual offences including rape or sexual penetration may remain suitable for trial in the Youth Court (see **5.07**). In such cases the court needs to consider the protocol for rape cases in the Youth Court issued by the Senior Presiding Judge in November 2007.

The protocol only applies to trials of rape offences in the Youth Court. It suggests that, in such cases, a Crown Court judge with an authorisation to try serious sexual offences should use his powers under s 66 of the

Courts Act 2003 (which effectively allow him to sit with all the powers of district judge) and sit in the Youth Court to hear the trial. Should there be a finding of guilt, it is highly desirable that the judge deals with the sentence.

If however the offence of rape, assault by penetration or sexual assault is alleged to be committed against a complainant under the age of 13, these are matters punishable with life imprisonment or 14 years in the case of an adult, which are likely to be designated a grave crime and committed to the Crown Court.

Following a conviction the court will need to carefully consider the Sentencing Guidelines Council's definitive guidelines on the Sexual Offences Act 2003. This came into force in May 2007 and applies to any offence sentenced on or after that date. Part 7 of the guidelines specifically deals with the sentencing of young offenders where the offences being dealt with (Sexual Offences Act 2003, ss 9 12) have a lower maximum sentence than in the case of an adult. In specific sexual offences the Youth Court must bear in mind the statutory requirement for a young offender to notify the police of his address for inclusion on the sex offenders register. The main offences requiring automatic registration in the case of the juvenile are those under ss 1, 2, 4, 5, 6 and 15 of the Act. Other sections do not require an automatic registration in the case of a juvenile. The statute only requires registration where there has been a 12-month sentence of imprisonment and the case of (:*R v Slocombe* [2005] EWCA Crim 2997 makes it clear that in the case of a juvenile this means a two-year detention and training order as only the detention part is to be regarded as imprisonment. A reprimand or warning will no longer automatically be caught by the Sex Offenders Act 2003 obliging the offender to notify the police of that name and address for inclusion on the register.

Since being brought into force in July 2008, s 140 of the Criminal Justice and Immigration Act creates a presumption in favour of releasing information to members of the public in relation to sex offenders but only where there is reasonable cause to believe that an offender poses a risk of serious harm to children or a particular child and that such disclosure is necessary to protect children from that harm.

Evidential problems

13.07 Although it will be extremely unusual for a juvenile to be unrepresented when charged with a sexual offence it is important to note that no defendant charged with the sexual offence may cross-examine *in person* a 'protected witness'. A protected witness is either the complainant in connection with that offence or in connection with any other offence charged in the proceedings or an alleged witness to the commission of the offence and is a child who falls to be cross-examined after giving evidence in chief by video recording or any other way (YJCEA 1999, ss 34 and 35). For the purposes of these sections 'child' has a special meaning and will encompass a person under the age of 14 where the offence charged is kidnapping, false imprisonment and offences under s 1 or 2 of the Child Abduction Act 1984 or an offence under s 1 of the Children and Young Persons Act 1933, or any offence involving an assault, injury or threat of injury. In respect of offences under the Protection of Children Act 1978 and Part 1 of the Sexual Offences Act 2003 the definition of child simply means a person under the age of 17.

When neither s 34 nor s 35 applies the prosecutor may make an application to the court for a direction that the witness be protected or the court may raise the issue of its own motion. The court may give a direction prohibiting the accused from cross-examining, or further cross-examining, the witness in person but only if satisfied it would not be contrary to the interests of justice and the witness' evidence is likely to be diminished if the cross-examination is conducted by the accused in person and would be improved by the making of a direction.

Before taking this step the court must have regard to the views of the witness, the nature of the likely questions to be asked, the behaviour of the accused during the proceedings, the relationship between the witness and the accused, whether any person other than the accused has been charged in the proceedings with the sexual offence or been made subject to a direction under s 34 or s 35. Whether the court makes such a direction or refuses an application for a direction or discharges such a direction it must give its reasons for so doing and enter them in the register of the proceedings. When a direction is made preventing the accused from cross-examining the complainant or protected witness in person the court must of course ensure that the defendant is offered legal representation. If the defendant fails during a period specified by the court to arrange for legal representation the court must consider whether it is necessary in the interests of justice for the witness to be cross-examined by a legal representative appointed to represent the interests of the accused. If it is necessary the court itself will appoint a qualified legal representative to conduct the cross-examination. A person so appointed is designated an officer of the court and shall not be responsible to the accused (YJCEA 1999, s 38(5)).

The Youth Justice and Criminal Evidence Act 1999 also prohibits the introduction of evidence or the asking of questions in cross-examination by or on behalf of the accused about the sexual behaviour of the complainant. Again the restriction applies to persons charged with a sexual offence but the definition in this case is found in s 62 of the Act. Sexual offence means any offence under Pt 1 of the Sexual Offences Act 2003 (YJCEA 1999, s 41).

The court may grant leave for questions relating to the sex life of the complainant in one of four situations but only where a refusal of leave might result in the court reaching an unsafe conclusion on any relevant issue in the case. The court must also be satisfied that the evidence in question is relevant to one of the four issues. The first situation is where the issue to which the evidence is relevant is something other than the victim's consent. The second is where the issue is consent, and the evidence relates to the complainant's sexual behaviour which is alleged to have taken place at or about the same time as the event which is the subject matter of the charge. The third relates to the issue of consent where the evidence concerns earlier behaviour of the complainant that is alleged to be so similar to the accused's version of events that the similarity cannot reasonably be explained as a coincidence. The final situation is where the prosecution itself has led evidence about the complainant's sex life, and the accused wishes to explain or rebut the evidence by questioning (see *R v F (Complainant's sexual history)* (2005) Times, 16 March, CA).

The court will have to be aware of any possible infringement of Article 6 of the European Convention on Human Rights when dealing with such applications. However, the court must weigh up the overall fairness of the trial and balancing the effect of such cross-examination on the victim against the need of the defendant to challenge the character or credibility of the complainant. A defendant will not be precluded by s 41(3)(a), where his defence is a belief in consent by the complainant, from adducing evidence that they had recently taken part in sexual activity together. However, such evidence is admissible only in relation to the defendant's belief and not in relation to whether the complainant in fact consented (*R v Y* (15 January 2001, unreported), CA).

Reporting restrictions

13.08 The Youth Justice and Criminal Evidence Act 1999, s 44 sets out the restrictions on reporting alleged offences involving persons under the age of 18. It is important to note that the restrictions in criminal proceedings start at police investigation stage. Reporting restrictions are dealt with in detail in Chapter 6.

DEFENDANT'S BAD CHARACTER

13.09 Application may be made to admit evidence that the defendant has a bad character in the sense that he has criminal convictions or has otherwise misbehaved, which is defined in CJA 2003, s 98 as 'misconduct'. The definition of bad character therefore is wide enough to apply to conduct arising out of a conviction or where there has been an acquittal and, in the case of a person who has been charged with another offence, and trial is pending, the use of the evidence relating to that charge in the current proceedings. Misconduct is defined as the commission of any offence or other reprehensible behaviour. Reprehensible conduct must be looked at objectively, taking account whether a particular kind of behaviour could be regarded as reprehensible by the public. It is important to note that the court must not convict the defendant only because he has a bad character. The court is exercising a judgment, or a determination, as to whether the defendant's bad character is relevant to an important matter in issue between him and the prosecution. In making the decision the court is allowed certain latitude, but where the judgment is plainly wrong the decision will be overturned on appeal. The appeal courts have found it difficult to give definitive guidance because the decisions will be made on the factual basis found by the lower court and, as such, that decision will be largely individual in its nature. It is important that the court gives full and detailed reasons therefore for granting or refusing applications relating to bad character.

An exception to the rule that the court cannot convicted on bad character alone is similar fact evidence where there may be no direct evidence that the defendant committed the offence charged, but the prosecution rely *solely* on evidence of bad character in the form of evidence that the defendant has committed other similar offences.

Detailed discussion of evidential points is outside the scope of this work and readers are urged to have regard to the statutory provisions, namely ss 98 112 of the Criminal Justice Act 2003. The following guidance does however provide a framework for the making of decisions and the giving of advice.

Evidence of bad character may be admitted through one of the following gateways:

    (a) all parties to the proceedings have agreed to it;

    (b) the defendant has given evidence of his own bad character or been asked questions by his barrister/solicitor that brought it up;

    (c) it is important in order to understand other evidence in the case either in part or case as a whole;

    (d) it may help to resolve an important issue that has arisen between the prosecution and the defendant;

    (e) the evidence has substantial probative value in that it may help to resolve an important issue that has arisen between the defendant and his co-defendant;

    (f) the prosecution may adduce the evidence correct a false impression given by the defendant;

    (g) the defendant has made an attack on another's character.

Only if one or more of cases (a) to (f) above apply may the court use the evidence of the defendant's bad character for the particular purpose(s) outlined in the statute.

If (f) alone applies, and it is disputed that the defendant has given a false impression, the court must decide first if a false impression has been given. If they are unsure that the defendant has given a false impression, the evidence of his bad character should be disregarded altogether.

The court may use the evidence of the defendant's bad character by taking it into account when deciding whether or not the defendant's evidence was truthful. A person with a bad character may be less likely to tell the truth, but it does not follow that he is incapable of doing so. In some cases, for example (d) above, the defendant may argue that his character means that he is more likely to be telling the truth.

The court may also take evidence of bad character into account when deciding whether or not the defendant committed the offence charged. This is a double-edged sword; the prosecution may rely on the defendant's propensity to commit offences of a certain kind as showing that he is more likely to be guilty. The defence however may rely on the differences between his previous convictions and the offence charged as showing that he is less likely to be guilty.

Detailed guidance was provided by the Court of Appeal in the case of *R v Hanson* [2005] EWCA Crim 824, which may be summarised as follows:

(a) Parliament's intention in passing the legislation was to assist in the evidence-based conviction of the guilty, without putting those who are not guilty at risk of conviction by prejudice.

(b) If a propensity to commit the offence is to be relied upon (ss 101(1)(d) and 103(1)(a)) there are three questions to be considered:

    (i) whether the history of convictions establishes a propensity to commit offences of the kind charged;

    (ii) whether that propensity makes it more likely that the defendant committed the offence charged; and

    (iii) whether it is just to rely on convictions of the same type and, in any event, whether the proceedings would be unfair if they were admitted.

(c) Where propensity to untruthfulness is relied upon (ss 101)(1)(d) and 103(1)(b)) this is not the same as propensity to dishonesty. Previous convictions (whether for dishonesty or otherwise) are only likely to show propensity to be untruthful where truthfulness is in issue, for example where the offence committed shows a propensity for untruthfulness by making false representations.

(d) Where an attack on the character of another person is made by the defendant, s 101(1)(g) may be relied upon. The court may rely on the pre-2003 authorities and s 106 of the Act to assess whether such an attack has been made.

(e) The Court of Appeal will generally only interfere with the court's judgement if it exercises its discretion in a manner that is plainly *Wednesbury* unreasonable.

(f) The Crown needs to decide at the time of giving notice of the application whether it proposes to rely simply on the fact of conviction or also upon the circumstances of the conviction. It is generally expected that the relevant circumstances of previous convictions will be agreed.

(g) In any case in which evidence of bad character is admitted to show propensity either to commit offences or to be untruthful the legal advisor should advise the magistrates that:

    (i) they should not conclude that the defendant is guilty or untruthful merely because he has convictions;

    (ii) although the convictions might show a propensity, this does not mean that he committed the offence or has been untruthful in this case;

    (iii) whether they in fact show a propensity is for them to decide;

    (iv) they must take into account what a defendant has said about his previous convictions; and

    (v) although they are entitled, if they find propensity is shown, to take this into account when determining guilt, propensity is only one relevant factor and they must assess its significance in the light of all the other evidence in the case.

The overriding factor for Youth Court justices to bear in mind is that bad character cannot by itself prove that the defendant is guilty. Where an application to admit bad character is made, a defendant may apply to have such evidence excluded under sub-s (d) or (g) (where the evidence is relevant to an issue in the case between the prosecution and the defendant or has become admissible because of the defendant attack on another person).

In either of these circumstances the court must not admit such evidence if it appears to it that its admission would have an adverse effect on the fairness of the proceedings and that it ought to be excluded. In applying the test the court is directed to take account, in particular, the length of time that has expired since the previous events and the current charges.

This test in s 101(3) is designed to reflect the existing position under s 78 PACE 1984, whereby the judge or magistrates assess the probative value of the evidence to the issue in the case and its prejudicial effect if admitted. Balancing these factors evidence will be excluded if it would be unfair to allow it to be admitted.

However, the test to be applied under s 101(3) CJA 2003 is stricter than that under s 78 PACE 1984 where the court *may* refuse to admit the evidence. The 2003 Act states that the court *must* not admit such evidence if it would have an adverse effect on the fairness of the proceedings.

Where the court makes a relevant ruling it must state its reasons for doing so and, if it is a magistrate's court, it must cause the ruling and the reasons for it to be entered in the court register.

Introducing evidence of non-defendant's bad character

13.10 Evidence of the bad character of a person other than the defendant is admissible if, and only if:

(a) it is important explanatory evidence; or

(b) it has substantial probative value in relation to a matter which is (i) a matter in issue in the proceedings, and (ii) is of substantial importance in the context of the case as a whole; or

(c) all parties to the proceedings agree to the evidence being admissible.

The evidence may also be adduced to show the complainant had a propensity to act in the way asserted by the defendant.

Procedural issues

13.11 A prosecutor who wants to introduce evidence of a defendant's bad character or who wants to cross-examine a witness with a view to eliciting that evidence, under s 101 of the CJA 2003, must give notice in the form set out in the Practice Direction to the court and all other parties to the proceedings at the same time as the prosecutor complies or purports to comply with s 3 of the Criminal Procedure and Investigations Act 1996 and CPR 2005, r 35.4.

A party who wants to introduce evidence of a non-defendant's bad character or who wants to cross-examine a witness with a view to eliciting that evidence must, under s 100 of the CJA 2003, apply in the form set out in the Practice Direction. The application must be received by the court officer and all other parties to the proceedings not more than 14 days after the prosecutor has complied or purported to comply with s 3 of the Criminal Procedure and Investigations Act 1996 (initial disclosure by the prosecutor), or disclosed the previous convictions of that non-defendant, or as soon as reasonably practicable, where the application concerns a non-defendant who is to be invited to give (or has given) evidence for a defendant.

The prosecution may oppose the application by giving notice in writing not more than 14 days after receiving the application (CPR, r 35.3).

PROBLEMS CONNECTED WITH AGE

Under 10 years

13.12 A child below the age of 10 years is under the age of criminal responsibility and cannot be guilty of an offence. A juvenile, whether under the age of 10 or not, may be the subject of care proceedings brought under the Children Act 1989. Alternatively, the local authority may apply to the family proceedings court for a child safety order where a child has committed an act which would have constituted an offence if the child was 10 years or over. Care proceedings and applications for child safety orders are non-criminal applications normally brought by a local authority, whenever they believe that a court order is needed to ensure the juvenile's proper care and control. Such applications are made to a family court and are therefore outside the scope of this work.

Between 10 and 14 years

13.13 A juvenile within the age group of 10 to 13 inclusive is referred to as a child (CYPA 1933, s 107).

The Crime and Disorder Act 1998, s 34 abolished the rebuttable presumption in criminal law that a child below the age of 14 years could not be guilty of a criminal offence. The Court of Appeal clarified, in *R v T* [2008] EWCA Crim 815, that there is no authority for the existence of a separate defence from the presumption abolished by Parliament.

Between 14 and 18 years

13.14 A juvenile who has attained the age of 14 but is under 18 years is referred to as a young person (CYPA 1933, s 107 as amended). However, there are specific exceptions where 'young person' means someone who has attained the age of 14 but is under 17 years. These exceptions are referred to at the appropriate parts of the text.

Throughout the text, the description 'juvenile' is used to include both children and young persons, unless it is necessary to differentiate between them.

16- and 17-year-olds

13.15 Although 16- and 17-year-olds are not referred to as a specific group in any legislation, they are set apart from other juveniles in a number of important respects. First, they may attend court on their own without a parent. Second, a number of orders and sentences can only be made in respect of 16- and 17-year-olds. Finally, in respect of 17-year-olds only, they are still treated as adults for the purposes of the Bail Act and remand hearings. These differences are dealt with fully in the previous chapters and it is convenient to refer to the group of 16- and 17-year-olds as 'youths'.

The term 'juvenile' usually refers to any young person between the ages of 10-17 years to describe anyone whose case would normally be heard in the Youth Court. Note however that for the purposes of arrest, detention and charge under the Police and Criminal Evidence Act 1984 the term refers to a person of 10-16 years.

The term young offender has no legal definition and may refer to any person aged 10-20 who has offended against the criminal law. A persistent young offender is another term without statutory definition. The definition ascribed to it by the Home Office in the context of speeding up youth justice is 'a young person aged 10-17 who has been sentenced … on three separate occasions for one or more recordable offences'. The term can be found again in relation to the use of detention and training orders where the court is restricted in the use of those orders for an offender under the age of 15, unless the court considers he is a persistent offender. The Home Office definition does not apply here and courts must decide on the definition of persistence depending on the individual circumstances of the case and any guidance given by the higher courts.

Attaining adulthood

13.16   The Magistrates Courts Act 1980, s 24(1), states that 'where a person under the age of 18 appears or is brought before a magistrates' court on an information charging him with an indictable offence other than homicide, he shall be tried summarily unless one of the exceptions in the section applies'. *Note that CJA 2003, Sch 3 will amend procedures when fully in force.*

The initial problem with a 17-year-old is which court he is to appear in or to be brought before. This is a decision which the prosecution must take. It is submitted that the advice given by Donaldson LJ in *R v Amersham Juvenile Court, ex p Wilson* [1981] QB 969, is still pertinent (despite the main body of that judgment being disapproved of by the House of Lords in *Re Daley* [1983] 1 AC 347, HL). He suggested that, those who arrest and charge or lay an information against persons who are in the juvenile/adult borderline age group should take all reasonable steps to find out exactly when they will attain the age of 18. If they are to be brought or summoned to appear before a court for the first time on a date when they will have attained the age of 18, the court selected or specified in the summons should be an adult court. If they have not attained the age of 18, it should be a Youth Court.

Any charge preferred after the juvenile has attained the age of 18 should be directed to a magistrates' court. In *R v Chelsea Justices, ex p DPP* [1963] 3 All ER 657, a 16-year-old was charged with wounding before a juvenile (youth) court. The case was adjourned and during the adjournment he attained 17 (which at that time made him an adult). He was then charged with attempted murder arising out of the same facts. It was held that the latter charge had to be heard before an adult court and subsequently, of course, the then equivalent of the Crown Court, as the charge was one triable on indictment only.

Youth Courts must pay particular attention at all times to the age of the juvenile before them. This is especially important when he has attained 17 years of age. If the defendant is charged with a matter triable, in the case of an adult, on indictment only and the court is adjourning the case to a date beyond the defendant's 18th birthday, it should consider remanding for the purpose of committal proceedings to take place. Such an action would follow the judgment in *R v Newham Juvenile Court, ex p F (a minor)* [1986] 3 All ER 17, where a court was barred from committing a charge of robbery (which in the case of an adult is triable on indictment only) to the Crown Court on the juvenile's subsequent attainment of adulthood, because they had already agreed to hear a summary trial of the matter.

The provisions of CYPA 1933, s 48(1), provide a safety net for the court. The section states:

'A Youth Court sitting for the purpose of hearing a charge against … a person who is believed to be a child or young person may, if it thinks fit to do so proceed with the hearing and determination of the charge … notwithstanding that it is discovered that the person in question is not a child or young person.'

So in proceedings where there is some doubt and it subsequently appears that the juvenile has attained the age of 18 years, the hearing does not have to be aborted.

During proceedings

13.17   The attainment of 18 years of age by juveniles during the course of proceedings raises the question of the right to trial by jury. This is a question which troubled the higher courts at one time but was somewhat clarified by the case of *Re Daley* [1983] 1 AC 347, a House of Lords judgment. This was followed by *R v Lewes Juvenile Court, ex p Turner* (1985) 149 JP 186 and *R v Nottingham Justices, ex p Taylor* [1992] QB 557. In the latter case, it is suggested that the advice given in the *ex p Turner* case should be followed, where McNeal J suggested that where a person under the age of 18 pleads not guilty before a Youth Court, and the circumstances set out in the Magistrates Courts Act 1980, s 24 do not apply, when the Youth Court is not, there and then, able to take evidence in the trial which is to follow, the register of the court should be marked 'remanded for summary trial' [and] that would be the decisive and determinate date on which, for the purposes of the section, the defendant appeared or was brought before the court.

The position was explained thus in the *Nottingham Justices* case. If before a juvenile becomes 18, he appears before the court, whether it is for the first time or on remand, and he is charged with an indictable offence or an offence triable either way and:

(a)   he pleads not guilty when the charge is put directly to him; and

(b)   the mode of his trial is discussed with him or his legal representative, decided upon and the decision thereupon recorded in clear terms;

then whether evidence is called on that occasion or not, his becoming 18 before trial can have no effect upon the already determined mode of trial. In other words, he must be tried as though he was still 17 years of age. It is only if the mode of trial has not been determined that his becoming 18 years of age can have any material effect whatsoever.

This question was considered in the case of *R v West London Justices, ex p Siley-Winditt* [2000] Crim LR 926. The defendant was charged with violent disorder, an either-way offence, and appeared in the Youth Court when he was 17. He pleaded not guilty and the charge was adjourned to a pre-trial review but no date was fixed for the trial. At the pre-trial review the defendant attained 18. The district judge held that the Youth Court had determined the mode of trial when the plea was entered and therefore the Youth Court had jurisdiction. He declined to allow the defendant to elect trial in the Crown Court. The High Court upheld this decision even though the register of the court which took the plea and adjourned had not been marked 'remanded for summary trial'.

Mode of trial

13.18   It can be seen that if a young person charged with an either way offence in a Youth Court attains the age of 18 at any time before evidence is received, or he pleads guilty, or the court sets the matter down for summary trial, the court must give him a right to jury trial. The procedure for determining mode of trial is set out in MCA 1980, ss 18-22. *Note CJA 2003, Sch 3 as above.*

The first step is for the legal adviser to read, and if necessary explain, the charge to the adult defendant. The second step is to embark upon the plea before venue procedure. The procedure can be found in MCA 1980, s 17A. The legal adviser will explain to the defendant that he is to be asked to intimate a plea to the court. It must be explained that if a guilty plea is intimated that plea will normally be accepted and the case will proceed on the basis of an admission of guilt. However, if the defendant fails to intimate that plea or intimates a wish to plead not guilty the court must embark on a full mode of trial procedure. The defendant must be made aware of the court's powers to commit for sentence in the event that they find their own powers are insufficient to deal with the seriousness of the offence.

The full mode of trial procedure is a determination as to whether the offence appears more suitable to be heard by magistrates or by the Crown Court. In order to facilitate this determination, the court shall hear representations first from the prosecutor and second the defendant, as to which venue is more appropriate. The court is required to have regard to:

(a)   the nature of the case;

(b)   whether the circumstances make the offence one of a serious character;

(c)   whether the punishment which a magistrates' court would have power to inflict for the offence would be adequate; and

(d)   any other circumstances which appear to the court to make it more suitable for the offence to be tried in one way rather than the other (MCA 1980, s 19(3)).

'Any other circumstances' will not normally include such matters as previous convictions, as these do not relate to the offence but to the offender (*R v Colchester Justices, ex p North Essex Building Co Ltd* [1977] 3 All ER 567). An exception to the normal rule is the situation where the defendant is alleged to have committed a third or a further burglary of a dwelling house, in which case the offence itself becomes triable purely on indictment. This naturally involves the prosecutor informing the court about the defendant's previous convictions so that it may adopt the correct procedure. In that context the most recent case on whether previous convictions can be taken into account at a grave crime mode of trial is *R (Tullet) v Medway Magistrates' Court* [2003] EWHC Admin 2279, 167 JP 541.

The situation will be further clarified when the CJA 2003 is fully in force as it makes provision for previous convictions to be aired at mode of trial.

Magistrates, in deciding the mode of trial, should take into account all the other information which is available to them. If they decide to embark on summary trial, they may commit for sentence under PCC(S)A 2000, s 3, if on reconsideration of the seriousness of the offence the court believes that greater punishment should be inflicted than the Youth/ magistrates' court has power to impose (*R v North Sefton Magistrates' Court, ex p Marsh* [1994] Crim LR 865), The Lord Chief Justice has issued a Practice Note giving guidance to magistrates on mode of trial decisions. These are known as the *National Mode of Trial Guidelines* and are now found in, *Practice Direction (Criminal Proceedings: Consolidation)* [2002] 3 All ER 904. These guidelines will be relevant when considering the sort of aggravating factors that may make an either-way offence more suitable to be tried at the Crown Court rather than in a magistrates' court. The court may also be influenced by guidance given in the *National Sentencing Guidelines* and guidelines issued by the Sentencing Guidelines Council as to which cases are unsuitable for summary trial.

If the court considers the case more suitable to be heard in the Crown Court, the court must commit the defendant to that court.

Where the magistrates decide that the case is suitable to be heard in the magistrates' court, the 18-year-old must be told that:
  (a) it appears to the court more suitable for him to be tried summarily for the offence, and that he can consent either to be so tried or, if he wishes, to be tried by a jury; and
  (b) if he is tried and is convicted by the court he may be committed for sentence to the Crown Court under PCC(S)A 2000, s 3, if the

convicting court is of the opinion that the offence or the combination of the offence and other offences associated with it was so serious that greater punishment should be inflicted for the offence than the court has power to impose.

The 18-year-old must then be asked if he consents to trial before the magistrates or if he wishes to elect to be tried by a judge and jury at the Crown Court. If he consents to summary trial the magistrates will proceed to hear the case. If he elects trial by jury the court must transfer the case to the Crown Court unless the defendant makes a successful application for dismissal.

The mode of trial procedures described above are only applicable to the 18-year-old charged with an offence triable either way, the exception to this being the offence of criminal damage under the Criminal Damage Act 1971, s 1 or aggravated taking of a motor vehicle where damage under £5,000 is alleged. (Theft Act 1968, s 12A) In this case, if the damage alleged is less than £5,000 in value, the offence is triable summarily only. If the value is not clear to the court it must explain to the defendant that:

(a) he can, if he wishes, consent to be tried summarily for the offence and that if he so consents he will definitely be tried in that manner; and

(b) if he is tried summarily and convicted the maximum punishment will be either a fine or three months' imprisonment. The accused is then asked if he wishes to be tried summarily, and if he consents the court will proceed to hear the case. If he does not consent the offence must be treated as triable either way (MCA 1980, s 22(5)-(6)).

If the accused appears charged on the same occasion with two or more offences of criminal damage etc which constitute or form part of a series of offences of the same or a similar character, they shall be tried summarily if their aggregate value is less than £5,000 (MCA 1980, s 22(11)).

The 18-year-old in the Youth Court after a finding of guilt

13.19 When an 18-year-old consents to summary trial, after hearing evidence, the Youth Court may deal with the case to finality. Where evidence has been heard and the juvenile subsequently attains the age of 18, the court may proceed to a conviction. If the court convicts the defendant but he attains the age of 18 before an order is made, then CYPA 1963, s 29 still applies. Section 29 states that: 'Where proceedings in respect of a young person are begun for an offence and he attains the age of 18 before the conclusion of the proceedings, the court may deal with the case and make any order which it could have made if he had not attained that age.' This means that the 18-year-old may remain subject to any relevant Youth Court order.

This section applies equally in the Crown Court as it does in the Youth Court. This leaves the Crown Court with an option to sentence a young person committed to it to any of the available Youth Court orders if he attains the age of 18 during the course of the proceedings.

The main difference between the sentencing powers of the Youth Court and those of an adult court in respect of a person under 21 years of age is that the Youth Court may sentence to a detention and training order for up to 24 months. An adult magistrates' court is restricted in passing of a detention order in a young offenders institute to a six months maximum per offence or a 12 months maximum for two or more either-way offences.

Note that the reporting restrictions contained in CYPA 1933, s 49 no longer apply once a defendant reaches the age of 18 years (*DPP v Todd* [2003] EWHC 240 (Admin)).

THE IMPORTANCE OF AGE ON CONVICTION AND AT THE SENTENCING HEARING

13.20   Some sentencing options only become open to the court when the offender before them has attained a certain age. For example, no juvenile under the age of 15 may be sentenced to a detention and training centre order, unless the court certifies that they are a persistent young offender. Similar restrictions apply to requirements imposed on a youth rehabilitation order for intensive supervision and support or fostering, and an unpaid work requirement in a youth rehabilitation order may only be imposed on a 16- or 17-year-old (see Chapter 9 for details).

Care is particularly important where a detention and training order is contemplated. The statute is clear that the order is unavailable where 'a child or young person (that is to say, any person aged under 18) is *convicted* of an offence which is punishable with imprisonment in the case of a person aged 21 or over'. In *R v T (a juvenile)* [1979] Crim LR 588, a case involving a juvenile found guilty when 14 years old and subsequently committed to the Crown Court with a view to borstal training having attained the age of 15, the Crown Court held that the word 'conviction' should be construed as meaning the finding of guilt and not the date on which the case was finally disposed of. This point was reiterated in *R v Danga* [1992] QB 476 and *R v Starkey* [1994] Crim LR 380, CA, in connection with custodial sentences. These cases confirm that as a matter of statutory construction, for the purpose of sentence, the age of the offender was his age at the date of conviction or when the plea of guilty was made and accepted.

Although PCC(S)A 2000, s 9 gives a power to remit 18-year-olds to the adult court for sentence it is of little practical application. In *R v Cassidy* [2000] All ER (D) 1200 the defendant was 17 years old at the time of his conviction. He was not sentenced until he had attained the age of 18. The court held that a detention and training centre order was valid and would not be converted into detention in a young offenders institute. It is worth noting the effect of CPYA 1963, s 29 outlined above. Consequently, the court and advocates representing young people must pay due regard to the statute under which the court proposes to impose a particular sentence so as to ensure that the young person has attained the relevant age at the relevant time. See also *Aldis v DPP* [2002] EWHC 403 (Admin).

In terms of the approach to sentencing where a defendant crosses a relevant age threshold, ie between the date of commission of the offence and the date of conviction, the Court of Appeal have said that the starting point was the sentence the defendant would have been likely to receive if he had been sentenced at the date of the commission of the of offence: *R v Ghafoor* [2002] Crim LR 739, CA.

This case had been followed in *R v H* [2003] All ER (D) 143. Whilst it may be considered a 'settled principle', for sentencing purposes, that the age at the date of offence should be considered as the starting point, the Court of Appeal further considered this point in *R v Bowker* [2007] EWCA Crim 1608 and concluded that there is a need for flexibility. The defendant's age being a powerful but not the sole determining factor, there may be cases were the appropriate sentence required was a deterrent sentence, particularly as s 142 CJA 2003 applied to those convicted when 18 years old.

R v Robson [2006] EWCA Crim 1414 is authority for the important restriction on the Crown Court powers where an offender attains the age of 18 between committal for sentence and appearance before the judge under the 'dangerousness' provisions; the powers of the Crown Court are those that would be applicable to a 17-year-old.

JUVENILES APPEARING ALONE IN THE ADULT COURT

13.21 Where a juvenile appears alone before the adult court and the court, having no reason to believe that he is a juvenile, proceeds with the case, it is not prevented from hearing and determining the matter if it subsequently becomes known to the court that the person is in fact a juvenile. The adult courts' powers on a finding of guilt are limited by PCC(S)A 2000, s 8 to a discharge, a fine, or an order binding over the parent to exercise control over the juvenile. As noted above a referral order may also be made in appropriate circumstances.

The Children and Young Persons Act 1933, s 46(1), states that a joint charge against an adult and a juvenile 'shall' be heard by the adult court. Where the adult has absconded or cannot be traced it would be inappropriate to bring a juvenile before the adult court to stand trial alone. In such circumstances the prosecution should consider removing the joint element from the charge to allow the juvenile to appear or be brought before the Youth Court. The practice for most adult courts when faced with a juvenile charged jointly with an adult, but appearing alone, is to remand the juvenile to the Youth Court. It is important to appreciate, however, that the wording of s 46(1) is clear and unambiguous and no court could be criticised for keeping the juvenile before the adult court until it reached a stage when it was empowered to remit or deal with the juvenile.

In *R v Doncaster Justices, ex p Langfield* (1984) 148 JP 26, a juvenile jointly charged with adults failed to attend on the day upon which the co-accused were committed for trial to the Crown Court under the provisions of MCA 1980, s 6(2). He was subsequently brought to court and committed alone to join the co-accused in the Crown Court. On appeal against the validity of the transfer, the Divisional Court held that the decision to send for trial on indictment, taken under the provisions of MCA 1980, s 24, must be taken at a time when those jointly charged were together in court. Any subsequent committal proceedings need not necessarily be held in the presence of all the accused (See also *R v Coventry City Magistrates Courts, ex p M* [1992] Crim LR 810.).

Other examples of restrictions on the courts, which depend upon the age of the offender, occur relatively infrequently. They include the Contempt of Court Act 1981, s 12, which provides a general power for magistrates to commit to prison for contempt of court. The statutory restriction on the imposition of a sentence of imprisonment or the committal to prison of a person under 21 years of age applies (*R v Selby Justices, ex p Frame* [1992] QB 72) thereby making any such committal illegal. As a result the court's powers to deal with contempt by a young person under the age of 18 years are extremely limited (*R v Byas* [1995] Crim LR 439, CA).

Another such restriction is that placed upon the court who may wish to make an order of detention in default of payment of a fine or confiscation order. Again, due to the statutory restrictions, such an order may only be made on persons over the age of 18 years (*R v Basid* [1996] Crim LR 67).

GUILTY PLEA BY POST PROCEDURE

13.22   The Magistrates' Courts Act 1980, s 12 permits a defendant to enter a plea of guilty to minor summary offences without appearing before a court. This procedure is commonly used in road traffic cases. Although the MCA 1980, s 12, expressly excludes the use of the plea by post procedure in the Youth Court unless the juvenile has attained the age of 16 years.

Furthermore, if a guilty plea by letter is received by the clerk of the court in pursuance of s 12, and the offender was a child or young person, then if the court proceeds without reason or belief that the defendant is in fact a juvenile, he is deemed to have been an adult for the purpose of those proceedings (CYPA 1933, s 46(lA)).

Many 16- and 17-year-olds are now dealt with by fixed penalty ticket without court proceedings. See HOC 7/1997.

RECKLESSNESS

13.23 In cases involving recklessness there has been a change in emphasis in dealing with cases involving recklessness as an element.

The case of *R v Caldwell* [1982] AC 341, HL, established the definition of recklessness used for the past 20 years. Lord Diplock gave a model direction to juries setting down an objective test for such crimes as criminal damage and reckless driving. A different subjective test was set down in the case of *R v Cunningham* [1957] 2 QB 396, CCA for crimes of specific intent such as those under the Offences Against the Person Act 1861, ss 18 and 20.

In a more recent case of *DPP v A* [2000] All ER (D) 1247 two boys started a game in which they agreed to shoot at each other with air pistols. They wore cricket pads for protection and agreed to aim below the knee. A had suggested they wear crash helmets but none were available. During the game A fired a shot which hit his companion in the eye. A was charged with wounding his companion.

The question for the High Court was whether the prosecution had failed to prove beyond reasonable doubt that A had foreseen that his act of firing the air pistol would cause some physical harm. The court ruled that 'maliciously' for the purposes of s 20 of the Offences against the Person Act 1861 meant either actual intention or recklessness as to whether a particular type of harm might be done. It would be sufficient that only slight harm had been foreseen. In giving judgement the High Court applied the case of *R v Parmenter* [1991] 4 All ER 698 HL.

In *R v G & R* [2004] All ER 765, the House of Lords departed from *Caldwell*, saying that it made no allowance for a defendant's youth or lack of mental capacity. They stated that in a case of arson it was offensive to a sense of justice, and to the principle that a person should not be found guilty of a serious criminal offence unless he acted with the relevant *mens rea*, ie guilty intent.

In that case, the two defendants, aged 11 and 12 respectively, set fire to some newspaper and threw it under a wheelie bin believing it would burn out on the concrete floor of the yard. In fact the bin caught fire and then set buildings alight causing £1m worth of damage. The House of Lords said that a defendant could not be culpable under the criminal law of doing something to risk injury to another or damaging property if, due to his age or understanding, he genuinely did not perceive the risk.

Chapter 14

Anti-social behaviour orders in the Youth Court

14.01 An Anti-Social Behaviour Order (ASBO) can be made against anyone of 10 years or over. There are two types of order relevant to the Youth Court, an order on complaint (a free-standing order) and an order made ancillary to a sentence (or conditional discharge) imposed in criminal proceedings. It follows that an order may not be combined with an absolute discharge nor may it be imposed at the same time as the court defers sentence.

The behaviour or offences must have taken place or been committed after 1 April 1999, the commencement date of the legislation for the civil orders and for offences committed after 2 December 2002 for orders ancillary to sentences.

ORDERS ON COMPLAINT

The applicants

14.02 Only 'a relevant authority' may apply. They are defined as follows (CDA 1998, s 1(1A)):

  (a) the council for a 'local government area' (defined by s 1(12) as 'the area of a District Council');
  (b) the chief officer of police of any police force maintained for a police area;
  (c) the Chief Constable of the British Transport Police;
  (d) any person registered under the Housing Act 1996, s 1 as a social landlord who provides or manages any houses or hostel in a local government area;
  (e) a housing action trust established under the Housing Act 1988, s 62.

Consultation must take place before an application is made:
 (a) if the council intends to apply it must first consult the chief officer of police for the area;
 (b) if the chief officer of police intends to apply he must first consult the council for the area in which the proposed defendant resides or appears to reside;
 (c) any other relevant authority (unless a county council with no districts) who intends to apply must first consult both the council for the area in which the proposed defendant resides or appears to reside and the chief officer of police for the area.

The application itself is by way of complaint to the court whose commission area includes the local government area or police area concerned. The chief constable himself does not have to be the complainant (CDA 1998, s 1(3)).

Complaints are not matters assigned to the Youth Court under CYPA 1933, s 46, and so like complaints for bind overs (MCA 1980, s 115) and dangerous dog applications (Dogs Act 1871, s 2) the application must be heard by an adult court. This is somewhat academic as a Youth Court is only a specially constituted magistrates' court. The case of *V v United Kingdom and T v United Kingdom* (1999) 30 EHRR 121 set out the process for young people so as to avoid intimidation, distress and humiliation and ensure the involvement of the young person in that process.

It will be appropriate for proceedings to be conducted by Youth Court magistrates and to follow the Youth Court procedural rules (Practice Direction on the Composition of Benches [2006] 1All ER 886).The automatic press restrictions in the Youth Court do not apply nor do the restrictions on who can be present in court (see also **14.23–14.24**below).

The criteria

14.03 The court must be satisfied that the following conditions are both fulfilled:
 (a) the person against whom the order is sought ('the defendant') has acted in an anti-social manner, that is to say in a manner that caused or is likely to cause harassment, alarm or distress to one or more persons not of the same household as himself; and
 (b) such an order is necessary to protect 'relevant persons' from further anti-social acts by him.

Relevant persons are persons within the local government area of that council, if the council are the applicants. If the chief officer of police is the applicant they are persons within the police area.

If the Chief Constable of the British Transport Police is the applicant they are either:

(a) persons who are on or likely to be on 'policed premises' in a local government area. 'Policed premises' are, broadly speaking any railway land building structure or trains; (CDA 1998, s 1(12)) or

(b) persons who are in the vicinity of or likely to be in the vicinity of 'policed premises'.

If a social landlord or housing action trust is the applicant they are either:

(a) persons who are residing in or who are otherwise on or likely to be on premises provided or managed by the applicant; or

(b) persons who are in the vicinity of or likely to be in the vicinity of such premises.

The general rule about the time-limit for making complaints to the magistrates' court is contained in s 127 of the Magistrates' Courts Act 1980, namely: 'a magistrates' court shall not ...hear a complaint unless the ...complaint was made ...within six months from the time when the...matter of the complaint arose.' (See **14.11** below)

What the applicant must prove

14.04   The applicant must prove, in relation to the first criteria that an application for an ASBO under s 1(1)(a) of the Crime and Disorder Act 1998 is based on an allegation that the respondent has acted in a manner that 'was likely to cause harassment, alarm or distress to one or more persons not of the same household'.

It is not necessary to prove,

(a) any intent to cause harassment, etc, or

(b) where the conduct of a number of persons was involved, that the respondent was acting in concert with the others, or

(c) where harassment, etc, was likely to have been caused by the conduct of a number of people, including the respondent, that the respondent's conduct in isolation would have been of a sufficiently aggravated nature to have caused those effects (*Chief Constable of Lancashire v Potter* [2003] EWHC 2272, [2003]

42 LS Gaz R 31). When assessing the necessity for an order the court may take into account an act committed before the 1 April 1999 (the commencement of the legislation) (*Stevens v Southeast Surrey Magistrates' Court, Surrey Police* [2004] EWHC 1456 (Admin)).

The standard of proof required to satisfy the first limb is the criminal standard of proof, ie beyond reasonable doubt even though the proceedings are civil (so the justices have to be sure that the defendant has acted in an anti-social manner):.

In relation to the second criteria the court must be satisfied that such an order is necessary to protect persons from further anti-social acts by him:

'The inquiry under the second limb, namely that such an order is necessary to protect persons from further anti-social acts by him, does not involve a standard of proof: it is an exercise of judgement or evaluation'. (Per Lord Steyn in *R (on the application of McCann) v Crown Court at Manchester* [2003] 1 AC 787, HL)

and in assessing the necessity for an order the court may take into account acts committed before 1 April 1999 (the commencement of the legislation).

If both conditions are fulfilled the court may make an ASBO which prohibits the defendant from doing anything described in the Order.

Proceedings under s 1C are civil in nature and hearsay evidence is admissible. However, whether the defendant had acted in an anti-social manner has to be proved on the criminal standard of proof (see **14.14**). The second part of the application as to whether it was necessary to make an order to protect others from further anti-social behaviour was an exercise of judgement (*R (on the application of W) v Acton Youth Court* [2005] EWHC 954 (Admin)).

The High Court has held that where an ASBO is sought against a child, the magistrates must take into account the best interests of the child as a 'primary consideration' (*R (on the application of Kenny and M) v Leeds Magistrates' Court* [2004] 1 All ER 1333), when considering if an order is necessary.

Note this does not mean the *paramount consideration*, as the interests of the public are also a primary consideration.

An interesting point arose in the case of *R (M) v Sheffield Magistrates* [2004] EWHC Admin 1830 where a local authority applied for an ASBO against a child in its care and an issue arose as to how the interests of the child could be protected. The Administrative Court ruled that, although there was a conflict between a local authority discharging a duty that it owed to the residents and the locality affected by anti-social behaviour and the duty to act so as to promote the welfare of the child, which would lead it to hesitate before placing the child at risk of detention in custody, that did not disempower a local authority and preclude it from making an application for an ASBO.

The case also established that the solicitor having responsibility for the authority's ASBO application should not attend the meetings with the child's solicitor and social services representatives. Once a decision had been taken to apply for an ASBO there should be no contact on the issue between the ASBO team and the social services section without the child's solicitor being informed and consenting.

It should also be noted that an interim order should not be granted without notice and where there was no one present from social services. Furthermore, orders should contain prohibitions directed to anti-social behaviour and care should be taken not to include negative prohibitions that in truth amounted to mandatory orders to do something specific.

Civil Evidence

14.05 In these proceedings the Magistrates' Courts (Hearsay and Evidence in Civil Proceedings) Rules 1999 and the Civil Evidence Act 1995 will apply. The main effect of this is to allow for a statement made otherwise than by a person giving oral evidence to be tendered as evidence of the matters stated (Civil Evidence Act 1995, s 1(2)). The Rules require that a party who desires to give hearsay evidence at the hearing must serve a hearsay notice on the other party and the court not less than 21 days before the hearing. Such a notice must:

   (a) state that it is a hearsay notice;
   (b) identify the proceedings in which the hearsay evidence is to be given;
   (c) state that the party proposes to adduce hearsay evidence;
   (d) identify the hearsay evidence;
   (e) identify the person who made the statement which is to be given in evidence;

(f) state why that person will not be called to give oral evidence.

Such a notice may deal with hearsay evidence of more than one witness.

Failure to comply with the notice requirement will not affect the admissibility of the evidence but the court will take this into account when considering the weight which is given to that evidence. The time limits set may be altered by the court or a justices' clerk either on application or of its own motion. Where the facts of the case demand it the defendant must be given adequate time to prepare and to meet those allegations. Justices are entitled to expect that if there were a need for an adjournment an application would be made.

Hearsay evidence is admissible in accordance with the Civil Evidence Act 1995 but the court must carefully decide what weight to attach to it as it cannot be tested by cross-examination. The court must disregard any act of the defendant that he shows, presumably a legal burden on the balance of probabilities, was reasonable in the circumstances (CDA 1998, s 1(5)).

THE ORDER

14.06 Any restrictions can be attached to an order that are necessary for the purpose of protecting persons (whether 'relevant persons' or persons elsewhere in England and Wales) from further anti-social acts by the defendant. Although the court has to be satisfied that an ASBO is necessary to protect relevant persons, the prohibitions imposed need not be limited to those necessary for their protection but can include those necessary for the protection of persons elsewhere in England and Wales if relevant to the behaviour and incidents that comprise the anti-social behaviour.

Deciding what prohibitions are necessary involves the exercise of judicial discretion and judgement and, in view of the Human Rights Act 1998, the court must act fairly and proportionately. Prohibitions must be clear, easily understood and specific. They need not be confined to acts which are criminal in themselves but should be in terms that make it easy to determine and prosecute a breach. Positive requirements may not be imposed, only prohibitions. An order may be challenged on the ground that it is so vague that the respondent could have no certainty as to whether or not his actions would breach it (*R (M) v Sheffield Magistrates and Sheffield City Council* [2004] EWHC Admin 1051).

Courts must be vigilant to ensure that orders are clear, unequivocal and enforceable: see for example *R v McGrath* [2005] EWCA Crim 353.The respondent was prohibited from entering any car park within three counties, not to trespass on any land belonging to any person whether legal or natural, and not to possess in public any window hammer, screwdriver, torch or any tool or implement that could be used for breaking into motor vehicles. These prohibitions were determined as being too wide; as an example the phrase 'tool or implement' was difficult to determine and the prohibition on entering car parks would prohibit the respondent from accompanying someone to a supermarket for the purpose of food shopping.

In *DPP v T* [2006] All ER (D) 41 an ASBO was made prohibiting a juvenile from 'acting in an anti-social manner in the city of Manchester'. On subsequent conviction for another offence the prosecutor argued that the defendant had also breached his ASBO. The district judge questioned the validity of the order as the original requirements were vague and unclear. On appeal it was said that the court order should be treated as valid unless and until it was set aside. Additionally, as the subject of the ASBO could appeal against the order or apply for variation, it was wrong to treat the order as a nullity in the meantime.

The Court of Appeal gave the following guidance on making ASBOs in *R v Boness, R v Bebbington* [2005] EWCA Crim 2395:

   (a) An ASBO has to be precise and understandable to the offender so that the court can be satisfied that the defendant knows precisely what it is that he is prohibited from doing.
   (b) The purpose of an ASBO is not to punish. The order has to be necessary to protect persons from further anti-social acts by the defendant. Each separate direction prohibiting a person from doing a specified thing has to be necessary to protect persons from further anti-social acts by him. The use of an ASBO to punish a defendant is unlawful.
   (c) It follows that the court should not impose an order that prohibits a defendant from committing a specified criminal offence if the sentence that could be passed following conviction for the offence should be a sufficient deterrent.
   (d) Were the defendant to be liable, following conviction for the offence, to a custodial sentence, then an ASBO would add nothing other than to increase the sentence if the sentence for the offence is less than five years' custody. Logically, if the defendant is not

going to be deterred from committing the offence by a sentence of custody for his offending, the ASBO is unlikely to provide further deterrence and could not therefore be said to be 'necessary'. The court should not allow itself to be persuaded by the defendant's advocate to impose an ASBO when sentencing in the hope that the court would avoid the imposition of a custodial sentence. Better practice dictates that the court should decide the appropriate sentence and then move on to consider whether an ASBO should or should not been made after that sentence had been decided.

(e) The aim of an ASBO is to prevent anti-social behaviour, by enabling action to be taken before the anti-social behaviour it is designed to prevent takes place. A court should therefore normally refrain from imposing an order that prohibits a defendant from committing a specified criminal offence.

(f) The terms of the order also have to be proportionate to the risk of further anti-social behaviour. That was particularly important where an order might interfere with offenders' rights under the European Convention on Human Rights.

In terms of the general principles, the whole of the procedure should take place in the presence of the defendant; to whom it must be explained; the findings of fact giving rise to the making of the order must be recorded; the exact terms of the order must be pronounced in open court; and the written order must accurately reflect the order as pronounced (*R v P (Shane Tony)* [2004] EWCA Crim 287). There is no harm in reminding offenders that certain matters constitute criminal offences, by including such conduct in the order, but only comparatively minor offences should be expressly so included (*R v Parkin* (2004) Times, 19 February, CA).

The date of an ASBO, for the purposes of the Crime and Disorder Act 1998, s 1, is the date on which it was pronounced orally in court, and not the date on which the written order came into existence consequent upon that commencement (*Walking v DPP* (2003) 167 JP 65).

Length of order

14.07 The order can be for a fixed period of not less than two years or until further order.

Either the applicant or the defendant may apply by complaint to the court which made the order for its variation or discharge *but* it cannot be discharged within two years of its service on the defendant unless both parties consent (CDA 1998, s 1(7), (8) and (9)).

Interim orders

14.08 Interim orders are dealt with in CDA 1998, s 1D and may be made following an application by a relevant authority or by the court, either of its own volition or at the request of the prosecution. The court must consider that it is just to make such an order pending the determination of the final hearing. This power only exists once the offender has been convicted of the offence to which the application for the order on conviction relates. An interim order is a requirement that prohibits the defendant from doing anything prescribed in that order.

The prohibitions which may be imposed are those which may be included in a final ASBO and an order may be made if the court, before determining the full application, considers it just to do so. This clearly involves the exercise of judicial discretion and although the order may be of limited duration the penalty for a breach is up to five years' imprisonment as with the final order.

The procedure for making an interim ASBO is found in s 1D of the Crime and Disorder Act 1998 and is by way of application without notice as prescribed by r 5 of the Magistrates' Courts (Anti social Behaviour Orders) Rules 2002 (SI 2002/2784).

There is however no obligation on the court at this stage to find that the evidence in support of a full order 'discloses an extremely strong prima facie case' (*R(M) v Secretary of State for Constitutional Affairs and Lord Chancellor* (2004) Independent, 25 March, CA).

An interim order must be for a fixed period but can be reviewed. It may also be varied or discharged on the complaint of either the applicant or the defendant but shall, in any event, come to an end when the full application is determined (CDA 1998, s 1D(4)(b) and (c)).

Circumstances may arise where an interim order is deemed just but as a minimum the court should consider all the circumstances of the case, such as the nature, seriousness and frequency of the anti-social acts alleged against the defendant. The court should ascertain what persons require protection from him and whether they are vulnerable, and then decide whether the need to protect them is so immediate that an interim order is justified.

The power to make an interim order under s 1D arises when an application is made by the prosecutor, or the court considers making an order of its own motion, following the offender's conviction for an offence. However the court should bear in mind the case of *R v Lawson* [2008] EWCA Crim 416, which stated that where there is a need to control an individual's behaviour post-conviction but prior to sentence, bail conditions should be preferred. Interim orders may, however, be useful, in a situation where the substantive ASBO hearing is adjourned to a date after sentence in accordance with CDA 1998, s 1C(4A).

Following the decision in *R v Boness* [2005] EWCA Crim 2395, a request for an ASBO under CDA 1998, s 1C cannot be made until after sentence.

Ex parte interim order

14.09   The clerk to the justices can authorise an application for an interim order to be made without notice being given to the defendant (Magistrates:' Courts (Anti Social Behaviour Order) Rules 2002, r.5). Given the nature of prohibitions attaching to an ASBO and the consequences of breach, there would have to be clear and compelling reasons for both authorising and granting an *ex parte* application. Only in cases of clear and present urgency, where the court is satisfied that immediate protection to persons or property is required should an order be entertained.

Exparte orders are served on the defendant at the same time as the application for the ASBO itself and do not take effect until served. If not served within seven days they cease to have effect.

Exparte interim orders should be given as early a returndate as practicable to allow the defendant an opportunity to be heard quickly.

The relevant considerations were discussed in *R v Leeds Magistrates' Court and Leeds Council* [2004] EWCA Civil 213. The Court of Appeal, dismissing A's appeal against an interim ASBO, held:
   (a)   Although it is unusual for a court in this country to make an order against a person who has not been given notice of the proceedings, that course is adopted when it is necessary to do so, and subject to safeguards which enable the person affected at an early stage to have the order reviewed or discharged.
   (b)   The more intrusive the order the more the court will require proof that it is necessary that it should be made, and made in the particular

form sought, but there is nothing intrinsically objectionable about the power to grant an interim ASBO without notice.

It is important to note that an interim ASBO made without notice is ineffective until served and, when made as required in the standard form, it does make provision for all parties to attend at court, either on a return date or on a date fixed for the hearing of the full application. If the former, then it would be open to the court to re-consider the order, either to vary it or discharge it, if it considered that to be the appropriate course. The court were told by counsel that it is the practice at Leeds always to ask the court to fix an early return date – in the present case it was 13 days after the date of the order, and that seemed to the court to be desirable. The court was also of the opinion that:

(c) From the time that the order is served the person upon whom it is served can apply under reg. 6 to have the order varied or discharged, and the requirement that the magistrates' courts give not less than 14 days' notice of the hearing of the application was in the court's judgement a sensible and realistic procedural requirement, which does not undermine the right of the person affected to seek rapid relief. Nothing, in the court's judgement, could be made of the fact that under reg 6 it is for the parties and not for the court to seek a review.

(d) Because an application for an interim order without notice can only be made when the justices' clerk is satisfied that it is necessary for the application to be made without notice, and because the order can only be made for a limited period, when the court considers that it is just to make it, and in circumstances where it can be reviewed or discharged as indicated above, it was impossible to say that it undermined civil rights. Certainly for a time it restricts certain freedoms, and the restriction can be enforced by sanctions, but that is the nature of any interim order; so provided the interim order follows its normal course Article 6 of the European Convention will not be engaged. (Article 6 requires civil rights to be determined by an independent and impartial tribunal, a requirement that carried with it a range of procedural safeguards, such as the right to be heard – as a result of this finding Article 6 issues do not arise on applications for interim ASBOs.)

(e) Although Article 6 is not engaged the procedure must be fair, and there was no apparent unfairness in the procedure. In *R (on the application of M) v Secretary of State for Constitutional Affairs and Lord Chancellor* [2004] 2 All ER 531, CA, it was said that in deciding whether to make an interim order on a without notice application, the court must balance the need to protect the public against the impact on the defendant, taking account of the seriousness of the behaviour, the urgency of the situation and whether the order must be made without notice to be effective. The considerations in favour of injunctive relief should be sufficiently serious to warrant what might be a serious interference with the defendant's civil rights, but there was no warrant for glossing the statute with a test of 'exceptional circumstances' or 'compelling urgency'. On an application to discharge an interim order, there was no burden cast on the applicant; the burden was on the party who had sought the order, and the test remained that set out in s 1D(2).

A custodial sentence combined with an ASBO

14.10   The court may make an ASBO at the same time as it imposes a custodial sentence. The court may also suspend the requirements of that ASBO until the offender is released from custody (CDA 1998, s 1C(5)).

In *R v Parkin* (2004) Times, 19 February, CA, however, the Lord Chief Justice. Lord Woolf. held that:

'where a custodial sentence of more than a few months was passed and the offender was liable to be released on licence and therefore subject to recall, the circumstances in which there would be a demonstrable necessity to make a suspended anti-social behaviour order, to take effect on release, would be limited, although there would be cases in which geographical restraints could properly supplement licence conditions; an order should only be made where it is "necessary" to protect persons in any place in England and Wales from further anti-social acts by [the offender].

TIME LIMITS

14.11   Where an application is made to a magistrates' court for an ASBO it is made by way of a 'complaint' (CDA 1998, s 1(3)). The general rule about the time limit for making complaints to the magistrates' court is contained in s 127 of the Magistrates' Courts Act 1980, namely: 'a magistrates' court shall not ...hear a complaint unless the ...complaint was made ...within six months from the time when the ...matter of the complaint arose.'

The question arose in *Stevens v South East Surrey Magistrates Court* [2004] EWHC Admin 1456 as to how this affected the two-part test in s 1.The justices granted the police's application for an ASBO in respect of Mr Stevens: having considered the eight 'in-time' allegations, the court found the first condition proved. Mr Stevens had engaged in anti-social behaviour.

The court then went on to admit evidence of 30 more allegations said to have taken place more than six months before the application and which it had been argued were out of time. However, the High Court held that the evidence revealed a fairly regular and consistent pattern of 'out-of-time' anti-social behaviour, continuing seamlessly into the eight courses of conduct 'in-time' incidents. In the various and sometimes overlapping evidential forms they were capable of being regarded by the magistrates as relevant and as reliable indicators of what was needed by way of protection of the public.

The court said:

> 'Given the purpose of this legislation to provide effective protection to those vulnerable to and frightened by anti-social behaviour in their locality. I can see no unfairness in the magistrates' decision to admit this comprehensive and cogent evidence when considering the necessity for protection.'

Consequently 'out-of-time' evidence can be admitted to prove the second leg of the test for an order. However the court went on to say that an important factor going both to relevance and hence admissibility, and possibly to reliability, going to its weight, is the age of the earlier 'out-of-time' incidents to which magistrates are asked to have regard on this issue. (This also applies to evidence of such incidents where it is a candidate for admission as similar fact evidence in support of proof of harassment under s 1(1)(a).) If the incidents are very old and amount to only a single or a very few incidents, they may have little relevance or weight however reliable the evidence of them may be when looking at each incident on its own. On the other hand, if they indicate a solid and consistent line of anti-social behaviour beginning possibly well out of time and ending within time they would usually be highly relevant to the decision whether an order is, in the circumstances, necessary and to what form it should take.

ANTI-SOCIAL BEHAVIOUR ORDERS AFTER CRIMINAL CONVICTIONS

14.12 The court has power to make an ASBO where a person is convicted of any offence committed after 2 December 2002 (s 1C(1) and (10)). If he is convicted in the Youth Court that court will make the ASBO. An order can be made on request of the CPS or the court can act of its own motion (CDA 1998, s 1C). The order can only be made in addition to a sentence (including a conditional discharge). It remains a civil order 'on conviction'.

The prosecutor must serve a notice of intention to apply for such an order as soon as practicable (without waiting for the verdict) on the court officer, the defendant against whom the prosecutor wants the court to make the order, and any person on whom the order would be likely to have a significant adverse effect. The notice must be in the form set out in the Practice Direction and must:

(a) summarise the relevant facts;
(b) identify the evidence on which the prosecutor relies in support;
(c) attach any written statement that the prosecutor has not already served; and
(d) specify the order that the prosecutor wants the court to make.

The defendant must then serve written notice, identifying the evidence and attach any written statement that has not already been served, on the court officer, and the prosecutor as soon as practicable (without waiting for the verdict) (CPR 2005, r 50.3).

The criteria

14.13 The court must be satisfied that:

(a) the offender has acted in an anti-social manner, that is to say in a manner that caused or was likely to cause harassment, alarm or distress to one or more persons not of the same household as himself; and
(b) an order is necessary to protect persons in any place in England and Wales from further anti-social acts by him.

In *R (on the application of C) v Sunderland Youth Court* [2003] EWHC 2385 (Admin), 167 JP 596, the High Court indicated that:

(a) magistrates have a broad discretion under s 1C of the Crime and Disorder Act 1998, but it is not an unfettered discretion and must be exercised fairly, reasonably and having regard to all the relevant circumstances; where a court proposes to make such an order of its own motion, fairness requires the court to indicate the basis on which it provisionally considers an order may be appropriate, and the material on which it proposes to rely, so that the defendant can make meaningful submissions as to why the order should not be made at all or should not be made in the form provisionally proposed;

(b) since justice should be seen to be done, it would be unfair if the court appeared to take into consideration material which had not been given in open court;

(c) where an order was made, it was imperative that the terms of the order were clear so that the defendant should be in doubt as to exactly what was prohibited by the order;

(d) consistency in the exercise of discretionary powers is an important aspect of fairness, from which it followed that where a Youth Court had declined on one occasion to make an order under s 1C against the claimant (when dealing with him for a large number of offences), despite having been invited to do so, it would be prima facie unreasonable for that same court to make such an order of its own motion when dealing with him one month later in respect of two further matters (both committed before the previous hearing), subject to a change of circumstances. The justices' failure to give reasons for making the order left open the question of the extent to which they had had regard to the scale of offending before the court on the previous occasion, when the bench had declined to make an order.

This case demonstrates the need for care when considering ASBOs in the Youth Court, the need to exercise judicial discretion and analysis of the evidence before the court, and finally the need to give cogent reason for making an order or not doing so when so invited by the prosecution.

Evidential matters

14.14   As stated above the making of an ASBO in criminal proceedings is an ancillary order made as part of the sentencing process.

Whether proceedings under s 1C are civil or criminal is unclear since the amendments to the statute by the Anti-social Behaviour Act 2003.

What is clear is that an order under s 1C can only be made in criminal proceedings following a conviction, if the prosecutor asks it to do so or the court thinks it is appropriate to do so. An order under s 1C may be made in respect of a young offender in the Youth Court. The Youth Court is a criminal court and has no civil jurisdiction. To deem the consideration of an order under s 1C as separate civil proceedings after conviction is to confer a civil jurisdiction on an otherwise criminal court. In *R (On the application of Mills) v Birmingham Magistrates' Court* [2005] EWHC 2732 (Admin) it was said that 'the facts of the case must trigger the section' so that there must be evidence proving harassment alarm and distress resulting from that particular offence.

Section 1C(4A) does permit the court to adjourn an application for a post-conviction order even after the offender has been sentenced although it is poor sentencing practice to separate the process by sentencing for the offence and adjourning to consider an ancillary sentence, as this is an order 'in addition to a sentence imposed in respect of the relevant offence' (s 1C(4)). If the offender fails to attend the adjourned hearing the court has power to further adjourn the proceedings or issue a warrant for his arrest. There does not appear to be power to hear such an application in the defendant's absence as the Magistrates Courts Act 1980 ss 51 and 57 would not apply to proceedings for a post-conviction order as they are commenced by application and not on complaint. See **14.08** on the making of interim orders.

CDA 1998, s 1C further states that:

'(3A) For the purpose of deciding whether to make an order under this section the court may consider evidence led by the prosecution and defence, and

(3B) it is immaterial whether evidence led in pursuance of subsection 3A would have been admissible in the proceedings in which the offender was convicted.'

This suggests that evidence used to inform the court's decision on whether or not to make an ASBO ancillary to sentence is subject to civil procedure and r 50.6 of the Criminal Procedure Rules 2005. As the Civil Evidence Act requires notice to be served to enable 'hearsay' evidence to be admitted the whole sentencing process may have to be adjourned under

MCA 1980, s 10 for at least the 21-day period to allow for compliance with CPR 2005, rr 50.8 and 50.9 which allow sevenday notice periods for service of notice and the making of representations.

Subject to the court being satisfied that the defendant acted in an anti-social manner and judging it necessary, the offender may be prohibited from doing anything described in the order. As with 'free-standing' orders, any prohibition in the order needs to be proportionate in its terms.

The Magistrates' Courts (Anti-Social Behaviour Order) Rules 2002, SI 2002/2784 provide that an order under s 1C shall be in the form set out in Sch 4. There is corresponding provision for the Crown Court.

An order made under these provisions in respect of the juvenile under the age of 17 may specify a relevant authority other than the chief officer of police as being responsible for carrying out a review of the operation of the order under CDA 1998, s 1J.

Review of anti-social behaviour orders

14.15   Where an order is made in respect of a juvenile under the age of 17 either on complaint (CDA 1998, s 1) or in criminal proceedings (CDA 1998, s 1C) a review of the operation of the order must be carried out before the end of a review period. The review periods are 12 months beginning with the day on which the order was made or the date of any supplemental order made after that and then a period of 12 months beginning with the day after the end of the previous review period or the date of any supplemental order.

The responsibility for carrying out the review will fall to the police and local authority working in co-operation with each other and any other person specified under CDA 1998, s 1C(9ZA).

The review must consider the extent to which the person subject to the order has complied with it, the adequacy of any support available to him and any matters relevant to the question as to whether an application should be made for the order to be varied or discharged. Guidance is issued by the Secretary of State as to how the review should be carried out, what particular matters should be dealt with, and what actions would be appropriate as a consequence of the findings of the review.

PARENTING ORDERS AND ASBOs

14.16   The Anti-Social Behaviour Act 2003, s 25 provides for parenting contracts to be made where a child or young person has been referred to a youth offending team. The team may enter into a contract with a parent of the child or young person if a member of the team has reason to believe that the child or young person has engaged, or is likely to engage, in criminal conduct or anti-social behaviour. The contract requires the parent to abide by certain requirements and the team to provide support with respect thereto. Section 26 makes provision for parenting orders to be made by a magistrates' court on the application of a youth offending team. The court may make such an order if satisfied that the child or young person has engaged in criminal or anti-social behaviour, and that making the order would be desirable in the interests of preventing the child or young person from engaging in further such conduct.

Ideally a juvenile found to be causing anti-social behaviour should be referred to the YOT at an early stage rather than proceedings being brought to court for an order.

It should be borne in mind that ASBOs are a preventative measure and not a short cut to custody for juveniles whose criminal offences are not serious enough to warrant that outcome.

However if an ASBO is made in relation to a juvenile under 16 years the court must make a parenting order if the conditions are fulfilled (CDA 1998, s 9(1B)).

If the court is not satisfied that an order would be desirable in the interests of preventing anti-social behaviour it must state its reasons in open court (CDA 1998, s 9(1B)).

If, while a parenting order is in force, the parent without reasonable excuse fails to comply with any requirement included in the order, or specified in directions given by the responsible officer, he shall be liable on summary conviction to a fine not exceeding level 3. See **12.26-12.30**.

The various forms of complaints, variation and discharge can be found in the Magistrates' Courts (Parenting Orders) Rules 2004, SI 2004/247.

INDIVIDUAL SUPPORT ORDERS

14.17   Individual support orders (ISOs) were introduced by CDA 1998, s 1AA as inserted by ss 322 and 323 of the Criminal Justice Act 2003 and amended by the CJ&IA 2008. Where a court makes an ASBO, or considers an application in respect of an existing ASBO, in respect of a defendant who is a child or young person it must consider whether the individual support conditions are satisfied and must make the ISO if they are so satisfied.

Although the Home Office guidance suggest, that the ISO is restricted to stand alone civil ASBOs, the legislation makes no such distinction. Logically, however, a court making an ancillary order in criminal proceedings can address rehabilitative and behavioural issues in its sentencing.

The conditions which must be met are that:
   (a)   an individual support order would be desirable in the interests of preventing any repetition of the kind of behaviour which led to the making of the ASBO or an order varying it;
   (b)   the defendant is not already subject to an individual support order; and
   (c)   the court has been notified by the Secretary of State that arrangements for implementing individual support orders are available in the area in which it appears to it that the defendant resides or will reside and the notice has not been withdrawn.
If the court is not satisfied that the individual support conditions are fulfilled, it shall state in open court that it is not satisfied and why it is not.

If the conditions are satisfied that court may make an order for a period not exceeding six months requiring the defendant to comply with any directions given by the responsible officer in connection with the requirements imposed under the order.

An ISO made on a subsequent application in relation to an ASBO (CDA 1998, s 1AA(1A)) must not be longer than the remaining term of the ASBO and if the ASBO as a result of which an ISO was made ceases to have effect, the ISO (if it has not previously ceased to have effect) ceases to have effect when the ASBO does (CDA, s 1AB(5A)).

The requirements

14.18   The requirements that may be specified are those that the court considers desirable in the interests of preventing any repetition of the kind of behaviour which led to the making of an ASBO.

Requirements included in an individual support order, or directions given under such an order by a responsible officer, may require the defendant to do all or any of the following things:

    (a) to participate in activities specified in the requirements or directions at a time or times so specified;

    (b) to present himself to a person or persons so specified at a place or places and at a time or times so specified;

    (c) to comply with any arrangements for his education so specified.

Requirements included in, or directions given under, such an order may not require the defendant to attend (whether at the same place or at different places) on more than two days in any week; and 'week' here means a period of seven days beginning with a Sunday. Further they may not interfere with attendance at school or other educational establishment.

Before making an order the court should obtain information from the YOT to help determine if the conditions are fulfilled and what requirements should be imposed in the order.

BREACH OF AN ISO

14.19   The order and the consequences of breach should be explained to the juvenile in ordinary language before he leaves court.

A breach may be dealt with by a fine, in the case of a 14-year-old and above of up to £1,000 and below that age up to £250.

Breach of an ASBO and sentence

14.20   Somewhat unusually breach of an ASBO is a criminal offence punishable in the adult court by a fine or imprisonment and on indictment by up to five years' imprisonment. Definitive guidance can be found at www.sentencing-guidelines.gov.uk, in particular section E on sentencing young offenders.

Legal representation will be available through the magistrates' court both for the original criminal offence, if the order is under s 1C, and for the offence of breach. Interestingly a civil application under s 1 can also be granted a representation order but the application must be made to the Legal Services Commission (Criminal Defence Service (General) (No 2) Regulations 2000, regs 3(b) and 6(3)).

Conviction for a breach of an ASBO may be treated seriously by the court. In the adult court a three-year prison sentence was upheld in the case of *R v Braxton* [2004] EWCA Crim 1374, for a second breach involving aggressive begging.

In *R v Thomas* [2004] EWCA Crim 1178 a sentence of 18 months' imprisonment was upheld for stealing from a shop which the defendant was prohibited from entering. The breach was a second breach and occurred within days of his release on licence following a five months' sentence for the first breach.

There is power to suspend some or all the provisions of an ASBO pending an offender's release from custody presumably so that the order is not largely nullified by a lengthy prison sentence (see **14.10**).

It is for the prosecutor to prove that the defendant was the person made subject of the ASBO in question although the offence of breaching the order does not require proof of a mental element. The defence may raise the defence of reasonable excuse and, if the evidential burden is satisfied, it is for the prosecution to prove, to the criminal standard, that the defendant had no reasonable excuse (*R v Nicholson* [2006] EWCA Crim 1518).

A mistake of fact may only provide a defence if it amounts to a reasonable excuse for what the defendant did. Questions about the validity of the order cannot be raised as a defence in proceedings for its breach. However, where the prohibition that is being enforced is too vague to be enforceable, a defence of reasonable excuse may be raised (*CPS v T* [2006] EWHC 728 (Admin)).

In sentencing a breach, the court should have regard to the nature and seriousness of the behaviour that constituted a breach, and whether that behaviour caused or could have caused harassment, alarm or distress to another person. In *R v Lamb* [2005] EWCA Crim 2487, the Appeal Court drew a distinction between breaches that involved no anti-social behaviour but constituted breach, for example by the respondent entering a prohibited zone, and breaches that did not involve such behaviour but were triggered by further criminal offending.

In the Youth Court the court must of course have regard to the welfare of the juvenile, the need to prevent further offences and the seriousness of any breach before it considers its sentence. Indeed, offences of breach are dealt with following procedures in place for any criminal offence committed by a juvenile; as a consequence the police in consultation with the youth offending team would normally make an assessment of the seriousness of the breach and of the juvenile's offending history. Where a breach is a flagrant one, then the offender is likely to be charged unless there are some very usual circumstances.

Note that it is not open to the court to impose a conditional discharge for a breach offence.

FURTHER OFFENCES

14.21   It may occur that a defendant breaches his ASBO conditions and is charged with a separate criminal offence at the same time and based on the same facts. Section 18 of the Interpretation Act 1978 reads:

> 'Where an act or omission constitutes an offence under two or more Acts, or both under an Act and at common law, the offender shall, unless the contrary intention appears, be liable to be prosecuted and punished under either or any of those Acts or at common law, but shall not be liable to be punished more than once for the same offence.'

The section makes no reference to whether the prosecutions should proceed concurrently or not. If a prosecution was commenced for breach of the ASBO after a court had dismissed a charge of the offence arising out of the same facts, there may follow an argument that the later charge could fail on the *autrefois acquit* rule: *R v Beedie* [1998] QB 356, CA.

It seems unlikely that this is an abuse of process. It is lawful for the defendant to be convicted of both offences. The court however must sentence on the seriousness of the incident and ensure that the defendant is not punished twice for the same conduct. In the case of *R v Lawson* [2006] All ER (D) 52 the defendant was convicted of assault and pleaded guilty to the breach of an ASBO. He was sentenced to consecutive terms of imprisonment. On appeal the High Court said there was nothing inherently wrong with passing a consecutive sentence for breach of an ASBO.

VARIATION AND DISCHARGE

14.22   From the time that the order is served, the person upon whom it is served can apply under r 6 of the Magistrates' Courts (Anti-Social Behaviour Orders) Rules 2002 to have it varied or discharged, as may a relevant authority as defined in s 1(1A).The requirement that the court give not less than 14 days' notice of the hearing of an application for variation or discharge does not undermine the right of the person affected to seek rapid relief.

Although an ASBO may be on application by the subject of the order or a relevant authority as defined in s 1(1A), if it is to include discharging the order before the end of the two years beginning with the date of the order both parties have to agree to the application being made (CDA 1998, s 1(8) and (9)). Such an application may properly take account of an offender's changed circumstances which may lead magistrates to think the prohibition can be lifted.

In *Leeds City Council v LG* [2007] EWHC 1612 (Admin) the court held that there is a power to extend an ASBO by way of variation. However, in such circumstances the court should examine closely why they are being asked do so rather than make a new order.

Variation is a civil procedure and there is no right of appeal to the Crown Court against a variation (*R (On the application of Langley) v Preston Crown Court* [2008] EWCA 2632 (Admin).

PRESS RESTRICTIONS

In the magistrates' court (civil proceedings)

14.23   An adult magistrates' court, unlike a Youth Court, is open to the general public and the presumption is that reporting restrictions do not apply unless the court decides to impose them under s 39 of the Children and Young Persons Act 1933 to protect the identity of a juvenile connected with the proceedings.

There need not be a request to impose reporting restrictions; it is a matter for the court in individual cases.

Section 39 states that; in relation to any proceedings in any court, the court may direct that:

(a) no newspaper report of the proceedings shall reveal the name, address, or school, or include any particulars calculated to lead to the identification of any child or young person concerned in the proceedings, either as being the person by or against or in respect of whom the proceedings are taken, or as being a witness therein;

(b) no picture shall be published in any newspaper as being or including a picture of any child or young person so concerned in the proceedings as aforesaid; except in so far (if at all) as may be permitted by the direction of the court;

Any person who publishes any matter in contravention of any such direction shall on summary conviction be liable in respect of each offence to a fine not exceeding level 5 on the standard scale.

A guide to ASBOs published by the Home Office jointly with the Association of Chief Police Officers and Youth Justice Board in August 2006 suggests a number of useful practice issues. For example, the guide notes that a sentence for breach of an ASBO should be proportionate to the behaviour that constituted the breach. On the subject of publicity it notes the need to record considerations of the human rights implications of such publicity and, if a different court imposed reporting restrictions when the order was made, there should be a presumption in favour of their imposition in any breach hearing.

The sort of arguments the court will have to consider include the need for identification of the offender, unless the nuisance is extremely localised, the general public need to be aware of the existence of the order and against whom it is made, as against the fact that most local communities know the nuisances within their population, and are prepared to tell other residents.

The view that communities need to know that something is being done about disorder in their neighbourhoods, against the need to rehabilitate the young person and work towards their social inclusion needs to be balanced.

Effective enforcement requires the ability to identify those subject to ASBOs, which requires publication of photographs, balanced by the knowledge that much press coverage is sensationalist in its nature and may give young people a notoriety which they feel they have to live up to thus negating the effectiveness of the order.

The case of *McKerry v Teesside Justices* (2000) 164 JP 355, emphasised that the power to dispense with anonymity must be exercised with great care, caution and circumspection. The public interest criterion will rarely be satisfied and it is wholly wrong to exercise the power as an additional punishment or for 'naming and shaming'. In order to determine whether it is in the public interest to dispense with restrictions, it is entirely proper for the court to ask reporters present in court if they had any representations to make.

The application of s 39 of the Children and Young Persons Act 1933 where a juvenile is the subject of an ASBO was considered in *R v St Albans Crown Court, ex p T* [2002] EWHC 1129 (Admin) and *Chief Constable of Surrey v J H-G and D H-G* [2002] All ER (D) 308 (May). The following considerations were identified as relevant by the court when considering imposing or removing reporting restrictions:

(a) In deciding whether to impose or thereafter to lift reporting restrictions, the court will consider whether there are good reasons for naming the defendant.

(b) In each case there will be a wide variety of factors that have to be fully considered and, a balance has to be struck between the desirability of public disclosure on one hand and the need to protect the welfare of the juvenile on the other hand.

(c) In reaching its decision, the court will give considerable weight to the age of the offender and the potential damage to any young person of public identification as a criminal before the offender has the benefit or burden of adulthood.

(d) By virtue of s 44 of the CYPA 1933, the court must have regard to the welfare of the child or young person.

(e) The prospect of being named in court with the accompanying disgrace is a powerful deterrent and the naming of a defendant in the context of his punishment serves as a deterrent to others. These deterrents are proper objectives for the court to seek.

(f) There is strong public interest in open justice and in the public knowing as much as possible about what has happened in court, including the identity of those who have committed crime.

(g) The weight to be attributed to the different factors may shift at different stages of the proceedings, and, in particular, after the defendant has been found, or pleads, guilty and is sentenced. It may then be appropriate to place greater weight on the interest of the public in knowing the identity of those who have committed particularly serious and detestable crimes.

(h) The fact that an appeal has been made may be a material consideration.

(i) Where an ASBO has been imposed, that is a factor that reinforces, and in some cases may strongly reinforce, the general public interest in the public disclosure of court proceedings.

(j) The court should not have regard to the impact of publicity on the other members of the youth's family.

The court also has to balance any decision with its obligations under Arts 8 and 10 of ECHR.

R (on the application of K) v Knowsley Metropolitan Borough Council (2004) 168 JP 461 makes the point that on an application for an interim order it is necessary to bear in mind that the allegations are unproven at that stage and that they may or may not be proved at the hearing for a full order. Where justices had failed to attach sufficient importance to the interim nature of the proceedings, the order would be quashed. It was not the case that a direction under s 39 should be the norm in applications for interim ASBOs, because the very nature of the allegations of the anti-social behaviour reinforce the importance of the public interest in public disclosure.

The case of *Medway Council v BBC* [2002] 1 FLR 104, Fam Div, suggests, as outlined above, that in most cases it would be inappropriate for the court thus to inhibit identification by the press of a child who is made the subject of such an order, for the efficacy of the order may well depend on the awareness of the local community not only of the acts that it prohibits but also of the identity of the persons against whom it is made.

Finally, the case of *R (on the application of Kenny) v Leeds Magistrates' Court* [2003] EWHC 2963 (Admin), reminds courts that when contemplating making an ASBO on someone under 18 one of their considerations must be the best interests of that child. While *Todd v CPS* (2003) Times, 13 October, is authority for the proposition that reporting restrictions in relation to the identification of a young person involved in proceedings fall away once that person reaches the age of 18, the legislation should be construed in the light of the judgement in *C v CPS* [2008] EWHC 854 and the general freedom of the press to report proceedings in adult courts.

In the Youth Court

14.24   Section 86(3) of the Anti-social Behaviour Act 2003 amends CDA 1998, s 1C so that the normal automatic restrictions of CYPA 1969, s 49 as amended do not apply to an ASBO made on conviction. The Youth Court is therefore in the same position as the adult court as outlined above in deciding whether or not to apply CYPA 1969, s 39 restrictions.

Chapter 15

The mentally ill juvenile

INTRODUCTION

15.01   The incidents of mentally ill juveniles appearing before the Youth Court are fortunately relatively infrequent. The involvement of the health authority in the youth offending team is a positive change. In some areas the police employ a psychiatric nurse or doctor to visit arrested persons in the cells with a view to diverting them away from the criminal justice system. Nevertheless, when a mentally ill juvenile does appear before the court there is a need for special care both in respect of the young person and the law as it applies.

The mentally ill juvenile may appear before the Youth Court in criminal proceedings as the result of involvement in crime. Where the court has an indication of a mental illness in a juvenile, it should call for medical reports to determine if treatment is required.

CJA 2003, s 157 specifically requires the court to obtain a medical report before passing a custodial sentence where it appears that the defendant may be mentally disordered. The court is required to consider any information before it which relates to the offender's mental condition, whether in a medical report, a pre-sentence report or otherwise. It is also required to consider the likely effect of such a sentence on the offenders' mental condition and on any treatment which may be available for it.

The court will be assisted in finding out what facilities are available for diverting an offender to hospital by the primary care trust, or local health board in Wales, who are under a duty to provide said information to the court where defendant was last resident in their area (Mental Health Act 1983, s 39).

The orders which are specifically designed for the mentally ill juvenile are hospital orders, guardianship orders and youth rehabilitation orders with a condition of treatment by a specified medical practitioner. Hospital and guardianship orders may be appropriate where the court, having heard evidence about the juvenile's mental condition, decides that he needs to be committed to a specified hospital or placed under the guardianship of the local health authority or a person approved by the authority so that he may receive treatment for his illness.

DEFINITIONS

15.02   A hospital order authorises the juvenile's treatment in a hospital or as an outpatient. A guardianship order allows the child to remain as an outpatient, but vests the parental rights and duties in the guardian to ensure that treatment is received. In each case, the court must comply with the provisions of the Mental Health Act 1983 (MHA 1983, s 37 as amended).

In the Act, 'mental disorder' means a medical determination that the person is under any disorder or disability of the mind.

'Mental illness' , 'mental impairment' and 'psychopathic disorder' are all undefined.

Persons with learning disabilities are not mentally disordered for the purposes of most provisions of the Act by reason of that disability alone, unless the disability is associated with abnormally aggressive or seriously irresponsible conduct on the part of the person concerned.

Dependence on drugs or alcohol is specifically excluded from the definition of mental disorder. However a drug or alcohol dependent person who has another mental disorder (even if that disorder is associated with alcohol or drug use) is not excluded from the definition (MHA 1983, s 1(3)).

'Place of safety' has the same meaning as in CYPA 1933, s 107 and includes *inter alia* a doctor's surgery, a hospital, a community home and a police station, but not a prison establishment.

'In custody' here means for juveniles aged less than 17 years in local authority accommodation, unless the juvenile is male, aged 15 years and over and the statutory criteria are satisfied for remanding to a remand centre or prison. For offenders aged 17 and over 'custody' means a remand centre or prison.

PRE-TRIAL CONSIDERATIONS

15.03   The court may be faced with a number of legal issues that may best be tackled at a pre-trial review, although some of the issues can only be dealt with as the trial progresses. Indeed, where it is apparent that insanity is alleged or there is potential for an order under the Mental Health Act 1983 it may be advisable to allocate the case to a district judge as in *R (on the application of Singh) v Stratford Magistrates' Courts* [2007] 4 All ER 407.

The court may be faced with a suggestion that the juvenile defendant is unfit to plead, that he is insane or that the trial should be halted on the basis that it would be an abuse of process given the juvenile's inability to take an effective part in the trial.

Insanity is a defence in law under the Criminal Procedure (Insanity) Act 1964, ss 1 and 4 and is a valid basis for an acquittal in the magistrates' courts (*R v Horseferry Road Magistrates Court, ex p K* [1996] 3 All ER 719).

Where the issue is not one of insanity but it is suggested that a juvenile defendant is unfit to plead the court may proceed to hear the evidence and determine whether they are satisfied that the he did the act or made the omission charged. The Youth Court has the power, to try the issues and reach a conclusion, without convicting or acquitting the accused, provided that the conditions for making a hospital or guardianship order under s 37(3) are met.

The availability of this procedure was confirmed in the case of the *Crown Prosecution Service v P* [2007] 4 All ER 628 and it is worth noting that such a procedure does not infringe the defendant's rights under Art 6 to a fair trial as there is no finding of guilt (*R v H (Tyrone)* [2002] EWCA 2988). The case law also explored the possibility of the court applying the doctrine of 'doli incapax', but the Court of Appeal has in a subsequent case made it clear that the defence of 'doli incapax' has been abolished by s 34 of the Crime and Disorder Act 1998, (*R v T* [2008] EWCA Crim 815).

The final issue that may arise is the suggestion that the case should be halted as an abuse of process on the basis that a juvenile defendant's mental impairment or lack of capacity prohibits him from taking a full part in the trial. Whilst the court has an inherent jurisdiction to stay proceedings as an abuse of process at any stage, it is limited to issues directly affecting the fairness of the trial of the juvenile before them, and does not extend to any sort of wider supervisory jurisdiction such as may be exercised by the High Court. In *CPS v P* above, the court made it clear that only in exceptional circumstances should this power be exercised, before evidence was heard, on the ground that one or more of the capacity issues made it unlikely that the juvenile would receive a fair trial. It was pointed out that the court has a duty to keep under continuing review the question of whether the trial should continue. If at any stage the court concluded that the juvenile was unable to participate effectively it can decide to halt the trial. Even then, it was pointed out that the court may consider that it is in the best interests of the child that the trial should continue if, for example, the prosecution evidence is weak and there may be no case to answer.

Medical evidence may be influential in the court's decision. However it should almost always be set in the context of other evidence relating to the child, such as his understanding, mental capacity and ability to participate effectively in trial. The issue as to whether the juvenile will receive a fair trial is for the court to decide. Where the court proceeds with the trial it will wish to ensure that the child understands each stage of the process. This will necessarily involve exchanges between the bench and the child. The manner in which the trial is conducted by the child's legal representative will inform the court as to whether he does or does not have adequate instructions on which to cross-examine witnesses. Therefore, in most cases medical evidence will be considered as part of the evidence in the case and not the sole evidence of a freestanding application (*R (on the application of P) v West London Youth Court* [2006]1 All ER 477). Again, it is the court's opinion (rather than that of a medical practitioner) of the child's level of understanding that will determine whether the trial proceeds of not (*R (on the application of P) v Barking Youth Court* [2002] EWHC 734 (Admin)).

If the court does halt a criminal trial on the basis that the juvenile cannot take an effective part in proceedings, it may then consider switching to a fact-finding exercise as to whether the defendant did the act charged, in a procedure set out in the *Barking Youth Court* case. In essence, proceedings should only be stayed as an abuse of process before a fact-finding exercise if it is clear that no useful purpose at all could be served by embarking on that procedure. If the court finds that the defendant did not do the acts alleged then a finding of not guilty should be recorded and the defendant acquitted.

A good deal of court time and stress to the juvenile can be avoided by good pre-court communication between the CPS and defence solicitors. The Crown always has an obligation to consider the public interest and, when faced with appropriate medical history and opinion, may take the view that a prosecution is unnecessary, especially where a treatment plan is already in existence. A defence solicitor must consider whether the best interests of the client are served by embarking on a process that could result in a hospital order following a fact-finding exercise when appropriate research and representations to the Crown may result in a more beneficial outcome.

SPECIAL MEASURES AT TRIAL

15.04 A juvenile offender may give evidence in criminal proceedings in a Youth/Magistrates' Court (or Crown Court) using a live link if:

  (a) his ability to participate effectively in the proceedings as a witness giving oral evidence is compromised by his level of intellectual ability or social functioning; and

  (b) his ability to participate effectively would be improved by giving evidence over a live link (s 33A(4) Youth Justice and Criminal Evidence Act 1999 as inserted by s 47 of the Police and Justice Act 2006); and

  (c) the court is satisfied that it is in the interests of justice for the youth to give evidence through a live link.

A live link is defined in s 33B of the Youth Justice and Criminal Evidence Act 1999 as an arrangement by which the accused, while absent from the place where the proceedings are being held, is able to see and hear a person there, and to be seen and heard by the justices, co-accused, legal representatives and interpreters, or any other person appointed by the court to assist the accused.

The defence must apply for a live link direction, which then prevents the defendant from giving oral evidence in the proceedings in any manner other than through a live link (s 33A(6)). The court may discharge a live link direction at any time, if it appears in the interests of justice to do so, of its own motion or on application by any party (s 33A(7)). The court must give reasons in open court for giving or discharging a live link direction or for refusing an application for or the discharge of a live link direction. Those reasons must be recorded on the register of proceedings where the decision was made in the magistrates' court (s 33A(8)).

THE ORDERS

Requirements for hospital and guardianship orders

15.05   In criminal proceedings the orders may be made after the court has made a finding of guilt for an offence which carries imprisonment in the case of an adult. The power applies notwithstanding the restrictions contained in PCC(S)A 2000, ss 109–111 (imposition of minimum sentences) or under s 51A(2) of the Firearms Act 1968, or under any of the provisions of ss 225–228 of the Criminal Justice Act 2003, as nothing in those provisions shall prevent the court from making an order under s 37(1) for the admission of the offender to a hospital.

The court must be satisfied, on the written or oral evidence of two registered medical practitioners that the juvenile is suffering from a mental disorder.

In addition, before detaining any person under the Act for treatment, the court must be satisfied that medical treatment is available to that person, which is not only clinically appropriate to their condition, but also to their personal circumstances.

The court must further be satisfied that:
- (a) it is of the opinion that the hospital order is the most suitable method of disposing of the case; or
- (b) in the case of an offender who has attained the age of 16 years, the mental disorder is of a nature or of a degree which warrants his reception in guardianship, and the court is of the opinion, having regard to all the circumstances including the nature of the offence and the character and antecedents of the offender, and to the other available methods of dealing with him, that the most suitable method of disposing of the case is by means of an order (MHA 1983, s 37(2)(b)).

The court may make an order under MHA 1983, s 37 without making a finding of guilt if, having heard all the evidence including medical evidence, it is satisfied that the offender 'did the act or made the omission charged.' This provision allows the court to make a hospital or guardianship order in cases where the juvenile's mental condition is such that the court cannot be satisfied that the juvenile intended his action or had the necessary mental element in the criminal offence. For example, the juvenile may be charged with an offence of theft; normally the court would have to be satisfied beyond reasonable doubt that the juvenile had a dishonest intention to permanently deprive the owner of the goods in question. If the court has evidence of a mental illness it need only be satisfied that the juvenile performed the *actus reus* of theft without regard to his intentions. In the case of *R v Lincolnshire (Kesteven) Justices, ex p O'Connor* [1983] 1 All ER 901 it was held that this power should be exercised rarely, and usually only if those acting for the defendant consented to such an order being made.

In *R (on the application of P) v Barking Youth Court* [2002] EWHC 734 (Admin) a youth's fitness to plead was queried and the magistrates made their decision based on an expert's report and their own observations. The Divisional Court remitted the case back to the Youth Court reminding them that they were a specially constituted magistrates' court and, as such, the procedures in PCC(S)A 2000, s 11(1) applied. The court should have determined by evidence whether he did the act or omission charged (not necessarily whether he was guilty or not) and then adjourned for medical reports. The procedure may also be applicable in cases where a defendant is unable to consent to mode of trial due to a mental disorder (*R v Lincolnshire (Kersteven) Justices, ex p O'Connor* [1983] 1 WLR 335).

Note that where this procedure is employed there can be no conviction and therefore the criminal charge provisions of Article 6 do not apply to such proceedings (*R v M* [2001] EWCA Crim 2024 and *Re H* [2002 EWCA 2988).

A Youth Court may only make an order without a finding of guilt in respect of a person suffering from a mental disorder as defined above.

In the case of a hospital order, the court must be satisfied that arrangements have been made to admit the juvenile to a hospital within 28 days. Such evidence must be the written or oral evidence of the approved clinician who would be in charge of the offender's treatment, or of some other person representing the managers of the hospital named in the order (MHA 1983, s 37(4)). Pending the juvenile's admission to the hospital which has agreed to accept him the court may, on making the hospital order, direct that he be taken and detained in a place of safety. The offender must be admitted to the specified hospital within 28 days unless it appears to the Secretary of State that an emergency or other special circumstance has arisen whereby he may give directions for admission to another hospital. Alternatively the patient may be returned to the court for a further order to be made giving a further 28-day period in which a bed may become available.

When making a guardianship order, the court must be satisfied that either the local authority or the person under whose guardianship he is to be placed is willing to receive the juvenile into guardianship. It should be noted that a guardianship order may only be made in respect of a juvenile who has attained 16 years.

The court may not, at the same time as making a hospital or guardianship order in respect of an offender, make a custodial order; impose a fine, or a YRO. Nor may the court make an order for the offender's parent or guardian to enter into a recognisance or an order to take proper care of and exercise proper control over him.

In the case of a hospital order the court shall not make a referral order in respect of the offence.

MEDICAL REPORTS

15.06 The court must be satisfied on the evidence of two approved clinicians that the juvenile is suffering from such mental disorder as to render either a hospital or guardianship order necessary. One of the approved clinicians giving evidence must be recognised by the Secretary of State as having special experience in the diagnosis or treatment of mental disorders. (MHA 1983, s 12 as amended)

The medical evidence may be received for the purposes of MHA 1983, s 37 in a written form. Any such report in writing must be signed by an approved clinician under MHA 1983, s 12, as having special experience in the treatment of diagnosis of mental disorders (MHA 1983, s 54(2)).

Where the medical evidence is by way of written report, with a view to an order under MHA 1983, s 37, a copy must be given to the juvenile's counsel or solicitor if he is represented. Where he is not so represented 'the substance of the report shall be disclosed' to his parent or guardian present in court (MHA 1983, s 54(3)).

RESTRICTION ORDERS

15.07 Where the offender is a young person over the age of 14 and the court is satisfied that the conditions under MHA 1983, s 37 exist so as to make a hospital order, but it appears to the court that there should also be an order restricting the offender's discharge, the court may commit him in custody to the Crown Court to be dealt with (MHA 1983, s 43(4) & (4A)). The power to commit to the Crown Court with a view to a restriction order being made only arises on a finding of guilt, not on a finding that the accused did the act or made the omission charged.

A restriction order gives authority to detain the patient for the duration of the order, although it can be discharged by the Secretary of State.

In most circumstances, the committal will be in custody but if the court is satisfied that arrangements have been made to admit the offender to a hospital the court may order his admission pending his appearance at the Crown Court (MHA 1983, s 44).

In deciding whether to commit to the Crown Court with a view to a restriction order, the court shall take into account the nature of the offence, the antecedents of the offender and the risk of his committing further offences if released. In the case where it is necessary to protect the public from serious harm a Crown Court may order an offender to be subject to special restrictions. In doing so the court may require information from the PCT or LHB (in Wales) about the availability of suitable facilities for an offender under the age of 18 years. See (for the principles involved) *R v Birch* (1989) 11 Cr App Rep (S) 202, CA, and *R v Nwohia* [1996] 1 Cr App Rep (S) 170, CA.

EFFECTS OF A HOSPITAL ORDER AND RESTRICTION ORDER

15.08   A hospital order only gives the responsible clinician power to detain a patient for six months in the first instance (*R v Birch* (1989) 11 Cr App Rep (S) 202). This period can be reviewed and extended if necessary in the interests of the patient's health or safety or for the protection of others. A patient who is 16 or over or his nearest relative can apply to a mental health review tribunal for a discharge. On the other hand the responsible clinician can discharge the patient at any time. A patient who absents himself without leave effectively ceases to be detained.

As a consequence of this offenders who are thought to be dangerous or who do need to be detained are usually sent to the Crown Court where a restriction order can be made (see **15.07**). The authority for such a committal is contained in MHA 1983, s 43 and is restricted to juveniles of or over the age of 14 years. Guidance has been given in the case of *R v Gardiner* [1967] 1 All ER 895, CA, on the appropriateness of the two orders.

APPEAL

15.09　After a finding of guilt and the making of an order under MHA 1983, s 37, a juvenile may appeal against any sentence or order. Appeals are dealt with in Chapter 16.

If an order has been made without a finding of guilt, that is the court has found that the juvenile did the act or made the omission charged, he has the same rights of appeal as if it has been made after a finding of guilt. The appeal may be brought by the juvenile or his parent or guardian on his behalf (MHA 1983, s 45).

YOUTH REHABILITATION ORDER WITH A REQUIREMENT OF MEDICAL TREATMENT

15.10　The court may make a youth rehabilitation order that includes a requirement that the offender undertakes treatment for a mental condition.

The provisions are subject to the general requirements and restrictions on making Youth rehabilitation orders found at **9.02 9.07.** Perhaps the most important of these is that the offence itself must be serious enough to merit the making of a YRO, which may not always be the case where the defendant is suffering from a mental condition.

Mental health treatment requirement

15.11　This requires the offender to submit, during periods specified in the order, to treatment by or under the direction of a registered medical practitioner or a chartered psychologist (or both, for different periods) with a view to the improvement of the offender's mental condition.

The treatment required must be one of the following kinds of treatment as may be specified in the relevant order:

    (a)　treatment as a resident patient in an independent hospital or care home within the meaning of the Care Standards Act 2000 or a hospital within the meaning of the Mental Health Act 1983, but not in hospital premises where high security psychiatric services within the meaning of that Act are provided;

(b) treatment as a non-resident patient at such institution or place as may be specified in the order;

(c) treatment by or under the direction of such registered medical practitioner or chartered psychologist (or both) as may be so specified.

The nature of the treatment may not to be specified in the order except as mentioned in (a), (b) or (c) above.

A court may not include a mental health treatment requirement in an order unless:

(a) the court is satisfied, on the evidence of a registered medical practitioner approved for the purposes of s 12 of the Mental Health Act 1983, that the mental condition of the offender:

(i) is such as requires and may be susceptible to treatment, but

(ii) is not such as to warrant the making of a hospital order or guardianship order within the meaning of that Act;

(b) the court is also satisfied that arrangements have been or can be made for the treatment intended to be specified in the order (including arrangements for the reception of the offender where he is to be required to submit to treatment as a resident patient); and

(c) the offender has expressed his willingness to comply with such a requirement.

While the offender is under treatment as a resident patient in pursuance of a mental health requirement, his responsible officer shall carry out the supervision of the offender to such extent only as may be necessary for the purpose of the revocation or amendment of the order.

Note that sub-ss (2) and (3) of s 54 of the Mental Health Act 1983 have effect with respect to proof for the purposes of sub-s (3)(a) of an offender's mental condition as they have effect with respect to proof of an offender's mental condition for the purposes of s 37(2)(a) of that Act.

Mental health treatment at place other than that specified in order

15.12 Where the medical practitioner or chartered psychologist, treating the offender in pursuance of a mental health treatment requirement, is of the opinion that part of the treatment can be better or more conveniently given in or at an institution or place which:

(a) is not specified in the relevant order, and

(b) is one in or at which the treatment of the offender will be given by or under the direction of a registered medical practitioner or chartered psychologist,

he may, with the consent of the offender, make arrangements for him to be treated accordingly.

These arrangements may provide for the offender to receive part of his treatment as a resident patient in an institution or place notwithstanding that the institution or place is not one which could have been specified for that purpose in the relevant order.

Where any such arrangements are made for the treatment of an offender the medical practitioner or chartered psychologist by whom the arrangements are made shall give notice in writing to the offender's responsible officer giving details of the place and the treatment provided as it is deemed to be treatment to which the offender is required to submit to as part of the order.

REMANDS TO HOSPITAL

15.13 The Mental Health Act 1983, ss 35 and 36, allows a court to remand an accused person to a hospital for a report on his mental condition if:

(a) he has been found guilty of an offence punishable with imprisonment in the case of an adult; or

(b) he has been charged with such an offence and the court is satisfied that he did the act or made the omission charged; or

(c) he has consented to the exercise by the court of this power so to remand (MHA 1983 s 35(2)(b)).

The court has to be satisfied on the written or oral evidence of one medical practitioner, approved by the Secretary of State as having special experience in the diagnosis or treatment of mental disorders, that there is reason to suspect that the accused person is suffering from a mental disorder. In addition to this the court has to be of the opinion that it would be impracticable for a report on the offender's mental condition to be made if he were remanded on bail. After such a remand the court may further remand the accused if it appears on evidence, either written or oral, by the doctor preparing the report that a further remand is necessary for completing the assessment of the accused's mental condition. A remand to hospital must not exceed 28 days at a time or more than 12 weeks in all.

The court shall not remand an accused person to a hospital unless satisfied on the written and oral evidence of the doctor making the report, or a representative of the hospital management, that arrangements have been made for his admission to that hospital within a seven-day period beginning with the date of remand. If the court is so satisfied it may, pending his admission, give directions for his detention in a place of safety. The power to further remand under MHA 1983, s 36 may be exercised by the court without the juvenile patient being brought before the court, if he is represented by counsel or solicitor and such representative is given an opportunity of being heard. Any such further remand may only be made where the responsible medical officer warrants it as necessary. A notice of the remand must be sent to the hospital manager by the court (CPR 2005, r 49.1).

INTERIM HOSPITAL ORDERS

15.14   The Mental Health Act 1983, s 38 gives the court power to make interim hospital orders. The court must be satisfied on the written or oral evidence of two medical practitioners that:

    (a) the offender is suffering from a mental disorder;

    (b) there is reason to suppose that the mental disorder from which the offender is suffering is such that it may be appropriate for a hospital order to be made in his case.

An interim order initially may not last for more than 12 weeks, and thereafter may be renewed for further periods of 28 days at a time, but the order may not continue in force for more than six months in all.

The power to renew an interim hospital order may be exercised without the offender being brought before the court if he is represented by counsel or a solicitor who is given an opportunity of being heard.

An interim hospital order may be made into a full hospital order without the offender being brought before the court, subject to the relevant medical evidence being available and the offender's solicitor or counsel being given an opportunity of being heard. Before making either a full or an interim hospital order or remanding to a hospital, the court must be satisfied on written or oral evidence that arrangements have been made for the admission of the offender to a hospital. This evidence may be given by the approved clinician who would be in charge of the offender's treatment or of preparing the report or by some other persons representing the managers of the hospital in question (MHA 1983, ss 36(3) and 38(4)).

The power to make an interim hospital order and the power to remand to hospital have significant differences. A remand will be for the purpose of obtaining information about the mental condition of an offender. To make an interim hospital order in criminal proceedings, the offender must have been found guilty (or arraigned before the court and not yet dealt with) of an offence punishable with imprisonment and there must be reason to suppose that it may be appropriate for a hospital order to be made. When remanding to hospital the court must be satisfied that provision has been made to admit the defendant to hospital.

Chapter 16

Appeals

GENERAL POINTS

16.01   Appeals from the Youth Court may be heard either by the Crown Court, or by way of case stated by the Divisional Court. At the Crown Court, the case proceeds, except for agreed evidence, by rehearing all the evidence.

Appeal by way of case stated to the Divisional Court is reserved for appeals which involve a point of law that requires the opinion of the High Court.

Appeal against a Youth Court's decision to withhold bail and remand in custody is made in the first instance to the Crown Court.

APPEAL TO THE CROWN COURT IN CRIMINAL CASES

Applicability

16.02   An appeal to the Crown Court is applicable in cases where the appellant is aggrieved at the magistrates' decision on questions of fact or, in the case of a juvenile, where his parent or guardian is aggrieved at a decision ordering either of them to pay a fine, costs or compensation imposed in respect of the case involving his child (PCC(S)A 2000, s 137). A juvenile found guilty by a youth or an adult court may appeal to the Crown Court:

  (a) if he pleaded guilty to the offence, against his sentence or order; or

  (b) if he did not plead guilty to the offence against the finding of guilt and sentence or order.

'Sentence' means any order made on a finding of guilt, including an order of conditional discharge, an order for contempt of court and orders made on breach of a YRO. Sentence does not include an order for costs (MCA 1980, s 108).

The various routes of appeal against conviction and sentence in contempt of court cases are explored in *Haw v Westminster Magistrates Court* [2007] EWHC 2960 (Admin). The judgement establishes that there is an appeal to the Crown Court for both conviction and sentence despite the wording of s 12(5) of the Contempt of Court Act 1981. The terms of the Magistrates' Courts Act 1980, s 111 provide for and are wide enough to encompass an appeal by way of case stated to the High Court but there is no right of appeal under s 30 of the Administration of Justice Act 1960.

A defendant may also appeal against conviction if the Youth Court treats an equivocal plea as a guilty plea. In *R v Birmingham Crown Court, ex p Sharma* [1988] Crim LR 741, an equivocal plea was defined as a plea of guilty when the defendant had added a qualification which, if true, may show that they would not guilty of the offence charged.

Notice of appeal

16.03   An appeal is commenced by the appellant's notice of appeal. Under the Criminal Procedure Rules 2005, r 63.2 the appellant has 21 days in which to lodge notice in writing with magistrates' courts appropriate officer and any other party (usually the prosecutor).. In criminal proceedings the notice must state whether the appeal is against the finding of guilt or the order or both. Details of the appeal notice and documentation can be found in r 63.3 of the Criminal Procedure Rules 2005.

Time limits for appeal

16.04   The time limit of 21 days is from the date of the court's order and not the date of any finding of guilt, even if the appeal is against a finding of guilt only. The period excludes the day of the decision but includes the 21st day thereafter, as held in *Stewart v Chapman* [1951] KB 792.This is a case which involved time limits in road traffic cases, although the same principles apply to all time limits. The 21-day time limit may be extended by the Crown Court on receipt of an application in writing specifying the grounds of the application. The application should be sent to the appropriate officer at the Crown Court. If the extension of time is allowed then the appropriate officer at the Crown Court will notify the office for the appropriate Youth Court. The appellant must notify any other party to the appeal.

Abandonment of an appeal to the Crown Court

16.05   The appellant may abandon his appeal at any time by giving notice in writing to the appropriate officer at the magistrates' court and Crown Court not later than the third day before that fixed for the hearing of the appeal (not including Saturdays, Sundays and Bank Holidays) (Criminal Procedure Rules 2005, r 63.5). Once a notice of abandonment of appeal has been validly given the Crown Court cannot entertain an appeal: *R v Essex Quarter Sessions Appeals Committee, ex p Larkin* [1961] 3 All ER 930, in which a defendant had been convicted by magistrates and gave notice of appeal to Quarter Sessions. He then gave notice of abandonment of appeal. Subsequently he sought to withdraw the notice of abandonment but the Quarter Sessions refused to allow him to do so. The Divisional Court upheld the Quarter Sessions decision.

Once the appeal has been abandoned by the appellant giving notice, the court against whose decision the appeal was brought may enforce that decision and issue any process necessary for enforcement subject to anything already suffered or done under it by the appellant. The costs of the appeal may be ordered against the appellant (MCA 1980, s 109).

The powers of the Crown Court

16.06   On hearing an appeal in criminal proceedings against conviction, the Crown Court may uphold the conviction, quash it, or remit the case to the magistrates with their opinion upon it.

The hearing at the Crown Court, subject to provisions to avoid unreasonable delay, will be before the judge sitting with two youth panel members so that the tribunal consists of both a man and a woman (CPR 2005, r 63.9).

A youth panel magistrate may not sit on the appeal of a matter upon which they adjudicated in the youth court (CPR 2005, r 63.9).

On appeal against sentence alone or against conviction and sentence, the Crown Court may award a punishment the magistrates could have awarded whether it is more or less severe than the sentence appealed against (Supreme Court Act 1981, s 48).

APPEAL BY WAY OF CASE STATED FROM THE YOUTH COURT

Applicability

16.07 The justices adjudicating may be asked to state a case for the opinion of the High Court by any party or any person who believes himself to be aggrieved by a conviction, order or other determination, on the ground that it was wrong in law or in excess of jurisdiction (MCA 1980, s 111).

In *James v Chief Constable of Kent* (1986) Times, 7 June, Woolf LJ emphasised that an appeal by way of case stated was for an examination as to whether the justices had erred on matters of law. If the defendant was aggrieved by a decision of the justices as to matters of fact, the proper remedy was an appeal to the Crown Court not the Queen's Bench Divisional Court.

In *R v Ealing Justices, ex p Scarfeld* [1994] RTR 195 it was made clear that the most appropriate way for an appellant to challenge a sentence imposed on him by justices was on appeal to the Crown Court as opposed to the High Court by way of case stated. This is confirmed in the recent case of *Spillman v DPP* (unreported, 5 May 2006, Court of Appeal).

Persons who may apply

16.08 Any person or party to the proceedings may include, for example the prosecutor, victim of a crime who has not been given compensation, or a person adversely affected by an order for the restitution of stolen property, as in the case of *Moss v Hancock* [1899] 2 QB 111. A juvenile, being under 18, requires a 'litigation friend' in proceedings in the Crown Court. These will usually be the parent or guardian or if no parent is willing to act it could be any responsible adult.

The application

16.09   The application must be made within 21 days of the justices' decision, in writing, and signed by or on behalf of the applicant. The application must identify the question or questions of law or jurisdiction on which the opinion of the High Court is sought. If the contention of the applicant is that the decision is perverse, then the applicant must state the questions of fact which it is claimed cannot be supported by evidence. The submission in law for the High Court being that no reasonable tribunal, honestly applying its mind to the question, could reach the conclusion reached on the facts adduced in evidence. The application should then be sent to the appropriate officer of the court whose decision is questioned (CPR 2005, r 64.1)).

The case stated itself should include the facts found by the court, and the question or questions of law or jurisdiction upon which the opinion of the High Court is sought. It should also include the representations of the parties, and the opinion or decision of the Youth Court. The question for the High Court should be as simple as possible reflecting the findings of fact, and seeking an answer that will decide whether the conviction or order can be upheld.

Time limits

16.10   The application itself must be lodged with the appropriate officer within 21 days of the decision, ie the day on which the court makes its order or otherwise deals with the juvenile. Within 21 days of receipt of the application, the appropriate officer must supply the applicant or his solicitor, and the respondent or his solicitor, with a copy of the draft case. The parties to the application then have a further 21 days in which to make representations in writing, signed by or on behalf of the applicant, and sent to the appropriate officer concerned (CPR 2005, r 64.2)).

At the end of the 21-day period for representations the justices whose decision is being questioned have a further 21 days to consider the representations and make amendments to the draft case. The case itself, which may be stated on behalf of the justices by any two or more of them, shall contain a statement of facts found and the question of law or jurisdiction on which the opinion of the High Court is sought.

Unless the applicant contends that the decision was perverse, the case shall not contain a statement of evidence. The case shall be signed by the justices or, if they so direct, by their Justices' Clerk, and sent forthwith to the applicant or his solicitor (CPR 2005, rr 64.3 and 64.6).

The justices have power to require a recognisance from the appellant before they state a case, the condition of which is that he prosecutes the appeal without delay and submits to the judgment of the High Court: MCA 1980, s 114.

Extensions of time

16.11 At each 21-day stage, the time limit may be extended, although there is no power to extend the original 21-day time limit within which the application must be lodged. Where any delay has occurred in drafting the case stated, the appropriate officer shall attach to the case at each stage a statement of the delay and the reasons therefore (CPR 2005, r 64.4).

Once the applicant is in receipt of the case stated the applicant must lodge it, within 10 days, with the Crown Office of the Divisional Court. Within a further four days the applicant must serve on the respondent a notice of the entry of the appeal together with a copy of the case.

Failure to state a case

16.12 Where the justices feel an application is frivolous they may refuse to state a case (MCA 1980, s 111(5)). Frivolous may be taken to mean, futile, misconceived, hopeless or academic (see Lord Bingham in *ex p Forest Health District Council* (1997) 161 JP 401) or as having no prospect of success because the case is unarguable (*R v Betting Licensing Committee for Cardiff Petty Sessions, ex p les Croupiers Casino Ltd* (1994) 158 (20) JP and 311). Where such a refusal is made the applicant may appeal to the High Court directly for an order of mandamus requiring the justices to state a case.

The powers of the Divisional Court

16.13 The appeal to the Divisional Court by way of case stated does not proceed by a rehearing of the evidence but takes the form of legal argument before the High Court judges. The Divisional Court may reverse, affirm or amend the determination in respect of which the case had been stated, or remit the matter to the justices with the opinion of the court thereon or make such other order in relation to the matter as it sees fit (Summary Jurisdiction Act 1857, s 6 as amended).

Upon applying to the justices to state a case an appellant loses the right to appeal to the Crown Court (MCA 1980, s 111(4)). Thus, in the case of *R v Winchester Crown Court, ex p Lewington* (1982) 4 Cr App Rep (S) 224, it was held that an appellant who applied for a case stated, and subsequently withdrew the application, was debarred from appealing to the Crown Court against his conviction.

Bail pending appeal

16.14 Where a person who has given notice of appeal to the Crown Court against the decision of a Youth Court, or has applied to the Youth Court to state a case for the opinion of the High Court, is in custody the Youth Court may grant him bail (MCA 1980, s 113). The court has discretion as to whether or not to grant bail. The general right of accused persons to bail under the Bail Act 1976, s 4, does not apply.

The Youth Court will be reluctant to grant bail pending appeal when an expedited hearing of the appeal would be more appropriate. In *Re W (B) (an infant)* [1969] 2 Ch 50, CA, a respondent was committed to prison for contempt of court. He was subsequently granted bail, pending appeal, and Wimm LJ commented at the appeal hearing before the Divisional Court:

'It would be inappropriate today for this court to make any order which had the effect of returning S to prison, for it is well recognised that the court has greater reluctance in dismissing an appeal against sentence where bail has been granted during the period since sentence was imposed.'

The reasoning behind this is that bail pending appeal inevitably raises the defendant's hopes for a successful appeal, only for them to be dashed if the appeal is in fact unsuccessful. This point is illustrated by the case of *R v Lancastle* [1978] Crim LR 367, where an appellant had been released on bail pending appeal, and the Divisional Court commented: 'It was to be regretted that [the appellant] had been granted bail pending her appeal. It would have been preferable had she remained in custody and the hearing of her appeal been expedited.'

In the case of *R v Watton* (1978) 68 Cr App Rep 293, the Court of Appeal gave guidance as to how the court should exercise its discretion in the matter of bail pending appeal. The court indicated it only granted bail where the appeal seemed likely to succeed or where the sentence might have been served by the time the appeal was heard. Lord Lane CJ concluded that: 'the true question is, are there exceptional circumstances which would drive the court to the conclusion that justice can only be done by the granting of bail?'

A case involving a juvenile in which the question of bail pending appeal was considered is *R v Imdad Shah* (1978) 144 JP 460. Here the Crown Court sentenced a boy of 16 years to three months in a detention centre. He appealed to the Court of Appeal and was released on bail pending appeal. The result of this was that if his appeal was dismissed he would be due to go back to the detention centre for only one month, and the court was reluctant to send him back for that short period. If bail had not been granted he would, with remission, have served the full sentence.

The Court of Appeal said that bail should not be granted where the sentence appealed against was short. Instead the judge should take steps to see that the appeal was expedited. Roskill LJ again stressed that bail pending appeal should be granted only in exceptional circumstances.

Prosecution right of appeal

16.15   Where bail is granted to a person charged with an offence punishable in the case of an adult with imprisonment the prosecution may appeal to a Crown Court judge. They may only appeal if they made representations against the granting of bail. The prosecution must give oral notice at the end of the remand proceedings and written notice within two hours. The bailed person is then kept in custody until the appeal is heard and the hearing must be commenced within 48 hours from the date on which the notice was given (Bail Amendment Act 1993).

APPEAL FROM THE CROWN COURT

16.16   Although strictly outside the ambit of this work it is worth noting that young people appearing in the Crown Court may also appeal. Juveniles may appear in the Crown Court as a result of being jointly charged with an adult or having been committed subject to a grave crime. An appeal from the Crown Court in these circumstances is made to the Court of Appeal. However, unlike an appeal from the Youth Court to the Crown Court an appeal may only proceed where the trial judge grants a certificate confirming that the case is a suitable one. This is known as a grant of leave to appeal. An application for leave to appeal may also be made to a High Court Judge who will consider the application by reference to the papers. If he refuses leave the application may be renewed to the full Court of Appeal. Notice of application for leave to appeal must be lodged within 28 days of the decision of the court and must include the grounds of the appeal.

Appeal by the prosecution

16.17   Also limited to young persons appearing in the Crown Court is the power given to the prosecution to appeal a sentence passed by the Crown Court which is unduly lenient. There is no such power to appeal from the case heard in the Youth Court. The Attorney-General must lodge notice of appeal to the Court of Appeal within 28 days of the decision complained of following the procedure in CJA 1988, ss 35-36 as amended by CJ & IA 2008,s 46.

Appendix A

Magistrates' Courts (Children and Young Persons) Rules 1992 (1992 No 2071)

PART I
GENERAL

I Citation and commencement

These Rules may be cited as the Magistrates' Courts (Children and Young Persons) Rules 1992 and shall come into force on 1st October 1992.

2 Interpretation

(1) In these Rules—
   'the Act of 1933' means the Children and Young Persons Act 1933;
   'the Act of 1969' means the Children and Young Persons Act 1969;
   'the Act of 1989' means the Children Act 1989;
   'the Act of 2000' means the Powers of Criminal Courts (Sentencing) Act 2000;]
   'child' means a person under the age of fourteen;
   'court'—
   - (a) in Parts II and IV and, subject to rule 13(2), in Part III, means a youth court, and
   - (b) in rules 26 to 29, means a magistrates' court whether a youth court or not;
   'court computer system' means a computer or computer system which is used to assist to discharge and record the business of the court;]
   'guardian' has the meaning given in section 107(1) of the Act of 1933;
   'register' means the separate register kept for the youth court pursuant to rule 25 of these Rules; and
   'young person' means a person who has attained the age of fourteen and is under the age of eighteen.

(2) In these Rules, unless the context otherwise requires, references to a parent in relation to a child or young person are references—
   - (a) where a local authority has parental responsibility for him under the Act of 1989, to the local authority, and

323

(b) in any other case, to a parent who has parental responsibility for him under that Act.

(3)   In these Rules, unless the context otherwise requires, any reference to a rule, Part or Schedule shall be construed as a reference to a rule contained in these Rules, a Part thereof or a Schedule thereto, and any reference in a rule to a paragraph shall be construed as a reference to a paragraph of that rule.

3 Revocations and savings etc

(1)   Subject to paragraph (3), the Rules specified in Schedule 1 are hereby revoked to the extent specified.

(2)   Subject to paragraph (3), the provisions of the Magistrates' Courts Rules 1981 shall have effect subject to these Rules.

(3)   Nothing in these Rules shall apply in connection with any proceedings begun before the coming into force thereof.

PART II
. . .

4–12 . . .

. . .

PART III
PROCEEDINGS IN CERTAIN OTHER MATTERS

13 Application and interpretation of Part III

(1)   This Part applies in connection with proceedings in a court in the case of any child or young person in relation to whom proceedings are brought or proposed to be brought under—
   (a) section 72 or 73 of the Social Work (Scotland) Act 1968 (persons subject to supervision requirements or orders moving from or to Scotland), or
   (b) regulations made under section 25 of the Act of 1989 (authority to retain child in secure accommodation),

except that rules 14,16(2), 20 and 21 do not apply in connection with proceedings under the enactments mentioned in sub-paragraph (a) above.

(2)   In this Part—

'the applicant' means the person by whom proceedings are brought or proposed to be brought;

'court', in relation to proceedings of the kind mentioned in paragraph (1)(b), means a magistrates' court, whether a youth court or not, but does not include a family proceedings court: and

'the relevant minor' means the person in relation to whom proceedings are brought or proposed to be brought as mentioned in paragraph (1).

14 Notice by person proposing to bring proceedings

(1)   The applicant shall send a notice to the designated officer] for] the court specifying the grounds for the proceedings and the names and addresses of the persons to whom a copy of the notice is sent in pursuance of paragraph (2).

(2)   Without prejudice to section 34(2) of the Act of 1969 and regulations made under section 25 of the Act of 1989, the applicant shall—

  (a)   send to each of the persons mentioned in paragraph (3) a copy of the said notice, and

  (b)   notify each of those persons of the date, time and place appointed for the hearing unless a summons is issued for the purpose of securing his attendance thereat.

(3)   The persons referred to in paragraph (2) are—

  (a)   the relevant minor, unless it appears to the applicant inappropriate to notify him in pursuance of paragraph (2), having regard to his age and understanding,

  (b)   the parent or guardian of the relevant minor if the whereabouts of such parent or guardian is known to the applicant or can readily be ascertained by him, and

  (c)   where the father and mother of the relevant minor were not married to each other at the time of his birth, any person who is known to the applicant to have made an application for an order under section 4 of the Act of 1989 (acquisition of parental responsibility by father) which has not yet been determined.

15 Rights of parents and guardians

Without prejudice to any provision of these Rules which provides for a parent or guardian to take part in proceedings, the relevant minor's parent or guardian shall be entitled to make representations to the court at any such stage after the conclusion of the evidence in the hearing as the court considers appropriate.

16 Adjournment of proceedings and procedure at hearing

(1)   The court may, at any time, whether before or after the beginning of the hearing, adjourn the hearing, and, when so doing, may either fix the date, time and place at which the hearing is to be resumed or leave the date, time and place to be determined later by the court; but the hearing shall not be resumed at that date, time and place unless the court is satisfied that the applicant, the respondent and any other party to the proceedings have had adequate notice thereof.

(2)   Subject to the provisions of the Act of 1969, sections 56, 57 and 123 of the Magistrates' Courts Act 1980 (non-appearance of parties and defects in process) shall apply to the proceedings as if they were by way of complaint and as if any references therein to the complainant, to the defendant and to the defence were, respectively, references to the applicant, to the relevant minor and to his case.

(3)   Rules 14 and 16(1) of the Magistrates' Courts Rules 1981 (order of evidence and speeches and form of order) shall apply to the proceedings as if they were by way of complaint and as if any references therein to the complainant, to the defendant and to the defence were, respectively, references to the applicant, to the relevant minor and to his case.

17 Duty of court to explain nature of proceedings

Except where, by virtue of any enactment, the court may proceed in the absence of the relevant minor, before proceeding with the hearing the court shall inform him of the general nature both of the proceedings and of the grounds on which they are brought, in terms suitable to his age and understanding, or if by reason of his age and understanding or his absence it is impracticable so to do, shall so inform any parent or guardian of his present at the hearing.

18 Conduct of case on behalf of relevant minor

(1)   Except where the relevant minor or his parent or guardian is legally represented, the court shall, unless the relevant minor otherwise requests, allow his parent or guardian to conduct the case on his behalf, subject, however, to the provisions of rule 19(2).

(2)   If the court thinks it appropriate to do so it may, unless the relevant minor otherwise requests, allow a relative of his or some other responsible person to conduct the case on his behalf.

19 Power of court to hear evidence in absence of relevant minor and to require parent or guardian to withdraw

(1)   Where the evidence likely to be given is such that in the opinion of the court it is in the interests of the relevant minor that the whole, or any part, of the evidence should not be given in his presence, then, unless he is conducting his own case, the court may hear the whole or part of the evidence, as it thinks appropriate, in his absence; but any evidence relating to his character or conduct shall be heard in his presence.

(2)   If the court is satisfied that it is appropriate so to do, it may require a parent or guardian of the relevant minor to withdraw from the court while the relevant minor gives evidence or makes a statement; but the court shall inform the person so excluded of the substance of any allegations made against him by the relevant minor.

20 Duty of court to explain procedure to relevant minor at end of applicant's case

If it appears to the court after hearing the evidence in support of the applicant's case that he has made out *a prima facie* case it shall tell the relevant minor or the person conducting the case on his behalf under rule 18 that he may give evidence or make a statement and call witnesses.

21 Consideration of reports: secure accommodation proceedings

(1)   The court shall arrange for copies of any written report before the court to be made available, so far as practicable before the hearing to—
  (a) the applicant,
  (b) the legal representative, if any, of the relevant minor,
  (c) the parent or guardian of the relevant minor, and
  (d) the relevant minor, except where the court otherwise directs on the ground that it appears to it impracticable to disclose the report having regard to his age and understanding or undesirable to do so having regard to potential serious harm which might thereby be suffered by him.

(2)   In any case in which the court has determined that the relevant criteria are satisfied, the court shall, for the purpose of determining the maximum period of authorisation to be specified in the order, take into consideration such information as it considers necessary for that purpose, including such information which is provided in pursuance of section 9 of the Act of 1969.

(3)   Any written report may be received and considered by the court without being read aloud.

22 Duty of court to explain manner in which it proposes to deal with case and effect of order

(1)   Before finally disposing of the case, the court shall in simple language inform the relevant minor, any person conducting the case on his behalf, and his parent or guardian, if present, of the manner in which it proposes to deal with the case and allow any of those persons so informed to make representations; but the relevant minor shall not be informed as aforesaid if the court considers it undesirable or, having regard to his age and understanding, impracticable so to inform him.

(2)   On making any order, the court shall in simple language suitable to his age and understanding explain to the relevant minor the general nature and effect of the order unless it appears to it impracticable so to do having regard to his age and understanding and shall give such an explanation to the relevant minor's parent or guardian, if present.

PART IV
. . .

23–24 . . .

. . .

PART V
MISCELLANEOUS

25–29 . . .

. . .

SCHEDULE I
Revocations

Rule 3

Rules revoked	References	Extent of revocation
The Magistrates' Courts (Children and Young Persons) Rules 1988	SI 1988/913	The whole Rules
The Magistrates' Courts (Criminal Justice Act 1988) (Miscellaneous Amendments) Rules 1988	SI 1988/2132	Rule 4
The Family Proceedings Courts (Matrimonial Proceedings etc) Rules 1991	SI 1991/1991	Paragragh 7 of Schedule 2

SCHEDULE 2
Forms

Rule 29

Forms I-6

. . .

Revoked by SI 2003/1236, rr 64, 71.
Date in force: 20 June 2003: see SI 2003/1236, r 1.

Form 7

. . .

Revoked, on the coming into force of the Criminal Procedure Rules 2005, SI 2005/384, by provision of r 2.1 thereof, the Courts Act 2003, the Courts Act 2003 (Commencement No 6 and Savings) Order 2004, SI 2004/2066 and the Courts Act 2003 (Consequential Amendments) Order 2004, SI 2004/2035.

Date in force: 4 April 2005: see SI 2005/384, r 2.1(3); for savings see SI 2004/2066, art 3 and SI 2005/384, r 2.1(3).

Forms 8-9

. . .

Revoked by SI 2003/1236, rr 64, 71.
Date in force: 20 June 2003: see SI 2003/1236, r 1.

Form 10

Revoked, on the coming into force of the Criminal Procedure Rules 2005, SI 2005/384, by provision of r 2.1 thereof, the Courts Act 2003, the Courts Act 2003 (Commencement No 6 and Savings) Order 2004, SI 2004/2066 and the Courts Act 2003 (Consequential Amendments) Order 2004, SI 2004/2035.
Date in force: 4 April 2005: see SI 2005/384, r 2.1(3); for savings see SI 2004/2066, art 3 and SI 2005/384, r 2.1(3).

Forms 11-54

. . .

Revoked by SI 2003/1236, rr 64, 71.
Date in force: 20 June 2003: see SI 2003/1236, r 1.

Appendix B

The Youth Courts (Constitution of Committees and Right to Preside) Rules 2007 (SI 2007 No 1611)

Citation and commencement

1. These Rules may be cited as the Youth Courts (Constitution of Committees and Right to Preside) Rules 2007 and shall come into force on 13th July 2007.

Interpretation

2. In these Rules—
    'the 2007 Rules' means the Justices of the Peace (Training Development and Committee) Rules 2007;
    'BTDC' means the Bench Training and Development Committee established in accordance with the 2007 Rules;
    'ILYTDC' means the Inner London Youth Training and Development Committee established in accordance with the 2007 Rules;
    'Inner London area' means the local justice areas covering the London Boroughs listed in Part 2 of Schedule I to the 2007 Rules;
    'justice' means a lay justice and, in relation to a local justice area, means a justice assigned to that area;
    'justices' clerk', in relation to a local justice area, means a justices' clerk assigned to that area and includes any person acting as such;
    'outgoing panel' means—
        (a) in relation to the Inner London area, the youth panel for the metropolitan area established in accordance with Schedule 2 of the Children and Young Persons Act 1933; and
        (b) in any other case, the youth panel formed for a local justice area in accordance with the Youth Courts (Constitution) Rules 1954;
    'youth election meeting' means the meeting held by the youth panel between 1st September and 30th November each year in accordance with rule 4; and
    'youth justice' means a justice authorised to sit as a member of a youth court.

Formation of Youth Panels

3.—(1) Subject to rule (5), there shall be a Committee, to be known as a youth panel, for each local justice area.

(2) The youth panel shall consist of the youth justices for the local justice area to which the youth panel relates.

Meetings of Youth Panels

4.—(1) A youth panel shall meet as often as necessary but not less than twice a year.

(2) One of the meetings of the youth panel, to be known as the youth election meeting, shall take place between the 1st September and 30th November each year.

Combined Panels

5.—(1) Where, immediately before 13th July 2007, two or more outgoing panels had formed a combined panel, there shall be a combined youth panel for the local justice areas covered by the combined outgoing panel.

(2) There shall be a combined youth panel for the Inner London area.

(3) The Lord Chief Justice may, on the application of the youth panels concerned and after consultation with the Area Director, give approval for—
  (a) the formation of a combined youth panel in respect of two or more local justice areas; or
  (b) or dissolution of a combined youth panel (including a combined youth panel referred to in paragraph (1) or (2)).

Chairman and deputy chairmen of Youth Panels

6.—(1) A person who, immediately before 13th July 2007, held office as a chairman of an outgoing panel or a combined outgoing panel shall hold office as chairman of the youth panel for the corresponding local justice area or areas for a term beginning on 13th July 2007 and ending on 31st December 2007.

(2) The members of each youth panel shall elect, by secret ballot, a chairman and one or more deputy chairmen in accordance with this rule, to hold office for a term of one year from the 1st January following the date of appointment.

(3) At the youth election meeting in 2007 the members of the youth panel shall elect the chairman and one or more deputy chairmen to hold office from 1st January 2008.

(4) At the youth election meeting in 2007 and each subsequent youth election meeting the members of the youth panel shall decide—
  (a) whether the election in the following year shall take place—
      (i) at the youth election meeting; or
      (ii) by postal ballot to be conducted prior to the youth election meeting; and
  (b) if appropriate, the method of conducting a postal ballot.

(5) Nominations for the chairman and one or more deputy chairmen may be made by the members of the youth panel to the justices' clerk.

(6) If a vacancy occurs in the chairmanship or deputy chairmanship, the members of the youth panel shall, as soon as practicable, elect by secret ballot a chairman or, as the case may be, deputy chairman, to hold office for the remainder of the period for which the person replaced would have served.

Eligibility for re-election of chairman or deputy chairman

7.—(1) In this rule—
  (a) 'previous chairman' means a youth justice who has held office as chairman of a youth panel established under these Rules or of an outgoing panel or combined outgoing panel; and
  (b) references, however phrased, to periods of office shall include periods of office held as chairman or deputy chairman, as the case may be, of an outgoing panel or combined outgoing panel.

(2) A previous chairman shall not be eligible for re-election as chairman if, on 1st January after the election, he will have held such office for periods totalling more than two years unless at least six years have elapsed since he last held office.

(3) In any event a previous chairman shall not be eligible for re-election as chairman if, on the 1st January after the election, he will have held office for periods totalling more than five years.

(4) A youth justice who has held office as deputy chairman of a youth panel established under these Rules ... shall not be eligible for reelection as deputy chairman if on 1st January after the election he will have held such office for periods totalling more than five years.

Conduct of ballots

8.—(1) Where there is an equality of votes between any candidates in a ballot and the addition of a vote would entitle one of them to be elected the justices' clerk shall decide between the candidates by lot.

(2) Where a ballot paper is returned unmarked or marked in such a manner that there is a doubt as to the identity of the justice or justices for whom the vote is cast the ballot paper or the vote, as the case may be, shall be rejected when the votes are counted.

Functions of Youth Panels

9.   A youth panel shall—
  (a) make recommendations to—
      (i)   the BTDC for its local justice area; or
      (ii) in the case of the Inner London area, the ILYTDC, in relation to the number of new justices required to sit and preside in youth courts; and
  (b) liaise with other bodies in order to share information and represent the views of youth justices.

Constitution of youth courts

10.—(1) A youth court shall consist of either—
  (a) a District Judge (Magistrates' Courts) sitting alone; or
  (b) not more than three justices who shall include a man and a woman.

(2) Paragraph (3) applies if it is not possible to comply with paragraph (1)(b) because—
  (a) no man or no woman is available due to circumstances unforeseen when the justices to sit were chosen; or
  (b) the only man or the only woman present cannot properly sit as a member of the court.

(3) Where this paragraph applies, the court may be constituted without a man, or as the case may be, a woman if the other members of the youth court think it inexpedient in the interests of justice for there to be an adjournment.

(4) Nothing in this rule shall be construed as requiring a youth court to include both a man and a woman in any case where a single justice has by law jurisdiction to act.

Chairmanship of youth courts

11.—(1) A youth court, other than one consisting of a District Judge

(Magistrates' Courts) sitting alone, shall sit under the chairmanship of—
- (a) a District Judge (Magistrates' Courts) if he is sitting as a member of the court; or
- (b) a youth justice who is on the list of approved youth court chairmen.

(2) A youth justice may preside before he has been included on a list of approved youth court chairmen only if—
- (a) he is under the supervision of a youth justice who is on a list of approved youth court chairmen; and
- (b) he has completed the training courses prescribed by rule 31 of the 2007 Rules.

(3) In this rule 'list of approved youth court chairmen' means a list kept by the ILYTDC or BTDC as appropriate in accordance with rules 32 and 36 of the 2007 Rules.

Absence of youth justice entitled to preside

12.—(1) The youth justices present may appoint one of their number to preside in a youth court to deal with any case in the absence of a justice entitled to preside under rule 11 if—
- (a) before making such appointment the youth justices present are satisfied as to the suitability for this purpose of the justice proposed; and
- (b) except as mentioned in paragraph (2), the justice proposed has completed or is undergoing a chairman training course in accordance with rule 31(f) of the 2007 Rules.

(2) The condition in paragraph (1)(b) does not apply if by reason of illness, circumstances unforeseen when the youth justices to sit were chosen or other emergency no justice who complies with that condition is present.

Revocation

13. The Youth Courts (Constitution) Rules 1954 are hereby revoked.

Appendix C

Criminal Procedure Rules 2005
(SI 2005 No 384)

PART I
THE OVERRIDING OBJECTIVE

Contents of this Part

1.1 The overriding objective

(1)   The overriding objective of this new code is that criminal cases be dealt with justly.

(2)   Dealing with a criminal case justly includes—
   (a) acquitting the innocent and convicting the guilty;
   (b) dealing with the prosecution and the defence fairly;
   (c) recognising the rights of a defendant, particularly those under Article 6 of the European Convention on Human Rights;
   (d) respecting the interests of witnesses, victims and jurors and keeping them informed of the progress of the case;
   (e) dealing with the case efficiently and expeditiously;
   (f) ensuring that appropriate information is available to the court when bail and sentence are considered; and
   (g) dealing with the case in ways that take into account—
      (i)   the gravity of the offence alleged,
      (ii) the complexity of what is in issue,
      (iii) the severity of the consequences for the defendant and others affected, and
      (iv) the needs of other cases.

1.2 The duty of the participants in a criminal case

(1)   Each participant, in the conduct of each case, must—
  (a) prepare and conduct the case in accordance with the overriding objective;
  (b) comply with these Rules, practice directions and directions made by the court; and
  (c) at once inform the court and all parties of any significant failure (whether or not that participant is responsible for that failure) to take any procedural step required by these Rules, any practice direction or any direction of the court. A failure is significant if it might hinder the court in furthering the overriding objective.

(2)   Anyone involved in any way with a criminal case is a participant in its conduct for the purposes of this rule.

1.3 The application by the court of the overriding objective

The court must further the overriding objective in particular when—
  (a) exercising any power given to it by legislation (including these Rules);
  (b) applying any practice direction; or
  (c) interpreting any rule or practice direction.

PART 2

UNDERSTANDING AND APPLYING THE RULES

Contents of this Part

2.1 When the Rules apply

(1)   In general, the Criminal Procedure Rules apply—
  (a) in all criminal cases in magistrates' courts and in the Crown Court; and
  (b) in all cases in the criminal division of the Court of Appeal.

(2)   If a rule applies only in one or two of those courts, the rule makes that clear.

(3)   The Rules apply on and after 4th April, 2005, but do not affect any right or duty existing under the rules of court revoked by the coming into force of these Rules.

[(4)   The rules in Part 33 apply in all cases in which the defendant is charged on or after 6 November 2006 and in other cases if the court so orders.]

[(5)   The rules in Part 14 apply in cases in which one of the events listed in sub-paragraphs (a) to (d) of rule 14.1(1) takes place on or after 2nd April 2007. In other cases the rules of court replaced by those rules apply.

(6)   The rules in Part 28 apply in cases in which an application under rule 28.3 is made on or after 2nd April 2007. In other cases the rules replaced by those rules apply.]

[(7)   The rules in Parts 65, 66, 67, 68, 69 and 70 apply where an appeal, application or reference, to which one of those Parts applies, is made on or after 1st October 2007. In other cases the rules replaced by those rules apply.]

[(8)   The rules in Parts 57–62 apply in proceedings to which one of those Parts applies that begin on or after 1st April 2008. In such proceedings beginning before that date the rules in those Parts apply as if—
  (a) the amendments made to them by The Criminal Procedure (Amendment No 3) Rules 2007 had not been made; and
  (b) references to the Director of the Assets Recovery Agency or to that Agency were references to the Serious Organised Crime Agency.]

[(9)   The rules in Part 50 apply in cases in which the defendant is charged on or after 7th April 2008 and in other cases if the court so orders. Otherwise, the rules replaced by those rules apply.

(10)   The rules in Part 74 apply where an appeal, application or reference, to which Part 74 applies, is made on or after 7th April 2008. In other cases the rules replaced by those rules apply.]

[(11)   The rules in Part 7 apply in cases in which on or after 6th October 2008—
  (a) a prosecutor serves an information on the court officer or presents it to a magistrates' court;
  (b) a public prosecutor issues a written charge; or
  (c) a person who is in custody is charged with an offence.

In other cases the rules replaced by those rules apply.

(12) The rules in Part 63 apply in cases in which the decision that is the subject of the appeal, or reference, to which that Part applies is made on or after 6th October 2008. In other cases the rules replaced by those rules apply.]

[*[Note. The rules replaced by the first Criminal Procedure Rules (The Criminal Procedure Rules 2005) were revoked when those Rules came into force by provisions of the Courts Act 2003, The Courts Act 2003 (Consequential Amendments) Order 2004 and The Courts Act 2003 (Commencement No 6 and Savings) Order 2004. The first Criminal Procedure Rules reproduced the substance of all the rules they replaced.]*]

2.2 Definitions

(1) In these Rules, unless the context makes it clear that something different is meant:

['business day' means any day except Saturday, Sunday, Christmas Day, Boxing Day, Good Friday, Easter Monday or a bank holiday;]

'court' means a tribunal with jurisdiction over criminal cases. It includes a judge, recorder, District Judge (Magistrates' Courts), lay justice and, when exercising their judicial powers, the Registrar of Criminal Appeals, a justices' clerk or assistant clerk;

'court officer' means the appropriate member of the staff of a court;

. . .

['live link' means an arrangement by which a person can see and hear, and be seen and heard by, the court when that person is not in court;]

'Practice Direction' means the Lord Chief Justice's Consolidated Criminal Practice Direction, as amended[; and]

['public interest ruling' means a ruling about whether it is in the public interest to disclose prosecution material under sections 3(6), 7A(8) or 8(5) of the Criminal Procedure and Investigations Act 1996.]

(2) Definitions of some other expressions are in the rules in which they apply.

2.3 References to Acts of Parliament and to Statutory Instruments

In these Rules, where a rule refers to an Act of Parliament or to subordinate legislation by title and year, subsequent references to that Act or to that legislation in the rule are shortened: so, for example, after a reference to the Criminal Procedure and Investigations Act 1996 that Act is called 'the 1996 Act'; and after a reference to the Criminal

Procedure and Investigations Act 1996 (Defence Disclosure Time Limits) Regulations 1997 those Regulations are called 'the 1997 Regulations'.

2.4 The glossary

The glossary at the end of the Rules is a guide to the meaning of certain legal expressions used in them.

[2.5 Representatives]

[(1)   Under these Rules, unless the context makes it clear that something different is meant, anything that a party may or must do may be done—
  (a) by a legal representative on that party's behalf;
  (b) by a person with the corporation's written authority, where that party is a corporation;
  (c) with the help of a parent, guardian or other suitable supporting adult where that party is a defendant—
    (i) who is under 18, or
    (ii) whose understanding of what the case involves is limited.

(2)   Anyone with a prosecutor's authority to do so may, on that prosecutor's behalf—
  (a) serve on the magistrates' court officer, or present to a magistrates' court, an information under section 1 of the Magistrates' Courts Act 1980; or
  (b) issue a written charge and requisition under section 29 of the Criminal Justice Act 2003.

[Note. See also section 122 of the Magistrates' Courts Act 1980. A party's legal representative must be entitled to act as such under section 27 or 28 of the Courts and Legal Services Act 1990.

Section 33(6) of the Criminal Justice Act 1925, section 46 of the Magistrates' Courts Act 1980 and Schedule 3 to that Act provide for the representation of a corporation.

Part 7 contains rules about starting a prosecution.]]

PART 3
CASE MANAGEMENT

Contents of this Part

3.1 The scope of this Part

This Part applies to the management of each case in a magistrates' court and in the Crown Court (including an appeal to the Crown Court) until the conclusion of that case.

[Note. Rules that apply to procedure in the Court of Appeal are in Parts 65 to 73 of these Rules.]

3.2 The duty of the court

(1) The court must further the overriding objective by actively managing the case.

(2) Active case management includes—
    (a) the early identification of the real issues;
    (b) the early identification of the needs of witnesses;
    (c) achieving certainty as to what must be done, by whom, and when, in particular by the early setting of a timetable for the progress of the case;
    (d) monitoring the progress of the case and compliance with directions;
    (e) ensuring that evidence, whether disputed or not, is presented in the shortest and clearest way;
    (f) discouraging delay, dealing with as many aspects of the case as possible on the same occasion, and avoiding unnecessary hearings;
    (g) encouraging the participants to co-operate in the progression of the case; and
    (h) making use of technology.

(3)   The court must actively manage the case by giving any direction appropriate to the needs of that case as early as possible.

3.3 The duty of the parties

Each party must—
- (a)   actively assist the court in fulfilling its duty under rule 3.2, without or if necessary with a direction; and
- (b)   apply for a direction if needed to further the overriding objective.

3.4 Case progression officers and their duties

(1)   At the beginning of the case each party must, unless the court otherwise directs—
- (a)   nominate an individual responsible for progressing that case; and
- (b)   tell other parties and the court who he is and how to contact him.

(2)   In fulfilling its duty under rule 3.2, the court must where appropriate—
- (a)   nominate a court officer responsible for progressing the case; and
- (b)   make sure the parties know who he is and how to contact him.

(3)   In this Part a person nominated under this rule is called a case progression officer.

(4)   A case progression officer must—
- (a)   monitor compliance with directions;
- (b)   make sure that the court is kept informed of events that may affect the progress of that case;
- (c)   make sure that he can be contacted promptly about the case during ordinary business hours;
- (d)   act promptly and reasonably in response to communications about the case; and
- (e)   if he will be unavailable, appoint a substitute to fulfil his duties and inform the other case progression officers.

3.5 The court's case management powers

(1)   In fulfilling its duty under rule 3.2 the court may give any direction and take any step actively to manage a case unless that direction or step would be inconsistent with legislation, including these Rules.

(2)   In particular, the court may—
- (a)   nominate a judge, magistrate, justices' clerk or assistant to a justices' clerk to manage the case;
- (b)   give a direction on its own initiative or on application by a party;

    (c) ask or allow a party to propose a direction;

    (d) for the purpose of giving directions, receive applications and representations by letter, by telephone or by any other means of electronic communication, and conduct a hearing by such means;

    (e) give a direction without a hearing;

    (f) fix, postpone, bring forward, extend or cancel a hearing;

    (g) shorten or extend (even after it has expired) a time limit fixed by a direction;

    (h) require that issues in the case should be determined separately, and decide in what order they will be determined; and

    (i) specify the consequences of failing to comply with a direction.

(3)   A magistrates' court may give a direction that will apply in the Crown Court if the case is to continue there.

(4)   The Crown Court may give a direction that will apply in a magistrates' court if the case is to continue there.

(5)   Any power to give a direction under this Part includes a power to vary or revoke that direction.

[(6) If a party fails to comply with a rule or a direction, the court may—

    (a) fix, postpone, bring forward, extend, cancel or adjourn a hearing;

    (b) exercise its powers to make a costs order; and

    (c) impose such other sanction as may be appropriate.]

[Note. Depending upon the nature of a case and the stage that it has reached, its progress may be affected by other Criminal Procedure Rules and by other legislation. The note at the end of this Part lists other rules and legislation that may apply.

[See also rule 3.10.

The court may make a costs order under—

    (a) section 19 of the Prosecution of Offences Act 1985, where the court decides that one party to criminal proceedings has incurred costs as a result of an unnecessary or improper act or omission by, or on behalf of, another party;

    (b) section 19A of that Act, where the court decides that a party has incurred costs as a result of an improper, unreasonable or negligent act or omission on the part of a legal representative;

    (c) section 19B of that Act, where the court decides that there has been serious misconduct by a person who is not a party.

Under some other legislation, including Parts 24, 34 and 35 of these Rules, if a party fails to comply with a rule or a direction then in some circumstances—

(a) the court may refuse to allow that party to introduce evidence;
(b) evidence that that party wants to introduce may not be admissible;
(c) the court may draw adverse inferences from the late introduction of an issue or evidence.

See also—

section 81(1) of the Police and Criminal Evidence Act 1984 and section 20(3) of the Criminal Procedure and Investigations Act 1996 (advance disclosure of expert evidence);

section 11(5) of the Criminal Procedure and Investigations Act 1996 (faults in disclosure by accused);

section 132(5) of the Criminal Justice Act 2003 (failure to give notice of hearsay evidence).*]]*

3.6 Application to vary a direction

(1)   A party may apply to vary a direction if—
(a) the court gave it without a hearing;
(b) the court gave it at a hearing in his absence; or
(c) circumstances have changed.

(2)   A party who applies to vary a direction must—
(a) apply as soon as practicable after he becomes aware of the grounds for doing so; and
(b) give as much notice to the other parties as the nature and urgency of his application permits.

3.7 Agreement to vary a time limit fixed by a direction

(1)   The parties may agree to vary a time limit fixed by a direction, but only if—
(a) the variation will not—
(i)   affect the date of any hearing that has been fixed, or
(ii) significantly affect the progress of the case in any other way;
(b) the court has not prohibited variation by agreement; and
(c) the court's case progression officer is promptly informed.

(2)   The court's case progression officer must refer the agreement to the court if he doubts the condition in paragraph (1)(a) is satisfied.

3.8 Case preparation and progression

(1)   At every hearing, if a case cannot be concluded there and then the court must give directions so that it can be concluded at the next hearing or as soon as possible after that.

(2) At every hearing the court must, where relevant—
  (a) if the defendant is absent, decide whether to proceed nonetheless;
  (b) take the defendant's plea (unless already done) or if no plea can be taken then find out whether the defendant is likely to plead guilty or not guilty;
  (c) set, follow or revise a timetable for the progress of the case, which may include a timetable for any hearing including the trial or (in the Crown Court) the appeal;
  (d) in giving directions, ensure continuity in relation to the court and to the parties' representatives where that is appropriate and practicable; and
  (e) where a direction has not been complied with, find out why, identify who was responsible, and take appropriate action.

[(3) In order to prepare for a trial in the Crown Court, the court must conduct a plea and case management hearing unless the circumstances make that unnecessary.]

3.9 Readiness for trial or appeal

(1) This rule applies to a party's preparation for trial or (in the Crown Court) appeal, and in this rule and rule 3.10 trial includes any hearing at which evidence will be introduced.

(2) In fulfilling his duty under rule 3.3, each party must—
  (a) comply with directions given by the court;
  (b) take every reasonable step to make sure his witnesses will attend when they are needed;
  (c) make appropriate arrangements to present any written or other material; and
  (d) promptly inform the court and the other parties of anything that may—
      (i) affect the date or duration of the trial or appeal, or
      (ii) significantly affect the progress of the case in any other way.

(3) The court may require a party to give a certificate of readiness.

[3.10 Conduct of a trial or an appeal]

[In order to manage a trial or (in the Crown Court) an appeal—
  (a) the court must establish, with the active assistance of the parties, what disputed issues they intend to explore; and
  (b) the court may require a party to identify—
      (i) which witnesses that party wants to give oral evidence,
      (ii) the order in which that party wants those witnesses to give their evidence,

(iii) whether that party requires an order compelling the attendance of a witness,

(iv) what arrangements are desirable to facilitate the giving of evidence by a witness,

(v) what arrangements are desirable to facilitate the participation of any other person, including the defendant,

(vi) what written evidence that party intends to introduce,

(vii) what other material, if any, that person intends to make available to the court in the presentation of the case,

(viii) whether that party intends to raise any point of law that could affect the conduct of the trial or appeal, and

(ix) what timetable that party proposes and expects to follow.]

[[*Note. See also rule 3.5.*]]

3.11 Case management forms and records

(1) The case management forms set out in the Practice Direction must be used, and where there is no form then no specific formality is required.

(2) The court must make available to the parties a record of directions given.

[*Note. Case management may be affected by the following other rules and legislation:*

Criminal Procedure Rules

Parts 10.4 and 27.2: reminders of right to object to written evidence being read at trial

Part 12.2: time for first appearance of accused sent for trial

Part 13: dismissal of charges sent or transferred to the Crown Court

Part 14: the indictment

Part 15: preparatory hearings in serious fraud and other complex or lengthy cases

Parts 21–26: the rules that deal with disclosure

Parts 27–36: the rules that deal with evidence

Part 37: summary trial

Part 38: trial of children and young persons

Part 39: trial on indictment

Appendix C

Regulations

Prosecution of Offences (Custody Time Limits) Regulations 1987

Criminal Justice Act 1987 (Notice of Transfer) Regulations 1988

Criminal Justice Act 1991 (Notice of Transfer) Regulations 1992

Criminal Procedure and Investigations Act 1996 (Defence Disclosure Time Limits) Regulations 1997

[Crime and Disorder Act 1998 (Service of Prosecution Evidence) Regulations 2005]

Provisions of Acts of Parliament

Sections 5, 10 and 18, Magistrates' Courts Act 1980: powers to adjourn hearings

Sections 128 and 129, Magistrates' Courts Act 1980: remand in custody by magistrates' courts

Part 1, Criminal Procedure and Investigations Act 1996: disclosure

Schedule 2, Criminal Procedure and Investigations Act 1996: use of witness statements at trial

Section 2, Administration of Justice (Miscellaneous Provisions) Act 1933: procedural conditions for trial in the Crown Court

Section 6, Magistrates' Courts Act 1980: committal for trial

Section 4, Criminal Justice Act 1987: section 53, Criminal Justice Act 1991: section 51 [and (so far as it is in force) section 51A], Crime and Disorder Act 1998: other procedures by which a case reaches the Crown Court

Section 7, Criminal Justice Act 1987; Parts III and IV, Criminal Procedure and Investigations Act 1996: pre-trial and preparatory hearings in the Crown Court

Section 9, Criminal Justice Act 1967: proof by written witness statement]

PART II
TRANSFER FOR TRIAL OF SERIOUS FRAUD CASES OR CASES
INVOLVING CHILDREN

Contents of this Part

11.1 Interpretation of this Part

(1)   In this Part:
'notice of transfer' means a notice referred to in section 4(1) of the Criminal Justice Act 1987 or section 53(1) of the Criminal Justice Act 1991.

(2)   Where this Part requires a document to be given or sent, or a notice to be communicated in writing, it may, with the consent of the addressee, be sent by electronic communication.

(3)   Electronic communication means a communication transmitted (whether from one person to another, from one device to another or from a person to a device or vice versa)—
  (a)   by means of an electronic communications network (within the meaning of the Communications Act 2003); or
  (b)   by other means but while in an electronic form.

[Note. Formerly rule 2 of the Magistrates' Courts (Notice of Transfer) Rules 1988 and rule 2 of the Magistrates' Courts (Notice of Transfer) (Children's Evidence) Rules 1992. See also sections 4 and 5 of the Criminal Justice Act 1987 and section 53 of, and Schedule 6 to, the Criminal Justice Act 1991. On the coming into force of Schedule 3 to the Criminal Justice Act 2003 those provisions will be replaced with sections 51B and 51C of the Crime and Disorder Act 1998, which are to similar effect. For the duties of the prosecuting authority see the Criminal Justice Act 1987 (Notice of Transfer) Regulations 1988 and the Criminal Justice Act 1991 (Notice of Transfer) Regulations 1992.]

11.2 Transfer on bail

(1)   Where a person in respect of whom notice of transfer has been given—
  (a)   is granted bail under section 5(3) or (7A) of the Criminal Justice

Act 1987 by the magistrates' court to which notice of transfer was given; or

(b) is granted bail under paragraph 2(1) or (7) of Schedule 6 to the Criminal Justice Act 1991 by the magistrates' court to which notice of transfer was given,

the magistrates' court officer shall give notice thereof in writing to the governor of the prison or remand centre to which the said person would have been committed by that court if he had been committed in custody for trial.

(2) Where notice of transfer is given under section 4(1) of the 1987 Act in respect of a corporation the magistrates' court officer shall give notice thereof to the governor of the prison to which would be committed a male over 21 committed by that court in custody for trial.

[Note. Formerly rule 3 of the Magistrates' Courts (Notice of Transfer) Rules 1988 and rule 3 of the Magistrates' Courts (Notice of Transfer) (Children's Evidence) Rules 1992. For bail generally, see Part 19.]

11.3 Notice where person removed to hospital

Where a transfer direction has been given by the Secretary of State under section 47 or 48 of the Mental Health Act 1983 in respect of a person remanded in custody by a magistrates' court and, before the direction ceases to have effect, notice of transfer is given in respect of that person, the magistrates' court officer shall give notice thereof in writing—

(a) to the governor of the prison to which that person would have been committed by that court if he had been committed in custody for trial; and

(b) to the managers of the hospital where he is detained.

[Note. Formerly rule 4 of the Magistrates' Courts (Notice of Transfer) Rules 1988 and rule 4 of the Magistrates' Courts (Notice of Transfer) (Children's Evidence) Rules 1992.]

11.4 Variation of arrangements for bail

(1) A person who intends to make an application to a magistrates' court under section 3(8) of the Bail Act 1976 as that subsection has effect under section 3(8A) of that Act shall give notice thereof in writing to the magistrates' court officer, and to the designated authority or the defendant, as the case may be, and to any sureties concerned.

(2) Where, on an application referred to in paragraph (1), a magistrates' court varies or imposes any conditions of bail, the magistrates' court officer shall send to the Crown Court officer a copy of the record made

in pursuance of section 5 of the 1976 Act relating to such variation or imposition of conditions.

[Note. Formerly rule 5 of the Magistrates' Courts (Notice of Transfer) Rules 1988.]

11.5 Documents etc to be sent to Crown Court

As soon as practicable after a magistrates' court to which notice of transfer has been given has discharged the functions reserved to it under section 4(1) of the Criminal Justice Act 1987 or section 53(3) of the Criminal Justice Act 1991, the magistrates' court officer shall send to the Crown Court officer—

(a) a list of the names, addresses and occupations of the witnesses;

(b) a copy of the record made in pursuance of section 5 of the Bail Act 1976 relating to the grant of withholding of bail in respect of the accused;

(c) any recognizance entered into by any person as surety for the accused together with a statement of any enlargement thereof;

(d) a copy of any representation order previously made in the case; and

(e) a copy of any application for a representation order previously made in the case which has been refused.

[Note. Formerly rule 7 of the Magistrates' Courts (Notice of Transfer) Rules 1988 and rule 6 of the Magistrates' Courts (Notice of Transfer) (Children's Evidence) Rules 1992.]

PART 16
RESTRICTIONS ON REPORTING AND PUBLIC ACCESS

Contents of this Part

16.1 Application for a reporting direction under section 46(6) of the Youth Justice and Criminal Evidence Act 1999

(1) An application for a reporting direction made by a party to any criminal proceedings, in relation to a witness in those proceedings, must be made in the form set out in the Practice Direction or orally under rule 16.3.

(2) If an application for a reporting direction is made in writing, the applicant shall send that application to the court officer and copies shall be sent at the same time to every other party to those proceedings.

[Note. Formerly rule 2 of the Magistrates' Courts (Reports Relating to Adult Witnesses) Rules 2004and rule 2 of the Crown Court (Reports Relating to Adult Witnesses) Rules 2004. Section 46 of the Youth Justice and Criminal Evidence Act 1999 applies to adult witnesses the quality of whose evidence, or whose co-operation, is likely to be diminished if their identity is made public. For reporting restrictions generally see direction I.3 in the Practice Direction.]

16.2 Opposing an application for a reporting direction under section 46(6) of the Youth Justice and Criminal Evidence Act 1999

(1) If an application for a reporting direction is made in writing, any party to the proceedings who wishes to oppose that application must notify the applicant and the court officer in writing of his opposition and give reasons for it.

(2) A person opposing an application must state in the written notification whether he disputes that the—
    (a) witness is eligible for protection under section 46 of the Youth Justice and Criminal Evidence Act 1999; or
    (b) granting of protection would be likely to improve the quality of the evidence given by the witness or the level of co-operation given by the witness to any party to the proceedings in connection with that party's preparation of its case.

(3) The notification under paragraph (1) must be given within five

business days of the date the application was served on him unless an extension of time is granted under rule 16.6.

[Note. Formerly rule 3 of the Magistrates' Courts (Reports Relating to Adult Witnesses) Rules 2004 and rule 3 of the Crown Court (Reports Relating to Adult Witnesses) Rules 2004.]

16.3 Urgent action on an application under section 46(6) of the Youth Justice and Criminal Evidence Act 1999

(1) The court may give a reporting direction under section 46 of the Youth Justice and Criminal Evidence Act 1999 in relation to a witness in those proceedings, notwithstanding that the five business days specified in rule 16.2(3) have not expired if—
  (a) an application is made to it for the purposes of this rule; and
  (b) it is satisfied that, due to exceptional circumstances, it is appropriate to do so.

(2) Any party to the proceedings may make the application under paragraph (1) whether or not an application has already been made under rule 16.1.

(3) An application under paragraph (1) may be made orally or in writing.

(4) If an application is made orally, the court may hear and take into account representations made to it by any person who in the court's view has a legitimate interest in the application before it.

(5) The application must specify the exceptional circumstances on which the applicant relies.

[Note. Formerly rule 4 of the Magistrates' Courts (Reports Relating to Adult Witnesses) Rules 2004 and rule 4 of the Crown Court (Reports Relating to Adult Witnesses) Rules 2004.]

16.4 Excepting direction under section 46(9) of the Youth Justice and Criminal Evidence Act 1999

(1) An application for an excepting direction under section 46(9) of the Youth Justice and Criminal Evidence Act 1999 (a direction dispensing with restrictions imposed by a reporting direction) may be made by—
  (a) any party to those proceedings; or
  (b) any person who, although not a party to the proceedings, is directly affected by a reporting direction given in relation to a witness in those proceedings.

(2) If an application for an excepting direction is made, the applicant must state why—

(a) the effect of a reporting direction imposed places a substantial and unreasonable restriction on the reporting of the proceedings; and

(b) it is in the public interest to remove or relax those restrictions.

(3)   An application for an excepting direction may be made in writing, pursuant to paragraph (4), at any time after the commencement of the proceedings in the court or orally at a hearing of an application for a reporting direction.

(4)   If the application for an excepting direction is made in writing it must be in the form set out in the Practice Direction and the applicant shall send that application to the court officer and copies shall be sent at the same time to every party to those proceedings.

(5)   Any person served with a copy of an application for an excepting direction who wishes to oppose it, must notify the applicant and the court officer in writing of his opposition and give reasons for it.

(6)   The notification under paragraph (5) must be given within five business days of the date the application was served on him unless an extension of time is granted under rule 16.6.

[Note. Formerly rule 5 of the Magistrates' Courts (Reports Relating to Adult Witnesses) Rules 2004 and rule 5 of the Crown Court (Reports Relating to Adult Witnesses) Rules 2004.]

16.5 Variation or revocation of a reporting or excepting direction under section 46 of the Youth Justice and Criminal Evidence Act 1999

(1)   An application for the court to—
  (a) revoke a reporting direction; or
  (b) vary or revoke an excepting direction,

may be made to the court at any time after the commencement of the proceedings in the court.

(2)   An application under paragraph (1) may be made by a party to the proceedings in which the direction was issued, or by a person who, although not a party to those proceedings, is in the opinion of the court directly affected by the direction.

(3)   An application under paragraph (1) must be made in writing and the applicant shall send that application to the officer of the court in which the proceedings commenced, and at the same time copies of the application shall be sent to every party or, as the case may be, every party to the proceedings.

(4)   The applicant must set out in his application the reasons why he seeks to have the direction varied or, as the case may be, revoked.

(5)   Any person served with a copy of an application who wishes to oppose it, must notify the applicant and the court officer in writing of his opposition and give reasons for it.

(6)   The notification under paragraph (5) must be given within five business days of the date the application was served on him unless an extension of time is granted under rule 16.6.

[Note. Formerly rule 6 of the Magistrates' Courts (Reports Relating to Adult Witnesses) Rules 2004 and rule 6 of the Crown Court (Reports Relating to Adult Witnesses) Rules 2004.]

16.6 Application for an extension of time in proceedings under section 46 of the Youth Justice and Criminal Evidence Act 1999

(1)   An application may be made in writing to extend the period of time for notification under rule 16.2(3), rule 16.4(6) or rule 16.5(6) before that period has expired.

(2)   An application must be accompanied by a statement setting out the reasons why the applicant is unable to give notification within that period.

(3)   An application must be sent to the court officer and a copy of the application must be sent at the same time to the applicant.

[Note. Formerly rule 7 of the Magistrates' Courts (Reports Relating to Adult Witnesses) Rules 2004 and rule 7 of the Crown Court (Reports Relating to Adult Witnesses) Rules 2004.]

16.7 Decision of the court on an application under section 46 of the Youth Justice and Criminal Evidence Act 1999

(1)   The court may—
   (a)   determine any application made under rules 16.1 and rules 16.3 to 16.6 without a hearing; or
   (b)   direct a hearing of any application.

(2)   The court officer shall notify all the parties of the court's decision as soon as reasonably practicable.

(3)   If a hearing of an application is to take place, the court officer shall notify each party to the proceedings of the time and place of the hearing.

(4)   A court may hear and take into account representations made to it by any person who in the court's view has a legitimate interest in the application before it.

[Note. Formerly rule 8 of the Magistrates' Courts (Reports Relating to Adult Witnesses) Rules 2004 and rule 8 of the Crown Court (Reports Relating to Adult Witnesses) Rules 2004.]

16.8 Proceedings sent or transferred to the Crown Court with direction under section 46 of the Youth Justice and Criminal Evidence Act 1999 in force

Where proceedings in which reporting directions or excepting directions have been ordered are sent or transferred from a magistrates' court to the Crown Court, the magistrates' court officer shall forward copies of all relevant directions to the Crown Court officer at the place to which the proceedings are sent or transferred.

[Note. Formerly rule 9 of the Magistrates' Courts (Reports Relating to Adult Witnesses) Rules 2004.]

16.9 Hearings in camera and applications under section 46 of the Youth Justice and Criminal Evidence Act 1999

If in any proceedings, a prosecutor or defendant has served notice under rule 16.10 of his intention to apply for an order that all or part of a trial be held in camera, any application under this Part relating to a witness in those proceedings need not identify the witness by name and date of birth.

[Note. Formerly rule 9 of the Crown Court (Reports Relating to Adult Witnesses) Rules 2004.]

16.10 Application to hold a Crown Court trial in camera

(1)   Where a prosecutor or a defendant intends to apply for an order that all or part of a trial be held in camera for reasons of national security or for the protection of the identity of a witness or any other person, he shall not less than 7 days before the date on which the trial is expected to begin serve a notice in writing to that effect on the Crown Court officer and the prosecutor or the defendant as the case may be.

(2)   On receiving such notice, the court officer shall forthwith cause a copy thereof to be displayed in a prominent place within the precincts of the Court.

(3)   An application by a prosecutor or a defendant who has served such

a notice for an order that all or part of a trial be heard in camera shall, unless the Court orders otherwise, be made in camera, after the defendant has been arraigned but before the jury has been sworn and, if such an order is made, the trial shall be adjourned until whichever of the following shall be appropriate—

(a) 24 hours after the making of the order, where no application for leave to appeal from the order is made; or

(b) after the determination of an application for leave to appeal, where the application is dismissed; or

(c) after the determination of the appeal, where leave to appeal is granted.

[Note. Formerly rule 24A of the Crown Court Rules 1982. As to the procedure for appealing against an order, see rule 67.2.]

16.11 Crown Court hearings in chambers

(1) The criminal jurisdiction of the Crown Court specified in the following paragraph may be exercised by a judge of the Crown Court sitting in chambers.

(2) The said jurisdiction is—

(a) hearing applications for bail;

(b) issuing a summons or warrant;

(c) hearing any application relating to procedural matters preliminary or incidental to criminal proceedings in the Crown Court, including applications relating to legal aid;

(d) jurisdiction under rules 12.2 (listing first appearance of accused sent for trial), 28.3 (application for witness summons), 63.2(5) (extending time for appeal against decision of magistrates' court), and 64.7 (application to state case for consideration of High Court);

(e) hearing an application under section 41(2) of the Youth Justice and Criminal Evidence Act 1999 (evidence of complainant's previous sexual history);

(f) hearing applications under section 22(3) of the Prosecution of Offences Act 1985 (extension or further extension of custody time limit imposed by regulations made under section 22(1) of that Act);

(g) hearing an appeal brought by an accused under section 22(7) of the 1985 Act against a decision of a magistrates' court to extend, or further extend, such a time limit, or brought by the prosecution under section 22(8) of the same Act against a decision of a magistrates' court to refuse to extend, or further extend, such a time limit;

(h) hearing appeals under section 1 of the Bail (Amendment) Act 1993 (against grant of bail by magistrates' court); and

(i) hearing appeals under section 16 of the Criminal Justice Act 2003 (against condition of bail imposed by magistrates' court).

[Note. Formerly rule 27 of the Crown Court Rules 1982. As to hearing restraint and receivership proceedings under the Proceeds of Crime Act 2002in chambers see rule 61.4.]

PART 19
BAIL IN MAGISTRATES' COURTS AND THE CROWN COURT

Contents of this Part

19.1 Application to a magistrates' court to vary conditions of police bail

(1)   An application under section 43B(1) of the Magistrates' Courts Act of 1980 [or section 47(1E) of the Police and Criminal Evidence Act 1984] shall—

    (a) be made in writing;

    (b) contain a statement of the grounds upon which it is made;

    [(c) where the applicant has been bailed following charge, specify the offence with which he was charged and, in any other case, specify the offence under investigation;]

    (d) specify, or be accompanied by a copy of the note of, the reasons given by the custody officer for imposing or varying the conditions of bail; and

    (e) specify the name and address of any surety provided by the applicant before his release on bail to secure his surrender to custody.

(2)   Any such application shall be sent to the court officer for—

    (a) the magistrates' court . . . appointed by the custody officer as the court before which the applicant has a duty to appear; or

    (b) if no such court has been appointed, a magistrates' court acting for the local justice area in which the police station at which the applicant was granted bail or at which the conditions of his bail were varied, as the case may be, is situated,

. . .

[(3)   The court officer to whom an application is sent under paragraph (2) above shall serve notice in writing of the date, time and place fixed for the hearing of the application on—

    (a) the applicant;

    (b) the prosecutor or, if the applicant has not been charged, the chief officer of police or other investigator, together with a copy of the application; and

(c) any surety in connection with bail in criminal proceedings granted to, or the conditions of which were varied by a custody officer in relation to, the applicant.]

(4)   The time fixed for the hearing shall be not later than 72 hours after receipt of the application. In reckoning for the purposes of this paragraph any period of 72 hours, no account shall be taken of Christmas Day, [Boxing Day,] Good Friday, any bank holiday, or any Saturday or Sunday.

(5)   . . .

(6)   If the magistrates' court hearing an application under section 43B(1) of the 1980 Act [or section 47(1E) of the 1984 Act] discharges or enlarges any recognizance entered into by any surety or increases or reduces the amount in which that person is bound, the court officer shall forthwith give notice thereof to the applicant and to any such surety.

(7)   In this rule, 'the applicant' means the person making an application under section 43B(1) of the 1980 Act [or section 47(1E) of the 1984 Act].

[*[Note. This rule derives in part from rule 84A of the Magistrates' Courts Rules 1981. See also section 43B of the Magistrates' Courts Act 1980 and section 47 of the Police and Criminal Evidence Act 1984].*]

19.2 Application to a magistrates' court to reconsider grant of police bail

(1)   The appropriate court for the purposes of section 5B of the Bail Act 1976 in relation to the decision of a constable to grant bail shall be—
  (a) the magistrates' court . . . appointed by the custody officer as the court before which the person to whom bail was granted has a duty to appear; or
  (b) if no such court has been appointed, a magistrates' court acting for the local justice area in which the police station at which bail was granted is situated.

(2)   An application under section 5B(1) of the 1976 Act shall—
  (a) be made in writing;
  (b) contain a statement of the grounds on which it is made;
  (c) specify the offence which the proceedings in which bail was granted were connected with, or for;
  (d) specify the decision to be reconsidered (including any conditions of bail which have been imposed and why they have been imposed);
    . . .

(e) specify the name and address of any surety provided by the person to whom the application relates to secure his surrender to custody[; and

(f) contain notice of the powers available to the court under section 5B of the 1976 Act].

[(3)   The court officer to whom an application is sent under paragraph (2) above shall serve notice in writing of the date, time and place fixed for the hearing of the application on—

(a) the prosecutor who made the application;

(b) the person to whom bail was granted, together with a copy of the application; and

(c) any surety specified in the application.]

(4)   The time fixed for the hearing shall be not later than 72 hours after receipt of the application. In reckoning for the purpose of this paragraph any period of 72 hours, no account shall be taken of Christmas Day, Good Friday, any bank holiday or any Sunday.

(5)   . . .

(6)   At the hearing of an application under section 5B of the 1976 Act the court shall consider any representations made by the person affected (whether in writing or orally) before taking any decision under that section with respect to him; and, where the person affected does not appear before the court, the court shall not take such a decision unless it is proved to the satisfaction of the court, on oath or in the manner set out by rule 4.2(1), that the notice required to be given under paragraph (3) of this rule was served on him before the hearing.

(7)   Where the court proceeds in the absence of the person affected in accordance with paragraph (6)—

(a) if the decision of the court is to vary the conditions of bail or impose conditions in respect of bail which has been granted unconditionally, the court officer shall notify the person affected;

(b) if the decision of the court is to withhold bail, the order of the court under section 5B(5)(b) of the 1976 Act (surrender to custody) shall be signed by the justice issuing it or state his name and be authenticated by the signature of the clerk of the court.

(8)   . . .

[Note. [This rule derives in part from] rule 93B of the Magistrates' Courts Rules 1981. See also section 5B of the Bail Act 1976.]

19.3 Notice of change of time for appearance before magistrates' court

Where—

(a) a person has been granted bail under the Police and Criminal Evidence Act 1984 subject to a duty to appear before a magistrates' court and the court before which he is to appear appoints a later time at which he is to appear; or

(b) a magistrates' court further remands a person on bail under section 129 of the Magistrates' Courts Act 1980 in his absence,

it shall give him and his sureties, if any, notice thereof.

[Note. Formerly rule 91 of the Magistrates' Courts Rules 1981.]

19.4 Directions by a magistrates' court as to security, etc

Where a magistrates' court, under section 3(5) or (6) of the Bail Act 1976, imposes any requirement to be complied with before a person's release on bail, the court may give directions as to the manner in which and the person or persons before whom the requirement may be complied with.

[Note. Formerly rule 85 of the Magistrates' Courts Rules 1981. See also section 3 of the Bail Act 1976. As to the estreatment of recognizances in magistrates' courts on failure to surrender see section 120 of the Magistrates' Courts Act 1980. For the procedure where a defendant fails to surrender see also direction I.13 in the Practice Direction.]

19.5 Requirements to be complied with before release on bail granted by a magistrates' court

(1) Where a magistrates' court has fixed the amount in which a person (including any surety) is to be bound by a recognizance, the recognizance may be entered into—

(a) in the case of a surety where the accused is in a prison or other place of detention, before the governor or keeper of the prison or place as well as before the persons mentioned in section 8(4)(a) of the Bail Act 1976;

(b) in any other case, before a justice of the peace, a justices' clerk, a magistrates' court officer, a police officer who either is of the rank of inspector or above or is in charge of a police station or, if the person to be bound is in a prison or other place of detention, before the governor or keeper of the prison or place; or

(c) where a person other than a police officer is authorised under section 125A or 125B of the Magistrates' Courts Act 1980 to execute a warrant of arrest providing for a recognizance to be entered into by the person arrested (but not by any other person), before the person executing the warrant.

(2)   The court officer for a magistrates' court which has fixed the amount in which a person (including any surety) is to be bound by a recognizance or, under section 3(5), (6) or (6A) of the 1976 Act imposed any requirement to be complied with before a person's release on bail or any condition of bail shall issue a certificate showing the amount and conditions, if any, of the recognizance, or as the case may be, containing a statement of the requirement or condition of bail; and a person authorised to take the recognizance or do anything in relation to the compliance with such requirement or condition of bail shall not be required to take or do it without production of such a certificate as aforesaid.

(3)   If any person proposed as a surety for a person committed to custody by a magistrates' court produces to the governor or keeper of the prison or other place of detention in which the person so committed is detained a certificate to the effect that he is acceptable as a surety, signed by any of the justices composing the court or the clerk of the court and signed in the margin by the person proposed as surety, the governor or keeper shall take the recognizance of the person so proposed.

(4)   Where the recognizance of any person committed to custody by a magistrates' court or of any surety of such a person is taken by any person other than the court which committed the first-mentioned person to custody, the person taking the recognizance shall send it to the court officer for that court:

Provided that, in the case of a surety, if the person committed has been committed to the Crown Court for trial or under any of the enactments mentioned in rule 43.1(1), the person taking the recognizance shall send it to the Crown Court officer.

[Note. Formerly rule 86 of the Magistrates' Courts Rules 1981.]

19.6 Notice to governor of prison, etc, where release from custody is ordered by a magistrates' court

Where a magistrates' court has, with a view to the release on bail of a person in custody, fixed the amount in which he or any surety of such a person shall be bound or, under section 3(5), (6) or (6A) of the Bail Act 1976, imposed any requirement to be complied with before his release or any condition of bail—

(a) the magistrates' court officer shall give notice thereof to the governor or keeper of the prison or place where that person is detained by sending him such a certificate as is mentioned in rule 19.5(2); and

(b) any person authorised to take the recognizance of a surety or do anything in relation to the compliance with such requirement shall, on taking or doing it, send notice thereof by post to the said governor or keeper and, in the case of a recognizance of a surety, shall give a copy of the notice to the surety.

[Note. Formerly rule 87 of the Magistrates' Courts Rules 1981.]

19.7 Release when notice received by governor of prison that recognizances have been taken or requirements complied with

Where a magistrates' court has, with a view to the release on bail of a person in custody, fixed the amount in which he or any surety of such a person shall be bound or, under section 3(5) or (6) of the Bail Act 1976, imposed any requirement to be complied with before his release and given notice thereof in accordance with this Part to the governor or keeper of the prison or place where that person is detained, the governor or keeper shall, when satisfied that the recognizances of all sureties required have been taken and that all such requirements have been complied with, and unless he is in custody for some other cause, release him.

[Note. Formerly rule 88 of the Magistrates' Courts Rules 1981.]

19.8 Notice from a magistrates' court of enlargement of recognizances

(1) If a magistrates' court before which any person is bound by a recognizance to appear enlarges the recognizance to a later time under section 129 of the Magistrates' Courts Act 1980 in his absence, it shall give him and his sureties, if any, notice thereof.

(2) If a magistrates' court, under section 129(4) of the 1980 Act, enlarges the recognizance of a surety for a person committed for trial on bail, it shall give the surety notice thereof.

[Note. Formerly rule 84 of the Magistrates' Courts Rules 1981. See also section 129 of the Magistrates' Courts Act 1980.]

19.9 Further remand of minors by a youth court

Where a child or young person has been remanded, and the period of remand is extended in his absence in accordance with section 48 of the

Children and Young Persons Act 1933, notice shall be given to him and his sureties (if any) of the date at which he will be required to appear before the court.

[Note. Formerly rule 12 of the Magistrates' Courts (Children and Young Persons) Rules 1992.]

19.10 Notes of argument in magistrates' court bail hearings

Where a magistrates' court hears full argument as to bail, the clerk of the court shall take a note of that argument.

[Note. Formerly rule 90A of the Magistrates' Courts Rules 1981.]

19.11 Bail records to be entered in register of magistrates' court

Any record required by section 5 of the Bail Act 1976 to be made by a magistrates' court (together with any note of reasons required by section 5(4) to be included and the particulars set out in any certificate granted under section 5(6A)) shall be made by way of an entry in the register.

[Note. Formerly rule 90 of the Magistrates' Courts Rules 1981. See also section 5 of the Bail Act 1976. As to the general requirement to keep a register, see rule 6.1.]

19.12 Notification of bail decision by magistrate after arrest while on bail

Where a person who has been released on bail and is under a duty to surrender into the custody of a court is brought under section 7(4)(a) of the Bail Act 1976 before a justice of the peace, the justice shall cause a copy of the record made in pursuance of section 5 of that Act relating to his decision under section 7(5) of that Act in respect of that person to be sent to the court officer for that court:

Provided that this rule shall not apply where the court is a magistrates' court acting for the same local justice area as that for which the justice acts.

[Note. Formerly rule 92 of the Magistrates' Courts Rules 1981. See also section 7 of the Bail Act 1976.]

19.13 Transfer of remand hearings

(1)   Where a magistrates' court, under section 130(1) of the

Magistrates' Courts Act 1980, orders that an accused who has been remanded in custody be brought up for any subsequent remands before an alternate magistrates' court, the court officer for the first-mentioned court shall, as soon as practicable after the making of the order and in any case within 2 days thereafter (not counting Sundays, Good Friday, Christmas Day or bank holidays), send to the court officer for the alternate court—

(a) a statement indicating the offence or offences charged;

(b) a copy of the record made by the first-mentioned court in pursuance of section 5 of the Bail Act 1976 relating to the withholding of bail in respect of the accused when he was last remanded in custody;

(c) a copy of any representation order previously made in the same case;

(d) a copy of any application for a representation order;

(e) if the first-mentioned court has made an order under section 8(2) of the 1980 Act (removal of restrictions on reports of committal proceedings), a statement to that effect.

(f) a statement indicating whether or not the accused has a solicitor acting for him in the case and has consented to the hearing and determination in his absence of any application for his remand on an adjournment of the case under sections 5, 10(1) and 18(4) of the 1980 Act together with a statement indicating whether or not that consent has been withdrawn;

(g) a statement indicating the occasions, if any, on which the accused has been remanded under section 128(3A) of the 1980 Act without being brought before the first-mentioned court; and

(h) if the first-mentioned court remands the accused under section 128A of the 1980 Act on the occasion upon which it makes the order under section 130(1) of that Act, a statement indicating the date set under section 128A(2) of that Act.

(2)   Where the first-mentioned court is satisfied as mentioned in section 128(3A) of the 1980 Act, paragraph (1) shall have effect as if for the words 'an accused who has been remanded in custody be brought up for any subsequent remands before' there were substituted the words 'applications for any subsequent remands of the accused be made to'.

(3)   The court officer for an alternate magistrates' court before which an accused who has been remanded in custody is brought up for any subsequent remands in pursuance of an order made as aforesaid shall, as soon as practicable after the order ceases to be in force and in any case within 2 days thereafter (not counting Sundays, Good Friday, Christmas Day or bank holidays), send to the court officer for the magistrates' court which made the order—

(a) a copy of the record made by the alternate court in pursuance of section 5 of the 1976 Act relating to the grant or withholding of bail in respect of the accused when he was last remanded in custody or on bail;

(b) a copy of any representation order made by the alternate court;

(c) a copy of any application for a representation order made to the alternate court;

(d) if the alternate court has made an order under section 8(2) of the 1980 Act (removal of restrictions on reports of committal proceedings), a statement to that effect;

(e) a statement indicating whether or not the accused has a solicitor acting for him in the case and has consented to the hearing and determination in his absence of any application for his remand on an adjournment of the case under sections 5, 10(1) and 18(4) of the 1980 Act together with a statement indicating whether or not that consent has been withdrawn; and

(f) a statement indicating the occasions, if any, on which the accused has been remanded by the alternate court under section 128(3A) of the 1980 Act without being brought before that court.

(4)   Where the alternate court is satisfied as mentioned in section 128(3A) of the 1980 Act paragraph (2) above shall have effect as if for the words 'an accused who has been remanded in custody is brought up for any subsequent remands' there shall be substituted the words 'applications for the further remand of the accused are to be made'.

[Note. Formerly rule 25 of the Magistrates' Court Rules 1981.]

19.14 Notice of further remand in certain cases

Where a transfer direction has been given by the Secretary of State under section 47 of the Mental Health Act 1983 in respect of a person remanded in custody by a magistrates' court and the direction has not ceased to have effect, the court officer shall give notice in writing to the managers of the hospital where he is detained of any further remand under section 128 of the Magistrates' Courts Act 1980.

[Note. Formerly rule 26 of the Magistrates' Courts Rules 1981.]

19.15 Cessation of transfer direction

Where a magistrates' court directs, under section 52(5) of the Mental Health Act 1983, that a transfer direction given by the Secretary of State under section 48 of that Act in respect of a person remanded in custody by a magistrates' court shall cease to have effect, the court officer shall give notice in writing of the court's direction to the managers of the hospital specified in the Secretary of State's direction and, where the period of remand has not expired or the person has been committed to the Crown Court for trial or to be otherwise dealt with, to the Governor of the prison to which persons of the sex of that person are committed by the court if remanded in custody or committed in custody for trial.

[Note. Formerly rule 110 of the Magistrates' Courts Rules 1981. As to the requirement to give notice to the prison governor and hospital authorities when a defendant subject to a transfer direction is transferred, committed or sent to the Crown Court for trial, see rules 11.3 and 19.20.]

19.16 Lodging an appeal against a grant of bail by a magistrates' court

(1)   Where the prosecution wishes to exercise the right of appeal, under section 1 of the Bail (Amendment) Act 1993, to a judge of the Crown Court against a decision to grant bail, the oral notice of appeal must be given to the justices' clerk and to the person concerned, at the conclusion of the proceedings in which such bail was granted and before the release of the person concerned.

(2)   When oral notice of appeal is given, the justices' clerk shall announce in open court the time at which such notice was given.

(3)   A record of the prosecution's decision to appeal and the time the oral notice of appeal was given shall be made in the register and shall contain the particulars set out.

(4)   Where an oral notice of appeal has been given the court shall remand the person concerned in custody by a warrant of commitment.

(5)   On receipt of the written notice of appeal required by section 1(5) of the 1993 Act, the court shall remand the person concerned in custody by a warrant of commitment, until the appeal is determined or otherwise disposed of.

(6)   A record of the receipt of the written notice of appeal shall be made in the same manner as that of the oral notice of appeal under paragraph (3).

(7)   If, having given oral notice of appeal, the prosecution fails to serve a written notice of appeal within the two hour period referred to in section 1(5) of the 1993 Act the justices' clerk shall, as soon as practicable, by way of written notice (served by a court officer) to the persons in whose custody the person concerned is, direct the release of the person concerned on bail as granted by the magistrates' court and subject to any conditions which it imposed.

(8)   If the prosecution serves notice of abandonment of appeal on a court officer, the justices' clerk shall, forthwith, by way of written notice (served by the court officer) to the governor of the prison where the person concerned is being held, or the person responsible for any other establishment where such a person is being held, direct his release on bail as granted by the magistrates' court and subject to any conditions which it imposed.

(9)   A court officer shall record the prosecution's failure to serve a written notice of appeal, or its service of a notice of abandonments.

(10)   Where a written notice of appeal has been served on a magistrates' court officer, he shall provide as soon as practicable to a Crown Court officer a copy of that written notice, together with—
  (a) the notes of argument made by the court officer for the court under rule 19.10; and
  (b) a note of the date, or dates, when the person concerned is next due to appear in the magistrates' court, whether he is released on bail or remanded in custody by the Crown Court.

(11)   References in this rule to 'the person concerned' are references to such a person within the meaning of section 1 of the 1993 Act.

[Note. Formerly rule 93A of the Magistrates' Courts Rules 1981.]

19.17 Crown Court procedure on appeal against grant of bail by a magistrates' court

(1)   This rule shall apply where the prosecution appeals under section 1 of the Bail (Amendment) Act 1993 against a decision of a magistrates' court granting bail and in this rule 'the person concerned' has the same meaning as in that Act.

(2)   The written notice of appeal required by section 1(5) of the 1993 Act shall be in the form set out in the Practice Direction and shall be served on—
  (a) the magistrates' court officer; and
  (b) the person concerned.

(3)   The Crown Court officer shall enter the appeal and give notice of the time and place of the hearing to—
  (a) the prosecution;
  (b) the person concerned or his legal representative; and
  (c) the magistrates' court officer.

(4)   The person concerned shall not be entitled to be present at the hearing of the appeal unless he is acting in person or, in any other case of an exceptional nature, a judge of the Crown Court is of the opinion that

the interests of justice require his to be present and gives him leave to be so.

(5)   Where a person concerned has not been able to instruct a solicitor to represent him at the appeal, he may give notice to the Crown Court requesting that the Official Solicitor shall represent him at the appeal, and the court may, if it thinks fit, assign the Official Solicitor to act for the person concerned accordingly.

(6)   At any time after the service of written notice of appeal under paragraph (2), the prosecution may abandon the appeal by giving notice in writing in the form set out in the Practice Direction.

(7)   The notice of abandonment required by the preceding paragraph shall be served on—
   (a) the person concerned or his legal representative;
   (b) the magistrates' court officer; and
   (c) the Crown Court officer.

(8)   Any record required by section 5 of the Bail Act 1976 (together with any note of reasons required by subsection (4) of that section to be included) shall be made by way of an entry in the file relating to the case in question and the record shall include the following particulars, namely—
   (a) the effect of the decision;
   (b) a statement of any condition imposed in respect of bail, indicating whether it is to be complied with before or after release on bail; and
   (c) where bail is withheld, a statement of the relevant exception to the right to bail (as provided in Schedule 1 to the 1976 Act) on which the decision is based.

(9)   The Crown Court officer shall, as soon as practicable after the hearing of the appeal, give notice of the decision and of the matters required by the preceding paragraph to be recorded to—
   (a) the person concerned or his legal representative;
   (b) the prosecution;
   (c) the police;
   (d) the magistrates' officer; and
   (e) the governor of the prison or person responsible for the establishment where the person concerned is being held.

(10)   Where the judge hearing the appeal grants bail to the person concerned, the provisions of rule 19.18(9) (informing the Court of any earlier application for bail) and rule 19.22 (conditions attached to bail granted by the Crown Court) shall apply as if that person had applied to the Crown Court for bail.

[(11)   The notices required by paragraphs (3), (5), (7) and (9) of this rule may be served under rule 4.6 (service by fax, e-mail or other electronic means) and the notice required by paragraph (3) may be given by telephone.]

[Note. [This rule derives in part from] rule 11A of the Crown Court Rules 1982.]

19.18 Applications to Crown Court relating to bail

(1)   This rule applies where an application to the Crown Court relating to bail is made otherwise than during the hearing of proceedings in the Crown Court.

(2)   Subject to paragraph (7) below, notice in writing of intention to make such an application to the Crown Court shall, at least 24 hours before it is made, be given to the prosecutor and if the prosecution is being carried on by the Crown Prosecution Service, to the appropriate Crown Prosecutor or, if the application is to be made by the prosecutor or a constable under section 3(8) of the Bail Act 1976, to the person to whom bail was granted.

(3)   On receiving notice under paragraph (2), the prosecutor or appropriate Crown Public Prosecutor or, as the case may be, the person to whom bail was granted shall—

   (a)   notify the Crown Court officer and the applicant that he wishes to be represented at the hearing of the application;

   (b)   notify the Crown Court officer and the applicant that he does not oppose the application; or

   (c)   give to the Crown Court officer, for the consideration of the Crown Court, a written statement of his reasons for opposing the application, at the same time sending a copy of the statement to the applicant.

(4)   A notice under paragraph (2) shall be in the form set out in the Practice Direction or a form to the like effect, and the applicant shall give a copy of the notice to the Crown Court officer.

(5)   Except in the case of an application made by the prosecutor or a constable under section 3(8) of the 1976 Act, the applicant shall not be entitled to be present on the hearing of his application unless the Crown Court gives him leave to be present.

(6)   Where a person who is in custody or has been released on bail desires to make an application relating to bail and has not been able to instruct a solicitor to apply on his behalf under the preceding paragraphs of this rule, he may give notice in writing to the Crown Court of his

desire to make an application relating to bail, requesting that the Official Solicitor shall act for him in the application, and the Court may, if it thinks fit, assign the Official Solicitor to act for the applicant accordingly.

(7) Where the Official Solicitor has been so assigned the Crown Court may, if it thinks fit, dispense with the requirements of paragraph (2) and deal with the application in a summary manner.

(8) Any record required by section 5 of the 1976 Act (together with any note of reasons required by section 5(4) to be included) shall be made by way of an entry in the file relating to the case in question and the record shall include the following particulars, namely—

(a) the effect of the decision;
(b) a statement of any condition imposed in respect of bail, indicating whether it is to be complied with before or after release on bail;
(c) where conditions of bail are varied, a statement of the conditions as varied; and
(d) where bail is withheld, a statement of the relevant exception to the right to bail (as provided in Schedule 1 to the 1976 Act) on which the decision is based.

(9) Every person who makes an application to the Crown Court relating to bail shall inform the Court of any earlier application to the High Court or the Crown Court relating to bail in the course of the same proceedings.

[Note. Formerly rule 19 and paragraph (1) of rule 20 of the Crown Court Rules 1982. As to applications for bail before committal for trial see also direction V.53, and for bail during trial see also direction III.25, in the Practice Direction.]

19.19 Notice to governor of prison of committal on bail

(1) Where the accused is committed or sent for trial on bail, a magistrates' court officer shall give notice thereof in writing to the governor of the prison to which persons of the sex of the person committed or sent are committed or sent by that court if committed or sent in custody for trial and also, if the person committed or sent is under 21, to the governor of the remand centre to which he would have been committed or sent if the court had refused him bail.

(2) Where a corporation is committed or sent for trial, a magistrates' court officer shall give notice thereof to the governor of the prison to which would be committed or sent a man committed or sent by that court in custody for trial.

[Note. Formerly rule 9 of the Magistrates' Courts Rules 1981. For the equivalent provision where a defendant is transferred for trial,

see rule 11.2. On the coming into force of Schedule 3 to the Criminal Justice Act 2003committal for trial will be abolished and cases triable either way will be sent to the Crown Court under sections 51 and 51A of the Crime and Disorder Act 1998in the same way as cases triable only on indictment.]

19.20 Notices on committal of person subject to transfer direction

Where a transfer direction has been given by the Secretary of State under section 48 of the Mental Health Act 1983 in respect of a person remanded in custody by a magistrates' court and, before the direction ceases to have effect, that person is committed or sent for trial, a magistrates' court officer shall give notice—

   (a) to the governor of the prison to which persons of the sex of that person are committed or sent by that court if committed or sent in custody for trial; and

   (b) to the managers of the hospital where he is detained.

[Note. Formerly rule 10 of the Magistrates' Courts Rules 1981. For the equivalent provision where a defendant is transferred for trial see rule 11.3. On the coming into force of Schedule 3 to the Criminal Justice Act 2003 committal for trial will be abolished and cases triable either way will be sent to the Crown Court under sections 51 and 51A of the Crime and Disorder Act 1998 in the same way as cases triable only on indictment.]

19.21 Variation of arrangements for bail on committal to Crown Court

Where a magistrates' court has committed or sent a person on bail to the Crown Court for trial or under any of the enactments mentioned in rule 43.1(1) and subsequently varies any conditions of the bail or imposes any conditions in respect of the bail, the magistrates' court officer shall send to the Crown Court officer a copy of the record made in pursuance of section 5 of the Bail Act 1976 relating to such variation or imposition of conditions.

[Note. Formerly rule 93 of the Magistrates' Courts Rules 1981. See also section 5 of the Bail Act 1976. For the equivalent provision where a defendant is transferred to the Crown Court, see rule 11.4. On the coming into force of Schedule 3 to the Criminal Justice Act 2003 committal for trial will be abolished and cases triable either way will be sent to the Crown Court under sections 51 and 51A of the Crime and Disorder Act 1998 in the same way as cases triable only on indictment.]

19.22 Conditions attached to bail granted by the Crown Court

(1)   Where the Crown Court grants bail, the recognizance of any surety required as a condition of bail may be entered into before an officer of the Crown Court or, where the person who has been granted bail is in a prison or other place of detention, before the governor or keeper of the prison or place as well as before the persons specified in section 8(4) of the Bail Act 1976.

(2)   Where the Crown Court under section 3(5) or (6) of the 1976 Act imposes a requirement to be complied with before a person's release on bail, the Court may give directions as to the manner in which and the person or persons before whom the requirement may be complied with.

(3)   A person who, in pursuance of an order made by the Crown Court for the grant of bail, proposes to enter into a recognizance or give security must, unless the Crown Court otherwise directs, give notice to the prosecutor at least 24 hours before he enters into the recognizance or gives security as aforesaid.

(4)   Where, in pursuance of an order of the Crown Court, a recognizance is entered into or any requirement imposed under section 3(5) or (6) of the 1976 Act is complied with (being a requirement to be complied with before a person's release on bail) before any person, it shall be his duty to cause the recognizance or, as the case may be, a statement of the requirement to be transmitted forthwith to the court officer; and a copy of the recognizance or statement shall at the same time be sent to the governor or keeper of the prison or other place of detention in which the person named in the order is detained, unless the recognizance was entered into or the requirement was complied with before such governor or keeper.

(5)   Where, in pursuance of section 3(5) of the 1976 Act, security has been given in respect of a person granted bail with a duty to surrender to the custody of the Crown Court and either—
-   (a)   that person surrenders to the custody of the Court; or
-   (b)   that person having failed to surrender to the custody of the Court, the Court decides not to order the forfeiture of the security,

the court officer shall as soon as practicable give notice of the surrender to custody or, as the case may be, of the decision not to forfeit the security to the person before whom the security was given.

[Note. Formerly paragraphs (2), (3), (5), (6) and (7) of rule 20 of the Crown Court Rules 1982.]

19.23 Estreat of recognizances in respect of person bailed to appear before the Crown Court

(1)   Where a recognizance has been entered into in respect of a person granted bail to appear before the Crown Court and it appears to the Court that a default has been made in performing the conditions of the recognizance, other than by failing to appear before the Court in accordance with any such condition, the Court may order the recognizance to be estreated.

(2)   Where the Crown Court is to consider making an order under paragraph (1) for a recognizance to be estreated, the court officer shall give notice to that effect to the person by whom the recognizance was entered into indicating the time and place at which the matter will be considered; and no such order shall be made before the expiry of 7 days after the notice required by this paragraph has been given.

[Note. Formerly rule 21 of the Crown Court Rules 1982. As to forfeiture of recognizances on failure to surrender, see rule 19.24.]

19.24 Forfeiture of recognizances in respect of person bailed to appear before the Crown Court

(1)   Where a recognizance is conditioned for the appearance of an accused before the Crown Court and the accused fails to appear in accordance with the condition, the Court shall declare the recognizance to be forfeited.

(2)   Where the Crown Court declares a recognizance to be forfeited under paragraph (1), the court officer shall issue a summons to the person by whom the recognizance was entered into requiring him to appear before the Court at a time and place specified in the summons to show cause why the Court should not order the recognizance to be estreated.

(3)   At the time specified in the summons the Court may proceed in the absence of the person by whom the recognizance was entered into if it is satisfied that he has been served with the summons.

[Note. Formerly rule 21A of the Crown Court Rules 1982. As to the estreat of recognizances on failure to comply with conditions of bail, see rule 19.23. For the procedure where a defendant fails to surrender see also direction I.13 in the Practice Direction.]

PART 29
SPECIAL MEASURES DIRECTIONS

Contents of this Part

29.1 Application for special measures directions

(1)   An application by a party in criminal proceedings for a magistrates' court or the Crown Court to give a special measures direction under section 19 of the Youth Justice and Criminal Evidence Act 1999 must be made in writing in the form set out in the Practice Direction.

(2)   If the application is for a special measures direction—
    (a)   enabling a witness to give evidence by means of a live link, the information sought in Part B of that form must be provided;
    (b)   providing for any examination of a witness to be conducted through an intermediary, the information sought in Part C of that form must be provided; or
    (c)   enabling a video recording of an interview of a witness to be admitted as evidence in chief of the witness, the information sought in Part D of that form must be provided.

(3)   The application under paragraph (1) above must be sent to the court officer and at the same time a copy thereof must be sent by the applicant to every other party to the proceedings.

(4)   The court officer must receive the application—
    (a)   in the case of an application to a youth court, within 28 days of the date on which the defendant first appears or is brought before the court in connection with the offence;
    (b)   in the case of an application to a magistrates' court, within 14 days of the defendant indicating his intention to plead not guilty to any charge brought against him and in relation to which a special measures direction may be sought; and
    (c)   in the case of an application to the Crown Court, within 28 days of

    (i) the committal of the defendant, or

    (ii) the consent to the preferment of a bill of indictment in relation to the case, or

    (iii) the service of a notice of transfer under section 53 of the Criminal Justice Act 1991, or

    (iv) where a person is sent for trial under section 51 of the Crime and Disorder Act 1998, the service of copies of the documents containing the evidence on which the charge or charges are based under paragraph 1 of Schedule 3 to that Act, or

    (v) the service of a Notice of Appeal from a decision of a youth court or a magistrates' court.

(5)   A party to whom an application is sent in accordance with paragraph (3) may oppose the application for a special measures direction in respect of any, or any particular, measure available in relation to the witness, whether or not the question whether the witness is eligible for assistance by virtue of section 16 or 17 of the 1999 Act is in issue.

(6)   A party who wishes to oppose the application must, within 14 days of the date the application was served on him, notify the applicant and the court officer, as the case may be, in writing of his opposition and give reasons for it.

(7)   Paragraphs (5) and (6) do not apply in respect of an application for a special measures direction enabling a child witness in need of special protection to give evidence by means of a live link if the opposition is that the special measures direction is not likely to maximise the quality of the witness's evidence.

(8)   In order to comply with paragraph (6)—

    (a) a party must in the written notification state whether he—

      (i) disputes that the witness is eligible for assistance by virtue of section 16 or 17 of the 1999 Act,

      (ii) disputes that any of the special measures available would be likely to improve the quality of evidence given by the witness or that such measures (or a combination of them) would be likely to maximise the quality of that evidence, and

      (iii) opposes the granting of a special measures direction; and

    (b) where the application relates to the admission of a video recording, a party who receives a recording must provide the information required by rule 29.7(7) below.

(9)   Except where notice is received in accordance with paragraph (6), the court (including, in the case of an application to a magistrates' court, a single justice of the peace) may—

(a) determine the application in favour of the applicant without a hearing; or
(b) direct a hearing.

(10)   Where a party to the proceedings notifies the court in accordance with paragraph (6) of his opposition to the application, the justices' clerk or the Crown Court must direct a hearing of the application.

(11)   Where a hearing of the application is to take place in accordance with paragraph (9) or (10) above, the court officer shall notify each party to the proceedings of the time and place of the hearing.

(12)   A party notified in accordance with paragraph (11) may be present at the hearing and be heard.

(13)   The court officer must, within 3 days of the decision of the court in relation to an application under paragraph (1) being made, notify all the parties of the decision, and if the application was made for a direction enabling a video recording of an interview of a witness to be admitted as evidence in chief of that witness, the notification must state whether the whole or specified parts only of the video recording or recordings disclosed are to be admitted in evidence.

(14)   In this Part:
'an intermediary' has the same meaning as in section 29 of the 1999 Act; and
'child witness in need of protection' shall be construed in accordance with section 21(1) of the 1999 Act.

[Note. Formerly rules 1 and 2 of the Magistrates' Courts (Special Measures Directions) Rules 2002and rules 1 and 2 of the Crown Court (Special Measures Directions and Directions Prohibiting Cross-examination) Rules 2002. See also chapter I of Part II of the Youth Justice and Criminal Evidence Act 1999.]

29.2 Application for an extension of time

(1)   An application may be made in writing for the period of 14 days or, as the case may be, 28 days specified in rule 29.1(4) to be extended.

(2)   The application may be made either before or after that period has expired.

(3)   The application must be accompanied by a statement setting out the reasons why the applicant is or was unable to make the application within that period and a copy of the application and the statement must be sent to every other party to the proceedings.

(4)   An application for an extension of time under this rule shall be determined by a single justice of the peace or a judge of the Crown Court without a hearing unless the justice or the judge otherwise directs.

(5)   The court officer shall notify all the parties of the court's decision.

[Note. Formerly rule 3 of the Magistrates' Courts (Special Measures Directions) Rules 2002 and rule 3 of the Crown Court (Special Measures Directions and Directions Prohibiting Cross-examination) Rules 2002.]

29.3 Late applications

(1)   Notwithstanding the requirements of rule 29.1—
   (a) an application may be made for a special measures direction orally at the trial; or
   (b) a magistrates' court or the Crown Court may of its own motion raise the issue whether a special measures direction should be given.

(2)   Where an application is made in accordance with paragraph (1)(a)—
   (a) the applicant must state the reasons for the late application; and
   (b) the court must be satisfied that the applicant was unable to make the application in accordance with rule 29.1.

(3)   The court shall determine before making a special measures direction—
   (a) whether to allow other parties to the proceedings to make representations on the question;
   (b) the time allowed for making such representations (if any); and
   (c) whether the question should be determined following a hearing at which the parties to the proceedings may be heard.

(4)   Paragraphs (2) and (3) do not apply in respect of an application made orally at the trial for a special measures direction—
   (a) enabling a child witness in need of special protection to give evidence by means of a live link; or
   (b) enabling a video recording of such a child to be admitted as evidence in chief of the witness,

if the opposition is that the special measures direction will not maximise the quality of the witness's evidence.

[Note. Formerly rule 4 of the Magistrates' Courts (Special Measures Directions) Rules 2002 and rule 4 of the Crown Court (Special Measures Directions and Directions Prohibiting Cross-examination) Rules 2002. [An application to make or vary a special measures direction also may be made in the time allowed under rule 36.6.]]

29.4 Discharge or variation of a special measures direction

(1)   An application to a magistrates' court or the Crown Court to discharge or vary a special measures direction under section 20(2) of the Youth Justice and Criminal Evidence Act 1999 must be in writing and each material change of circumstances which the applicant alleges has occurred since the direction was made must be set out.

(2)   An application under paragraph (1) must be sent to the court officer as soon as reasonably practicable after the change of circumstances occurs.

(3)   The applicant must also send copies of the application to each party to the proceedings at the same time as the application is sent to the court officer.

(4)   A party to whom an application is sent in accordance with paragraph (3) may oppose the application on the ground that it discloses no material change of circumstances.

(5)   Rule 29.1(6) to (13) shall apply to an application to discharge or vary a special measures direction as it applies to an application for a direction.

[Note. Formerly rule 5 of the Magistrates' Courts (Special Measures Directions) Rules 2002 and rule 5 of the Crown Court (Special Measures Directions and Directions Prohibiting Cross-examination) Rules 2002.]ot:

29.5 Renewal application following a material change of circumstances

(1)   Where an application for a special measures direction has been refused by a magistrates' court or the Crown Court, the application may only be renewed ('renewal application') where there has been a material change of circumstances since the court refused the application.

(2)   The applicant must—
   (a) identify in the renewal application each material change of circumstances which is alleged to have occurred; and
   (b) send the renewal application to the court officer as soon as reasonably practicable after the change occurs.

(3)   The applicant must also send copies of the renewal application to each of the parties to the proceedings at the same time as the application is sent to the court officer.

(4)   A party to whom the renewal application is sent in accordance with paragraph (3) above may oppose the application on the ground that it discloses no material change of circumstances.

(5)   Rules 29.1(6) to (13), 29.6 and 29.7 apply to a renewal application as they apply to the application which was refused.

[Note. Formerly rule 6 of the Magistrates' Courts (Special Measures Directions) Rules 2002 and rule 6 of the Crown Court (Special Measures Directions and Directions Prohibiting Cross-examination) Rules 2002.]

29.6 Application for special measures direction for witness to give evidence by means of a live television link

(1)   Where the application for a special measures direction is made, in accordance with rule 29.1(2)(a), for a witness to give evidence by means of a live link, the following provisions of this rule shall also apply.

(2)   A party who seeks to oppose an application for a child witness to give evidence by means of a live link must, in order to comply with rule 29.1(5), state why in his view the giving of a special measures direction would not be likely to maximise the quality of the witness's evidence.

(3)   However, paragraph (2) does not apply in relation to a child witness in need of special protection.

(4)   Where a special measures direction is made enabling a witness to give evidence by means of a live link, the witness shall be accompanied at the live link only by persons acceptable to the court.

(5)   If the special measures directions combine provisions for a witness to give evidence by means of a live link with provision for the examination of the witness to be conducted through an intermediary, the witness shall be accompanied at the live link only by—
    (a) the intermediary; and
    (b) such other persons as may be acceptable to the court.

[Note. Formerly rule 7 of the Magistrates' Courts (Special Measures Directions) Rules 2002 and rule 7 of the Crown Court (Special Measures Directions and Directions Prohibiting Cross-examination) Rules 2002. As to the provision of support for witnesses giving evidence by live television link see also direction III.29 in the Practice Direction.]

29.7 Video recording of testimony from witnesses

(1)   Where an application is made to a magistrates' court or the Crown Court for a special measures direction enabling a video recording of an interview of a witness to be admitted as evidence in chief of the witness, the following provisions of this rule shall also apply.

(2)   The application made in accordance with rule 29.1(1) must be accompanied by the video recording which it is proposed to tender in evidence and must include—

   (a) the name of the defendant and the offence to be charged;

   (b) the name and date of birth of the witness in respect of whom the application is made;

   (c) the date on which the video recording was made;

   (d) a statement as to whether, and if so at what point in the video recording, an oath was administered to, or a solemn declaration made by, the witness;

   (e) a statement that, in the opinion of the applicant, either—

      (i) the witness is available for cross-examination, or

     (ii) the witness is not available for cross-examination and the parties have agreed that there is no need for the witness to be so available;

   (f) a statement of the circumstances in which the video recording was made which complies with paragraph (4) of this rule; and

   (g) the date on which the video recording was disclosed to the other party or parties.

(3)   Where it is proposed to tender part only of a video recording of an interview with the witness, the application must specify that part and be accompanied by a video recording of the entire interview, including those parts which it is not proposed to tender in evidence, and by a statement of the circumstances in which the video recording of the entire interview was made which complies with paragraph (4) of this rule.

(4)   The statement of the circumstances in which the video recording was made referred to in paragraphs (2)(f) and (3) of this rule shall include the following information, except in so far as it is contained in the recording itself—

   (a) the times at which the recording commenced and finished, including details of interruptions;

   (b) the location at which the recording was made and the usual function of the premises;

   (c) in relation to each person present at any point during, or immediately before, the recording—

      (i) their name, age and occupation,

     (ii) the time for which each person was present, and

(iii) the relationship, if any, of each person to the witness and to the defendant;
(d) in relation to the equipment used for the recording—
    (i) a description of the equipment,
    (ii) the number of cameras used,
    (iii) whether the cameras were fixed or mobile,
    (iv) the number and location of the microphones,
    (v) the video format used; and
    (vi) whether it offered single or multiple recording facilities and, if so, which were used; and
(e) the location of the mastertape if the video recording is a copy and details of when and by whom the copy was made.

(5) If the special measures directions enabling a video recording of an interview of a witness to be admitted as evidence in chief of the witness with provision for the examination of the witness to be conducted through an intermediary, the information to be provided under paragraph (4)(c) shall be the same as that for other persons present at the recording but with the addition of details of the declaration made by the intermediary under rule 29.9.

(6) If the special measures directions enabling a video recording of an interview of a witness to be admitted as evidence in chief of the witness with provision for the witness, in accordance with section 30 of the Youth Justice and Criminal Evidence Act 1999, to be provided with a device as an aid to communication during the video recording of the interview the information to be included under paragraph (4)(d) shall include also details of any such device used for the purposes of recording.

(7) A party who receives a recording under paragraph (2) must within 14 days of its receipt, notify the applicant and the court officer, in writing—
(a) whether he objects to the admission under section 27 of the 1999 Act of any part of the video recording or recordings disclosed, giving his reasons why it would not be in the interests of justice for the recording or any part of it to be admitted;
(b) whether he would agree to the admission of part of the video recording or recordings and, if so, which part or parts; and
(c) whether he wishes to be represented at any hearing of the application.

(8) A party who seeks to oppose an application for a special measures direction enabling a video recording of an interview of a child witness to be admitted as evidence in chief of the witness must, in order to comply with rule 29.1(6), state why in his view the giving of a special measures direction would not be likely to maximise the quality of the witness's

evidence.

(9)   However, paragraph (8) does not apply if the witness is a child witness in need of special protection.

(10)   Notwithstanding the provisions of rule 29.1 and this rule, any video recording which the defendant proposes to tender in evidence need not be sent to the prosecution until the close of the prosecution case at the trial.

(11)   The court may determine an application by the defendant to tender in evidence a video recording even though the recording has not, in accordance with paragraph (10), been served upon the prosecution.

(12)   Where a video recording which is the subject of a special measures direction is sent to the prosecution after the direction has been made, the prosecutor may apply to the court for the direction to be varied or discharged.

(13)   An application under paragraph (12) may be made orally to the court.

(14)   A prosecutor who makes an application under paragraph (12) must state—
   (a)   why he objects to the admission under section 27 of the 1999 Act of any part of the video recording or recordings disclosed, giving his reasons why it would not be in the interests of justice for the recording or any part of it to be admitted; and
   (b)   whether he would agree to the admission of part of the video recording or recordings and, if so, which part or parts.

(15)   The court must, before determining the application—
   (a)   direct a hearing of the application; and
   (b)   allow all the parties to the proceedings to be present and be heard on the application.

(16)   The court officer must notify all parties to the proceedings of the decision of the court as soon as may be reasonable after the decision is given.

(17)   Any decision varying a special measures direction must state whether the whole or specified parts of the video recording or recordings subject to the application are to be admitted in evidence.

[Note. Formerly rule 8 of the Magistrates' Courts (Special Measures Directions) Rules 2002 and rule 8 of the Crown Court (Special Measures Directions and Directions Prohibiting Cross-examination) Rules 2002. As to the use of video-recorded evidence in chief see also direction IV.40 in the Practice Direction.]

29.8 Expert evidence in connection with special measures directions

Any party to proceedings in a magistrates' court or the Crown Court who proposes to adduce expert evidence (whether of fact or opinion) in connection with an application or renewal application for, or for varying or discharging, a special measures direction must, not less than 14 days before the date set for the trial to begin—

    (a) furnish the other party or parties [and the court] with a statement in writing of any finding or opinion which he proposes to adduce by way of such evidence [and notify the expert of this disclosure; and]

    (b) where a request is made to him in that behalf by any other party to those proceedings, provide that party also with a copy of (or if it appears to the party proposing to adduce the evidence to be more practicable, a reasonable opportunity to examine) the record of any observation, test, calculation or other procedure on which such finding or opinion is based and any document or other thing or substance in respect of which any such procedure has been carried out.

[Note. Formerly rule 9 of the Magistrates' Courts (Special Measures Directions) Rules 2002 and rule 9 of the Crown Court (Special Measures Directions and Directions Prohibiting Cross-examination) Rules 2002. [Part 33 contains rules about the duties of an expert and the content of an expert's report.]]

29.9 Intermediaries

The declaration required to be made by an intermediary in accordance with section 29(5) of the Youth Justice and Criminal Evidence Act 1999 shall be in the following form:

> 'I solemnly, sincerely and truly declare that I will well and faithfully communicate questions and answers and make true explanation of all matters and things as shall be required of me according to the best of my skill and understanding.'

[Note. Formerly rule 9A of the Magistrates' Courts (Special Measures Directions) Rules 2002 and rule 9A of the Crown Court (Special Measures Directions and Directions Prohibiting Cross-examination) Rules 2002.]

PART 35
EVIDENCE OF BAD CHARACTER

Contents of this Part

35.1 When this Part applies

This Part applies in a magistrates' court and in the Crown Court when a party wants to introduce evidence of bad character as defined in section 98 of the Criminal Justice Act 2003.

[Note. For the introduction of evidence of bad character in the Court of Appeal see rule 68.21.]

35.2 Introducing evidence of non-defendant's bad character

A party who wants to introduce evidence of a non-defendant's bad character or who wants to cross-examine a witness with a view to eliciting that evidence, under section 100 of the Criminal Justice Act 2003 must apply in the form set out in the Practice Direction and the application must be received by the court officer and all other parties to the proceedings—

    [(a) not more than 14 days after the prosecutor has—
        (i) complied or purported to comply with section 3 of the Criminal Procedure and Investigations Act 1996 (initial disclosure by the prosecutor), or
        (ii) disclosed the previous convictions of that non-defendant; or]
    (b) as soon as reasonably practicable, where the application concerns a non-defendant who is to be invited to give (or has given) evidence for a defendant.

[Note. Formerly rule 72A(1) of the Magistrates' Courts Rules 1981and rule 23E(1) of the Crown Court Rules 1982.]

35.3 Opposing introduction of evidence of non-defendant's bad character

A party who receives a copy of an application under rule 35.2 may oppose that application by giving notice in writing to the court officer and all other parties to the proceedings not more than 14 days after receiving that application.

[Note. Formerly rule 72A(2) of the Magistrates' Courts Rules 1981 and rule 23E(2) of the Crown Court Rules 1982.]

35.4 Prosecutor introducing evidence of defendant's bad character

(1)   A prosecutor who wants to introduce evidence of a defendant's bad character or who wants to cross-examine a witness with a view to eliciting that evidence, under section 101 of the Criminal Justice Act 2003 must give notice in the form set out in the Practice Direction to the court officer and all other parties to the proceedings.

(2)   Notice under paragraph (1) must be given—
    (a) in a case to be tried in a magistrates' court, at the same time as the prosecutor complies or purports to comply with section 3 of the Criminal Procedure and Investigations Act 1996; and
    (b) in a case to be tried in the Crown Court, not more than 14 days after—
        (i)   the committal of the defendant, or
        (ii) the consent to the preferment of a bill of indictment in relation to the case, or
        (iii) the service of notice of transfer under section 4(1) of the Criminal Justice Act 1987 (notices of transfer) or under section 53(1) of the Criminal Justice Act 1991 (notices of transfer in certain cases involving children), or
        (iv) where a person is sent for trial under section 51 of the Crime and Disorder Act 1998 (sending cases to the Crown Court) the service of copies of the documents containing the evidence on which the charge or charges are based under paragraph 1 of Schedule 3 to that Act.

[Note. Formerly rule 72A(3) of the Magistrates' Courts Rules 1981 and rule 23E(3) of the Crown Court Rules 1982.]

35.5 Co-defendant introducing evidence of defendant's bad character

A co-defendant who wants to introduce evidence of a defendant's bad character or who wants to cross-examine a witness with a view to eliciting that evidence under section 101 of the Criminal Justice Act 2003 must give notice in the form set out in the Practice Direction to the court officer and all other parties to the proceedings not more than 14 days after the prosecutor has complied or purported to comply with section 3 of the Criminal Procedure and Investigations Act 1996.

[Note. Formerly rule 72A(4) of the Magistrates' Courts Rules 1981 and rule 23E(4) of the Crown Court Rules 1982.]

35.6 Defendant applying to exclude evidence of his own bad character

A defendant's application to exclude bad character evidence must be in the form set out in the Practice Direction and received by the court officer and all other parties to the proceedings not more than [14] days after receiving a notice given under rules 35.4 or 35.5.

[Note. Formerly rule 72A(5) of the Magistrates' Courts Rules 1981 and rule 23E(5) of the Crown Court Rules 1982.]

Appendix D

Code for Crown Prosecutors

The Crown Prosecution Service is the principal public prosecuting authority for England and Wales and is headed by the Director of Public Prosecutions. The Attorney General is accountable to Parliament for the Service.

The Crown Prosecution Service is a national organisation consisting of 42 Areas. Each Area is headed by a Chief Crown Prosecutor and corresponds to a single police force area, with one for London. It was set up in 1986 to prosecute cases investigated by the police.

Although the Crown Prosecution Service works closely with the police, it is independent of them. The independence of Crown Prosecutors is of fundamental constitutional importance. Casework decisions taken with fairness, impartiality and integrity help deliver justice for victims, witnesses, defendants and the public.

The Crown Prosecution Service co-operates with the investigating and prosecuting agencies of other jurisdictions.

The Director of Public Prosecutions is responsible for issuing a Code for Crown Prosecutors under section 10 of the Prosecution of Offences Act 1985, giving guidance on the general principles to be applied when making decisions about prosecutions. This is the fifth edition of the Code and replaces all earlier versions. For the purpose of this Code, 'Crown Prosecutor' includes members of staff in the Crown Prosecution Service who are designated by the Director of Public Prosecutions under section 7A of the Act and are exercising powers under that section.

1 INTRODUCTION

1.1   The decision to prosecute an individual is a serious step. Fair and effective prosecution is essential to the maintenance of law and order. Even in a small case a prosecution has serious implications for all involved — victims, witnesses and defendants. The Crown Prosecution Service applies the Code for Crown Prosecutors so that it can make fair and consistent decisions about prosecutions.

1.2   The Code helps the Crown Prosecution Service to play its part in making sure that justice is done. It contains information that is important to police officers and others who work in the criminal justice system and to the general public. Police officers should apply the provisions of this Code whenever they are responsible for deciding whether to charge a person with an offence.

1.3   The Code is also designed to make sure that everyone knows the principles that the Crown Prosecution Service applies when carrying out its work. By applying the same principles, everyone involved in the system is helping to treat victims, witnesses and defendants fairly, while prosecuting cases effectively.

2   GENERAL PRINCIPLES

2.1   Each case is unique and must be considered on its own facts and merits. However, there are general principles that apply to the way in which Crown Prosecutors must approach every case.

2.2   Crown Prosecutors must be fair, independent and objective. They must not let any personal views about ethnic or national origin, disability, sex, religious beliefs, political views or the sexual orientation of the suspect, victim or witness influence their decisions. They must not be affected by improper or undue pressure from any source.

2.3   It is the duty of Crown Prosecutors to make sure that the right person is prosecuted for the right offence. In doing so, Crown Prosecutors must always act in the interests of justice and not solely for the purpose of obtaining a conviction.

2.4   Crown Prosecutors should provide guidance and advice to investigators throughout the investigative and prosecuting process. This may include lines of inquiry, evidential requirements and assistance in any pre-charge procedures. Crown Prosecutors will be proactive in identifying and, where possible, rectifying evidential deficiencies and in bringing to an early conclusion those cases that cannot be strengthened by further investigation.

2.5 It is the duty of Crown Prosecutors to review, advise on and prosecute cases, ensuring that the law is properly applied, that all relevant evidence is put before the court and that obligations of disclosure are complied with, in accordance with the principles set out in this Code.

2.6 The Crown Prosecution Service is a public authority for the purposes of the Human Rights Act 1998. Crown Prosecutors must apply the principles of the European Convention on Human Rights in accordance with the Act.

3 THE DECISION TO PROSECUTE

3.1 In most cases, Crown Prosecutors are responsible for deciding whether a person should be charged with a criminal offence, and if so, what that offence should be. Crown Prosecutors make these decisions in accordance with this Code and the Director's Guidance on Charging. In those cases where the police determine the charge, which are usually more minor and routine cases, they apply the same provisions.

3.2 Crown Prosecutors make charging decisions in accordance with the Full Code Test (see section 5 below), other than in those limited circumstances where the Threshold Test applies (see section 6 below).

3.3 The Threshold Test applies where the case is one in which it is proposed to keep the suspect in custody after charge, but the evidence required to apply the Full Code Test is not yet available.

3.4 Where a Crown Prosecutor makes a charging decision in accordance with the Threshold Test, the case must be reviewed in accordance with the Full Code Test as soon as reasonably practicable, taking into account the progress of the investigation.

4 REVIEW

4.1 Each case the Crown Prosecution Service receives from the police is reviewed to make sure that it is right to proceed with a prosecution. Unless the Threshold Test applies, the Crown Prosecution Service will only start or continue with a prosecution when the case has passed both stages of the Full Code Test.

4.2 Review is a continuing process and Crown Prosecutors must take account of any change in circumstances. Wherever possible, they should talk to the police first if they are thinking about changing the charges or stopping the case. Crown Prosecutors should also tell the police if they believe that some additional evidence may strengthen the case. This gives the police the chance to provide more information that may affect the decision.

4.3 The Crown Prosecution Service and the police work closely together, but the final responsibility for the decision whether or not a charge or a case should go ahead rests with the Crown Prosecution Service.

5   THE FULL CODE TEST

5.1 The Full Code Test has two stages. The first stage is consideration of the evidence. If the case does not pass the evidential stage it must not go ahead no matter how important or serious it may be. If the case does pass the evidential stage, Crown Prosecutors must proceed to the second stage and decide if a prosecution is needed in the public interest. The evidential and public interest stages are explained below.

The evidential stage

5.2 Crown Prosecutors must be satisfied that there is enough evidence to provide a 'realistic prospect of conviction' against each defendant on each charge. They must consider what the defence case may be, and how that is likely to affect the prosecution case.

5.3 A realistic prospect of conviction is an objective test. It means that a jury or bench of magistrates or judge hearing a case alone, properly directed in accordance with the law, is more likely than not to convict the defendant of the charge alleged. This is a separate test from the one that the criminal courts themselves must apply. A court should only convict if satisfied so that it is sure of a defendant's guilt.

5.4 When deciding whether there is enough evidence to prosecute, Crown Prosecutors must consider whether the evidence can be used and is reliable. There will be many cases in which the evidence does not give any cause for concern. But there will also be cases in which the evidence may not be as strong as it first appears. Crown Prosecutors must ask themselves the following questions:

Can the evidence be used in court?

a   Is it likely that the evidence will be excluded by the court? There are certain legal rules which might mean that evidence which seems relevant cannot be given at a trial. For example, is it likely that the evidence will be excluded because of the way in which it was gathered? If so, is there enough other evidence for a realistic prospect of conviction?

Is the evidence reliable?

b   Is there evidence which might support or detract from the reliability of a confession? Is the reliability affected by factors such as the defendant's age, intelligence or level of understanding?

c   What explanation has the defendant given? Is a court likely to find it credible in the light of the evidence as a whole? Does it support an innocent explanation?

d   If the identity of the defendant is likely to be questioned, is the evidence about this strong enough?

e   Is the witness's background likely to weaken the prosecution case? For example, does the witness have any motive that may affect his or her attitude to the case, or a relevant previous conviction?

f   Are there concerns over the accuracy or credibility of a witness? Are these concerns based on evidence or simply information with nothing to support it? Is there further evidence which the police should be asked to seek out which may support or detract from the account of the witness?

5.5   Crown Prosecutors should not ignore evidence because they are not sure that it can be used or is reliable. But they should look closely at it when deciding if there is a realistic prospect of conviction.

The public interest stage

5.6   In 1951, Lord Shawcross, who was Attorney General, made the classic statement on public interest, which has been supported by

Attorneys General ever since: 'It has never been the rule in this country
— I hope it never will be — that suspected criminal offences must
automatically be the subject of prosecution'. (House of Commons
Debates, volume 483, column 681, 29 January 1951.)

5.7   The public interest must be considered in each case where there is
enough evidence to provide a realistic prospect of conviction. Although
there may be public interest factors against prosecution in a particular
case, often the prosecution should go ahead and those factors should be
put to the court for consideration when sentence is being passed. A
prosecution will usually take place unless there are public interest factors
tending against prosecution which clearly outweigh those tending in
favour, or it appears more appropriate in all the circumstances of the
case to divert the person from prosecution (see section 8 below).

5.8   Crown Prosecutors must balance factors for and against
prosecution carefully and fairly. Public interest factors that can affect
the decision to prosecute usually depend on the seriousness of the
offence or the circumstances of the suspect. Some factors may increase
the need to prosecute but others may suggest that another course of
action would be better.

**The following lists of some common public interest factors, both
for and against prosecution, are not exhaustive. The factors that
apply will depend on the facts in each case.**

Some common public interest factors in favour of prosecution:

5.9   The more serious the offence, the more likely it is that a prosecution
will be needed in the public interest. A prosecution is likely to be needed
if:

a   a conviction is likely to result in a significant sentence;

b   a conviction is likely to result in a confiscation or any other order;

c   a weapon was used or violence was threatened during the
commission of the offence;

d   the offence was committed against a person serving the public
(for example, a police or prison officer, or a nurse);

e   the defendant was in a position of authority or trust;

f   the evidence shows that the defendant was a ringleader or an
organiser of the offence;

g   there is evidence that the offence was premeditated;

h   there is evidence that the offence was carried out by a group;

i   the victim of the offence was vulnerable, has been put in considerable fear, or suffered personal attack, damage or disturbance;

j the offence was committed in the presence of, or in close proximity to, a child;

k the offence was motivated by any form of discrimination against the victim's ethnic or national origin, disability, sex, religious beliefs, political views or sexual orientation, or the suspect demonstrated hostility towards the victim based on any of those characteristics;

l there is a marked difference between the actual or mental ages of the defendant and the victim, or if there is any element of corruption;

m the defendant's previous convictions or cautions are relevant to the present offence;

n the defendant is alleged to have committed the offence while under an order of the court;

o there are grounds for believing that the offence is likely to be continued or repeated , for example, by a history of recurring conduct;

p the offence, although not serious in itself, is widespread in the area where it was committed; or

q a prosecution would have a significant positive impact on maintaining community confidence.

Some common public interest factors against prosecution

5.10 A prosecution is less likely to be needed if:

a the court is likely to impose a nominal penalty;

b the defendant has already been made the subject of a sentence and any further conviction would be unlikely to result in the imposition of an additional sentence or order, unless the nature of the particular offence requires a prosecution or the defendant withdraws consent to have an offence taken into consideration during sentencing;

c the offence was committed as a result of a genuine mistake or misunderstanding (these factors must be balanced against the seriousness of the offence);

d the loss or harm can be described as minor and was the result of a single incident, particularly if it was caused by a misjudgement;

e there has been a long delay between the offence taking place and the date of the trial, unless:
- the offence is serious;
- the delay has been caused in part by the defendant;
- the offence has only recently come to light; or
- the complexity of the offence has meant that there has been a long investigation;

f a prosecution is likely to have a bad effect on the victim's physical or mental health, always bearing in mind the seriousness of the offence;

g the defendant is elderly or is, or was at the time of the offence, suffering from significant mental or physical ill health, unless the offence is serious or there is real possibility that it may be repeated. The Crown Prosecution Service, where necessary, applies Home Office guidelines about how to deal with mentally disordered offenders. Crown Prosecutors must balance the desirability of diverting a defendant who is suffering from significant mental or physical ill health with the need to safeguard the general public;

h the defendant has put right the loss or harm that was caused (but defendants must not avoid prosecution or diversion solely because they pay compensation); or

i details may be made public that could harm sources of information, international relations or national security.

5.11 Deciding on the public interest is not simply a matter of adding up the number of factors on each side. Crown Prosecutors must decide how important each factor is in the circumstances of each case and go on to make an overall assessment.

The relationship between the victim and the public interest

5.12 The Crown Prosecution Service does not act for victims or the families of victims in the same way as solicitors act for their clients. Crown Prosecutors act on behalf of the public and not just in the interests of any particular individual. However, when considering the public interest, Crown Prosecutors should always take into account the consequences for the victim of whether or not to prosecute, and any views expressed by the victim or the victim's family.

5.13 It is important that a victim is told about a decision which makes a significant difference to the case in which they are involved. Crown Prosecutors should ensure that they follow any agreed procedures.

6 THE THRESHOLD TEST

6.1 The Threshold Test requires Crown Prosecutors to decide whether there is at least a reasonable suspicion that the suspect has committed an offence, and if there is, whether it is in the public interest to charge that suspect.

6.2 The Threshold Test is applied to those cases in which it would not be appropriate to release a suspect on bail after charge, but the evidence to apply the Full Code Test is not yet available.

6.3 There are statutory limits that restrict the time a suspect may remain in police custody before a decision has to be made whether to charge or release the suspect. There will be cases where the suspect in custody presents a substantial bail risk if released, but much of the evidence may not be available at the time the charging decision has to be made. Crown Prosecutors will apply the Threshold Test to such cases for a limited period.

6.4 The evidential decision in each case will require consideration of a number of factors including:
- the evidence available at the time;
- the likelihood and nature of further evidence being obtained;
- the reasonableness for believing that evidence will become available;
- the time it will take to gather that evidence and the steps being taken to do so;
- the impact the expected evidence will have on the case;
- the charges that the evidence will support.

6.5 The public interest means the same as under the Full Code Test, but will be based on the information available at the time of charge which will often be limited.

6.6 A decision to charge and withhold bail must be kept under review. The evidence gathered must be regularly assessed to ensure the charge is still appropriate and that continued objection to bail is justified. The Full Code Test must be applied as soon as reasonably practicable.

7 SELECTION OF CHARGES

7.1 Crown Prosecutors should select charges which:
  a   reflect the seriousness and extent of the offending;
  b   give the court adequate powers to sentence and impose appropriate post-conviction orders; and
  c   enable the case to be presented in a clear and simple way.
This means that Crown Prosecutors may not always choose or continue with the most serious charge where there is a choice.

7.2 Crown Prosecutors should never go ahead with more charges than are necessary just to encourage a defendant to plead guilty to a few. In the same way, they should never go ahead with a more serious charge just to encourage a defendant to plead guilty to a less serious one.

7.3 Crown Prosecutors should not change the charge simply because of the decision made by the court or the defendant about where the case will be heard.

8 DIVERSION FROM PROSECUTION

Adults

8.1 When deciding whether a case should be prosecuted in the courts, Crown Prosecutors should consider the alternatives to prosecution. Where appropriate, the availability of suitable rehabilitative, reparative or restorative justice processes can be considered.

8.2 Alternatives to prosecution for adult suspects include a simple caution and a conditional caution.

Simple caution

8.3 A simple caution should only be given if the public interest justifies it and in accordance with Home Office guidelines. Where it is felt that such a caution is appropriate, Crown Prosecutors must inform the police so they can caution the suspect. If the caution is not administered, because the suspect refuses to accept it, a Crown Prosecutor may review the case again.

Conditional caution

8.4 A conditional caution may be appropriate where a Crown Prosecutor considers that while the public interest justifies a prosecution, the interests of the suspect, victim and community may be better served by the suspect complying with suitable conditions aimed at rehabilitation or reparation. These may include restorative processes.

8.5 Crown Prosecutors must be satisfied that there is sufficient evidence for a realistic prospect of conviction and that the public interest would justify a prosecution should the offer of a conditional caution be refused or the offender fail to comply with the agreed conditions of the caution.

8.6 In reaching their decision, Crown Prosecutors should follow the Conditional Cautions Code of Practice and any guidance on conditional cautioning issued or approved by the Director of Public Prosecutions.

8.7 Where Crown Prosecutors consider a conditional caution to be appropriate, they must inform the police, or other authority responsible for administering the conditional caution, as well as providing an indication of the appropriate conditions so that the conditional caution can be administered.

Youths

8.8 Crown Prosecutors must consider the interests of a youth when deciding whether it is in the public interest to prosecute. However Crown Prosecutors should not avoid prosecuting simply because of the defendant's age. The seriousness of the offence or the youth's past behaviour is very important.

8.9 Cases involving youths are usually only referred to the Crown Prosecution Service for prosecution if the youth has already received a reprimand and final warning, unless the offence is so serious that neither of these were appropriate or the youth does not admit committing the offence. Reprimands and final warnings are intended to prevent re-offending and the fact that a further offence has occurred indicates that attempts to divert the youth from the court system have not been effective. So the public interest will usually require a prosecution in such cases, unless there are clear public interest factors against prosecution.

9   MODE OF TRIAL

9.1   The Crown Prosecution Service applies the current guidelines for magistrates who have to decide whether cases should be tried in the Crown Court when the offence gives the option and the defendant does not indicate a guilty plea. Crown Prosecutors should recommend Crown Court trial when they are satisfied that the guidelines require them to do so.

9.2   Speed must never be the only reason for asking for a case to stay in the magistrates' courts. But Crown Prosecutors should consider the effect of any likely delay if they send a case to the Crown Court, and any possible stress on victims and witnesses if the case is delayed.

10   ACCEPTING GUILTY PLEAS

10.1 Defendants may want to plead guilty to some, but not all, of the charges. Alternatively, they may want to plead guilty to a different, possibly less serious, charge because they are admitting only part of the crime. Crown Prosecutors should only accept the defendant's plea if they think the court is able to pass a sentence that matches the seriousness of the offending, particularly where there are aggravating features. Crown Prosecutors must never accept a guilty plea just because it is convenient.

10.2   In considering whether the pleas offered are acceptable, Crown Prosecutors should ensure that the interests of the victim and, where possible, any views expressed by the victim or victim's family, are taken into account when deciding whether it is in the public interest to accept the plea. However, the decision rests with the Crown Prosecutor.

10.3 It must be made clear to the court on what basis any plea is advanced and accepted. In cases where a defendant pleads guilty to the charges but on the basis of facts that are different from the prosecution case, and where this may significantly affect sentence, the court should be invited to hear evidence to determine what happened, and then sentence on that basis.

10.4 Where a defendant has previously indicated that he or she will ask the court to take an offence into consideration when sentencing, but then declines to admit that offence at court, Crown Prosecutors will consider whether a prosecution is required for that offence. Crown Prosecutors should explain to the defence advocate and the court that the prosecution of that offence may be subject to further review.

10.5   Particular care must be taken when considering pleas which would enable the defendant to avoid the imposition of a mandatory minimum sentence. When pleas are offered, Crown Prosecutors must bear in mind the fact that ancillary orders can be made with some offences but not with others.

11 PROSECUTORS' ROLE IN SENTENCING

11.1   Crown Prosecutors should draw the court's attention to:
*   any aggravating or mitigating factors disclosed by the prosecution case;
*   any victim personal statement;
*   where appropriate, evidence of the impact of the offending on a community;
*   any statutory provisions or sentencing guidelines which may assist;
*   any relevant statutory provisions relating to ancillary orders (such as anti-social behaviour orders).

11.2   The Crown Prosecutor should challenge any assertion made by the defence in mitigation that is inaccurate, misleading or derogatory. If the defence persist in the assertion, and it appears relevant to the sentence, the court should be invited to hear evidence to determine the facts and sentence accordingly.

12 RE-STARTING A PROSECUTION

12.1   People should be able to rely on decisions taken by the Crown Prosecution Service. Normally, if the Crown Prosecution Service tells a suspect or defendant that there will not be a prosecution, or that the prosecution has been stopped, that is the end of the matter and the case will not start again. But occasionally there are special reasons why the Crown Prosecution Service will re-start the prosecution, particularly if the case is serious.

12.2   These reasons include:
a   rare cases where a new look at the original decision shows that it was clearly wrong and should not be allowed to stand;
b   cases which are stopped so that more evidence which is likely to become available in the fairly near future can be collected and

prepared. In these cases, the Crown Prosecutor will tell the defendant that the prosecution may well start again; and

c   cases which are stopped because of a lack of evidence but where more significant evidence is discovered later.

12.3   There may also be exceptional cases in which, following an acquittal of a serious offence, the Crown Prosecutor may, with the written consent of the Director of Public Prosecutions, apply to the Court of Appeal for an order quashing the acquittal and requiring the defendant to be retried, in accordance with Part 10 of the Criminal Justice Act 2003.

Appendix E

Final Warning Scheme
Guidance for the Police and Youth Offending Teams

1. INTRODUCTION

1.1 This guidance provides advice for the police and youth offending teams on the operation of the final warning scheme.

1.2 The principal aim of the youth justice system, established by section 37 of the Crime and Disorder Act 1998 (the 1998 Act), is to prevent offending by children and young people.

1.3 The final warning scheme aims to divert children and young people from their offending behaviour before they enter the court system.

1.4 The scheme was designed to do this by:
- ending repeat cautioning and providing a progressive and effective response to offending behaviour;
- providing appropriate and effective interventions to prevent re-offending; and
- ensuring that young people who do re-offend after being warned are dealt with quickly and effectively by the courts.

The scheme

1.5 The legislation governing the final warning scheme is contained in sections 65-66 of the 1998 Act. Following pilots in five areas, the scheme was introduced across England and Wales on 1 June 2000.

1.6 The final warning scheme introduced a system of reprimands and final warnings for 10-17 year old offenders. Depending on the seriousness of the offence, a reprimand is normally given for a first offence and a final warning for a second offence. If a young person who has been given a final warning commits a further offence he or she must be charged.

The only exception is where it is at least two years since the previous warning and the offence is not so serious as to require a charge to be brought, in which case a second warning may be given.

1.7 A final warning goes much further than an old style caution. Following a final warning, the police have a statutory duty to refer the young offender to the youth offending team (Yot). The Yot in turn has a statutory duty to carry out an assessment of the young offender and in most cases to provide an intervention programme aimed at preventing re-offending.

1.8 Compliance with the intervention programme is voluntary. However, if a young person goes to court, their final warning and any failure to participate in an intervention programme may be cited in the same way as previous convictions. Furthermore, if the young offender has received a final warning within the past two years the court can only give a conditional discharge in exceptional circumstances and should give reasons if they do so. The aim is to ensure that action is taken to tackle offending behaviour and to address the needs of victims.

Current position

1.9 The scheme has now been in operation for over two years and is proving its worth. The YJB report that in 2001, 28,339 young people received final warnings and 70% were accompanied by an intervention programme. Research shows that effective intervention at the final warning stage significantly reduces the rate of re-offending. The Youth Justice Board has set a target that 80% of all final warnings should have an intervention programme by 2004.

1.10 But while there is much good practice around the country, this needs to be applied more consistently by police forces and youth offending teams in all areas; and there is more to be done if the final warning scheme is to reach its full potential, particularly in terms of <u>victim satisfaction</u>.

Scope and status of this guidance

1.11 Section 65(6) of the 1998 Act, provides for the publication of guidance by the Secretary of State. Two separate documents, *Guidance for the Police and Guidance for Youth Offending Teams,* were issued, together with a covering circular, in March 2000.

1.12 Two small changes to the legislation were implemented on 1 February 2001. *Further Guidance for the Police and Youth Offending Teams* on these amendments was issued on 24 January 2001.

1.13 This guidance on the final warning scheme for the police and youth offending teams replaces all previous guidance. It should be used by police forces and youth offending teams as the basis for their operation of the final warning scheme.

1.14 It follows a Home Office/Youth Justice Board/Association of Chief Police Officers (ACPO) review of the operation of the scheme and takes account of research commissioned by the Youth Justice Board (YJB).

1.15 The police and Yots will also wish to take account of the independent and comprehensive research by Oxford University published in May 2002 by the Joseph Rowntree Foundation. Its findings are available at www.jrf.org.uk. This was a three year study on restorative conferencing and cautioning. It found that a restorative approach appeared to be significantly more effective than traditional cautioning in reducing the risk of re-offending and in having high levels of victim satisfaction and community support.

1.16 This guidance is issued jointly by the Home Office and the YJB, and is endorsed by ACPO and the Crown Prosecution Service.

1.17 This document is for guidance only and is not a substitute for legal advice. Those responsible for administering the final warning scheme should seek their own legal advice as they consider necessary.

1.18 The guidance in the main consolidates the previous guidance but it goes further in that it:
- sets out the decision-making process; —
- provides advice on the use of police bail;
- updates the ACPO gravity factors;
- encourages closer liaison between the police and Yots;
- explains the role of Yot Steering Groups in monitoring the effectiveness of the final warning scheme;
- further encourages a restorative approach to make final warnings more effective and meaningful;
- promotes the greater involvement of victims in both the delivery of warnings and intervention programmes; and
- is more detailed on intervention programmes in support of warnings.

Other initiatives

1.19 The YJB has introduced a new shorter version of ASSET, developed especially for final warning cases, which will be available electronically.

1.20 National Standards on reprimands and final warnings are included in the YJB National Standards for Youth Justice. The YJB is currently revising the Standards. This guidance is consistent with the revised Standards.

1.21 The YJB is also publishing Effective Practice Guidance designed for use by anyone working with young people involved in the final warning process. The Guidance describes the features that have been found, through research, to be most effective in working with this group of young offenders. It is a working tool that will be updated every two or three years in the light of new or further evidence of effective practice. It contains specific guidance for Yot Steering Groups, managers and practitioners, so it is important that these groups use it to develop and inform their practice.

1.22 The YJB is appointing consultants to act as national developers to provide operational advice and support for police and Yots on final warnings and restorative justice.

1.23 The YJB Board will be supporting these initiatives through the provision of nationally accredited training for Yot and police staff during 2003 to raise standards and reinforce the effective practice guidance.

Enquiries

1.24 Enquiries about this guidance should be addressed to:

Jewell Jackman-Jones Juvenile Offenders Unit Home Office Room 309, 50 Queen Anne's Gate London SW1H 9AT

Tel: 020 7273 2933 Fax: 020 7273 4345

Email: jewell.jackman-jones@homeoffice.gsi.gov.uk

Roger Cullen Youth Justice Board 11 Carteret Street London SW1H 9DL

Tel: 020 7271 2974 Fax: 020 7271 3030

Email: roger.cullen@yjb.gsi.gov.uk

Electronic version of this guidance

1.25 This guidance is available on the following websites:

www.homeoffice.gov.uk

www.youth-justice-board.gov.uk

www.acpo.police.uk

2. THE LEGISLATION

2.1 A summary of the relevant provisions in the 1998 Act is at Annex A.

2.2 There have been two legislative amendments to the scheme since it was introduced[1].These were designed to facilitate a restorative approach to the delivery of reprimands and final warnings, as experience has shown that the effect of a reprimand or final warning can be enhanced by delivering it as part of a restorative process involving the young offender, his or her parents and, where appropriate, the victim. The first amendment removed the requirement for reprimands and final warning to be delivered in a police station and the second gave the police an explicit power to bail a young offender pending the delivery of the reprimand or final warning. The amendments came into force on 1 February 2001.

3. THE AGENCIES INVOLVED IN THE FINAL WARNING SCHEME

3.1 The police have responsibility for making decisions on disposals under the final warning scheme but may ask the Yot to help by carrying out a prior assessment of the young offender. (See section 8).

3.2 The Yot is responsible for ensuring that effective interventions are delivered in support of final warnings.

3.3 The police and Yots must work closely together for the final warning scheme to be fully effective. (See section 6).

---

1   The 1998 Act was amended by section 56 of the Criminal Justice and Court Services Act 2000.

Role of the Yot Steering Group

3.4 The Yot Steering Group should monitor the effectiveness of the local final warning scheme and:

- agree the local protocol between the Yot and the police on final warning arrangements;
- ensure that YJB targets on final warning interventions are met; and
- regularly consider data evaluating local final warning procedures and outcomes, including completion and re-offending rates.

3.5 Where there is doubt about whether a prosecution should be brought, it may also be useful to seek the opinion of the Crown Prosecution Service at an early stage. As well as advising on points of law and the sufficiency of the evidence, they may also be able to give guidance on public interest considerations.

4. OPERATION OF THE FINAL WARNING SCHEME

Informal action

4.1 Following the introduction by the 1998 Act of the final warning scheme which has replaced cautioning for young offenders, there is only strictly limited discretion for the police to take informal action, such as 'firm advice' to a young person and his or her parents. Informal action should be taken only in exceptional circumstances where the police consider that it will be sufficient to prevent future offending. This will almost always be in cases of anti-social behaviour where the behaviour falls short of being 'criminal' or for very minor non-recordable offences. To ensure that the final warning scheme has a real impact on offending behaviour, any informal action should be confined to such circumstances.

4.2 In dealing with any offence committed by under 18s, the police have three options:

- reprimand;
- final warning; or
- charge.

4.3 The 1998 Act requires that a final warning should normally be supported by an intervention programme delivered by the local Yot.

4.4 The final warning scheme is structured and progressive. Depending on the seriousness of the offence, the response will normally be:

4.5 But the police must consider a range of factors when deciding which disposal is the most appropriate.

First offence   Reprimand
Second offence   Final warning
Third offence   Charge

The police decision-making process

4.6 At Annex B is a summary chart of the police decision-making process for action under the final warning scheme.

4.7 Before a reprimand or final warning can be administered, the following criteria must be met (s65(1) of the 1998 Act).

There must be:
  (a) evidence that the young person has committed an offence; and
  (b) the evidence is such that, if prosecuted for the offence, there would be a realistic prospect of a conviction;
  (c) an admission of guilt;
  (d) no previous conviction; and
  (e) the police are satisfied that it would not be in the public interest for the offender to be prosecuted.

4.8 This is a step-by-step guide to the decision-making process.

Step one what is the offence?

4.9 The first step is to decide what offence is supported by the evidence.

Step two: is there sufficient evidence against the young person to give a realistic prospect of conviction if he or she were to be prosecuted?

4.10 For action to be taken under the scheme, the evidence must meet the required standard:that it could be used and would be reliable, such that a jury or bench of magistrates properly directed in accordance with the law would be more likely than not to convict the young person.

4.11 If the police do not have this evidence, either the matter should be dropped or the police should seek further evidence as needed following their normal practice.

Step three: does the young person admit the offence?

4.12 A reprimand or warning can be given only if the young person makes a clear and reliable admission to all elements of the offence. This should include an admission of dishonesty and intent, where applicable.

4.13 Unlike adult cautions, the young person does not 'consent' to the reprimand or final warning. Under the legislation, it is a matter for the police to decide the appropriate disposal in accordance with the statutory criteria.

4.14 Young people and their parents/carers or other appropriate adults should have access to information about the options available including the final warning scheme so that they can make an informed decision before the question as to whether they admit the offence is put to them. For instance, they should be aware that the police will decide the appropriate disposal under the final warning scheme in the light of the statutory criteria. The status of a reprimand or final warning should also be explained, including:-

 *   the fact that a record will be kept for a minimum of five years or until the offender reaches 18 years of age whichever is the longer;

 *   that it can be cited in criminal proceedings;

 *   in some cases can be made available to employers;

 *   if the offence is listed under the Sex Offenders Act 1997, that a reprimand or final warning will also require them to register with the police for inclusion in the sex offenders register. (See paragraphs 12.14-12.16).

4.15 If the young person does not make an admission, he or she cannot be reprimanded or finally warned. The police will decide whether to take no further action or to charge the young person, and may seek the advice of the CPS before taking the decision. The CPS will review the case in accordance with the Code for Crown Prosecutors and will decide whether to continue the prosecution. The relevant extract from the Code is attached at Annex C.

Step four: has the young person previously been convicted of an offence (recordable or non-recordable)?

4.16 The young person's previous history, convictions, reprimands and final warnings are determined by a Police National Computer (PNC) and local police force and Yot checks.

4.17 The final warning scheme applies to all offences – recordable and non-recordable – committed by under 18s. Recordable[2] offences are kept on the Police National Computer: non-recordable offences should

---

2   Recordable offences are imprisonable offences plus those offences listed in the National Police Records (Recordable Offences) Regulations 2000.

be checked locally, including records held by the forces of other areas where the young person may have lived previously. Wherever possible, the police should also check the offending history with the Yot for the young person's home area to ensure that previous offences, particularly non-recordable offences, are not missed.

4.18 If the young person has previously been 4.24 The different gravity scores, and the convicted of an offence, he or she cannot be police action that should normally be taken in reprimanded or finally warned and should be response to them are: charged. The CPS will then consider, in the light of the facts of the case and in line with the Code for Crown Prosecutors, whether to proceed with the prosecution.

Step five: has the young person previously been reprimanded/finally warned?

4.19 If the young person has been finally warned for one offence more than two years previously or reprimanded, he or she cannot be reprimanded but may be warned or charged.

4.20 If the young person has previously been finally warned for two offences or warned at all in the past two years, he or she cannot be reprimanded or warned and should be charged. The CPS will then consider whether to proceed with the prosecution.

Step six: how serious is the offence?

ACPO Gravity Factor System

4.21 The decision whether to reprimand, finally warn or charge will depend on the seriousness of the offence. To help the police assess the seriousness – or gravity – of offences, the Association of Chief Police Officers (ACPO) has devised a Gravity Factor System, under which all offences can be given a gravity score of between '1' for the most minor offences and '4' for the most serious.

4.22 Other factors – either aggravating (e.g. the offence was motivated by the victim's racial or ethnic origin) or mitigating (e.g. the offender was influenced by others more criminally sophisticated) – may raise or lower the score for a particular offence.

4.23 The Gravity Factors will help in assessing whether a young person should be charged for an offence. They reflect the public interest principles in the Code for Crown Prosecutors.

Gravity score	*Police Action*
1	Always the minimum response applicable to the individual offender, ie reprimand, warning or charge.
2	Normally reprimand for a first offence. If offender does not qualify for a reprimand but qualifies for a warning then give warning. If offender does not qualify for a warning then charge.
3	Normally warn for a first offence. If offender does not qualify for a warning then charge. Only in exceptional circumstances should a reprimand be given. Decision-maker needs to justify reprimand.
4	*Always charge*

4.25 The ACPO gravity scores have been updated. Revised guidance on the System, with the updated gravity scores, is at Annex D.

Step seven: is it in the public interest for the young person not to be prosecuted?

Public interest considerations

4.26 A reprimand or final warning may be given only if the police are satisfied that it would not be in the public interest to prosecute.

4.27 Where the option to prosecute has not been ruled out and where there are risk factors present, the police should consider bailing the young person for a Yot assessment to inform the police's decision (see paragraphs 5.4 – 5.5).

4.28 The use of bail enables full consideration of the public interest test. The Yot can explore whether all the aggravating and mitigating factors have been identified and correctly applied to the gravity score. It also enables information from victims to be taken into account and the final warnings and interventions to be tailored to the offender and the offence.

General issues

Group offences

4.29 The experience and circumstances of offenders involved in group offences can vary greatly, as can the degree of their involvement. Although consistency and equity are important considerations in the decision whether to charge, warn or reprimand, each offender should be considered separately. Different disposals may be justified.

Multiple offences

4.30 The guidelines apply generally to individual offences but more than one offence can be included in a final warning if, overall, a final warning is deemed an appropriate and proportionate response.

4.31 Where multiple offences arise from the same incident, the most serious offence should be considered and the gravity factors applied to it in the decision-making process. Clearly the circumstances of the other offence(s) should also be considered and may aggravate or mitigate the gravity factors.

4.32 Where multiple offences arise from a number of separate incidents that have come to light at the same time (eg reported separately prior to arrest or further offences admitted during interview), the cumulative effect of the offences should be considered when making an overall decision.

18 year olds

4.33 Offenders who were 17 when the offence was committed, but are 18 at time of delivery, and who are eligible for a caution, should be given an adult caution provided they consent to this.

Relevance of previous cautions

4.34 Section 67(8) of the 1998 Act abolished cautions for children and young people. Schedule 9's transitional provisions provided that a previous caution should be treated in the same way as a previous reprimand, and two or more previous cautions in the same way as one previous warning.

4.35 So if the young person's most recent disposal is a caution that is more than two years old, the young person cannot be reprimanded but may be warned or charged.

5. USE OF BAIL

Bail powers

5.1 Section 56(2) of the Criminal Justice and Court Services Act 2000 amended section 34(5) of the Police and Criminal Evidence Act 1984 (PACE) to read:

> A person whose release is ordered under subsection (2) above shall be released without bail unless it appears to the custody officer:
> (a) that there is need for further investigation of any matter in connection with which he was detained at any time during the period of his detention; or
> (b) that, in respect of any such matter, proceedings may be taken against him or he may be reprimanded or warned under section 65 of the Crime and Disorder Act 1998, and, if it so appears, he shall be released on bail.

Reasons for bail

5.2 The police decision whether to bail will depend on the circumstances of each case. Reasons for bail can include:

Prior to decision to reprimand/finally warn/charge
(i) further investigation into the offence;
(ii) referral to the Yot to check local records of offending history, where there is no conviction recorded on PNC;
(iii) referral to the Yot for an assessment of the young person.

Following a decision to reprimand/finally warn
(iv) to enable the reprimand or warning to be delivered by a trained police officer, possibly at a final warning clinic;
(v) to enable the reprimand or final warning to be delivered by a trained police officer as part of a restorative process, possibly with the victim present.

5.3 The young person and parent/ guardian/appropriate adult should be informed of the reason for bail, e.g. that the police need more information before they can decide whether the young person will be reprimanded, warned or charged.

Bail for assessment

5.4 The amendment to s34 of PACE allows the police to bail a young person pending a decision on whether or not to deliver a reprimand or final warning. That power involves a power to bail pending assessment of whether or not prosecution would be in the public interest as this is one of the criteria for deciding whether or not a reprimand or final warning should be given.

5.5 In particular, the police should consider bailing for a full assessment by the Yot of the risk of re-offending in cases where they have identified risk factors such as homelessness, poor school attendance, mixing with offending peers, substance misuse (including alcohol), unsupportive parents, other offender in the household and unemployment.

Bail for delivery

5.6 Granting a young person a period on bail for the purpose of delivery, gives the police/Yot time to prepare for the delivery of the reprimand or final warning, while ensuring that there is an enforceable means of bringing the young offender back into police custody. It is not possible to impose bail conditions unless a person has been charged. Therefore, if the delivery of a reprimand or final warning is to take place at a venue other than a police station, the young person and his parents/guardian should be invited to the venue within the bail period. If the young person and their parent/guardian attend the venue and the reprimand or final warning is delivered the young person should be released from bail by serving on the young offender a standard letter which has been previously signed by the custody officer.

5.7 If for any reason the reprimand or final warning is not delivered, the young offender will still be required to answer bail or they will be in breach of bail.

5.8 If the reprimand or final warning has not been delivered but the young offender answers to bail, the police will have to decide whether to:

- deliver the standard reprimand or final warning (which if the offender is aged under 17, will still require the presence of a parent or other appropriate adult);
- grant a further period of bail pending the delivery of the reprimand or final warning; or
- charge.

5.9 Whether or not it would be appropriate to charge will be a matter for the police and Crown Prosecution Service to decide, depending on the circumstances of the case.

5.10 If the reprimand or final warning has not been delivered and the young offender does not answer to bail, he or she may be arrested for the substantive offence, as the young offender is still in jeopardy of being charged. The police will then have the options set out in paragraph 5.8. If the police decide to deliver a reprimand or final warning, or charge, this may be for both the substantive and the bail offences.

Length of the bail period

5.11 It is important that the consequences of the offending behaviour are brought home to the young person without delay. Early intervention with the young person may also minimise the chances of further offending whilst on bail. The police should have monitoring processes to minimise delay in youth cases and should require authorisation to exceed maximum permitted timescales.

5.12 The length of the period of bail will depend on the facts of each case and young defendants should be bailed for the minimum period necessary depending on the enquiries/arrangements to be made.

5.13 Where final warnings are being considered, the police should issue the final warning within 20 working days (4 weeks) from the date of bail, giving sufficient time for the Yot assessment and the arrangement of the appropriate delivery method.

5.14 In particular, those identified as high risk should be bailed for 20 working days for a Yot assessment and the Yot notified within one working day. The Yot, working to National Standards, should conduct their ASSET assessment and suitability for a restorative justice approach within 10 working days to engage the young offender while still in the youth justice process. The police should be notified of the ASSET assessment within a maximum of 15 working days so that any relevant issues can inform the final decision on disposal and be incorporated in the delivery of the reprimand or final warning at which the Yot officer should be present. The bail period will also give an opportunity to arrange for restorative processes, if appropriate.

5.15 In some cases, the police may be unsure as to whether a final warning is suitable. This will include occasions when the police have not yet been able to check the previous offending history with the Yot or where there is some question over reliability of certain evidence. On these occasions the police should bail for a decision as to disposal in the same timescales as above. The police decision will then normally be: to take no further action, to finally warn or to charge. During the bail period the Yot should conduct the ASSET assessment and suitability for restorative processes and feed any relevant issues into the police decision-making process.

6. LIAISON BETWEEN THE POLICE AND YOTS

Local protocols

6.1 Police services and Yots should draw up a joint protocol setting out locally agreed practice under the final warning scheme. The protocol should be approved by the Yot Steering Group and implementation regularly monitored. A draft specimen protocol is attached at Annex E.

6.2 The protocol should be agreed between the Yot and the police on the operation of the final warning scheme and should include:
- notification to the Yot by the police for assessment of the suitability of a final warning intervention
- arrangements for bail
- contact with victims by the police
- arrangements for the delivery of reprimands and final warnings
- use of restorative processes
- information to the police on the outcome of interventions
- arrangements for victims to be informed of the outcome
- the provision of information on the impact of the scheme, including completion and re-offending rates
- joint training arrangements for police and Yot staff.

Notification

6.3 The police must notify the Yot within one working day of the arrest of all young people who:
- have been reprimanded or finally warned

- are thought to be appropriate for a final warning intervention and who are being bailed for assessment by the Yot
- have been charged.

6.4 Arrangements should be made by the police to contact victims within 24 hours of the arrest. The joint protocol should include the arrangements for contacting victims. When the victim first reports the crime, where appropriate the police should give him/her appropriate information regarding the role of the Yot and obtain their consent to being contacted by the Yot.

Sharing police information with Yots

6.5 The Youth Justice Board's Guidance for Youth Offending Teams on Information Sharing includes guidelines for information-sharing between Yots and partner agencies.

6.6 The police and Yot should develop a protocol for sharing information about young offenders and their victims.

6.7 The police and Yots should clarify their joint information requirements on both individual offenders and at an aggregated level, including agreement on the core data to be collected and the development of common data definitions.

6.8 The type of reprimand and final warning resulting from a police/Yot process (ie. with or without intervention) should be recorded by the Yot. This information is required for the quarterly returns to the YJB.

6.9 Locating the police information systems in the Yot can facilitate the process of final warning and assessments and improve the quality of the information exchanged.

6.10 Aggregated information on the numbers and characteristics of those receiving reprimands, final warnings and prosecutions should be regularly shared between the police and Yots. This should enable a joint evaluation of trends and contribute to any strategic decisions with regard to any changes needed in policy and practice.

6.11 There should be a quality assurance process for information exchange in both agencies.

Offenders

6.12 The police should pass on the following information to the Yot within one working day of the arrest:

- details of the young person;
- details of the offence (including the ACPO gravity score);
- any previous offending history;
- the name and contact details of the police officer responsible for the case or the contact details of the case manager in the file preparation unit or similar; and
- any particular issues that the Yot may wish to bear in mind when carrying out the assessment.
- Victim contact details.

Victims

6.13 The investigating police officer should notify the Yot in writing of the victim's details at the point of referring the young person to the Yot, provided that the victim has already given consent to be referred to the Yot.

6.14 The police should ensure that victims are informed of developments in the case. This function may be performed by the Yot police officer or victim worker according to the local protocol.

6.15 Victims should have the opportunity to give fully informed consent to any involvement in the final warning process. Their involvement can be increased if they receive advanced notification that the Yot will be in contact with victims of the offence unless they request otherwise. Victims should be given the name and contact details of a Yot worker to ask for further information or talk through any concerns.

7. INVOLVEMENT OF VICTIMS

7.1 Extensive guidance on involving victims and on restorative processes is given in the Youth Justice Board's Effective Practice Guides for Final Warnings and Restorative Justice and Section 6 of the joint Home Office/YJB Guidance on Referral Orders and Youth Offender Panels. The Board also plans to provide Yots with guidance on developing Victim Policies. The National Standards for the Youth Justice System contains standards for work with victims.

7.2 It is important that the police and Yots make full use of the guidance provided by the YJB and seek to involve victims more fully under the final warning scheme. Without this involvement, victims can feel ignored and fail to understand that young offenders who have not been brought to court can still be subject to a challenging and rehabilitative process. There is an obligation on police and Yots to ensure that victims are kept fully informed and the process explained to them in order that victims' needs are fully met and that the final warning scheme has public support.

7.3 Police and Yots should ensure that victims are enabled to make informed choices about whether they wish to be involved in the final warning scheme and if so in what way. If victims are involved in a way that is appropriate for them, this can be helpful to their recovery after crime. It is vital that victims are not coerced into participating or that their involvement is simply a means of addressing the offending behaviour needs of the young offender. The victims' rights must be fully respected and the police and Yots must take all necessary steps to prevent further damage being caused to victims as a result of the process.

7.4 All contact with victims should be handled with sensitivity and in accordance with anti-discriminatory practice, ensuring that the needs of diverse communities are appropriately met, including any need for interpreting and translation services. Victims attending a meeting with the offender should be invited to bring someone to support them if they wish.

7.5 The first contact with victims should be made by the police and the victim's consent must be sought to being contacted by the Yot; to being kept informed; or to being involved in restorative processes. Victims need clear information about the options they have and time to make up their minds without pressure. Their decisions must be respected, including the right to change their mind at any stage. Each victim will have different needs for preparation and support in relation to the process and their individual needs must be addressed.

7.6 All staff contacting victims must be trained in victim awareness. Access to information on the victim should be restricted to those who need it and in any event such information should be kept separate from information on the young offender.

7.7 Intervention programmes must contain either an element of direct reparation to the victim or community, or victim awareness input.

8. YOT ASSESSMENTS

Assessing the young person

8.1 Where a young person has been referred to the Yot, the Yot should carry out an assessment of the young person to aid the police decision-making as part of the public interest test, to assess the likelihood and suitability of the young person engaging voluntarily with a Yot intervention and/or to determine the most appropriate intervention for the young person.

Role of the youth offending team

8.2 When the Yot has received a request for a prior assessment, the Yot manager or their nominated representative should allocate a member of staff to deal with the prior assessment of the young person. Once assigned to the case, the Yot team member should contact the young person to make arrangements for a meeting.

8.3 Yots must undertake an assessment of the young person within 10 working days of referral. All assessments must be concluded, and the police informed, within 15 working days from the date of bail in order to minimise delay in decision-making.

Undertaking the assessment

8.4. The Yot should undertake a risk assessment of the young person using the Final Warning ASSET. The assessment should be used to:
* assess the re-offending risk factors;
* determine the nature and content of the intervention programme that would be appropriate to deal with the risk factors;
* explore the young person's attitude to intervention and assess and encourage the likelihood of him or her engaging with an intervention programme;
* explore with the young person the possibility of their participating in a restorative conference for the delivery of the warning; x
* if the Yot is assessing a young person who is being considered for a warning for an offence listed in the Sex Offenders Act 1997, explain to the young person and his or her parents the implications of that Act.

8.5 There may be occasions when the shorter Final Warning ASSET is not adequate for a full assessment of risk of serious harm, in these circumstances the full ASSET should be used.

8.6 Participation in an intervention programme or a restorative conference is voluntary and there must be no suggestion of the warning being conditional on agreement to participate.

Views of the victim

8.7 Unless the victim has requested no contact, Yots should contact the victim within five working days of being notified in order to
  (i) establish their view about the offence and
  (ii) to carry out an assessment of their willingness to participate in a restorative process.

8.8 In assessing the views of the victim, further information on aggravating or mitigating factors may be uncovered.

8.9 Aggravating factors might include:
  • the offence being motivated by the victim's racial or ethnic origin;
  • the victim deliberately being put in considerable fear; or
  • the young person being the ringleader.

8.10 Mitigating factors might include:
  • the offender having reacted impulsively to provocation from the victim (e.g. in some cases where a victim of bullying attacks the bully); or
  • the offender having expressed regret and offered reparation to the victim.

8.11 Victims should not be involved in decisions on disposals for young offenders. The police are solely responsible for making the decision to reprimand, warn or charge and although the views of the victim will be an important factor in determining the seriousness of the offence, they will not be conclusive.

8.12 Yots should ensure that the expectations of victims are not raised unrealistically. This is relevant both in relation to the disposal to be used (for example victims must not be led to believe that a young person is going to court when a warning is more likely) and the form of any reparation activity.

8.13 Where the victim does not, for whatever reason, engage in the Yot assessment of the public interest, the Yot may wish to refer to any victim personal statement taken at the time of the offence.

8.14 The Yot assessment should enable the victim to make decisions based on informed consent about participating in a restorative process related to the warning or as part of an intervention programme.

8.15 It should be made clear to victims that they can choose not to have contact with the offender.

9. DELIVERY OF REPRIMANDS AND FINAL WARNINGS

Use of the bail period

9.1 Where the statutory criteria are met and the police have reached a decision to reprimand or finally warn, there are several options for delivery:

- In straightforward reprimand and final warning cases which do not present any risk factors, or cases where the young offender is only temporarily in the area, the reprimand or final warning may be delivered straightaway.
- However, delivery should be by a police officer who has been given appropriate training.
- Some forces have set up surgeries or clinics where all reprimands and final warnings are given by trained officers (paragraph 9.33-9.34); as explained in section 5, there is power to bail for this purpose.

9.2 Where the young person has been bailed, the bail period may be used to:

- consider whether a mainstream police force officer or Yot police officer should deliver the reprimand or final warning;
- select the most appropriate venue for the delivery of the reprimand or final warning; and
- prepare for the delivery of the reprimand or final warning as part of a restorative process.

9.3 In some areas, police officers in the Yot are responsible for the delivery of reprimands and final warnings and it takes place on Yot premises. Victims may also be involved in the process. Such arrangements have produced high rates of compliance with intervention programmes; reduced re-offending rates locally; and increased victim satisfaction.

9.4 If the final warning is being given at the police station, it is good practice to have a member of the Yot present who can explain the role of the Yot to the young person and the family and a date fixed to follow up the final warning. Experience has shown that young people are more likely to comply with an intervention programme following a final warning if the Yot has been involved at an early stage.

Category of police officer

9.5 Under the 1998 Act, all reprimands and final warnings must be given by a police officer.[3]

9.6 However, there is no prescription as to the rank of police officer able to deliver reprimands and warnings. The expertise of the officer will normally be a more important factor in this consideration than his or her rank.

9.7 Officers delivering reprimands and warnings do not have to be in uniform. However, there is a strong preference from ACPO that officers should normally be in uniform.

9.8 Research shows that emphasis on the formality of a final warning contributes to reducing re-offending.

9.9 The YJB will be delivering a new Learning and Development Programme for all practitioners in the youth justice system during 2003, as part of its commitment to improving standards and raising the skills of staff in Effective Practice. This training is accredited and will form part of a national qualification structure containing specialist elements in Final Warnings, restorative justice and all elements of youth justice. Local police services and Yots should work together in prioritising training need in this area.

---

3   S65 of the 1998 Act specifies that the decision-making delivery is carried out by a
     'constable'.

Explaining the effect of reprimands and final warnings

9.10 All reprimands and final warnings must be given orally, and supplemented with written information clearly explaining the effect of the reprimand/warning. A standard leaflet on final warnings is at Annex F.

9.11 In giving a reprimand the officer should specify the offence that has led to it and make clear that:

- the reprimand is a serious matter;
- any further offending will result in a final warning or prosecution in all but the most exceptional circumstances;
- a record of the reprimand will be kept by the police until the offender is 18 years old, or for five years, whichever is longer;
- the young person's reprimand may be cited in any future criminal proceedings;
- if the offence is one covered by the Sex Offenders Act 1997, the young person is required to register with the police for inclusion on the sex offenders register (see paragraphs 12.14-12.16).

9.12 In giving a final warning the officer should specify the offence that has led to it and make clear that:

- the final warning is a serious matter;
- any further offending will result in prosecution in all but the most exceptional circumstances;
- a record of the final warning will be kept by the police until the offender is 18 years old or for five years, whichever is longer;
- the final warning may be cited in any future criminal proceedings;
- if the young person is convicted of a further offence within two years of getting the warning, the option of conditional discharge will only be open to the courts in exceptional circumstances; the young person can expect a more serious sentence;
- if the offence is one covered by the Sex Offenders Act 1997, the young person is required to register with the police for inclusion on the sex offenders register;
- the final warning will be followed up by the local youth offending team (if the Yot is present at the delivery of the final warning, the date, time and venue of the young person's next appointment with the Yot may be fixed);
- the Yot will assess the young person and, unless they consider it inappropriate, devise an intervention programme designed to tackle the reasons for the offending behaviour, prevent any re-

offending and repair some of the harm done (this may involve direct reparation if the victim wishes it, or reparation to the wider community); and

• unreasonable non-compliance with the intervention programme will be recorded and could be cited in any future criminal proceedings.

9.13 Any questions about what will happen next should be put to the Yot. The officer should give the young person contact details for the Yot.

Appropriate adults

9.14 Where the young offender is under 17 years old, the reprimand or final warning must be given in the presence of a parent or guardian or other 'appropriate adult' (as determined by PACE). The parent/guardian or appropriate adult must also be given copies of any written information given to the young person.

9.15 Where a Yot officer is present, as envisaged in para 9.4, their presence is not as an appropriate adult and therefore is not a replacement for the young person's parent or guardian.

Signed records

9.16 Whenever a reprimand or final warning is given, the young person, the officer and any parent, guardian or appropriate adult present must sign a form to confirm that it was given for the offence indicated. In cases involving non-recordable offences in particular, this form will be needed in any subsequent criminal proceedings where decisions as to the availability or otherwise of a conditional discharge are being made. A standard pro forma for recording non-recordable offences is at Annex G. The form should be copied to the Yot.

Venues

9.17 When the 1998 Act was being drafted, it was considered appropriate that reprimands and final warnings should be delivered only in police stations. However, to provide greater flexibility in the delivery of reprimands and final warnings, the 2000 Act removed this requirement.

9.18 Where the young person is bailed for a Yot assessment of the public interest prior to the decision regarding the final warning, the bail period can be used to give consideration to the selection of the venue most appropriate for the delivery of the warning. Bail can also be given for the purpose of arranging delivery.

9.19 The selection of the right venue may have a restorative effect and help bring home to the young person the consequences of his or her behaviour. For example, if the offence was one of criminal damage to a school or youth club, the warning could be delivered on the premises. The local community centre may also be a more accessible and less threatening venue for victims attending a restorative conference than the police station.

9.20 All venues should be assessed for suitability; they must be easily accessible to all participants (in particular the victim); and secure. It would not be appropriate for reprimands or final warnings to be delivered on the street. Nor would it normally be appropriate for them to be delivered in an individual's home.

Yot premises

9.21 Local police services and Yots should give particular consideration to using Yot premises for the delivery of warnings, especially in cases where the young person has been bailed for a Yot assessment. This will provide greater continuity in the final warning process (as the Yot will already have engaged with the young person), and it can also facilitate the involvement of the victim in the delivery of the warning (as the Yot will normally already have been in contact with the victim). This should increase the likelihood both of the young person engaging with the intervention programme after the warning, and of the young person and the victim participating in a restorative process as part of the intervention programme. However, some victims may not wish to attend at Yot premises and it is important that victims' preferences are taken into account.

Restorative processes

9.22 A restorative approach can make final warnings more meaningful and effective. Experience in areas which have embraced restorative justice

427

principles in this work has been very positive. Research into the delivery of final warnings shows that the use of restorative processes reduces re-offending, particularly when the RJ process is linked to an intervention programme following the final warning, and can be of benefit to victims.

9.23 Wherever appropriate, restorative processes should be used in the delivery of reprimands and warnings. ACPO share the view of the need to use restorative justice processes and trained police officers.

9.24 There are two main options for using a restorative process in the delivery of a warning:

- a restorative warning involving the young person and his or her parents, wherever appropriate any other influential adults as necessary, with the views of the victim conveyed;
- a full restorative meeting/conference with the addition of the victim and victim supporter.

9.25 The impact of a final warning on a young offender can be significantly enhanced by delivering it as part of a restorative conference. If the victim does not want to take part, similar principles can be applied by giving a restorative warning. Delivery of a final warning as part of a restorative process makes the young offender confront the consequences of his or her offence. It also provides a forum in which those affected by the offence – primarily the victim and the victim's supporters but also the offender's parents and supporters can express their views.

9.26 Victims under 17 should be involved only with the agreement of their parents or primary carer, who should be given the opportunity to come to the conference.

9.27 A restorative warning can be delivered if the victim is willing to have his or her views conveyed by the police officer, a Yot member, or their representative (e.g. a close friend, family member or other representative).

9.28 Even where the victim chooses to have no involvement in the process, police officers should aim to deliver both reprimands and warnings in a way which is consistent with restorative processes (e.g. by talking to the young person about the actual or potential impact of their offending on the victim and the wider community).

9.29 In some cases, police officers may feel that it is appropriate to use a restorative approach when delivering a reprimand. This could be where a young offender is identified as being at high risk of further offending and it is proposed to refer them to the Yot team following the reprimand, or where there appears to be particular potential benefits for the victim. The restorative approach could take the form of a full restorative conference with the victim, or a restorative reprimand in their absence. In making their decision, police officers need to balance the views of the victim with the need not to overload young offenders at their first contact with the police. Final warnings should receive priority in the use of resources for restorative justice processes.

9.30 It is recognised that the use of restorative justice in the delivery of reprimands and warnings has resource implications for police forces and Yots. It will not always be appropriate or possible for the full range of restorative justice processes to be available for every young offender and victim. However the priority must be to deliver reprimands and final warnings in a way that will be most effective in preventing re-offending and in considering the views of victims.

9.31 Where a young person is bailed for a Yot assessment, the Yot should also make an assessment of the appropriateness and type of restorative justice intervention that might be used either for the delivery of the final warning or as part of the intervention programme. The YJB is developing an RJ Assessment Tool for this purpose.

9.32 Detailed guidance on how to operate both restorative conferences and restorative warnings is contained in the Youth Justice Board's Effective Practice Guides for Final Warnings and Restorative Justice.

Surgeries/clinics

9.33 In some areas, final warning 'surgeries' or 'clinics' have been established where reprimands and final warnings are delivered at regular intervals at one venue, with the Yot present.. They are normally held one or two days each week, often on the Yot premises or at a community venue. Warnings are delivered either by specially trained mainstream police officers or Yot police officers. The police officer may be in civilian dress but there is a strong ACPO preference that the police officer should be in uniform.

9.34 Victims are invited to attend and should, if they wish, be invited to participate. There may need to be alternative arrangements to meet the needs of victims for whom the hours or venue of the clinic are unsuitable.

10. INTERVENTION PROGRAMMES

Assessments

10.1 The 1998 Act made clear that a final warning should normally be supported by an intervention programme delivered by the local Yot. The YJB has set a target for Yots to deliver intervention programmes in support of 80% of warnings by 2004.

10.2 It is important that the young people who do not receive an intervention programme with a final warning are those who are least likely to re-offend.

10.3 There may also be cases of first time offenders who are given a reprimand where risk factors of re-offending have been identified. Such cases should also be referred to the Yot for assessment and consideration of an intervention programme.

10.4 Responsibility for final warning assessments and intervention programmes should not be limited to Yot police officers. Given the complexity of young offenders' needs it would be beneficial for the range of Yot workers/skills to be engaged in the process, as appropriate.

10.5 Yots should aim to assess all young people who normally reside in their area and who have been finally warned within ten working days of being notified by the police.

Citable/non-citable components

10.6 Unreasonable non-compliance with the intervention programme could be cited in any future criminal proceedings, should the young person re-offend and be prosecuted.

10.7 The Yot may offer and the young person may agree to voluntary involvement in addition to or following the ending of the formal part of the final warning intervention. Where the young person fails to complete this voluntary involvement, it is not citable if the young person re-offends.

Devising intervention programmes

10.8 Intervention programmes will vary in their intensity and duration. But an intervention programme must be separate from the assessment and must consist of at least one post-assessment contact.

10.9 The citable components of any intervention programme must not be longer than three months duration (non-citable/voluntary intervention work may continue to be offered for a longer period).

10.10 Final warning interventions are part of the core work of the Yot and must be given priority.

10.11 In devising the intervention programme for each individual young person, the Yot must use the ASSET assessment as mentioned in 8.4 above.

10.12 Yots should normally use the (shorter) Final Warning ASSET in most final warning cases. However, where the final warning ASSET score is more than 20, then a more comprehensive assessment will need to be carried out using the full ASSET.

10.13 The total ASSET score can be used to determine how high or low the risk of re-offending in each case is, and thereby the intensity and duration of the intervention programme (or the number of hours of intervention work) that will normally be appropriate.

10.14 In determining the appropriate levels of intervention, Yots may find it helpful to use the following matrix:

Total ASSET score	Risk of re-offending	Number of offending* hours on intervention work normally appropriate
0-9	Low	1-4
10-19	Risk Aware	3-9
20+	Risk Concern	10 +

*   These are the categories in the ASSET tool.

10.15 Restorative processes should be used in the delivery of intervention programmes wherever possible[4].The type of restorative justice intervention and level of reparation should be determined by the impact of the offence on the young person's family, victim and the wider

4   The YJB targets for Yots for 2002-03 include i) to ensure that restorative processes are used in 100% of referral orders and in at least 75 % of other Yot interventions by Mar 2003 and ii) that 70% of victims by 2004 who have been consulted or who have participated in RJ processes are either satisfied or very satisfied with the outcome.

community, and the needs and wishes of individual victims. The YJB's Restorative Justice Assessment Tool which is being developed, may be of assistance in determining the most appropriate restorative justice intervention.

10.16 When the Yot has made the final decision on the contents of the intervention programme, this should be documented and a copy given to the young person and appropriate adult. The document should set out:
- the citable components of the intervention programme that must be complied with for successful completion of the programme;
- the non-citable voluntary intervention work that has been offered; and
- the consequences of unreasonable non-compliance with the citable components of the programme.

10.17 Where the intervention programmes are run by organisations external to the Yot, it is important that the Yot retains responsibility for these programmes and therefore maintains close links with the programme providers through meetings and regular progress reports.

10.18 The Yot must ensure that there is a contract or protocol with the programme provider that addresses such arrangements as:
- criteria for referral
- health and safety
- Criminal Records Bureau checks
- the role and responsibilities of the Yot and emphasises the Yot's role in reducing offending behaviour.
- record keeping
- regular feedback/progress reports to the Yot
- feedback to victims and the police

Closure

10.19 The case must be closed when reasonable attempts have been made to enable the young offender to complete the programme. Attempts to engage the young person in an assessment and in an intervention programme should be recorded. Where a young offender has failed to attend appointments, this should be followed up by the Yot, preferably by making personal contact.

10.20 Case closure following final warning intervention programmes must be managed by the Yot. Such closure should document:

- whether or not the young person has successfully completed the intervention programme (i.e. compliance or non-compliance with the citable components of the intervention programme);
- the young person's views of the intervention work;
- the victim's views of the intervention work; and
- a manager's review of the case.

10.21 A re-assessment of the young person and his or her risk of re-offending should normally be carried out using the closure summary of the Final Warning ASSET.

10.22 If the victim requests or agrees to receive a progress report, this should be provided on completion of the intervention programme by the young person. During this process the victim's views can be sought.

10.23 The police should be routinely notified of the completion of all intervention programmes.

11. MONITORING AND EVALUATION

11.1 It is important to establish local processes to monitor and evaluate the impact of intervention programmes delivered in support of warnings, including completion and re-offending rates. The annual re-offending cohort framework required by the YJB might contribute to this.

11.2 Findings from the evaluation should be examined by the:
- police and Yot officers responsible for the local protocol;
- Yot steering group; and
- Yot members with responsibility for final warnings.

11.3 In the light of the evaluation, local final warning procedures and intervention programmes should be regularly reviewed and appropriate changes made.

11.4 Yots must complete quarterly returns to the YJB, including, for final warnings, data on the number of final warnings supported by intervention programmes. Percentage improvements in tackling offending behaviour can be demonstrated using analysis of ASSET data. Overall data is published annually in the YJB's annual review. Local data is published in area youth justice plans.

12. OTHER ISSUES

Fingerprinting

12.1 Where a reprimand or warning is given for an offence, supporting fingerprints are needed so that the warning can be cited in any future criminal proceedings or form part of the criminal record for employment purposes.

12.2 Under current law, if fingerprints are not taken from the young offender when he or she is reported for a recordable offence, it is not possible to obtain fingerprints at a later stage should the police decide to proceed with a reprimand or warning. Changes to PACE contained in the Criminal Justice and Police Act 2001 will allow them to be taken without consent when a person is cautioned, reprimanded or finally warned for recordable offences. However, these changes will not be implemented until early 2003.

12.3 Measures in the 2001 Act, amending PACE, allow for the retention of all fingerprints and DNA samples taken on suspicion of involvement in a recordable offence.

Recording reprimands and final warnings

Recordable offences

12.4 The National Police Records (Recordable Offences) Regulations 2000 require the police to keep on Police National Computer (PNC) details of reprimands and warnings given for those offences for which they currently record convictions, (recordable offences).

12.5. Reprimands and warnings for recordable offences should be recorded in the same way as cautions for recordable offences.

12.6 All reprimands and warnings for all offences should therefore be recorded as soon as possible after they are administered. If necessary Chief Officers should give priority to recording cases involving young offenders. The effective operation of the final warning scheme relies on accurate records, to ensure appropriate decisions if there is a further offence.

12.7 The record made shall cover only the offence(s) for which the reprimand or warning was given, not any more serious offence which was not pursued.

Non-recordable offences

12.8 All police forces should have their own central systems to record reprimands and warnings for non-recordable offences given by their own and other forces. Its information will need to mirror that kept on PNC in relation to reprimands and warnings for recordable offences and records will need to be weeded in the same way. A model form is attached at Annex G. It will also need to cover convictions of juveniles for non-recordable offences by courts in their own area and (where passed on) outside, because they would preclude the use of a reprimand or warning for any future offence.

12.9 Because of the importance of the young person's previous record to the operation of the final warning scheme, we recommend that where forces are dealing with a young person whose home is (or has recently been) in a different force area, the officer handling the case should, in addition to checking the PNC and any local records, ask any other force likely to have dealt with the young person whether they have previously received a reprimand, warning or conviction for a non-recordable offence. Checks should also be made of the Yot in the area where the young person lives.

Retention of records

12.10 Police records of reprimands and final warnings are held until the offender is 18 years old or for a minimum of five years, whichever is the longer.

12.11 To ensure the effective operation of the scheme, records of reprimands and final warnings given for recordable offences will be retained on the PNC in line with the principles outlined in the current ACPO weeding guidance.

Rehabilitation of Offenders Act 1974

12.12 At present, reprimands and final warnings are not covered by the provisions of the 1974 Act. It is proposed that amending legislation should bring reprimands and final warnings within the scope of the Act with the disposals becoming spent as soon as they are given. There would be no requirement to disclose them except in respect of those circumstances excepted from the scheme (which are currently set out the in the Rehabilitation of Offenders Act 1974 (Exceptions) Order, as amended).

12.13 A reprimand or final warning is not a conviction. Young offenders receiving a reprimand or final warning should be told that if asked by employers or insurers they are entitled to say that they do not have a criminal conviction. But if asked whether they have a caution, reprimand or final warning, they should not say they do not. The police record of their reprimand or final warning can be made available to potential employers in certain circumstances ie if relating broadly to work with children, the sick, the vulnerable, the administration of justice or where issues of financial probity are in question.

Sex offenders register

12.14 Part 1 of the Sex Offenders Act 1997 requires those convicted or cautioned for relevant sex offences listed in Schedule 1 to the Act to notify the police of their name and address and certain other details. This includes young offenders who have been reprimanded or finally warned.

12.15 The police officer must explain to a young offender and their parent/guardian/appropriate adult that on receiving a reprimand or final warning for such an offence they will be subject to the requirements of the Sex Offenders Act ('the register'). Where the Yot has carried out a prior assessment of a young person who has been reported for a sex offence, this is an opportunity for them to explain about the register to the young person and his or her parents.

12.16 Registration following a reprimand or final warning is required for a period of two and a half years.

Children/young persons involved in prostitution

12.17 Young persons under the age of 18 who come to notice as being involved in prostitution should be dealt with in accordance with the joint guidance 'Safeguarding Children in Prostitution* published by the Home

Office/Department of Health/Department of Education and Employment and the Welsh Assembly in May 2000. That guidance emphasises that males and females under 18 who are involved in prostitution are primarily victims of abuse who do not consent freely to prostitution. As such, they should if at all possible be diverted away from prostitution without recourse to the criminal justice system.

12.18 However, the guidance makes it clear that in exceptional cases, where diversion has repeatedly failed, the police may, after consultation with others in the multi-agency group, take criminal action against a person under the age of 18 for loitering, soliciting or importuning. Where the offence is admitted, the young person can be dealt with under the final warning scheme. The final warning scheme replaces all cautions for young people which means that a prostitute's caution can no longer be issued to females under 18.

12.19 There is a wide range of sanctions available to deal with those who seek to encourage or exploit the prostitution of children under the age of 18. One of the principal aims of the criminal law in this area is to tackle those who control or exploit the prostitution of others.

Non-police prosecuting agencies

12.20 Since 1 June 2000, non-police prosecuting agencies that had previously given cautions to young people have no longer been able to do so eg the Department for Work and Pensions and the RSPCA.

12.21 It is the responsibility of the non-police agency to make contact with their local police. The police need to be prepared to respond to approaches from these agencies and to have the necessary arrangements in place. Protocols should be developed to enable young people to receive reprimands and final warnings as needed. Annex H suggests what should be covered in the protocol.

Home Office/Youth Justice Board November 2002

Appendix F

Youth Court Asset Form

 Core Profile

Additional information on answering the questions marked by asterisks on this form is given in the guidance notes.

Personal details

Surname_____ First name(s)_____

Other names _____ Gender: Male / Female   Date of birth _____

*Unique ID _____ *Police National Computer number_____

*Address _____

_____ *Postcode _____

Phone numbers (home, mobile, work) _____

*Ethnic classification (2001 census)   Information not obtainable ☐

White	British ☐	Irish ☐	Other White ☐		
Black/Black British	Caribbean ☐	African ☐	Other Black ☐		
Asian/Asian British	Indian ☐	Pakistani ☐	Bangladeshi ☐	Other Asian ☐	
Mixed	White/Black Caribbean ☐	White/Black African ☐	White/Asian ☐	Other Mixed ☐	
Chinese/Other ethnic group	Chinese ☐	Any other ☐			

Preferred language (other than English) _____

Information used for assessment (Please tick all that apply.)

Interview ☐	Crown Prosecution Service ☐	General practitioner ☐
Case record ☐	Solicitor ☐	Mental health service ☐
Family/carer ☐	Previous convictions ☐	Other health service ☐
School ☐	Residential home/hostel ☐	Drug/alcohol service ☐
Social Services Department ☐	Housing association ☐	Young Offender Institution ☐
Victim ☐	Local education authority ☐	Secure unit ☐
Police ☐	Careers guidance service ☐	Voluntary organisation ☐
	*Common Assessment Framework ☐	Lead Professional ☐

Other (e.g. club, religious organisation, local youth projects) _____

Give details of any particular difficulties in obtaining information.

Specify any significant pieces of information still to be obtained.

Assessment completed by _____ Date completed _____

1

Appendix F

Offence details

*Primary index offence

Additional offences

*Seriousness score (1-8)

Outline of current offence(s)

*Case stage

Referral Order ☐   Pre-sentence report ☐   Post-sentence ☐

Mid-Detention and ☐   *Review ☐   End order ☐   *Other ☐
Training Order

*Victim/s (Please tick all that apply.)

*Specific, targeted victim ☐   *Vulnerable victim ☐   *Repeat victim ☐

Victim not known to him/her ☐   Racially motivated offence ☐

Details

Offence analysis

Please use the framework below to describe and analyse the young person's offending behaviour regarding current offences.

*Actions and intentions
• What was the offence?
• Where, when, and with whom was it committed?
• What methods were used?
• What degree of planning was involved?
• Were any weapons used?
• What was the value of money or property stolen?
• Were alcohol and/or drugs used at the time of the offence?
• Was it a group offence? If so, was the young person a leader or follower?
• What were the intentions of the young person?
• What were the differences between their intentions and their actions?
• Was the victim targeted/random/groomed/particularly vulnerable?
• Were there any other aggravating or mitigating factors?

*Outcomes and consequences
• What is the impact on the victim – in the immediate and the longer term?
• What are the consequences for the young person (e.g. reaction to arrest and detention, response from family)?

*Reasons and motives
• What were the young person's personal and social circumstances at the time?
• What were the young person's motives?
• What were the young person's attitudes?
• Does the young person have any particular attitudes/beliefs which might have influenced the offence (e.g. a belief that certain types of behaviour are justified, racial motivation, triggers, disinhibitors)?

*Patterns of offending behaviour
• Are there any similarities or differences with previous behaviour?
• Has there been an increase/decrease in seriousness and/or frequency?
• Does the young person show a specialisation/diversity of offences?
• Are there any gaps in offending patterns?
• Has the young person made previous attempts to desist?

Analysis and evidence

Criminal history

Age at first Reprimand/Caution	10	11	12	13	14	15	16	17	N/A	Don't know
	☐	☐	☐	☐	☐	☐	☐	☐	☐	☐

Age at first conviction	10	11	12	13	14	15	16	17	N/A	Don't know
	☐	☐	☐	☐	☐	☐	☐	☐	☐	☐

Number of previous convictions	10+	8-9	6-7	5	4	3	2	1	0	Don't know
	☐	☐	☐	☐	☐	☐	☐	☐	☐	☐

Previous custodial sentences	2+	1	0	Don't know
	☐	☐	☐	☐

*Time since last conviction or pre-court disposal	Up to... 3 months	6 months	12 months	1 year +	N/A	Don't know
	☐	☐	☐	☐	☐	☐

Previous disposals

Please indicate whether the young person has ever received any of the following disposals.

	Date/s		Date/s
Final Warning		Supervision Order	
Referral Order		Community Punishment Order	
Reparation Order		Community Rehabilitation Order	
Action Plan Order		*Other disposals, e.g. fine	
ASBO			

Have there been any instances of failing to complete or comply with previous disposals?	Yes	No	Don't know	N/A
	☐	☐	☐	☐

Details (Please explain reasons for any 'Don't know' responses.)

③ CORE PROFILE

	Yes	No	Don't know
Is the young person's name on the sex offenders' register?	☐	☐	☐
*Any other previous contact with Yot?	☐	☐	☐

(e.g. YISP, YIP, Splash, ABC, referral for Child Safety Order)

Details (This does not include the information recorded above about previous disposals.)

Care history and 'looked after' status

Please indicate whether any of the following apply to the young person.

	Current	Previous	Never	Don't know
Accommodated by voluntary agreement with parents (s20 Children Act 1989)	☐	☐	☐	☐
Subject to a care order (s31 Children Act 1989)	☐	☐	☐	☐
Remand to local authority accommodation (s23(1) Children and Young Person's Act 1969)	☐	☐	☐	☐

If the young person is 16 or 17 and you have ticked a 'current' or 'previous' box above:

	Yes	No	Don't know
*Is s/he an 'eligible child' (still in care and looked after for at least 13 weeks since the age of 14)?	☐	☐	☐
*(If 'No') Is s/he a 'relevant child' (has left care but was looked after for at least 13 weeks from the age of 14, and for some time while 16 or 17)?	☐	☐	☐

Other social services contact

	Current	Previous	Never	Don't know
His/her name has been placed on the child protection register	☐	☐	☐	☐
*Any other referrals to or contact with social services	☐	☐	☐	☐
Any social services involvement with siblings	☐	☐	☐	☐

Details (Please explain reasons for any 'Don't know' responses and outline any aspects of the young person's care history which you consider relevant.)

5

1. Living arrangements

*Who has the young person been mostly living with over the last six months?

Mother ☐	Grandparent/s ☐	Friend/s ☐
Father ☐	Other family ☐	Residents of home or institution ☐
Step-parent ☐	By self ☐	
Foster carer/s ☐	Partner ☐	Other/s ☐
Sibling/s ☐	Own child(ren) ☐	

If his/her *current* living arrangements are different, please specify below.

Please indicate whether any of the following
apply to the young person.

	Yes	No	Don't know
*No fixed abode	☐	☐	☐
*Unsuitable, does not meet his/her needs (e.g. overcrowded, lacks basic amenities)	☐	☐	☐
Deprived household (e.g. dependent on benefits, entitlement to free school meals)	☐	☐	☐
*Living with known offender/s	☐	☐	☐
Absconding or staying away (e.g. ever reported as missing person)	☐	☐	☐
*Disorganised/chaotic (e.g. different people coming and going)	☐	☐	☐
*Other problems (e.g. uncertainty over length of stay)	☐	☐	☐

Evidence (Please explain reasons for any 'Don't know' responses.)

*Rate the extent to which the young person's living arrangements
are associated with the likelihood of further offending.

0	1	2	3	4

(0 = not associated, 4 = very strongly associated)

6

2. Family and personal relationships

Which family members or carers has the young person been in contact with over the last six months?

Birth mother ☐	Grandparent/s ☐	Other significant ☐
Birth father ☐	Sibling/s ☐	adults (e.g. neighbour,
Adoptive parent/s ☐	Partner ☐	family friend)
Step-parent ☐	Own child(ren) ☐	Other/s ☐
Foster carer/s ☐	Other family ☐	

Please indicate whether any of the following apply to the young person.

	Yes	No	Don't know
*Evidence of family members or carers with whom the young person has been in contact over the last six months being involved in criminal activity	☐	☐	☐
*Evidence of family members or carers with whom the young person has been in contact over the last six months being involved in heavy alcohol misuse	☐	☐	☐
*Evidence of family members or carers with whom the young person has been in contact over the last six months being involved in drug or solvent misuse	☐	☐	☐
*Significant adults fail to communicate with or show care/interest in the young person	☐	☐	☐
Inconsistent supervision and boundary setting	☐	☐	☐
*Experience of abuse (i.e. physical, sexual, emotional, neglect)	☐	☐	☐
*Witnessing other violence in family context	☐	☐	☐
*Significant bereavement or loss	☐	☐	☐
*Difficulties with care of his/her own children N/A	☐	☐	☐
Other problems (e.g. parent with physical/mental health problem, loss of contact, acrimonious divorce of parents, other stress/tension)	☐	☐	☐

Evidence (Please explain reasons for any 'Don't know' responses.)

*Rate the extent to which the young person's family and personal relationships are associated with the likelihood of further offending.

0	1	2	3	4

(**0** = not associated, **4** = very strongly associated)

7

445

3. Education, training and employment

Engagement in education, training or employment (ETE)

*Is the young person of compulsory school age?   Yes ☐ No☐

Which of the following best describe his/her current ETE situation?
(Tick as many as apply.)

Mainstream school ☐   Work experience ☐   College/further education ☐

Special school ☐   Full time work ☐   Other training course ☐

Pupil referral unit ☐   Part time work ☐   Unable to work (e.g. incapacity) ☐

Other specialist unit ☐   Casual/temporary work ☐   Looking after family ☐

Community home with education ☐   Unemployed ☐   Nothing currently arranged ☐

   New Deal ☐   Other ☐

Home tuition ☐   Pre-employment/lifeskills training ☐

*How many hours of ETE are arranged each week? _____ hours

*How many hours of ETE is she/he currently engaged in/receiving per week?___ hours

*Is there evidence of non-attendance? (Please tick relevant reasons
and give details below.)   Yes ☐ No☐

Permanent exclusion ☐   Fixed-term exclusion ☐   Family issues ☐   Illness ☐

Other non-attendance (specify)_____

Evidence (Please explain reasons for any 'Don't know' responses.)

Educational attainment

	Yes	No	Don't know
Does s/he have any educational qualifications?	☐	☐	☐
Does s/he have vocational/practical qualifications?	☐	☐	☐
*Have special needs (SEN) been identified?	☐	☐	☐
If 'yes', does s/he have a statement of SEN? N/A	☐	☐	☐
Does s/he have difficulties with literacy?	☐	☐	☐
Does s/he have difficulties with numeracy?	☐	☐	☐
Does s/he have difficulties caused by a severe lack of English (or Welsh, if applicable) language skills?	☐	☐	☐

8

③ CORE PROFILE

Evidence (Please explain reasons for any 'Don't know' responses.)

Other factors relating to engagement in ETE	Yes	No	Don't know
Negative attitudes towards ETE	☐	☐	☐
Lack of attachment to current ETE provision (e.g. wants to leave, cannot see benefits of learning)	☐	☐	☐
*Bullied	☐	☐	☐
*Bullies others	☐	☐	☐
Poor relationships with most teachers/tutors/employers/colleagues	☐	☐	☐
Negative parental/carer attitudes towards education/training or employment	☐	☐	☐
Other problems (e.g. frequent changes of school/educational placement, school is unchallenging/boring, disability, lack of stable address meaning difficulties securing work, no money to buy books/tools/equipment).	☐	☐	☐

Evidence (Please explain reasons for any 'Don't know' responses.)

*Rate the extent to which the young person's education, training and employment is associated with the likelihood of further offending.

0	1	2	3	4

(0 = not associated, 4 = very strongly associated)

9

447

4. Neighbourhood

*Please give a brief description of the neighbourhood in which the young person spends most of their time.

Please indicate whether any of the following are a problem in the neighbourhood.

	Yes	No	Don't know
*Obvious signs of drug dealing and/or usage	☐	☐	☐
Isolated location/lack of accessible transport	☐	☐	☐
*Lack of age-appropriate facilities (e.g. youth clubs, sports facilities)	☐	☐	☐
Racial or ethnic tensions	☐	☐	☐
Other problems (e.g. lack of amenities such as shops or post office, opportunities to sell stolen goods, red-light district, tension between police and local community)	☐	☐	☐

Evidence (Please explain reasons for any 'Don't know' responses.)

*Rate the extent to which the young person's neighbourhood is associated with the likelihood of further offending.

0	1	2	3	4

(0 = not associated, 4 = very strongly associated)

10

5. Lifestyle

Please indicate whether the following are
characteristic of the young person's lifestyle.

	Yes	No	Don't know
*Lack of age-appropriate friendships	☐	☐	☐
*Associating with predominantly pro-criminal peers	☐	☐	☐
*Lack of non-criminal friends	☐	☐	☐
Has nothing much to do in spare time	☐	☐	☐
*Participation in reckless activity	☐	☐	☐
*Inadequate legitimate personal income	☐	☐	☐
Other problems (e.g. gambling, staying out late at night, loneliness)	☐	☐	☐

Evidence (Please explain reasons for any 'Don't know' responses.)

*Rate the extent to which the young person's lifestyle is
associated with the likelihood of further offending.

0	1	2	3	4

(0 = not associated, 4 = very strongly associated)

11

449

6. Substance use

Please answer the questions below to give details of substance use (based on the information currently available).

	*Ever used	*Recent use	Age at first use	Not known to have used
Tobacco	☐	☐	☐	☐
Alcohol (Please specify types of alcohol in evidence box.)	☐	☐	☐	☐
Solvents (glue, gas and volatile substances e.g. petrol, lighter fuel)	☐	☐	☐	☐
Cannabis	☐	☐	☐	☐
Ecstasy	☐	☐	☐	☐
Amphetamines	☐	☐	☐	☐
LSD	☐	☐	☐	☐
Poppers	☐	☐	☐	☐
Cocaine	☐	☐	☐	☐
Crack	☐	☐	☐	☐
Heroin	☐	☐	☐	☐
Methadone (obtained legally or illegally – specify in evidence box)	☐	☐	☐	☐
Tranquilisers	☐	☐	☐	☐
Steroids	☐	☐	☐	☐
Other (Please specify in evidence box.)	☐	☐	☐	☐

Please indicate whether any of the following apply to the young person.

	Yes	No	Don't know
*Practices which put him/her at particular risk (e.g. injecting, sharing equipment, poly-drug use)	☐	☐	☐
*Sees substance use as positive and/or essential to life	☐	☐	☐
*Noticeably detrimental effect on education, relationships, daily functioning	☐	☐	☐
Offending to obtain money for substances	☐	☐	☐
Other links to offending (e.g. offending while under influence, possessing/supplying illegal drugs, obtaining substances by deception)	☐	☐	☐

Evidence (Please explain reasons for any 'Don't know' responses.)

*Rate the extent to which the young person's substance use is associated with the likelihood of further offending.

0	1	2	3	4

(0 = not associated, 4 = very strongly associated)

12

3

CORE PROFILE

7. Physical health

Please indicate whether any of the following apply to the young person.

	Yes	No	Don't know
*Health condition which significantly affects everyday life functioning	☐	☐	☐
*Physical immaturity/delayed development	☐	☐	☐
*Problems caused by not being registered with GP	☐	☐	☐
*Lack of access to other appropriate health care services (e.g. dentist)	☐	☐	☐
*Health put at risk through his/her own behaviour (e.g. hard drug use, unsafe sex, prostitution)	☐	☐	☐
Other problems (prescribed medication, binge drinking, obesity, poor diet, smoking, hyperactivity, early or late physical maturation)	☐	☐	☐

Evidence (Please explain reasons for any 'Don't know' responses.)

*Rate the extent to which the young person's physical health is associated with the likelihood of further offending.

0	1	2	3	4

(0 = not associated, 4 = very strongly associated)

13

451

8. Emotional and mental health

Is the young person's daily functioning significantly affected by emotions or thoughts resulting from the following? Yes   No   Don't know

*Coming to terms with significant past event/s (e.g. feelings of anger, sadness, grief, bitterness)   ☐ ☐ ☐

*Current circumstances (e.g. feelings of frustration, stress, sadness, worry/anxiety)   ☐ ☐ ☐

*Concerns about the future (e.g. feelings of worry/anxiety, fear, uncertainty)   ☐ ☐ ☐

Evidence (Please explain reasons for any 'Don't know' responses.)

	Yes	No	Don't know
*Has there been any formal diagnosis of mental illness?	☐	☐	☐
*Any other contact with, or referrals to, mental health services?	☐	☐	☐

Evidence (Please explain reasons for any 'Don't know' responses.)

*Are there indications that any of the following apply to the young person?   Yes   No   Don't know

*S/he is affected by other emotional or psychological difficulties (e.g. phobias, eating or sleep disorders, suicidal feelings not yet acted out, obsessive compulsive disorder, hypochondria).   ☐ ☐ ☐

*S/he has deliberately harmed her/himself.   ☐ ☐ ☐

*S/he has previously attempted suicide.   ☐ ☐ ☐

Details (Specify type of illness, medication, whether she/he co-operates with treatment etc. Please explain reasons for any 'Don't know' responses.)

*Rate the extent to which the young person's emotional and mental health is associated with the likelihood of further offending.	0	1	2	3	4

(0 = not associated, 4 = very strongly associated)

14

3

CORE PROFILE

9. Perception of self and others

Please indicate whether any of the following apply to the young person.

	Yes	No	Don't know
*S/he has difficulties with self-identity.	☐	☐	☐
*S/he has inappropriate self-esteem (e.g. too high or too low).	☐	☐	☐
*S/he has a general mistrust of others.	☐	☐	☐
Sees him/herself as a victim of discrimination or unfair treatment (e.g. in the home, school, community, prison).	☐	☐	☐
*S/he displays discriminatory attitudes towards others (e.g. race, ethnicity, religion, gender, age, class, disability, sexuality).	☐	☐	☐
*S/he perceives him/herself as having a criminal identity.	☐	☐	☐

Evidence (Please explain reasons for any 'Don't know' responses.)

*Rate the extent to which the young person's perception of self and others is associated with the likelihood of further offending.

0	1	2	3	4

(0 = not associated, 4 = very strongly associated)

15

453

10. Thinking and behaviour

*Are the young person's actions characterised by
any of the following?

	Yes	No	Don't know
*Lack of understanding of consequences (e.g. immediate and longer term outcomes, direct and indirect consequences, proximal and distal consequences)	☐	☐	☐
*Impulsiveness	☐	☐	☐
*Need for excitement (easily bored)	☐	☐	☐
*Giving in easily to pressure from others (lack of assertiveness)	☐	☐	☐
Poor control of temper	☐	☐	☐
*Inappropriate social and communication skills	☐	☐	☐

*Does the young person display any of the following
types of behaviour?

	Yes	No	Don't know
*Destruction of property	☐	☐	☐
*Aggression towards others (e.g. verbal, physical)	☐	☐	☐
*Sexually inappropriate behaviour	☐	☐	☐
*Attempts to manipulate/control others	☐	☐	☐

Evidence (Please explain reasons for any 'Don't know' responses.)

*Rate the extent to which the young person's thinking and
behaviour is associated with the likelihood of further offending.

0	1	2	3	4

(0 = not associated, 4 = very strongly associated)

16

11. Attitudes to offending

*Please indicate whether the young person
displays any of the following attitudes.

	Yes	No	Don't know
*Denial of the seriousness of his/her behaviour	☐	☐	☐
*Reluctance to accept any responsibility for involvement in most recent offence/s	☐	☐	☐
*Lack of understanding of the effect of his/her behaviour on victims (if victimless, on society)	☐	☐	☐
*Lack of remorse	☐	☐	☐
*Lack of understanding about the effects of his/her behaviour on family/carers	☐	☐	☐
*A belief that certain types of offences are acceptable	☐	☐	☐
*A belief that certain people/groups are acceptable 'targets' of offending behaviour	☐	☐	☐
*S/he thinks that further offending is inevitable	☐	☐	☐

Evidence (Please explain reasons for any 'Don't know' responses.)

*Rate the extent to which the young person's attitudes to
offending is associated with the likelihood of further offending.

0	1	2	3	4

(0 = not associated, 4 = very strongly associated)

17

455

12. Motivation to change

Please indicate whether the young person displays any of the following attitudes.

	Yes	No	Don't know
*Has an appropriate understanding of the problematic aspects of his/her own behaviour	☐	☐	☐
Shows real evidence of wanting to deal with problems in his/her life	☐	☐	☐
*Understands the consequences for him/herself of further offending	☐	☐	☐
*Has identified clear reasons or incentives for him/her to avoid further offending	☐	☐	☐
*Shows real evidence of wanting to stop offending	☐	☐	☐
Will receive positive support from family, friends or others during any intervention	☐	☐	☐
Is willing to co-operate with others (family, Yot, other agencies) to achieve change	☐	☐	☐

Evidence (Please explain reasons for any 'Don't know' responses.)

*Rate the extent to which the young person's motivation to change is associated with the likelihood of further offending.
(0 = not associated, 4 = very strongly associated)

0	1	2	3	4

18

③ CORE PROFILE

457

Appendix F

Positive factors

Please tick the relevant boxes to indicate the presence of positive factors in the young person's life. If, for any question, there do not seem to be any positives (or you are unsure) please leave that particular box blank. Use the evidence boxes to explain what impact the different factors may have on the likelihood of reoffending.

Individual factors

Current (or potential)

Education/training/work experience that enhances confidence and self-esteem (e.g. good at certain subjects, demonstrates practical skills, recognition of achievements) ☐

Has obtained qualifications that will help him/her to obtain employment ☐

Has some friends who are not involved in offending, model positive social behaviour etc. ☐

Positive and constructive things to do in his/her spare time ☐

Evidence

20

Current (or potential)

A sense of self-efficacy (e.g. that she/he can take action to change things, displays optimism) ☐

A goal, ambition, sense of direction or something to 'aim at' in life ☐

Opportunities for 'turning points' (e.g. change of school, moving to a new area, new social opportunities) ☐

Resilience (e.g. copes well with difficulties, knows where to seek help, seems to spring back quickly from adversity) ☐

Has engaged well with previous interventions (e.g. from YISP, YIP, Positive Activities or other initiatives, interventions by other agencies) ☐

Evidence

Family factors

Current (or potential)

Strong, stable relationship with at least one parent or other family member ☐

Parent/s or carers who value education/training/employment ☐

Family members or carers who model pro-social behaviour and norms ☐

Evidence

Appendix F

Community factors

Current (or potential)

Professional help/support, e.g. receiving support/counselling, other agency involvement with family ☐

School is interested in the young person's progress, keen to get involved and help ☐

Strong, stable relationship with an adult outside of the family home (e.g. teacher, youth club leader, neighbour) ☐

Community offers opportunities for the young person to get involved with activities (e.g. youth centre, sports facilities that caters for the young person's interests, other interest groups) ☐

If applicable, young person receives strong support from cultural and ethnic communities ☐

Evidence

Any other positive factors that can be identified (e.g. stable accommodation, good transport links)

Details

3
CORE PROFILE

22

Indicators of vulnerability

This section focuses on the possibility of harm being caused to the young person.

The first three questions should be completed in all cases; the last two, regarding previous custodial sentences and current concerns about vulnerability in custody, are not always required, but can be used where a young person is likely to receive a custodial sentence and there are concerns about his or her vulnerability within a secure establishment.

*Is there evidence that s/he is likely to be vulnerable as a result of the following?

	Yes	No	Don't know
The behaviour of other people (e.g. bullying, abuse, neglect, intimidation, exploitation)	☐	☐	☐
Other events or circumstances (e.g. separation, anniversary of loss, change of care arrangements)	☐	☐	☐
His/her own behaviour (e.g. risk taking, ignorance, drugs, acting out, inappropriate response to stress)	☐	☐	☐

Evidence (Please explain reasons for any 'Don't know' responses.)

*Are there indications that s/he is at risk of self-harm or suicide?

Yes	No	Don't know
☐	☐	☐

Evidence (Please explain reasons for any 'Don't know' responses.)

461

*Are there any protective factors that may reduce his/her vulnerability?

Yes ☐ No ☐ Don't know ☐

> Evidence (Please explain reasons for any 'Don't know' responses.)

Are there any known problems during previous custodial sentences?

Yes ☐ No ☐ Don't know ☐

> If yes, please specify (i.e. self-harm, attempted suicide, or victim of bullying) and provide details

Are there any current concerns about vulnerability if s/he were to go to custody?

Yes ☐ No ☐ Don't know ☐

> If yes, please specify the nature of the problems, and circumstances in which they are likely to occur

24

Indicators of risk of serious harm to others

This section focuses on the possibility of the young person causing serious harm to other people. Serious harm is defined as 'death or injury (either physical or psychological) that is life threatening and/or traumatic and from which recovery is expected to be difficult, incomplete or impossible'.

	Yes	No	Don't know
*Do any of the following apply to the young person in relation to the current offence/s?	☐	☐	☐

	Yes	No	Don't know
S/he has been convicted of a serious specified offence	☐	☐	☐

	Yes	No	Don't know
S/he is being sentenced in the Crown Court for a specified offence	☐	☐	☐

	Yes	No	Don't know
A Youth Court has specifically requested that the pre-sentence report risk assessment should contribute to the court's assessment of 'dangerousness', in order to determine whether to remit the case to the Crown Court for sentencing	☐	☐	☐

	Yes	No	Don't know
*Has the young person ever been assessed as presenting 'a risk to children'?	☐	☐	☐

If you have answered 'yes' to either of the questions above, you must complete the full *Risk of Serious Harm* form. If none of these cases applies, please complete the questions below. Take account of known offences and other behaviour that may not have resulted in a conviction (e.g. behaviour within the family, at school, in institutions, towards staff). If you answer 'yes' to either of the questions, you must go on to complete the full *Risk of Serious Harm* form.

*Is there any evidence of the following?	Yes	No	Don't know
*Behaviour by the young person which resulted in actual serious harm being caused	☐	☐	☐
*Behaviour which indicates that s/he was intending or preparing to cause serious harm	☐	☐	☐
*Other (e.g. reckless or unintentional) behaviour that was very likely to have caused serious harm	☐	☐	☐

25

Do any of the following indicate that there may be a risk of serious harm?

	Yes	No	Don't know
*Other features of his/her offending (e.g. unduly sophisticated methods, use of weapons, targeting)	☐	☐	☐
*His/her attitudes and motives (e.g. driven by desires for revenge, control or by discriminatory beliefs)	☐	☐	☐
*Current interests or activities (e.g. fascination with military paraphernalia, networks/associates)	☐	☐	☐

*Do any of the following cause significant concern?

	Yes	No	Don't know
*Any other disconcerting or disturbing behaviour by the young person (e.g. cruelty to animals)	☐	☐	☐
*Young person has said, indicated or threatened that s/he might cause serious harm to others	☐	☐	☐
*Others (e.g. family, school) have expressed concern that the young person might cause serious harm to others	☐	☐	☐
*Any other intuitive or 'gut' feelings about possible harmful behaviour	☐	☐	☐

Details (Where there are 'don't know' responses, specify what additional information is needed in order to make a judgement.)

3 CORE PROFILE

26

Appendix G

Maximum fines

1 MAXIMUM FINE

The power of the courts to impose a fine is entirely controlled by statute. Therefore, the maximum fine for the offence may not be exceeded.

The maximum fine for the vast majority of offences which are only triable by magistrates is expressed as being one of five levels, each level representing a monetary limit. (The maximum for most offences triable either way is expressed as the 'statutory maximum' or 'prescribed sum'.) The standard scale is currently as follows:

Level 1   maximum fine is £200

Level 2   maximum fine is £500

Level 3   maximum fine is £1,000

Level 4   maximum fine is £2,500

Level 5   maximum fine is £5,000

Either way offences: prescribed sum is £5,000 (MCA 1980, s 32).

This is known as the standard scale of fines and it has been devised as an attempt to rationalise the maximum amounts of fines and to provide a simple means of increasing them in inflationary times.

2 JUVENILES

Offender under 14 (a child). Maximum fine is the amount in the statute creating the offence or £250, whichever is less.

Offender 14 – under 18 (young person). Maximum fine is the amount in the statute creating the offence or £1,000, whichever is the less.

Orders guide

SENTENCING OBJECTIVES – THE YOUTH COURT

- To determine the seriousness of the offence and make any restriction on liberty (a court order) proportionate to its seriousness.
- To have regard to the aim of preventing further offences.
- To have regard to the welfare of the child or young person.

Together with the purposes of sentencing, namely:
- (a) the punishment of offenders,
- (b) the reform and rehabilitation of offenders,
- (c) the protection of the public, and
- (d) the making of reparation by offenders to persons as affected by their or offences.

A Discharges: absolute/conditional

- Absolute: technically guilty but morally blameless.
- Conditional: inexpedient to inflict further punishment; not to commit further offences during a period up to three years after the order.
- May *not* be made within two years of a final warning without exceptional circumstances.

B Fines

- Must enquire into offender's circumstances or if the parent or guardian is going to pay them.
- Normally parents of offenders under 16 years old will pay unless they cannot be found or it would be unreasonable in the

circumstances of the case. Parents of 16 and 17 year olds *may* be directed to pay if the court believes it is reasonable and after giving the parents an opportunity to address the court.

| Maximum fine | 10-13 | £ 250 |
| | 14-17 | £1000 |

C   Referral order

Mandatory
- Custodial sentence or absolute discharge or hospital order not proposed.
- Offender has pleaded guilty to all offences.
- No previous convictions (including conditional discharge). The offence is imprisonable.

Period of order 3 to 12 months.

Discretionary
- Defendant pleaded guilty to at least one offence but not all the [connected] offences or
- he has pleaded guilty to a non-imprisonable offence and
- custodial sentence, hospital order or absolute discharge not proposed.

  [The order may not be combined with a youth community rehabilitation order, fine, reparation, conditional discharge, bind over or parental bind over.]

If a further offence is committed before the referral order was made, the court has discretion to extend the referral order.

If a further offence committed after the referral order was made, the court may, sentenced by way of an extension of the existing referral order in exceptional circumstances only. The order must not exceed the 12 months maximum.

D   Reparation order
- Written report required.
- Not to be combined with custody, or youth rehabilitation order. Maximum of 24 hours work to be completed within a three-month period.

- No conflict with religious beliefs, any other community order or attendance at school or work.
- Recipient of reparation consulted and consents.
- Reparation commensurate with the seriousness of offence(s).
  [Reasons required where reparation order available but not made.]
  [Compensation order remains available.]

YOUTH REHABILITATION ORDER – 'SERIOUS ENOUGH?'

Aim: Offence prevention and welfare considerations

The following requirements may be attached to a youth rehabilitation order. As stated above the details are found in Sch 1 of the Act and the relevant paragraph of the schedule is in brackets next to each of the requirements.

(a) an activity requirement (paras 6 8),

(b) a supervision requirement (para 9),

(c) in a case where the offender is aged 16 or 17 at the time of the conviction, an unpaid work requirement (see para 10),

(d) a programme requirement (para 11),

(e) an attendance centre requirement (para 12),

(f) a prohibited activity requirement (para 13),

(g) a curfew requirement (para 14),

(h) an exclusion requirement (para 15),

(i) a residence requirement (para 16),

(j) a local authority residence requirement (paras 17 and 19),

(k) a youth rehabilitation order with fostering requirement (paras 4,18 and 19) (imprisonable offences only),

(l) a mental health treatment requirement (paras 20 and 21),

(m) a drug treatment/drug testing requirement (paras 22 and 23),

(n) an intoxicating substance treatment requirement (para 24),

(o) an education requirement (para 25),

(p) an electronic monitoring requirement (see para26), and

(q) a youth rehabilitation order with intensive supervision and surveillance (para 2) (imprisonable offences only).

CUSTODY 'SO SERIOUS'

Aim: Punishment and deprivation of liberty

Detention and training order

- So serious or (violent or sexual offence) only custody adequate to protect public from serious harm from offender (or falls within criteria in CJA 2003 s152(3).
- Offender aged 12-18 and convicted of imprisonable offence.
- No order permissible for offenders aged 10 to 12, but in exceptionally serious cases offender may be committed to the Crown Court pursuant to s.91 PCC(S)A 200 & s.24 MCA 1980 as a grave crime.
- Offender legally represented or offered legal aid (subject to means).
- Pre-sentence report received.
- If offender aged under 15 at time of conviction, must be a persistent offender (reasons required).
- Order of at least four months required after discount for guilty plea and time spent on remand.
- [Sentence of 4, 6, 8, 10, 12, 18 or 24 months only permitted.]

ANCILLARY ORDERS FOR PARENTS

Parenting order

- If offender under 16 family circumstances report obtained (otherwise discretionary).
- Order desirable to prevent the commission of further offences.
- [Reasons must be given if order not made in case of offender under 16 years old, unless a referral order is made].
- Order may be made where a parent/guardian fails to attend youth offender panel meetings in respect of a referral order.

Parental bind over

- Child or young person convicted of offence. Parent or guardian can be bound over to ensure the juvenile behaves or complies with a youth rehabilitation order

- Bind over desirable in the interests of preventing the commission of further offences by the offender.
[Bind over must be made in case of offender aged under 16 or reasons given.
Discretionary for 16- or 17-year-old.]

Index

Please note that references are to Chapter (in bold) and paragraph numbers